Fa. Bacon

THE WINDING STAIR

THE WINDING STAIR

JESSE NORMAN

Biteback Publishing

First published in Great Britain in 2023 by
Biteback Publishing Ltd, London
Copyright © Jesse Norman 2023

ISBN 978-1-78590-792-0

10 9 8 7 6 5 5 4 3 2

A CIP catalogue record for this book is available from the British Library.

Set in Trade Gothic and Adobe Caslon Pro

Printed and bound in Great Britain by
CPI Group (UK) Ltd, Croydon CR0 4YY

FSC
www.fsc.org
MIX
Paper | Supporting
responsible forestry
FSC® C171272

For Kate, Sam, Nell and Noah

This is a novel. Much of it is made up; almost all of it is true. Any resemblance to actual persons and events, past or present, is unlikely to be coincidental.

All rising to great place is by a winding stair.
FRANCIS BACON, *ESSAYS*, 'OF GREAT PLACE'

*If you would work any man, you must either know his nature
and fashions, and so lead him; or his ends, and so persuade him; or
his weakness and disadvantages, and so awe him or those
that have interest in him, and so govern him.*
FRANCIS BACON, *ESSAYS*, 'OF NEGOTIATING'

*For a crowd is not company; and faces are but a gallery
of pictures; and talk but a tinkling cymbal,
where there is no love.*
FRANCIS BACON, *ESSAYS*, 'OF FRIENDSHIP'

CONTENTS

DRAMATIS PERSONAE

THE BACON FAMILY

Sir Francis Bacon, Viscount St Alban
his wife, Alice Barnham
his father, Sir Nicholas Bacon, Lord Keeper
his mother, Anne, Lady Bacon, sister to Mildred Burghley
his elder brother, Anthony Bacon

THE CECIL FAMILY

Sir William Cecil, Lord Burghley, Lord Treasurer and principal
    adviser to Queen Elizabeth
his elder son by his first wife, Sir Thomas Cecil, later 2nd Lord
    Burghley and Earl of Exeter
his second wife, Mildred, Lady Burghley, sister to Anne Bacon
their son, Sir Robert Cecil, Earl of Salisbury, Secretary of State and
    Lord Treasurer

THE COKE FAMILY

Sir Edward Coke
his first wife, Bridget Paston
their son, Robert Coke, among other children
his second wife, Elizabeth, Lady Hatton, daughter of Sir Thomas Cecil
their second daughter, Frances Coke

THE TUDOR COURT

Elizabeth I, Queen of England
Sir Robert Devereux, Earl of Essex
Sir Thomas Egerton, later Lord Ellesmere, Lord Chancellor
Sir Thomas Howard, Earl of Suffolk, Lord Treasurer
Sir Henry Wriothesley, Earl of Southampton, friend of Essex

THE STUART COURT

James I of England and VI of Scotland, King of Great Britain
his wife, Queen Anne of Denmark
their second son Charles I, King of Great Britain
Richard Bancroft, Archbishop of Canterbury, succeeded by
George Abbot, Archbishop of Canterbury
Sir Robert Carr, later Viscount Rochester and Earl of Somerset, a
  favourite
Sir Thomas Overbury, friend of Carr
Sir George Villiers, later Earl, Marquess and Duke of Bucking-
  ham, a favourite
Don Antonio Perez, diplomat and adventurer, friend of Essex
Don Diego Sarmiento, Count Gondomar, Ambassador of Spain
John Selden, lawyer, historian
Sundry other characters

I

GENESIS: 1570–1592

1

Revenge. It is a word, but what of the thing itself? What matter, of what kind and variety, do we find in it? Private retribution, public humiliation, yes; an act which repayeth where the law doth not stretch. A levelling, by which a man done down may raise himself against his adversary.

It is not to be borne on Earth. No prince can let men gain the habit of revenge, else for what purpose have courts and law? Justice to be justice must lack personality. Nor may any prince show it shrift himself, for greatness soareth above such insults. To God alone is it reserved. In the book of Romans: Vengeance is mine; I will repay, saith the Lord.

Of all revenge, the greatest is this: that which cometh suddenly, without expectation, upon a bravado in his pomp, that bringeth him to an inevitable and annihilating public ruin. And he to know the cause, the occasion and the revenger but, like Cassandra, not to be believed by others.

Men cannot all be princes. Talent demandeth its reward. And if a grief is ever green, then to bring it balm is not revenge, but mercy.

2

HAMPTON COURT, 1570

Red battlements, great iron-studded oaken doors, a long hall that opens out to streaming light. His father walking, not fast but with purpose, so that he must trot to keep up. Uncle Cecil catching them briefly, to exchange a word.

'Your timing is good. She is in spirits.'

They wait, it seems interminably. Then the wall of bodies suddenly parts, and there is a flash of white before them. A long silk dress, embroidered richly in gold to match her hair. Councillors on either side, some faces familiar: he sees Walsingham, Leicester, Gresham.

'Lord Keeper!'

'Your Majesty.'

'You have acquired a page?' An eyebrow, raised.

'I hope I may present my son, your Majesty. Francis, brother to Anthony.'

She sees the round face, the domed forehead, an air of composure, and her interest is piqued. 'Tell me, child, how old are you?'

He has expected this. Stepping forward, chest up and in a steady, high voice: 'I have the honour to be two years younger than your Majesty's happy reign.'

She smiles. 'And, child, you are reading the ancient authors? Which is your favourite?'

'Homer for war, Virgil for the woods and trees, Tully for statecraft, your Majesty.'

'And know you arithmetic? Sir Francis, you are our numerologist. Set the boy a task.'

Walsingham steps forward, not unkindly: 'Francis, what is the square of forty-seven?'

For this there can be no preparation. But, instantly: '2,209, sir. There is a trick to such numbers.'

The Queen is delighted. 'Sir Nicholas, your boy hath a wit, and more than that: a mind. See if he doth not surpass even his father.'

And to him, 'Well, my young Lord Keeper: guard your talent well. We may have need of it in future years.'

'Well, my young Lord Keeper: guard your talent well. We may have need of it in future years.' He will never forget those words. They are graven on his heart; in his bleakest moments they give solace. Time and again he returns to them, pondering meanings, divining intentions, reposing hopes.

'My young Lord Keeper': an idle remark, said in the moment. Of course. But also conferring status, acknowledging his father. After all, it could be said to no other, save Anthony, and Francis, though he loves his brother like none other, does not regard him as his equal in intellect. But tie it to her final words, and there is more. Surely prediction, even predestination? The Queen always speaks to some purpose.

He can feel that something is at stake. Even at nine years of age, Francis Bacon is not naïve about the world. He knows the scriptures, but he has also heard his father talking.

Only God can predestinate a man, for reasons and from causes unknown. Yet the Queen too, perhaps? Stories are told of how, through luck and the wiles of a Penelope, she kept the axe from her tender neck after the death of King Henry. But she is only a woman, and her enemies are gathering ever stronger. Northumberland and Westmoreland have raised open rebellion, put down at the cost of hundreds dead. Now the Pope has excommunicated her. They say there are secret Catholics everywhere, some aided by recusants who will not take the Queen's Oath of Supremacy, all pouring their sweet seductions into men's ears, planning to destroy her and topple over her Council like so many skittles. And what of Mary of Scotland, now held captive? The threat is there.

'Guard your talent well': this is the heart of it. With talent, the way is clear. And if the talent be clearer, then clearer too the way. But talent is no quiet pet, no gently calling songbird. It makes demands. It must be tamed and fed. And it cannot live out of the light.

Francis Bacon is not in any doubt that he has talent, even genius. People have spoken of it since his birth. And not just his parents, fond as they are. The household servants still talk of how young he was to speak. His tutors are dazzled by his speed and breadth of comprehension. He can mention Homer and Cicero to the Queen, lightly, but if she wishes to discuss the death of Patroclus or the trial of Catiline in their detail, he can do it; and if she is ever moved by a desire to debate the 32nd Proposition of the First Book of Euclid's *Elements*, he can do that too.

And he can turn a sentence as can few others. He can make words crack and split, so their meanings lie open like oysters in the shell. He can set forth people in words as Holbein has painted them. He can make words shine, and fall on other minds like sunlight streaming through church glass. And he can use them to shade, to obscure, to enfold, to deceive and to imprison.

But as for talent, one might say, these things are not the whole. They are just aspects of the whole.

3

GORHAMBURY, JUNE 1572

For Francis, the big house and its vast grounds and gardens are an Eden. When father is away, he and Anthony are the young masters, and there are few changes when father is in residence. This is Sir Nicholas's second family, and he is a man of business; the boys can take care of themselves.

It is early morning, prelude to a summer day of heat and breezes. Francis's eyes are shining as he rouses his older brother. There were shooting stars last night – did he see them? Are there flaws in the celestial spheres? Does the ether crack like glass? How else can the stars move so quickly? How can they go in different directions? Surely they cannot be angels.

If there are answers to such questions, they do not come at morning prayers, over which their mother keeps a watchful eye. After chapel, the boys head to the hen houses. It is not quite forbidden territory, though Sir Nicholas has told Francis to leave such matters to the household and devote his mind to his studies. But there is so much he wants to know: how eggs become chickens, and how they don't; why the birds lay when they do; could you get more eggs by feeding them more? There are twenty-eight birds in the first roost, and today they have laid seventeen eggs. Francis has a little notebook. He writes the numbers in and frowns, pondering why there are more eggs this month than last, and more then than the month before.

The boys dally. But the hen house is not their final goal. Nor is it the walled garden, another favourite place, nor the parterres or the Italian terraces. Francis races off like a colt, whooping with joy. Running on down the meadows, they eventually reach the ponds, breathless and hot despite the hour, Francis in the lead, Anthony who is slight and short in the lungs wheezing heavily as they sluice their faces with water. Anthony has always been sickly, and Francis is protective of him. He scans his brother's face, but all is well.

There are *vivaria* for breeding fish, *servatoria* for keeping them. In the shallows of a pool above, they have built a pond of their own, carrying rocks back and forth to mark it out, with an inlet for the water and a dam. And they have decorated the bottom with brightly coloured pebbles, for Francis has long had a fascination for mosaic, taken from his father's books. They have made fishes, even a sea monster. Look closely, and you see just the several stones; but step back, and you see the whole picture.

Their pond is a live and ever-changing source of fascination. Francis has watched it fill with frogs spawn in the spring and seen the heron gorge itself before Easter. He has seen the newts and sticklebacks grow. When duckweed starts to cover it, he clears the weed away, then does it again, and again. Now he notes the little beetles on the surface, and the rushes growing ever thicker. And seven small frogs, in the shallows and in the grass around. Aristophanes would be pleased, he thinks.

It all goes in the book.

When they get back to the house, however, it is to raised voices.

'My dear, it is decided. I will not dispute with you. I saw Beaumont last month, and now I have sent to confirm it. Anthony will go to Trinity in the spring, and Francis with him. I have placed the boys in Dr Whitgift's personal care. Walsall and the others have done well with them; Whitgift will do better.'

'My Lord, you cannot send Francis away at his age. It is not healthy. Cambridge will expose him to every manner of unbelief. He will be tempted by strong drink. And Whitgift is a wretch, who sees the ways of God as mere mounting steps to his own greatness.'

'Nonsense. He is a man of balance and moderation. The temptation to dissent is a great danger in the young. He will check it.'

'But, but…'

'Anne' – her first name is a reproof – 'I honour you as wife and mother. But I say again, I will not dispute the matter. As for me, as for their brothers, so for the younger boys. Yes, you will be sad to lose Frank, as shall I. But the matter is done. We have a busy day today, so let us make adjournment of our talk.'

His mother storms past them, unseeing, in a rage.

Though the occasion is new, the disagreement is not. Lady Bacon is Sir Nicholas's second wife, eighteen years younger than him and the stepmother of his three elder sons, Nathaniel, Nicholas and Edward, and three daughters. But she is not someone who makes deference her habit, to husband, age or family.

On the contrary, she is a woman of formidable education, and a classical scholar. Her father was companion and instructor to King Edward, and she Lady-in-Waiting to Princess Elizabeth, as the Queen then was. But in point of learning she outstrips even the Queen. Some women can write Latin and Greek and speak French. Anne Bacon can do all that, and throw in Hebrew, Spanish and Italian for good measure. Does her restless energy come despite her accomplishments, or because of them? Is it frustration or heresy that she fears? At any rate, in religion she is an unyielding Puritan. Were the utter extirpation of popery within her gift, she would will it without hesitation or regret.

Her husband, by contrast, channels his passions carefully, and in this world not the next. He has bitten his tongue, conformed to Romish rite under Queen Mary, and returned to the reformed Church under Elizabeth. But at heart he is a Stoic, who follows the Senecan maxim: *mediocria firma*. There is wisdom in it, for moderate things endure, and there is safety in moderation. Sir Nicholas believes in stability, careful government and the common weal, and they have served him well.

From modest beginnings he has come by ability and a politic disposition via the law to one of the highest offices of the land. He is the Queen's Lord Keeper and holds the Great Seal of England, the embodiment of royal power itself. It is an office for a commoner not a peer, yet particularly codified in statute as 'entitled to like place, pre-eminence, jurisdiction, execution of laws, and all other customs, commodities, and advantages as the Lord Chancellor'.

In recent times Sir Nicholas has grown a great mass of body, till he resembles King Henry VIII in his later years. As the Queen herself has remarked, his soul is well lodged. Lady Bacon has tried to moderate its growth. But that mass has its uses, to steady wavering colleagues or nudge an errant Member of Parliament back to right reason, and it conceals an inner lightness, of wit and courtesy and taste. Sir Nicholas is the first to speak for the Crown in Parliament. He does so with dignity, unmoved by fervour in matters of religion.

Save for my birth, I would be Lord Chancellor, he thinks.

But Sir Nicholas does not begrudge the Queen her choice. Nor too has he ever begrudged acclaim to William Cecil, who is at once the Queen's first councillor, the most powerful man in the realm, his brother-in-law and his closest friend. Cecil has brought him into the innermost chambers of the court, and for more than a decade the two men have worked together to guide, promote, protect – and not seldom to frustrate – their monarch.

But Cecil is lately made Baron Burghley, and building an immense house at Theobalds, just twenty miles away. And he is coming to visit that day at Gorhambury.

4

GORHAMBURY, JUNE 1572

'Anthony, Francis, why do you not take your cousins to explore the grounds?'

It is the late forenoon, and after the frustrations of the morning Lady Bacon has reasserted herself. With huge effort, dinner has been moved from the great hall into the open air. Heavy oak tables and chairs are now set beneath a tented canopy, rugs strewn out across the grass for the children.

The gentleman usher has been instructed, the deputy, the yeoman usher, the men of the ewery, the carver, the cooks, waiters and other servants have been marshalled, the wards and young men of the household pressed to work, and all have streamed to and from the house carrying items throughout the morning. With the visitors, they are over fifty at table, for soup and capon, duck and jellies, beef and game and sturgeon and salmon, nuts and puddings and tarts. Lady Bacon is too wise to seek to rival her sister, but a royal visit is in prospect. Nothing can be left to chance, and this is useful preparation.

Now, as the meal is winding down, Sir Nicholas has called for claret.

The children eye one another carefully. The two Cecil girls are friendly enough. Less so the boy, Robert. He is small, with an appraising gaze and a crook in his left shoulder that Anthony and Francis have been strictly instructed to ignore. The boys have met in regular encounters over the years. This is not to say they like each other.

It is an irritation to Francis that Robert too has been dignified by Her Majesty, who calls him her Pygmy. The boy rarely speaks, but when he does it is with care, and his words are cool. Yes, the meal was good, and he thanks them for it; his own father gave a dinner not two weeks ago at which they served 130 on plates of silver. Yes, he admires the house, now in preparation for the royal progress that summer; they have themselves just come from Theobalds, which has entertained Her Majesty. But for himself, he prefers the house in Lincolnshire, which would put a royal palace to shame.

So it goes on. When they reach the ponds, Robert sees the coloured fish and the sea monster, and Francis can already feel the weight of his judgement: 'You made this pool yourselves? We have our own mosaic at home, brought from Italy. They say the gardens are bigger than those at Hampton Court. And my father hath designed a vast water garden with fountains, and moats as for a castle.'

The words are careless, not meant to injure, but Anthony is hot. 'Yes, we made it,' he says with pride, 'and we'd ask you now to help us with the work, if you had the back for it.'

Robert flushes. 'You speak of my back, you, with your halting leg?'

'Yes, I do, you arrogant little runt. Whoever your father is.'

Maybe it is his back, the heat, the insult or mention of his father, but the reaction is immediate. Robert hurls himself at Anthony and starts to strike at him indiscriminately. The girls scream. Anthony is five years older than his attacker, and fends him off without difficulty. But even as Anthony pushes him away, Francis sees his brother trip and fall backwards.

And then he sees something else, something that makes his heart stop. His brother is winded, now coughing and wheezing. He cannot get up, cannot breathe. He is choking.

Robert has not seen it. In his fury he sits astride Anthony's chest, still pummelling him. Francis takes hold of him, but Robert is still frantic and will not let go. So he wrenches him bodily away.

As Robert falls, at water's edge he emits a scream of terror, shouting he cannot swim. The coloured pebbles, the fish, the monster they have made: all are scattered and destroyed by the impact. But the pond is shallow, and Francis turns to care for his gasping brother.

It is a moment, like any other moment. A thousand other things might have happened at that instant. Can a cause have multiple effects? Must not every fruit spring from its own special seed? Is a man's life set by God, or by chance? Or by the Devil?

Francis has studied the *trivium* and the *quadrivium*; he has immersed himself in rhetoric and the *topoi* and *tropoi* of the ancient masters. He can debate these metaphysical points as well as any, though to do so is not to his taste.

What he cannot do, in the years afterward, is think of that moment by the pond. But he cannot help thinking of it either. How can that be? It is both a mental disorder and a contradiction in logic. Surely he, surely one so confessedly brilliant, can resolve it?

The damage was to spirits, not to bodies. But bodies heal more readily than spirits. His father's anger – Sir Nicholas calls it vexation, but it is anger sure enough – at the news. His own shame, made worse by being soundly beaten so as to drive out the wickedness from his soul. Robert Cecil sick abed two days with a fever. The abject apologies, their gracious acceptance by Lord and Lady Burghley, the visit not cut short but even extended as a mark of continued amity. The whole, in short, mortifying to him in every particular.

It is made worse a few weeks later, when the Queen visits

Gorhambury during her summer progress. The incident is not to be spoken of, yet rumour is more than meat and drink at court, and somehow she has come to hear of it. It will not do to provoke discord between two of her great councillors if feelings are still tender. But, to twit them once the danger is past… that is too tempting.

The thrust and parry of words; it is the Elizabethan way. On her arrival at Gorhambury, she had commented to Sir Nicholas, 'My Lord, what a little house you have gotten.' He replied, 'Madam, my house is well, but you have made me too great for my house.' He chafes at her remark, and resolves on new construction; yet at least his reply was nicely done.

But when they walk the grounds today, he is less ready of phrase.

'Have you not lakes around your little house, my Lord?'

'Yes, your Majesty. They are very pretty, tranquil places.'

'And yet I heard the waters broken of late. Is there a Hydra? Or some Carcinus to clutch the foot of great Hercules in his claw?'

That is two quick hits from a single lunge. And when Sir Nicholas does not reply, 'What think you, my Lord?'

'Your Majesty, waters once parted swiftly mingle again, and leave no mark. So it is here.'

'I am glad to know it. There can be no discord between my young Lord Keeper and my Pygmy.'

Yet discord there is. And soon afterwards Sir Nicholas commissions new works at the house: a grand loggia laid out with Italian columns and a statue of Henry VIII in a special niche, a cloister, a long gallery above, engraved with Latin maxims and, evident to view, the family coat of arms, quartered with the crest of a striding boar set atop a mantled helmet of red and gold.

His particular joy is to install exquisite stained glass windows depicting plants and animals from the New World. He will not be caught out by the Queen again.

5

YORK HOUSE, LONDON: JANUARY 1576

Francis has always had a close relationship with his father, but separation brings them closer. So has the plague, which has twice broken out while the boys are at Cambridge, forcing their immediate withdrawal. They return with misgivings. For to come home means to leave their pastimes, their bows and arrows, their friendships and freedom, and live again under their mother's exacting eye.

Soon after Christmastide, with snow heavy on the ground and the family in London, he is summoned. Sir Nicholas is at the great desk in his study as always, surrounded by papers and wax candles, a fire burning at the hearth. He opens by asking about the university, and not merely the boy's studies but the arguments, debates, rumours. Where does he worship? With whom does he converse? What sermons has he heard?

Francis is respectful, but unsparing. He has spent many hours in fruitless labour and debate and cordially despises the methods of the schoolmen who are his teachers, with their antic *disputationes*, *quaestiones* and *sententiae*. Yes, he too reveres the ancients, but that is all to the point. Could anyone who loved them see the greatest works of philosophy reduced to mere forms of argument, rendered void and naked of substance, without the bile of an honest indignation rising in the throat? And as a system of instruction, brought to fruit in the university, no less… is it any wonder students despair of acquiring real knowledge?

Then, his father: 'Frank, what would you be? I fancy your mother has you marked for the Church.'

'Yes, Father,' with a smile, 'but the Church is not for me. I would set myself to be at court, or Parliament like you.'

So his father tells a little more of his own history: how he grew up in Kent, his own father a Suffolk sheep-reeve and farmer, nothing more; how he came via Cambridge to London; the long years of study at the Inn; his preferment under King Henry and Archbishop Cranmer.

Francis silently wonders about the first wife, Jane, the mother of his six older half-brothers and sisters. Of her, however, Sir Nicholas says nothing.

It is the latest of many conversations. They both know that while parental love rests on all the children, expectation rests on him alone. And Anthony – gentle, sweet, fragile, funny Anthony, Anthony who is his father's second firstborn son, of quicksilver mind, who can mimic any voice at first hearing and make instant mock of pompous churchman and tavern bore alike – Anthony, weak of sight and wind and limb, he knows it too.

So the father and the son talk, of many things but always of one subject: of power and its limits. They talk of Aristotle, of monarchy and despotism, of aristocracy and oligarchy, of democracy and ochlocracy, of the mob and the fall of Rome. They talk of divine power, of natural law, of grace, of the authority of Kings, anointment and the coronation oath. They talk of war and conquest, of enslavement and obedience. They talk of law, and history, of the Emperor Justinian's code of law, of the law of the Church and of the courts.

And as they talk, the father unfolds himself a little.

'There was a great change,' he says, 'in the time of Lord Cromwell. Now that was a man of power, Frank! He could make things happen just by the willing of them, and no one else would know it till they were done. I recall he had a painting by Master Holbein at his house that caught his strength, but I never much liked it.

'How came the great change he made? He understood the arts

of administration. He used the King's Parliaments to good effect. He knew men as well as measures, and fitted the one to the other like a horse to the bridle, the better to ride them. Come, boy, let us have a glass of sack and walk together in the garden. I need the outside air.'

Yet there is something missing. Francis does not quite see it – how to see an absence? – but he feels it.

There is something there, beyond his reach yet inside the span of his attention. Plato thinks of his Republic as mirroring the parts of the soul: there are the prudent, reasoning guardians, and the wild spirits of the mob. But between them are the desirous, the ambitious. Who are these people? What do they want? Where are they going?

Sir Nicholas is a man of discretion and indirection. He knows his own mind, and he feels the range of his son's by letting the boy wander and roam in their chat. He can indulge the boy, but he is also orderly, methodical; he has a plan. Talent is requisite, but so is industry. A young man ascends but through connections, by services rendered, and for these things too there must be education. As he himself did, so Francis will go to Gray's Inn. He has the mind for it, and though he may never practise as a lawyer, that is hardly the point. A gentleman's son goes to the Inns for the company, for the experience, for the starting point in life, not merely for book learning.

There must be property, he knows, for a man is nothing without property. Sir Nicholas has planned for that as well: as he has done with his other boys, to assemble estates and livings sufficient to secure Francis from want, that he be free to make his way at court in service of the Queen. And there must also be time spent abroad. He himself grew up in the shadow of the King's Great Matter, with England too often swinging in a Romish breeze. Spain still drips its poison in the ear of every Catholic sower of heresy and insurrection.

The Duke of Norfolk is lately dead, executed for his traitorous assistance to Ridolfi, who plotted to assassinate Her Majesty. But the Duke's Howard kith and kin are not the only Catholics or their sympathisers in England. There are many more who could step forward with money and connections in an instant. Francis must understand all this.

6

PARIS, AUTUMN 1576

*N*omen est omen; your name is your fate. In retrospect it feels inevitable to Francis that he will go to France, and he does so at the ripe age of fifteen, after Cambridge – having kissed hands, so happily, with Her Majesty – in the entourage of the Queen's ambassador, Sir Amias Paulet.

These are testing times, for France remains racked by religious conflict and her capital is furiously Catholic. Barely four years earlier, several thousands of Protestant Huguenots, come to Paris to celebrate the wedding of the young Prince Henry of Navarre to Margaret of Valois, have been slaughtered in the streets at the feast of Bartholomew the Apostle.

Nor, as Francis discovers, is there any fondness in Paris for the English, deemed co-conspirators with the Huguenots and their allies in the low countries. The shopkeepers are surly; nothing is sold but for ready money. The ambassador's servants are jostled and spat on in the street. The courtiers are aloof and brusque, so that months of painful negotiation are required before the new ambassador may present his credentials to the King.

Till then, the cost must be borne by Paulet himself. Little wonder he is so often short of gold, and temper.

Sir Amias is in any case a man of severe and exacting disposition. He breathes the clean air of Puritanism, and his task in Paris is not only to support the embattled Huguenots against oppression but to gather information and furrow the French court with a hundred unseen channels through which intelligence may flow back to Burghley and his Queen.

As for Francis, he will learn the tongue, study the ways of diplomacy and receive a practical education in the civil law: the law of peoples and princes, not like the unruly sprawl of the judge-made English common law but orderly, and vital to foreign treaties and international negotiations.

Even Lady Bacon can be reassured as to the spiritual wellbeing of her younger son. In the face of so much popery, Paulet's household will be an enclave of the orthodox. And the experience of life abroad, of language and custom and public service in a foreign court, will equip her son perfectly for the gleaming future that must await him on his return.

7

A DEATH, 1579

At night, after the city gates close and the streets empty of people, as Francis drops to sleep in a Parisian bed, the dream comes to him.

There, once more, is lovely Gorhambury in the distance. But something is amiss; he can feel fear slowly birthing in his belly. Too much darkness, too much shadow. When he comes close, he sees the house is plastered over with black mortar. The walls are drenched in it, it fills the doors and windows, seeps down the marble steps from the great hall and oozes from the gallery. As he goes upstairs, he feels his feet sink deep into it, his limbs start to slow, his body become colder and colder.

People from the house flow past him – servants, women of the kitchen, pages – their faces white with horror, till he hears the sound of dreadful anguished screams, and sees his mother kneeling before a Bible at the bedside, and his father's great body lain out, pale in death.

In later life Francis will always hold to the existence of secret passages of sympathy between persons of near blood, for, as he says, there be many reports in history that upon the death of persons of such nearness, men have had an inward feeling of it.

The date can never be effaced from his memory: 20 February 1579, in the twenty-first year of the reign of Queen Elizabeth, just a few days after the dream visited him. His father, sleeping by an open window, suddenly struck down by a terrible illness and dead within a few days. *The creeping darkness of disease has claimed him, and dressed the house of Bacon in black shrouds of death.* Francis will always think it so.

And after the sorrow, the funeral; the burial of Lord Keeper Bacon next to the tomb of John of Gaunt at St Paul's; Francis's own hurried return to England; and the reckoning. His father has long settled the three elder boys with estates. To Anthony will go Gorhambury after his mother's life interest, with other lands and a serviceable income. Yet for Francis there are but crumbs. The debts are far larger than expected, and their father has been struck down before he can make final provision for his youngest son. What is left must be split five ways. The interest in York House will be sold when a new Lord Keeper is made.

As with his property, so with his station. His half-brother Nicholas has been made a knight, Edward and Nathaniel are esquires with their lands, and Anthony too. But he, Francis, is now their inferior in rank. He is *Francis Bacon, Gent.*, and nothing more. For the day of the Lord cometh as a thief in the night.

This is the end of Eden. The garden of my childhood joy is destroyed. So Francis quickly comes to see. The great tree that shielded and nourished him has been cut down. The man he loved and admired more than any, his guardian, his protector, his guide and counsellor, has left him, and left him little. He can have dreams, but no expectations. He is neither well left, nor well friended.

Yet it is perhaps still worse than that. While his father lived, Francis believed in a world of order, of justice, of reward, in the deliverances of a providential and all-seeing God. A world in which a man might pursue his vocation, do great things and be known and thanked for them.

But now, what is justice? Where is God's mercy?

His mind is awhirl, as everything alters in the months that follow. The household is broken up, the servants are dismissed and all the young men sent away. Good servants are hard to come by, and Lady Bacon is zealous in placing hers with the best families. But even her sense of duty and love are tested by the change in fortunes when her sister Mildred takes seven of them for Cecil House, fourteen for Theobalds and a round dozen for the great house Lord Burghley is building in Lincolnshire.

And then Lady Bacon withdraws, devoting herself to prayer for hours every day, inconsolable with worry as well as grief. The elder boys are protective of what they have received in their father's will and feel no great warmth for her, who is but their stepmother; in time they will turn hostile. Anthony and Francis rest at home, then move with some relief to the old Lord Keeper's chambers at Gray's Inn. The rooms are near the hall and the library and much sought after. But they have been kept for the boys' use, as almost a home from home. The brothers can eat in commons there with little expense, and they are not burdened by formal duties of study.

After the loss of their father, Anthony has been seized by a great desire to visit foreign regions; he is now set for France, to travel and to remit intelligence in the service of Sir Francis Walsingham, the Secretary of State. In the meantime, however, he feasts on intrigue and fellowship. He has a wide circle of friends for drinking, gaming and chatter. The family name commands respect. All will be for the good.

Francis looks on, and absorbs. He has not much taste for people, he knows, whether wenches or pot-fellows. His natural habitation is the library, not the tavern. Unlike his brother he enjoys the disciplines of the law, the old yearbooks, the copying out of cases, notes and notations, debate, mooting.

But not as a trade. No: he has the tastes of a philosopher and the expectations of a gentleman, and these point not to the law courts but to the court of the Queen.

Francis is the son of the late Lord Keeper, the godson of the Earl of Bedford and the nephew to the Lord Treasurer. His father's coffin was followed up Ludgate Hill to St Paul's Church by a slow procession of all the great men of the kingdom; that must count for much, surely? He mourns his father, but even as an unbearded young man of eighteen he can see that alongside his debts Sir Nicholas has left behind a vast repository of political affection, a record of most honourable service to Her Majesty and close family connections both in the Palace of Whitehall and in Parliament. It argues no great conceit to think that Francis could, nay must, be of use in either place.

But not just any use. No, far from being cast down, Francis is soaring with ambition and ideas, framing a scheme, a project, of vast scope and possibility and immeasurable public good. Was it not Hilliard the portrait maker who painted a proud and perfect image of him and wrote around the outside, 'If only I could paint his mind!'? It is time to show that mind in action.

He has discussed his scheme at length with Anthony, his second self. He knows how it may be accomplished. And just by itself it will transform his prospects.

Taking his pen in hand, Francis dips it in the ink and starts to compose a letter to his uncle, William Cecil, Lord Burghley, the Queen's Lord Treasurer.

8

THE PALACE OF WHITEHALL, OCTOBER 1579

'**A** letter from your nephew, my Lord?'

'And asking me for assistance, Michael. It is not a surprise,' Lord Burghley reflects. 'But this one is something out of the ordinary, and I must yet reply to his mother's importunities as well. Truly, my mind is so full of state matters that I can hardly fathom it. See what you think.'

He gives the letter to his secretary. It is a good hand, clear and even, strong in its up and down strokes. Nothing smudged, crammed in or half-completed. A fair copy, then, to be passed on to others.

MY SINGULAR GOOD LORD, it begins, into whose benignant care an untimely fate has thrust me, snatching me away thereby from one no less dear to your Lordship than to myself, I pray it doth not presume on your Lordship's goodness to entertain a request from a relative for whom, as the Psalm sayeth, Your word is a lamp for my feet, a light on my path, at that first starting-point of life in which a Christian soul yearneth to set its own way in the cause of the publique wealth and the service of our most gracious sovereign, yet bringing withal to this task what some have been gracious to acknowledge as no common store of talent and resolution. I beg you may know, then...

Michael pauses, a bit lost. 'No common store of talent and resolution,' he repeats. Burghley nods, bleakly. The secretary reads on for a few moments.

... that at a time when our universities are but the birdcages of fine minds, closeted all in vain chattering disputation for which they invoke none other than the name of the great philosopher himself, prodigal in ingenious contention over a few empty husks of corn, yet oblivious to the granaries and fields of true knowledge without...

The letter ends: I pray that in the exercise of your great goodness your Lordship may see fit to endue this small suit with the grace of your benevolent authority, and, with whatever corrective amendment your Lordship may see fit to add, forward it to Her Majesty under your signet of truth and kindness. Your most dutiful and bounden nephew, B. Fra.

'Well, what do you make of it?'

'I cannot speak to the family connection, my Lord. But in substance it is surely a most bold and imaginative scheme, worthy of your Lordship's further consideration.'

Burghley grunts. Bold it is, that is for sure, and imaginative. His mind goes back thirty years to his old friend, dear Nick Bacon, and he feels the pang of loss once more. A different time to be sure, with great King Henry on the throne, Cromwell not to be stopped in Parliament and all good men engaged in the rectification of the Church. A time of betterment.

Such was his abundance of grace and inspiration that the King himself had also thought at that time to establish a new Inn of Court, a fifth Inn, in his own name, as a school for legislators and diplomats. It would take the sons of the rising men and teach them the civil law, history, the arts of the statesman, to speak and write a proper French tongue and not its bastard legal offspring, and Latin too. It would regulate the education of some of the best young men in the kingdom, for the King's service. A fitting establishment of new learning, all to be paid for from the monastic revenue.

So Cromwell had commissioned a report from Nick Bacon, Robert Cary and Tom Denton of the Middle Temple; good men all, but the germ of it and the energy were Nick's. How often they had discussed it in the years after! The Inns hated the scheme, of course, seeing the challenge of it and sensing they would be next for reformation. Still more the universities when they heard of it, and the King's new friends swarming all over to kill it for its expense, lest it suck out the revenue from the sale of Church estates and take it away from them. Burghley recalls the history of the Diocese of Lincoln, in his own country, when it had sought to set up a third university in England in the time of Edward III. Such had been the anxiety at Oxford and Cambridge that they had buried their mutual dislikes and made a joint petition to the King to kill the scheme. And he had done so.

Yet Nick's project might have happened, and the country all the better for it.

But when it failed Nick was nothing daunted, for he then pressed the need to reform the Court of Wards, and early in the new reign they had both guided the Queen to improve the teaching of Crown wards. And he used to scold Burghley that his attention to wards' lands and neglect of their minds was plainly to set the cart before the horse.

So, yes, Burghley fancies he knows the pedigree of this proposal. But its scope is of a quite different magnitude. It is for a great college, a new Lyceum, to bring the arts of administration and law and diplomacy together with natural philosophy under a single roof. Not only that, to draw in practical skills of every variety, from husbandry and agriculture to magnetism and medicine, from lead and iron and leather and wool production to the arts of war. It will have a library, furnaces, a mill, gardens of different plants, a zoo.

Even its location has been compassed, at Twickenham, close to Richmond Palace and Hampton Court. Scholars and men of practice in every field will be sought out and assembled from across Europe. It will breed students fit for the active civic life that Cicero himself had proclaimed the highest calling for a man. It will be a beacon of advanced thought, to the profit of England and the glory of the Crown.

As for the promoter, he writes that his own aspiration is modest: certainly not to direct or guide such an august institution, but merely to act as secretary to a board of commissioners charged to that effect. He has in preparation a note which could act as draft for an instruction.

The Queen has a fascination with clever men and the play of the mind. She loves youth and energy. She will wish to see this letter, if she hears of it, perhaps even to question her young Lord Keeper in person. Yet in Burghley the letter stirs a strange mixture of emotions. He feels the filial piety, and the shadow of the father behind it. It comes from family, and family comes first. It is itself, for all its flattering and intricate language, a work of real intellect and imagination. All these things count for it.

But Burghley does not trust men of intellect any more, and he does not admire imagination. He has had the eloquence bled out of him. Take this new establishment for what it is, and it is serious work, at great cost and with no revenue attached. The old opponents of King Henry's scheme will spring into the attack, and to their number will be added the licence-holders, the concessionaries and guilds from the brasiers to the wax chandlers, and all hot at any infringement of their trades. Nor will the great foreign courts take kindly to their finest minds being lured westwards by Protestant English gold.

And there is something else, though it takes time to rise to the surface. Under Sir Nicholas's will, Burghley has been charged with the care of Anthony and Francis Bacon. He has known them both from birth. Yet – he is too proud to admit it – he has, he has long had, a… what? … a *disrelish* of Francis. Too much self-conceit, too much glister. No sense of doubt within him, no knowledge of the rocks that lie beneath even the most placid seas, of the froward fortune that put Burghley himself in the Tower for eight weeks under

King Edward VI, and made him take the sacraments of mass and give confession under Mary, though the words stuck like fish bones in his throat.

This letter makes the very point. It is couched in tones of obsequy. It slips and slides past obvious difficulties with a honeyed tongue. But – yes, this is it; this is what grates most – at its core is a presuming and equalising spirit, which would put its sender on a level with Lord Burghley himself. Burghley has seen many young men of good birth and still higher self-estimation over the years; his house has been almost a school for his many dozens of wards. Some have gone on to greatness. Some have been grievous to him, such as de Vere, the Earl of Oxford, who allured his beloved daughter Anne, married her, made her pregnant, and then disclaimed and denounced her for adultery.

So Burghley knows the cock-horse type. That this pup Bacon would send such a letter just at a time when Burghley has been constantly distracted from administration by the need to settle Nick's debts and bequests, let alone to calm the warring factions of Bacon brothers and Bacon wife and mother… well, that in itself argues a want of judgement as well as courtesy. To say nothing of his duty as Lord Treasurer and principal counsellor to protect the Queen, who is still crying betrayal at the secret marriage of her sweet Robin, the Earl of Leicester; or to manage the Privy Council, which is split on the match he has been exploring for Her Majesty with the Duke of Anjou.

The Queen hates expense, which must surely doom this college scheme. But what if Her Majesty were taken with it? All young Bacon's faults would be magnified and compounded by the success. Intolerably so. He would be placed at the heart of a new institution, which might itself disturb the balance of government. The way would lie open to rapid preferment at court, and that could be nothing good for the chances of his own son Robert, whose merits are signal but would be cast into dark shadow by the brilliance of his cousin.

Robert, who has no glister, but splayed feet, a misshapen back and constant pain. Little Robert, cruelly dealt with by the same fortune that his cousin Francis Bacon seeks to ride to glory. Robert, on whom his family's future and his father's hopes depend.

Lord Burghley puts the letter down. Perhaps it will go missing.

9

GRAY'S INN, SPRING 1580

The stone is dropped, it falls. Francis waits to hear the echo.

He is filled with hope and expectation. Urged on by a wafting breeze, surely a letter from the young Lord Keeper must land happily with the Queen? Yes, the scheme would be a new venture, even an ambitious one. It is not without risk. But look at Drake: he has been right round the world, discovered new lands and captured mountains of Spanish gold, all on the Queen's commission. What is Francis Bacon's own project but to sail the seas of human thought, discover unimagined continents, chart them, quarry their treasure and bring those riches back to England? And gold and silver are used up, treasure is spent. But knowledge remains forever, untouched by time and fortune.

Anthony is still more excited, for other reasons. He leaves for France shortly thereafter, bearing with him a letter of recommendation from Lord Burghley; a letter which particularly plays upon the family connection, the bearer being as Burghley says by the testament of his honourable good father committed to me, and by his mother referred absolutely to my consideration.

A promising augury indeed, supported when they meet by words of approbation and interest in Francis's scheme! The brothers celebrate with an extended evening at The Game Cock, and an order by Francis for six yards of green damask silk, for a coat lined in grey and finished with blue grosgrain at thirty shillings a yard. The silk must

31

be imported from Florence, and it will be ruinously expensive, but Anthony waves his worries away.

'The truth, dear brother,' he says, calling for another tankard, 'is that you have no choice. You cannot be ill-dressed if you would make your way at court, for nothing less is requisite in the service of the Queen. Mark my words, Frank: Nothing. Less.'

'It is the same for me,' Anthony continues gaily. 'God hath given me a genius for life, as he hath given you a genius for work. When I call for physic, or for almond milk to soothe my digestion, I do it to sustain me, but only for those difficult days to come when I must eat and drink my way with Ned Selwyn through France. Pity me, Frank, that I am so bounden to my calling.'

'Ha! If your travels are anything like mine, you may get a hotter reception than you know,' says Francis.

Anthony laughs.

'But, brother, you were in harness then with Paulet, while I shall be free. My duties will be to make new friends, talk like a gossip, compose sonnets when I desire, and write when it shall please me to Secretary Walsingham who will be my master.

'No, Frank,' Anthony continues, 'your task is to watch over our mother, ensure she remits regular sums of money to me from the estate, and above all see she does not marry one of her preachers. Lose her and we lose Gorhambury, and that is ruin for us both.'

By Easter there is still no word from Burghley touching the letter Francis has sent.

Perhaps six months is not so long, he reflects, with such mighty personages. There are great matters of state at hand: revolt in the Spanish Netherlands, Catholic treasons at home, the vexed matter of the succession. His scheme is a novel and weighty one. Give it time.

Still, he is uneasy, and to relieve his mind he mentions his letter on a visit to his mother at Gorhambury. Anthony need not fear for any marriage by her, no doubt of that, for the house is all but empty now.

The great hall, the gallery, the state rooms need a mass of servants to fill them, to polish the furniture and keep the fires burning, to dust the books and tapestries, to clean the magnificent stained glass. With just a few old retainers left, the rooms are ever in shadow, and Francis feels the dread anew of the dream he had before his father's death. As for the gardens, they are unkempt, the grass overgrown, weeds amid the parterres.

His mother keeps to her privy rooms, but they meet for chapel and for walks and meals. She too is dark, in dress and in the spirit with which she rails at her idle and ungodly tenants, but she lightens at his words.

'You have writ to Lord Burghley, and your letter is before the Queen? But Francis, this is good news indeed! Your uncle is a wise man, a good man. He is careful, but he has an eye for young men of ability. He has been kind to me in fending off your ravenous half-brothers from what little patrimony still remains in my name. And he is, as is my sister Mildred, someone who knows the value of a family connection. I do not doubt of your success. William has strings to pull with any man of rank across the land. See if he does not do something for you, and it may be passing good.'

'Mother, it is but early in the play; we cannot tell what will issue.'

'*You* cannot, my boy. But I know how it ends, though I care nothing for mummery. You shall have preferment, you must have it, for that you can set forth what is in your teeming mind. And if not what you seek today, then why not a reversion, or a clerkship *sine cura* in the Court of Chancery, or the Exchequer?'

'Mother...'

'Or may he not give you a letter of introduction to the father of some marriageable young lady of substantial fortune? He is Master of the Court of Wards, after all. Ah, if only your father were still alive to superintend such an alliance! I feel my own insufficiency so keenly where matters of business are concerned.'

'Mother!'

'… And if it please God then let any of this be so, and right soon, for your brother's steward Mantell is forever pressing me for money to send to France. Though he may scant the detail I cannot, and every shilling passed over is a shilling I cannot use for you, or the estate. Provided, of course, that same shilling does not end up in Mantell's own knavish pocket. That is all I will say.'

Back at Gray's Inn, Francis writes to Anthony. Loving and beloved brother, I long to tell you how matters fare with our uncle, but the waters have closed over my letter and no dove yet appeareth with leaf of olive to show it still liveth. If for yourself you give him good service, as must be, it may tip the balance of my suit in his affections. Our mother continues undiminished in voice and opinions. If you will remit me £10 I will be forever grateful for I am sore pressed till Lammas. Send me what you have, of news or credit. Your entire loving brother.

May passes, then June, and it is stifling in London.

Francis does not sleep, he cannot. Surely, he must have an answer, for letters such as this cannot go unanswered. Maybe the reply is a negative, and his uncle is shielding the blow. Maybe his own letter has been lost, or they do not feel its full weight and merit. Maybe the Queen has turned against him, but for what reason? It would surely be presumptuous to send again, as though to call Lord Burghley to his duty. But not to know, and to consign so fair a project to an unconsidered dust, is not to be borne.

Finally, he takes pen to hand once more. First to his mother, to seek her support with his uncle. And second, some weeks later, to Lord Burghley himself.

MY SINGULAR GOOD LORD, he writes, in excuse of my motion, lest it should appear to your Lordship altogether undiscreet and unadvised, so my hope to obtain it resteth only upon your Lordship's good affection toward me and grace with Her Majesty... if it may please your Lordship both herein and elsewhere to be my patron, and to make account of me as one in whose well-doing your Lordship hath interest... I cannot account your Lordship's service distinct from that which I owe to God and my Prince; the performance whereof to best proof and purpose is the meeting point and rendezvous of all my thoughts.

Intricate words again! Yet his deeper meaning is not hard to divine: *I beg you, love me, take me into your charge, and I will repay you with service equal to that I owe God and our Queen.*

It is no easy thing to swallow pride, to set oneself at the foot of the great and seek with thanks to gather up the scrapings from their table.

Francis takes care to flatter his uncle with the full energies of his mind, forcing himself to feel the proper devotion of a loving suppliant in hope his words will carry his conviction. It must be done, for that which is requisite must be done.

His new coat finally arrives. It is magnificent.

10

LONDON, MARCH 1590

Think, think. The numbers float out of focus, and he must force himself to drag them back, to reckon and tally. They are written on whatever serves the purpose; small papers, bits of wood, scraps of cloth. Often there are words too: silk, bere, linnen, paper, holland shirts, silver buckles, rose oil, portwine. And they are everywhere.

All I have is books and bills, he thinks. My books come with bills, and my bills come in books. Some are so ancient they seem to have taken up a residence of their own in chambers; they are the senior benchers of my penury. Some are mere mendicants, moving from pocket to bag to pot to desk to table. Some are new acquaintances, met with from time to time again, without pleasure. But when I see them, all accost me like footpads, with vicious little stabs to the gut.

And these are the ones he still has hold of, the ones he cannot bring himself to hand over. Time was when his steward Henry would see him every few months, and lay down the big leather-bound ledger before asking for money to pay what was due. All the numbers carefully tabulated, with a separate page for income received and expected. Now it feels like every other week. And, as they both know, Francis never has the stomach to put all the tallies on the table.

These are not really debts, he thinks. They are power, control. These men come for me because they can. The hares scatter in the face of the pack, but I am the hare that cannot run, and if I cannot escape by other means I will be torn in pieces, or drawn like Nicholas Horner the Catholic at Smithfield lately. If I had a position at court, I could be rid of these papers, pay them off, thrust them into the grate or – he glows at the thought – take the whole pile and burn them one by one in front of my creditors, they all scowling behind their smiles.

Francis Bacon looks in the glass, and he does not see a bad man. Now in his thirtieth year, he has hazel eyes, luxuriant brown hair, which he wears long in the fashion of the time, and a brown beard and moustaches. In disposition he is kind, often soft. He gives Christian alms with money he does not have, and he cannot resist a petitioner in straitened circumstance.

But he must live like a gentleman. He must dress finely – as witness his latest acquisition, a doublet in French cherry velvet with black piping, slashes on the sleeves revealing blue. He must be properly shaven, and his beard regularly clipped and pointed. And he must be able to dispense favour, and return it. A hogshead of oysters, a haunch of venison... he longs for a day when he can scatter these *nugae* as little acts of grace, without thought of recompense.

He has no income, but gentlemen with capital can and do live without income the land over. The problem is that he has no capital either. All he has are his name and his talent, and no one is interested.

Nearly ten years have now passed since that letter to Burghley. Francis keeps up his attendance at the Inn, but with only half a heart. Of his great project he heard nothing more, bar a few muttered words of acknowledgment from his uncle.

The cup of patronage has not been entirely dry: he has acted as interpreter at a great banquet for the French in pursuit of the royal marriage, thanks to Burghley. But what has flowed has been honorific, not pecuniary, and it has largely come through others. He is made the Member of Parliament for Bossiney in 1581, but that is thanks not to Burghley but to the Earl of Bedford, who is Francis's godfather. When the Queen summons a parliament in 1584, Burghley finally puts him in at the last moment for Gatton, and is then visibly disconcerted and irritated when Francis has to reveal that he has already accepted the nomination at Weymouth, owing to Bedford.

And Parliament? To be a Member of Parliament carries an air of distinction, to be sure, especially in a young man of just twenty-three years, for whom greatness must surely be marked out. Parliament itself fills his days from eight of the morning till dinner, with committee work in the afternoon. It gives him employment and, with over a dozen of his relatives in the House, good opportunities to build his connections. But it brings nothing in to his leather-bound ledger. On the contrary, it is all expense, for entertaining, fees and tips. And it is now nine years since he was first named Member, and six since he took his seat. Six years in which he has looked, constantly and without reward, for means to ascend.

His name, family and connections have long been debated and digested by the older Parliament men whom he joins at Westminster. And in truth he has quietly revelled in their tavern mutterings of respect, envy or contempt alike. 'Ah, there goeth Nick Bacon's latest son.' 'Another? Are we not full up with them?' 'Full up and fed, fed up and full.' 'Never too many to vote the Queen's business, methinks. He'll fly past you and me, just you watch.'

They speak of promise. But Francis knows his duty too, and when the Bill came in to prevent men from leasing out their rights to wardship and denying the Crown its due, a Bill much hated by the rising men across the Chamber, he spoke in favour of it in his first speech, working in a mention of his father and drawing upon his own experience as a fifth son to thank the monarch for her bounty. 'He talketh much on himself,' 'too much matter in the speech,' they said, and he felt the anger of many Members afterwards, but

Secretary Walsingham and Speaker Puckering both congratulated him.

Perhaps I am not the hare but the young hound after the course, he had thought, blooded from the body of the killed.

Two years later, his loyalty was on show again. To all appearance it was no real test, for the parliament of 1586 had but one true purpose: to condemn Mary Stuart of Scots for her treasonous foreknowledge and involvement in a dastardly plot to assassinate the Queen of England. And condemn her it did, with energy and dispatch, calling in aid rumour and evidence of designs for insurrection and invasion from Spain.

But such windy passion was not in Francis Bacon's heart. He felt the pull of the true Church, of course. But he had also read, read and voted for, the Act for the Queen's Surety, with its studied silence about Mary of Scots. And he had read the Instrument of Association, drafted by Burghley and Walsingham, by which the Act authorised all subjects 'by all forcible and possible means to pursue to death every one of such wicked persons, by whom or by whose means assent or privity any such invasion or rebellion shall be in form aforesaid denounced to have been made, or such wicked act attempted, or other thing compassed or imagined against Her Majesty's person'.

To use such a temporal power to kill a queen, God's own anointed representative on Earth, and by such a manifest, intended and enmeshing snare of law... is that justice? Did not Queen Elizabeth extend herself to protect Mary of Scots on just this ground for many a year?

But that was not the moment for let or cavil. To equivocate on such an issue, to debate the corners of natural justice in the face of such an Act... even to contemplate the question with the House roaring death and vengeance, that would have risked the end of all his hopes, and perhaps a visit to the Tower. When the moment came Francis took special care to drown his doubts and strangle his scruples. It was an honour for a junior Member to be called to speak in such a debate, and he obliged his political friends by adding his voice loudly to the call for execution.

All this public loyalty has been noted by the finely coated Privy Council men who occupy the government bench, and shortly thereafter Francis is nominated to a Council panel of inquiry into Catholic prisoners.

He is now so anxious for favour that he snatches at it. Anything to have status in some degree, a voice.

11

LONDON, MARCH 1590

Yet with time the mutterings start to weigh on him. These men read me, he thinks, and they see nothing inside. They expect great things of me, yet what am I, and what do I have to show for all my family and connections? I do not advance, yet I behold the rising men in Parliament, these Gawdys, Hydes and Stanhopes, all preening for notice and jostling for preferment. None doubtful of his own worth, and all the stronger for it.

Nor are matters better at the Inn. Men who have toiled over their yearbooks mislike his ability, which he does not trouble to disguise, and his diligence, which is not solely devoted to the trade of lawyering. They wonder at the Lord Keeper's chambers staying with his sons long after the Lord Keeper himself is dead, and the more with new building work and the lease even extended.

But comment becomes contempt when, as a mere student, Francis is seen sporting an utter barrister's robes in the city, years before they are his due. *Facies est fortuna*. Men dress, by law and by custom, according to their station and their honours. The Inn has always been strict in such matters, and this over-reaching is an impertinence which will not lightly be forgotten. And the offence is magnified when Francis presses to be made a full Bencher of the Inn at an unseasonably early age.

News of men's ill opinion reaches the Lord Treasurer's ears. So Francis must write yet again to his uncle, to confute and deny the hard words of men that did misaffect me... I protest simply before God,

that I sought therein an ease in coming within bars, and not any extraordinary or singular note of favour... I find that such persons as
are of nature bashful (as myself is), whereby they want that plausible
familiarity which others have, are often mistaken for proud. But once I
know well, and I most humbly beseech your Lordship to believe, that
arrogancy and overweening is so far from my nature, as if I think well
of myself in any thing it is in this, that I am free from that vice.

Such letters are painful to write, painful to receive. To have the
Bacon name sullied, and at his own Inn where the Queen herself
is Patron Lady, is not to be borne, and the infection must not be
allowed to spread. So Lord Burghley at last pulls one of his strings
and smoothes Francis's path a little to make him first Bencher of
the Inn, then Reader. And then he pulls another and Francis receives a reversion on the clerkship of the Star Chamber. A high
recognition, with few duties, and carrying with it the handsome
sum of £1,600 a year.

But, Francis bitterly reflects, this is not a position at court, but a
cul-de-sac suited to a scholarly life. Had not his father been made
Solicitor to the Court of Augmentations at the age of twenty-
seven, without ever having practised? It was the perfect position
for a man on the rise, with its constant stream of lands from the
dissolved monasteries and abbeys. No, uncle Burghley has done
enough for himself, but not enough for Francis, so much is plain.
And the income will be delayed till the present clerk dies or gives it
up, which is like to mean years of wait.

All this may mend his prospect, but it does not fill his barn. It
brings no occupation to his agitated mind, no place to sport his fine
clothes, and nothing new to come into the leather-bound ledger.

But Francis has not been idle. He has written papers, tracts, pamphlets, all designed to make himself pleasing to the great and gain
attention in certain corners of the court.

His range is wide, if not yet prodigious. He defends the Queen in matters of religion, and slips quietly sideways from the true reformed Church of his mother to the *via media* of his father. He drafts diplomatic letters for Walsingham. More helpfully still, in the parliament of 1589 he crafts a legal form of words which eases the passage of a double subsidy needed to maintain the fight against the Spanish. This preamble to the Bill is ingenious. Backbenchers hate the expense of a double subsidy, but it is drafted in such a way as to limit any precedent set; Burghley insists the Bill be done quickly, and the Queen just wants the money. So all are well pleased. Yet still no preferment follows.

This is a time of flux. The Spanish *Gran Armada* has been destroyed amid the storms of the Channel, but, though no one speaks of it, Drake's expedition of the following year against the Spanish also sustained grievous losses from weather and disease. And there has been a change in the balance of forces at court as well. The Earl of Leicester, beloved of the Queen, is dead; Leicester, whose men have been Her Majesty's excited audience on the shore at Tilbury. Chancellor Mildmay is gone, and now Walsingham is rumoured near the grave. Hatton remains to dance a galliard at court, but the coming man is Leicester's stepson and Burghley's ward, the Earl of Essex.

Francis knows these men of old, yet now it is as if they are the shimmering stars, which a man can reach out to but never touch. And Robert Cecil... can the talk be true? Does the Queen's Pygmy now bid fair to overtake her young Lord Keeper? They say Burghley intends to make his own son Secretary of State, responsible above all for foreign matters, and he is already active in the business. Certainly Cecil is everywhere at court. He bustles through the Palace of Whitehall holding papers, he attends the Queen on her summer progress, he coos sweet counsel into her proffered ear.

And Francis has noticed something else over the years, something that fills him with jealousy. In Parliament, at family gatherings, Robert is no longer the same cold and private youth he was.

And he has never mentioned, there is no sign that he even recalls, that fateful moment at the ponds in Gorhambury all those years before.

No, Francis thinks with a shudder: *he is become gracious.* He has fine words for everyone around him, he scatters kindness like corn before guinea fowl. And they all eagerly peck it up.

12

LONDON, MARCH 1590

Beloved father, thou whose kindly eye
Kept careful watch for me o'er all my youth
Whose warmth of heart no man on earth could buy
Nor steady judgement e'er seduce from truth
If I have failed to honour thee in act
Have scorned thy memory, forgot thy aid
Then heed me not. But if to thee in fact
Thy love a loving son hath oft repaid
Then by the God above whom all revere
Attend me now, turn back this evil crone
Ill fortune whose entoiling hate and fear
Will else destroy me ere my work is done.
'Cross all man's arts my thoughts the world bestride
And will, if thou wilt only be my guide.

Truly, neglect is the mother of ambition, Francis reflects.

What is poetry when every upward path is closed? Every day, he seems to feel time itself flow past him, and dissipate itself away with nothing to show. He is a man of no effect or consequence. Yet still a restless yearning drives on the clockwork of his mind like a vast pendulum, pushing its escapement from side to side, ceaselessly back and forth.

Francis despises the schoolmen as arid sifters of the sands or panners for fool's gold, men who search vainly through syllogisms to weed out falsehood and establish true knowledge. That is all very well: but what does he have to show for himself? What alternative does he propose?

After all, the question is not what do you attack, but what do you defend. On a wax tablet, Francis likes to say, you cannot write anything new until you rub out the old. With the mind it is not so; there you cannot rub out the old till you have written in the new. If men have better knowledge, then what was old was not knowledge at all, but mere superstition. It must be attacked, undermined and exploded, and their faith in it withal. But how?

And so, closeted in his chambers at the Inn, lonely, angry and spurning company, driven on by his thoughts and fears, Francis sets himself a new task, to question the very foundations of true knowledge. For this, he must know where the greatest sages have erred, and how and why. So he summons up the thinkers of the past, and subjects them to a searching cross-examination.

It is as though they come to a court: a court not of law or of Kings but of human inquiry. He, Francis, stands at the manteltree, as prosecuting counsel; there at the table in sad succession sit Aristotle, Plato, Galen and others, these ancient sages all to face indictment for their false coinages, vague inductions and bogus panaceas. Evidence to be called, not from priests or professors but from geometers and builders, farmers and husbandmen, metalworkers and alchemists and navigators and foundrymen. And nature itself in the chair, to pronounce final judgment.

And as he thinks on this and on his dreams of greatness, as he reflects on the contrast between his outward stagnation and inner energy, between the soaring scope of his ambition and the infirmity of his prospects, something shifts. Deep inside him there is a movement in the clockwork; a great cog revolves, the gears turn, a hammer strikes.

The force of recognition makes him sweat. Enough of weakness, he thinks, enough of doubt. None will help me but myself. I must chart a new course, or go to the grave unloved, unpitied and unfeared.

Quisque faber fortunae suae, every man is maker of his own fortune. So will I be.

13

GORHAMBURY, SUMMER 1591

Lady Bacon can never say exactly when her hopes finally faded; perhaps they still have not.

Her Lord and she discussed the matter regularly when the boys were young. There was playful joshing about the charms of young mistress this or lady that, and quieter rumination about the advantages of a well-chosen wife. A marriage is always between families, Sir Nicholas used to say. He was hardly the man to miss its possibilities, and all his first three boys have been well lodged. Their sisters too, for that matter. And there has been a large clutch of grandchildren.

But with Anne's boys, matters are different. Not for the want of trying, though. Sir Nicholas had gone through a considerable process of alliance with one Master Paget, himself well married three times, full of wealth and a Sheriff of the City of London. The Paget daughter Dowsabell had been destined for Anthony at sixteen. The papers were all drawn up, with allowances, estates, an annuity and a large bequest at her parents' death. And then... the dish long prepared grew suddenly stale. Anthony would not have it, and nor would she.

Quite why not, Lady Bacon cannot tell, not at least till long afterwards. And then her husband dies and her world suddenly shrinks in upon itself almost to nothing.

She worries that her two boys do not pray enough and need the guidance of a father's authority. Anthony is in France, and she hears little of him; little, that is, apart from money matters pressed by his insolent Popish servants, and vague, disquieting rumours. She fears for his soul and frets about his health.

But Francis? Why should he not take a wife who can make him happy, and extend the family? There are plenty more Pagets and their like in London, rich merchants on the rise who would give a handsome dowry to have their daughters tied to the Bacon name, if it could just be arranged. She has dreams of Gorhambury full of noisy grandchildren falling over each other in sport and playing with their Cecil cousins, all those fair little girls of Thomas's, Mary, Dorothy, Eliza and Frances. The family renewed, and its fortunes likewise.

But slowly, softly, dimly, she comes to believe that there will be no marriage for Francis, no grandchildren, and no sportive bruiting to fill the halls of Gorhambury. She must make do with the servants, with divines come to talk the scriptures, and with silence.

II

HUBRIS: 1592–1601

14

LONDON, JANUARY 1594

Sir Robert Cecil and the Earl of Essex are in a carriage, driving away after the interrogation of the Queen's doctor, Lopez. Cecil asks Essex who his candidate is for the vacant position of Attorney General.

Essex says, 'I wonder that you should ask me that question, seeing it could not be unknown unto you that I stand resolutely against all whosoever for Francis Bacon.'

'Good Lord, I wonder that your Lordship should go about to waste your strength in so unlikely or impossible a matter.'

'A younger than Francis, of lesser learning and of no greater experience, sueth and shoveth with all force for an office of far greater importance, greater charge and greater weight than the Attorneyship.'

'I know your Lordship means myself,' says Cecil.

'Although my years and experience are small,' he goes on, 'yet weighing the school I studied in and the great wisdom and learning of my schoolmaster, and the pains and observations I daily passed, yet I deem my qualifications to be sufficient. The added entitlement of my father's long service will make good the rest.'

Cecil adds, 'I beg your Lordship to consider of it, if at least your Lordship had spoken of the Solicitorship for Bacon, that might be of easier digestion to Her Majesty.'

'Digest me no digestions!' Essex snorts. 'It is the Attorneyship that I must have for Francis, and in that I will spend all my power, mine authority, and amity, and with tooth and nails defend and procure the same for him against whomsoever, and whosoever getteth this office out of my hands for any other, before he have it, it shall cost him the coming by, and this be you assured of, Sir Robert, for now do I fully declare myself.

'And for your own part, Sir Robert, I find strange both of my Lord Treasurer and you that can have the mind to seek the preferment of a stranger before so near a kinsman as a first cousin.'

15

LONDON, OCTOBER 1592

But O, methinks, how slow
This old moon wanes! She lingers my desires,
Like to a stepdame or a dowager
Long withering out a young man's revenue.

Yet all this lies in the future. For the present, Francis Bacon has not given up his quest for knowledge. But now a new course and a new patron beckon to his earthly ambitions.

And the Earl of Essex is not *terra incognita*. He is the soldier into whose hand Sir Philip Sidney thrust his sword as he was taken mortally wounded from the battlefield of Zutphen. Sidney, warrior, writer of sonnets, author of *Astrophil and Stella*, and champion of the reformed Church.

Essex is not quite twenty-seven years of age, four years younger than Francis, and he is many things. He is martial valour, courage, the brightest colours of youth and spirit. But he is also style, wit, history, refined letters and an eye for beauty in all things, a scholar of the University of Cambridge who has performed the public exercises and been declared *magister artium*. He has *sprezzatura*, the studied nonchalance of the gentleman. Nay, more, he is everything Castiglione himself could want in a courtier, and yet he carries with him too the English chivalry of old.

Compared to such a man, Lord Burghley is the grey of greyness bidden towards the grave. His *sprezzatura* has long since faded, if it ever was. His seventieth birthday celebrations two years before were magnificent in their feasting and pageant and music. The houses he has built are marvels of grandeur and artistry. But Francis has also seen his uncle flinch with the gout, his hands gnarled, struggling even to hold a pen.

And it is not only Burghley who declines, for the Queen is now in her sixtieth year. It is treason to compass her death, not wise even to consider the possibility. But the unasked, unanswered questions of the succession hang over court and nation, make the times uncertain and set men against each other in rivalry for power.

Though none dare speak of it, none can miss the cracks of age that show through her painted mask of white. Least of all Essex, her Master of Horse, who, though thirty years and more her junior, is regularly in her closet. Or so men say.

This is the autumn of her years, and must surely yield to winter. The times are shaking men from their moorings, and it is well to be prepared. Where is the spring? There will be a new dispensation, but from whom, and when?

Several years before, Francis had bid for Essex's support in a letter to Leicester. It was an act of prudence, intended to register an affinity with the Queen's new likely favourite. Since then the two men have developed an acquaintance that has ripened into friendship. Essex has enlisted Francis to help in the writing of devices and masques. For his part, Francis has introduced his friend Thomas Phelippes, a great expert in codes and ciphers, to Essex and urged the Earl to develop the network of foreign informants fitting to a statesman.

Yet, as Francis knows well, the politics are delicate. Essex was entrusted by his father on his deathbed to the guardianship of Burghley. He grew up at Cecil House, and so is all but kin to Robert Cecil the Pygmy. His family are from Wales and of noble origin, but he has no rich estates nor any great wealth – or had none at least, till the Queen let him take over her monopoly on sweet wines when Leicester died. Yet the rapid rise of Essex is plain for all to see.

As for Robert Cecil, his rise too has continued, without check. Francis had noted with some pain that Cecil was made Privy Councillor and then knighted in the year before.

Sooner or later there must be a collision, he thinks. Is Essex still friend to the Cecils, or is he now their enemy? Can Francis press his suit on both sides, with Burghley and Essex, or must he choose?

As Francis ponders these questions, there comes the sweetest sound he knows: the voice of his brother, at last returned from overseas. Odysseus took ten long years to voyage back from Troy, and Anthony has spent ten long years in France and more, working as intelligencer and spy on his travels from Paris to Marseille to Bordeaux, and on to Béarn and the southern Kingdom of Navarre. How each has changed to the other, both now grown men of three- and one-and-thirty!

Anthony has brought back with him his lute and virginals, his love of song and poetry and endless tales of adventure. And books and friendships and information too, for he is on terms with men so diverse and great in their way as would astonish, from King Henry IV to Montaigne the essayist and Beza the Protestant cleric of Geneva – alongside a diverse crowd of several dozen quiet informers and projectors whom he quietly nourishes across the continent.

Yet in all that time, despite great risk, ill health and weakness, especially in his legs, he has had little thanks and less reward for his work. Sir Francis Walsingham the great spymaster is dead. As for Burghley: his words, Anthony says, make fools fain, and yet even in these is there no offer or hopeful assurance of real kindness, which I thought I might justly expect at the Lord Treasurer's hands, who had inned my ten years' harvest into his own barn without any halfpenny charge.

Francis is hale, but he sees his brother lame and older than his years. He eats late and sleeps little. Yet for all that, and his pretty new French ways, under the surface Anthony is little changed. He still loves finery and hates parsimony as much as he ever did, if not more so from his time at the French court. It is a source of distraction to Lady Bacon that he must keep a carriage. It is rather for his dignity than for his health, and leaves him with more debts than ever.

But Anthony's spirits are continuously in flight, soaring and diving like swallows between exuberance and melancholia. There is a sense of desperation behind them. His business in France ended in a welter of recrimination from powerful enemies in Montauban and Bordeaux. It seems another marriage has been spurned. Now a former friend, one Ridley, calls him a sodomite – a man can be *brûlé vif*, burned alive, for that in France – and threatens to denounce him to the Privy Council as a Catholic sympathiser.

Perhaps all this is the true reason why Anthony will not stir from Gray's Inn, and after a time retreats to Gorhambury, pleading the renewal of plague in the city. Perhaps it is why he can never bring himself to go to court, despite the pleas of his family and the Queen's inquiries. Or perhaps it is gout and the stone, by both of which he is assailed, or his ever-increasing use of physic, of whose evil effects both his mother and Walsingham had often warned him.

To Francis, Anthony is like the lettuce that bodies forth so well in early summer, then bolts to seed in the heat for lack of water. But his brother's warmth is undimmed, his mind unaltered, his talk resolute. And he is all in all for the Earl of Essex.

16

TWICKENHAM PARK, OCTOBER 1592

'Frank, do you not see that in Essex all our prayers may be answered?'

They are walking in the garden at Twickenham. Francis has the rent of a house, and Anthony is there to recover health and spirits.

'Brother,' says Francis, 'his Lordship is the coming man, no doubt. But what can you and I do to assist him?'

'Sooth, man, but he needs us. He is deep in the Queen's affections, and must surely be made Privy Councillor ere long. 'Tis plain as plain he intendeth to succeed Lord Burghley and supplant his son, who is not our friend. Essex is a man of arms, but he will come to see that that is not enough. He hath his soldiers and men of business, but he must want good counsel and intelligence. And he has a great admiration for you and for your gifts.

'Well, Francis, you can be his counsel and I his intelligencer! I can give him full benefit of my friends abroad. Did I not write the Queen herself a survey of opinion in France, Italy, Spain, Austriche, the German dukes and landgraves, Sweden? How can the Earl refuse us?'

'Believe me, he will find a way to refuse, if my experience of these great men be true.'

'Nay, Francis. See how he acts. Can you not see how he loves and reverences you? And see his company. The Earl of Southampton is never far from his side, and he is much admired. Essex hath assured the publication of *Arcadia*, and an array of wits and scholars cluster about him. I was at his house last week and I saw Fulke Greville and Henry Savile at his table. Spenser is his intimate, as he was to Leicester before him. And there will be others. It is not to be doubted.'

'Our uncle will hear of it.'

'And what's to it? Hath Burghley been so great a patron that you cannot forswear him? Every letter I have had from you these last ten years hath borne the stamp of his disregard. Yes, the Earl of Essex is ambitious, but his is a fine and manly ambition, to do good by God and his Queen.

'And mark this, brother – he is not afraid of men of talent. He will get that which he seeks. And we can help him.'

Anthony and the Earl of Essex fell into the harmony of deep friendship from their first meeting, so much is clear to Francis. Essex liked his brother's wit and warmth and breadth of knowledge, true enough, but was also touched by his frailty and delicacy of temper. As for Anthony, he has always longed for someone to admire, a lord, almost a prince, who would unite power and principle, and all the more that Anthony is so out of sorts with Burghley and his son.

Still, Francis is not quite persuaded. Even now he cannot cut the cord to family, however frayed it may be. So once again, as though for the last time, he petitions his uncle Burghley. Only this time he cannot stop himself, but pours his soul into a letter at once pleading and smouldering with anger and contention.

MY LORD – With as much confidence as mine own honest and faithful devotion unto your service and your honourable correspondence unto me and my poor estate can breed in a man, do I commend myself unto your Lordship.

I wax now somewhat ancient: one-and-thirty is a great deal of sand in the hour-glass... I ever bare a mind to serve Her Majesty, as a man born under an excellent sovereign, that deserveth the dedication of all men's abilities.

I confess that I have as vast contemplative ends, as I have moderate civil ends. For I have taken all knowledge to be my province; and if I could purge it of two sorts of rovers, whereof the one with frivolous disputations, confutations, and verbosities, the other with blind experiments and auricular traditions and impostures, hath committed so many spoils, I hope I should bring in industrious observations, grounded conclusions, and profitable inventions and discoveries; the best state of that province.

Francis continues, saying this, whether it be curiosity, or vainglory, or nature, or *philanthropia*, is so fixed in my mind as it cannot be removed. If your Lordship will not carry me on, I will not do as Anaxagoras did, who reduced himself with contemplation unto voluntary poverty. But this I will do; I will sell the inheritance that I have, and purchase some lease of quick revenue, or some office of gain that shall be executed by deputy, and so give over all care of service, and become some sorry book-maker, or a true pioneer in that mine of truth, which lay so deep.

This which I have writ unto your Lordship is rather thoughts than words, being set down without all art, disguising, or reservation... And even so I wish your Lordship all happiness, and to myself means and occasion to be added to my faithful desire to do you service. From my lodging at Gray's Inn, Fra Bacon.

I have as vast contemplative ends, as I have moderate civil ends. For I have taken all knowledge to be my province... This is both his confession and his manifesto. Indeed, it is the manifesto of a future undreamed of by others.

Yet Francis's letter fails, again. There is acknowledgement from his uncle, but nothing more. And so the clockwork of his mind moves ever on.

17

THE PALACE OF WESTMINSTER, FEBRUARY 1593

The Queen has summoned another parliament, and again she has but a single purpose: the supply of fresh revenue to the Crown. There are reports of the plague near London, and she intends this parliament will be short and simple. New taxes, but no new Bills, which might distract and divide men from their duty.

This time Francis and Anthony have both been returned as Members, for Middlesex and for Wallingford in Berkshire. But as they take their seats in the Commons Chamber, they notice not the joy of the newly elected among their colleagues, but mutterings and signs of mounting concern.

There are the usual anxieties over the succession, and agitations against the bishops. Yet the ill feeling runs deeper. What is to be the size of this new subsidy? Surely not less than a double, yet the last was only lately paid out. Lord Keeper Puckering has spoken eloquently of the threat from Spain, her alliance with Scotland, her new ships now better fitted for English waters, their own exhausted Exchequer, the drain on the Queen's own privy moneys and the need to build and arm the navy.

Raleigh and his friends press hard for war. Yet, say more moderate men, there is no imminent threat, no declaration of war from Spain. So wherefore so many new imposts on a plague-struck nation? Are we to be taxed every year? Men cannot bear the load.

It was ever thus: licentious speech and religious provocations are irritations, sometimes more, and must be dealt with. But parliamentary spirits are most perturbed and enraged by matters of taxation.

Sitting some way back from the government bench, Francis sees his now knighted cousin Sir Robert Cecil instructing his fellow Privy Councillors, whose job it is to move about the Members, calm the querulous and marshal the undecided. How odd that Francis cannot see Cecil fully in his new estate, can never rid himself of that image of the pool at Gorhambury and the sodden, weeping, angry boy who might have killed his brother? And if he cannot, how much less can Robert have forgotten it?

Then he inspects the new Speaker. Edward Coke is older than him, known but not familiar. Yet as Francis has come to discover, it is as though the two men's lives have always been intertwined. Coke too was a student of Whitgift's at Trinity College in Cambridge, almost a decade of years before Francis. He too has gone on to the bar, first to Clifford's Inn, then to the Inner Temple. He has built a considerable reputation as a lawyer and a scholar of the law, to judge by his summer readings of Littleton on the law of property at the Inn. He too sat in the last parliament, and he is now returned for Norfolk… alongside Francis's half-brother Nathaniel. Coke might almost be an affectionate elder brother himself, if there were affection between them.

But there, as Francis learns, comparison must end. For Coke has done everything Francis has not. He has built up a wide and successful legal practice; the family names of Howard, Gresham, and indeed of Bacon, are among his many clients. Francis's own half-brother Nicholas has long been Coke's close friend. Coke has married an heiress, of the great Norfolk family of Paston, with a vast fortune some have estimated at £30,000. Coke has made himself close to Burghley, bought and sold wardships from the old man and thereby added to his riches. And Coke has had preferment from the Queen, who has made him her Solicitor General only months before. And now Speaker.

So, yes, Francis knows about the new Speaker, and the knowledge gives him pain. This is not envy, he tells himself. It doth not touch the man himself, and envy is a gadding passion, and walketh the streets, and doth not keep home. Coke has a brusque manner, but he is cordial enough when they meet, and Francis is careful to be sweet in his own words of greeting or reply.

Yet if not envy, then what? For to Francis this Coke is but a tympanum of boar's hide, rough to the touch, booming to the ear, empty of all matter within. As for his supposed scholarship, tenures in fee simple, fee tail and the rest of them, well, the man is nothing but a black letter plodder of the law. He trudges through his readings like a weary ploughman on the way home after a long day, dragging every scrap of mud from the field back with him and shaking it off on his unhappy auditors.

But Francis's pain is sharpened when, at the opening of Parliament, he hears the Lord Keeper addressing Coke directly and congratulating him in the name of Her Majesty on an oration modest, wise and well composed. And it is sharpened again when he sees Coke at work in the chair. There can be no denying the new Speaker's capacity of decision, as he quickly shows in handling parliamentary business.

But Francis and Anthony have other reason to rejoice, for only in the past few days the Earl of Essex has been appointed to the Privy Council. Essex has long deplored the lack of noble blood at the Council table: now he has been placed there, in the innermost chamber of royal government, alongside Burghley and his son. He will be, he must be, both warrior and counsellor, fit to argue peace and war, laws and taxes. The Master of Horse has leapt off his mount and taken up pen and parchment in place of sword and armour. It is a signal mark of royal favour, paid to person not to rank, for the Earl is what he is now by, and only by, the Queen's grace. And from it great preferment shall flow, to the Earl and to his followers.

This is the moment, the brothers reflect, that their diligence and loyalty to the Earl must yield rewards. This is the moment for a new power to arise in the Queen's service: an instrument of change that is free of corruption, mindful of friends and dedicated not to its own prolongation and reward but to the monarch and her nation.

And, Francis decides, this is the moment in which he himself can step forward and make a mark as a leader in Parliament, a mark that men shall not long forget.

18

THE PALACE OF WESTMINSTER, FEBRUARY 1593

Francis's path is to be the middle, the moderate way, as his father always preferred. *Mediocria firma*. He has not forgotten the last parliament, and his small but palpable triumph in amending the preamble to the subsidy Bill. That pleased Crown and Commons alike. So it will be here.

Nor have others forgotten. And he is now a knight of the Shire of Middlesex; not a real knighthood, he regrets, but even so a mark of his loyalty to the Crown. So it is no surprise when he is called early in the debate, in a full House, to support the motion for the subsidy.

Yet his speech is a strange one: he supports the Bill, but he talks not of money but of laws. He evokes the memory of his father, the great Lord Keeper, who thirty years before had called upon the House for a reformation and codification of the laws. Now his son seeks the same, a purging of statutes and a reduction in their volume, they being so many in number that neither common people can half-practise them, nor the lawyer sufficiently understand them. The sovereign and her people are joined together by ties of mutual obligation, he says, that with the advice and consent of Parliament the Queen supplies laws to benefit her people, and through Parliament the people provide the wherewithal in subsidy to support her government.

Such a legal matter is hardly to the point, and debate passes swiftly on to others. Francis sees a puzzled look from Robert Cecil, who is managing the Bill, and in whispered conversation with the Speaker.

A few days later, after conference with the Lords, Cecil reports their demand that the triple subsidy should be paid to Her Majesty in three years, not six as expected, and that the Lords and Commons should debate the matter together. This is cunningly wrought, for it is both substance and distraction. The subsidy, if difficult to stomach over three years, will at least be shortly ended. But a joint debate between the Houses to decide a question of taxation, well, that is a different thing, which would set such a precedent as to destroy centuries of hard-won parliamentary privilege. It is for the Commons as a matter of right to debate and decide questions of supply: every green Member of Parliament fresh from the shires knows that. Little wonder there is uproar in the Chamber.

So Francis steps forward with a middle way. First, that the subsidy be granted; but as to joining with the Lords, he says, they could not do this but with prejudice to the privileges of this House. He cites a precedent in support from the time of the last King Henry.

His motion is well liked of the House, and so resolved. But afterwards he is beckoned outside by Cecil, who is evidently in some heat.

'Francis, what is your purpose? Do you mean to set yourself in opposition to Her Majesty?'

'God's truth, no. Why should you think so?'

'For one, your speech in the debate seemed to have a levelling intent. There is no mutual obligation of which you speak between Parliament and Her Majesty. The Queen may summon a parliament and she may dismiss it, as she will. She and she alone sets the laws to be debated, and she must have subsidies to wage war and keep the peace. Men may petition her as they wish, but there is no *alterum quid pro quo*, no bargaining to be had between them and their Queen, and that's the sum of it.

'And now this! You have ever shown yourself a loyal supporter of Her Majesty, yet here you come forward with a motion directly contrary to her intent. Let there be no double meaning: she wished a joint conference with the Lords, and you have denied it to her.'

'Nay, cousin, it is not so. The original proposition was stirring men up against her. It is I who have calmed them. The subsidy remains untouched.'

'Cousin,' Cecil is hissing now, jabbing him in the chest. 'I would be clearly understood. We have no need of independent minds. It is not for you to make such choices, but rather to rally behind your Queen in her hour of need. That means silence, and support. I say again: silence, and support.'

And in case the message goes missing, the Speaker too addresses him outside the Chamber.

'Master Bacon!'

Their eyes meet, steadily. Coke is a little taller than Francis, and nearly a decade older. He has spent hours without number at his desk, poring over the yearbooks, Bracton, Fortescue, Littleton, the Statutes and Acts of Parliament, the chronicles and treatises of the law. You might expect a pallid little shrimp of a man, Francis thinks, that he can sift and feed on such minutious matter with relish. Yet Coke has the seasoned face of the huntsman; his beard is full, brown and well groomed, his garb rich but not gaudy. He feels like a man who is used to command.

'Master Bacon, I am the servant of this House but, as we all are, also of our gracious sovereign lady. I wonder how men, especially men of wit, can find a contradiction between the two, where in reality there is none.

'I do not offer advice unsought or unpaid. But in my experience men who indulge themselves, men who thwart Her Majesty, even in small matters, rarely flourish.

'Make of that what you will.'

19

ESSEX HOUSE, MARCH 1593

'They set the dogs on you!' The Earl of Southampton tosses his girlish tresses with glee. 'I doubt there be much Bacon left after such a course, to judge by the way my hounds go after the scrapings.'

'This is matter for a new tract, Francis. Surely Paracelsus has words to describe such corruptions in the body politic. Or Pythagoras, or Aristotle, or one of those fellows.'

'The toad hath bit you!'

'Write to Burghley! Petition the Queen for relief from grievances against her corrupt councillors!'

Anthony and Francis are at Essex House, dining with the Earl and his company. The wines have flowed and the others are all in high spirits. It is a mixed table, of peers and military men, family, scholars and secretaries. But Francis is still somewhat shaken from his encounters.

Essex enjoys the gaiety, but not when others mock his friend.

'Gentlemen, this is no matter for jest. Francis, you were in the right, and you will win through, we will see to it.'

'But my Lord, Burghley now demands a triple subsidy, to be paid not in six years, but in three.'

'That is twice what was before,' adds Anthony, 'and we know not where it will end. Will any man be safe in his own property?'

Francis goes to the point.

'Yes, but can men pay it? Will it not merely stoke up discontent and rancour against Her Majesty and her advisers? It must seem the whole nation is awash in debts. Many will be ruined.'

There is a sudden silence, as each man present considers what lands he has and how they are encumbered, what he owes and what debts remain. This is no pretty matter for thought. And it may be of deeper consequence.

Looking down at the Commons from the Speaker's Chair, Coke sees, as ever, a squabbling multitude. But there is one particular man he must attend to.

Coke has no doubt that after his chastisements Francis Bacon has seen the error of his ways, and, given the chance, will make a public profession of it. It will be a correction of the will and an example to others; both are things of value. So he is careful to call on Bacon early to speak when the Bill returns to Parliament for a final debate and vote.

The motion is for a triple subsidy, but now to be paid in four years, not three. Cecil and his men have counted noses; they know how the votes will tally, and the concession of an extra year for payment is a small price to pay to get the Bill through quickly.

Bacon's speech starts well. As he says, the Lord Keeper has stated in plain words the cause and reason for this subsidy, and in matters of peace and war it is meet to attend with reverent care to the testimony of those supplied by information from foreign courts and battlefields. Among which…

The attention of the House starts to wander. This is Bacon the parasite, and his language ever turns back on itself; not many of the Members can follow what he says. Coke presides benignly.

But what is this? The Speaker suddenly wakes up.

Yet while I willingly assent to these three subsidies, Francis is saying, yet I cannot support their payment in under six years. The House broke new ground four years ago, and it will break new ground again here with an imposition on such terms. On the matter of the Bill, I would beg this House consider three grounds for longer payment: those of impossibility or difficulty of payment, of danger or discontentment, and of a better manner of supply. Each would suffice as reason for delay, but together they show its great advantage.

The House has caught the scent; men are suddenly listening. Coke looks down at Cecil on the Privy Council bench. Cecil glares back, and starts whispering feverishly to his neighbours. But Francis has the Chamber, and he continues. For impossibility, the poor men's rent is such as they are not able to yield it... The gentlemen must sell their plate and the farmers their brass pots ere this will be paid... We are not to persuade ourselves of their wealth more than it is.

The danger is this, he says, that we breed discontentment in the people. In a cause of jeopardy, Her Majesty's safety must consist more in the love of her people than in their wealth. And therefore we should beware not to give them cause of discontentment...

A member of the Cecil clan turning against the old fox and his cub, and on nothing less than a subsidy! This is worthy of note. Now there are hostile interventions, men urged on by Robert Cecil, men who are standing, beckoning to Francis for his attention, seeking to interrupt his flow of words with their questions. He waves them to be silent, imperiously, like a schoolmaster with a class of quarrelsome children.

This being granted in this sort, he continues, other princes hereafter will look for the like, so we shall put an ill precedent on ourselves and to our posterity. And in histories, it is to be observed that of all nations the English care not to be subject, base or taxable. The manner of supply may be by levy or imposition when need may most require. So when Her Majesty's coffers are empty, they may be imbursed by these means.

Members of Parliament have few skills, on the whole. But over centuries they have perfected the art of murmuring assent so loudly as to be unmistakable, yet so indistinctly that none can be held to account for it. When Francis touches on England's history and the ancient privileges of their House, when he hints at the need for a regular accounting to Parliament by the Queen, the response from the Chamber is immediate: a noisy and extended rumble of approbation from the utter benches, a rumble rendered still bolder by the breadth of its anonymity. No one can mistake its meaning or intent.

Francis sits down. Coke's face is Delphic, almost amused. Cecil looks like thunder.

20

WHITEHALL, MARCH 1593

'**M**aster Bacon did what?!'

Her Majesty does not credit her ears.

'He defied the Bill, your Grace, sought to amend it, said it would cause discontentment among your people, and called for the subsidy not to be paid sooner than six years.'

'Francis Bacon, my Lord? Francis Bacon, your own nephew, son of the late Lord Keeper? You do not mean his brother Anthony? That perhaps I could deem possible.'

'I am afraid it is so. It is of little consequence, your Majesty. Robert made sure to have those who spoke afterwards address and confute everything he said, and there was no other sign of opposition. He did not press it, and the Bill passed *nemo contradicente*.'

'It is of consequence, my Lord, and it is I who am contradicted. In the King my father's time a lesser offence than that would have seen a man banished his presence forever. I do not like rebellion, and I do not expect it from a member of your family.'

Burghley winces.

'Not rebellion, Majesty. He was misled. He thinketh Parliament is for the perfection of legislation.'

'Well, then he is a fool indeed. But I will teach him true knowledge.'

So Francis finds himself obliged to write once again to his uncle Burghley:

IT MAY PLEASE YOUR LORDSHIP – I was sorry to find by your Lordship's speech yesterday that my last speech in Parliament, delivered in the discharge of my conscience and duty to God, Her Majesty, and my country was offensive.

If it were misreported, he says, I would be glad to attend your Lordship to disavow anything I said not. If it were misconstrued I would be glad to expound my self, to exclude any sense I meant not. If my heart be misjudged by imputation of popularity or opposition by any envious or officious informer, I have great wrong; and the greater, because the manner of my speech did most evidently show that I spake simply; and only to satisfy my conscience, and not with any advantage or policy to sway the cause; and my terms carried all signification of duty and zeal towards Her Majesty and her service.

Misreported... misconstrued... misjudged. Burghley notes the tricolon. He has expected an apology. But this is no apology; it is rhetoric.

There is here no regret, no admission, nor even any consciousness of offence. The letter offers nothing to heal the wound inflicted. He cannot report back to the Queen and speak of a spirit chastised, a soul full of shame and contrition.

Burghley has long suspected a weakness of character in Francis Bacon. This is his judgement's final confirmation.

But when the Earl of Essex hears the news, his response is very different. Essex rejoices in the story as though it were a military action, demands it be told and retold. That evening, when he and his men are in their cups, he makes Francis stand and act it out, casting the other parts like a maker of theatricals: You here as Cecil, man, you as Coke, who will be putting questions? Come Francis, recount again your speech, you all be the other Members. Now! Go to it.

And the Earl has seen a new citadel to be captured. For the office of Attorney General is now vacant. Essex wants that office; for his friend Francis Bacon, and for himself.

21

ESSEX HOUSE, SUMMER 1593

The Master of the Rolls, Gilbert Gerard, is newly dead and the Queen is moving to replace him. They say Attorney General Egerton will be the next Master. So the Attorneyship will lie vacant. It is everything Francis could dream of.

'It is a considerable position, and it must be yours, Master Bacon,' says Essex. 'Nay, it shall be. She cannot deny your learning, and she shall not deny my suit on your behalf.'

'My Lord, I thank you, but how can it be so? I am deep mired in her displeasure. She has forbidden me from court. Yet I confess I still struggle to know what I did wrong. I did not cross her on the subsidy, but pleaded an easement fit to sugar the medicine.

'She cannot surely contemn me for speaking in Parliament. What is Parliament? It should be the high Chamber for counsel of the realm, fit to discuss such matters, not some marketplace for sycophants and ranters.'

'You will ever go to the very heart of things, Francis. And that is why we love you: for your wit, your counsel and your service. Yet 'tis clear the Queen hesitateth over the matter. With the old fox and Monsieur le Bossu the hunchback ever in her presence, we must expect them to be all for Coke, who is their creature.'

Francis says, 'Burghley writeth to me as my loving uncle, yet he placeth me second in the lists. My cousin Cecil kindly warns me of the Queen's choler. Yet I fear he seeks the good opinion of us all, while he worketh for the Huddler underhand.'

'Coke the Huddler!' Anthony interjects.

'Yes, the Huddler,' continues Essex. 'But mark me, gentlemen, we have points to make of our own against their candidate.

'Coke is just lately made Solicitor, and now Speaker, so he hath had favour enough. If the Queen spreadeth her balm more widely, she does not lose him, but she will gain you. And she liketh it ill that he acteth in defence of crooked men, men who but for his words would face condign justice. She hath told me so to my face.'

Anthony again: 'Yet, my Lord, nothing is won unless it be carefully prepared and executed. They speak of Brograve and Branthwayt, but it is Coke who is our opponent. To see him off we must cultivate friends and soften foes. Our friends may set the scene, they can bring her forward, and they can deflect the whispers of our enemies.'

Essex nods assent, for he seeks to build his power on every front. He has taken over much of the patronage of his stepfather, the Earl of Leicester. His Welsh interests, from Pembroke to Brecknock to Cardigan, give him a base in Parliament, which he eagerly tends. He gathers high stewardships like so many bushels of corn, and they give him the power of nomination of Members of Parliament. The retainers of his household ceaselessly tread the Strand and ply the Thames between London and Westminster in their green and gold livery.

Essex plucks fine young men from the universities, Smith, Reynolds, Cuffe and others, to be his secretaries, and regularly takes counsel with scholars and men of expert knowledge. He has the patronage of dozens of clergymen and many men who would be bishops, and allies himself with Whitgift against Burghley to make Richard Bancroft the next Bishop of London.

And now, thanks to Anthony, Essex has to hand a net of foreign intelligencers fit to rival Burghley's own for information and diplomacy. Even Don Antonio Perez, former Secretary to King Philip, has come to London as a fugitive of justice. He is laden with secrets of the Spanish government and empire, and resides at Essex House as a paid guest of the Earl.

To have Francis placed as Attorney General would be a further advance. Not the Solicitor; to Essex that is but drudgery without influence, and besides, the post has come and gone to Coke.

No, the Attorney it must be, and set aside Francis's own silly doubts and cavils. How sweet to have the younger man by nine years overleap the older, his own candidate against Burghley's, and how much a testimony to the Earl of Essex's own powers of patronage! *He persuaded the Queen, and it was done. His Councillor is now Attorney General. Honi soit qui mal y pense.*

Yet Essex is moved by more than a ceaseless quest for advantage. For he gives himself wholeheartedly to those around him. Burghley hath climbed the ladder of success and then pulled it out of the reach of others, they say. Not so Essex. He wants his friends nearby, but from his service he urges them on to positions of influence and authority elsewhere; as it seems without regard for himself, and with a natural and unfeigned generosity that demands no reward.

Shuttling from court to a tiny room by the Commons Chamber, Robert Cecil follows it all. He notes the slights and insults that have always followed him, without response.

As he remarks to himself, it feels like there is a court quietly gestating in the womb of Essex House. Yet the severing of the head of Mary of Scots from her shoulders witnesses this, that there cannot be two courts in a land.

22

ESSEX HOUSE, SUMMER 1593

And so the canvass begins.

Thomas Cecil, older brother of Robert, writing to their father Lord Burghley: It may please your Lordship... at this time I must confess I am importuned with my will to be a motioner unto your Lordship for one nearly allied to your house, and whose gifts and qualities of mind I know will not think unfit for the place he seeketh. It is Mr Francis Bacon, who hearing of late that the Attorney General is likened for the Master of the Rolls, his desire is to be remembered by me unto your Lordship's good acceptance and conceit of him for that place which Mr Attorney shall leave, and thereby to be recommended by your Lordship to Her Majesty.

There are letters from Francis, Anthony, their mother; from Fulke Greville, who has regular access to Her Majesty; from persons of influence, among them Sir Thomas Egerton, the outgoing Attorney and a notable catch; and above all from the Earl of Essex himself. They go to Burghley, to Cecil, to Privy Councillors who may be able to assist, and to the Queen.

From Robert Cecil comes this letter to Francis in May, mixing truth with courtesy. Cousin, he says, I have received your letter wherein you request my help and advice. For the first, I do and will assure you of it as firmly and honestly as any man that can do it powerfully. But for the second, I must be tender with you, because the effect may be doubtful in things that are here so variable... make it your first object to gain access to Her Majesty again through the Earl of Essex, for without such access aught hope of preferment is like to be premature.

All Francis's hopes rest on Essex. So much is clear.

In June, Anthony reports clear signs to their mother that Essex is making progress, saying that from his speeches the Queen was at length thoroughly appeased, and she stood only on the exception of Francis's years for his present preferment. But Essex doubts not that he shall overcome that difficulty very soon, and that Her Majesty will show it to good effects.

It is time, Essex suggests, for Francis to write directly to Her Majesty. She has been prepared and, as he says, how often in the past have soft sweet breezes dispelled the clouds of her anger?

The letter starts well enough. Madam, Francis says, remembering that your Majesty had been gracious to me both in countenancing me and conferring upon me the reversion of a good place, and perceiving your Majesty had taken some displeasure towards me, both these were arguments to move me to offer unto your Majesty my service, to the end to have means to deserve your benefit and to repair my error.

As the Queen reads it, she starts to smile. She knows what is to come. She is ready, she is gracious, and she is disposed to welcome the confession, the apology, the humble servant begging pardon from a gracious sovereign for his foolish offence...

But Francis cannot do it. He has tried, he has written one copy after another in search of meaning. He wants words that will please her, but with sweetness not surrender. Normally, such words come unbidden, as though the Muse herself has taken his hand in hers and guided it across the page. Or, if they do not, he can ascend into high philosophical talk, to shade and shroud his words with double import.

Not so today. Instead, there comes: Upon this ground I affected myself to no great matter, but only a place of my profession, such as I do see divers younger men, and men of no great note, do without blame aspire unto…

This is nothing humble, thinks the Queen. This is justification. There is pride here, and peevishness.

Francis continues, Your Majesty's favour indeed, and access to your royal person, I did ever, encouraged by your own speeches, seek and desire; and I would be very glad to be reintegrate in that. But my mind turneth upon other wheels than those of profit. The conclusion shall be that I wish your Majesty served answerable to yourself. *Principis est virtus maxima nosse suos.* Thus I most humbly crave pardon of my boldness and plainness. God preserve your Majesty.

A prince's greatest virtue is to know the measure of his men. So Bacon instructs his Queen. He deigns to say he would be glad of access, but does not seek it. He wishes preferment but not, of course, to profit by it. He confesses error, but only in relation to his own simple ambition to seek the good. So she is supposed to conclude.

Foolish, obstinate, perverse of spirit! The Queen fancies she has Master Bacon's measure; that is for sure. She has given him time to beg her pardon and make amends. If need be, she might even give him more. But till he does that, he can wait.

She takes up a candle, holds his letter in its flame, and burns it to a cinder.

23

GRAY'S INN, SUMMER 1593

The canvass continues. But Master Harvey is pressing for his money, and the sum weighs heavy in Francis's big ledger book of debts.

First Harvey was courteous, even kind, out of deference for the Bacon name, saying that *resting in your good faith it has ever been an honour to me to extend…* Then he was orderly, seeking settlement on terms agreed, that *the fortnight wherein you willed me to send unto you for the money due unto me being now fully expired, I make bold…*

Now he is insistent; *I am sore pressed myself,* he says, and failure to make payment will be ruinous to me and thrust me into the hands of the moneylenders.

In the meantime many months have passed, and Francis has lived them through hope, expectation, shame, anger and despair, oblivious to and yet always feeling the burden of what he owes.

Anthony sees his brother struggling. He too has little head for business, but he is Crassus himself, the richest man in ancient Rome, compared to Francis, who has never had income to manage nor property to dispose of. Something must be sold to pay Harvey off, Anthony suggests, and why not the Marks estate?

The lands belong to Francis, but the sale of them requires their mother's consent.

So Anthony makes himself the interlocutor, and puts the matter in a letter to their mother. Lady Bacon has time enough, more time than she can happily dispose of, and her temper is sharpened by her solitude. Her answer is not long in coming.

I have been too ready for you both, she remarks, till nothing is left. And surely though I pity Francis, yet so long as he pitieth not himself but keepeth that bloody Percy – or is it Perez? She writes Peerce, but Anthony cannot make it out – as I told him then, yea as a coach companion and bed companion – a proud profane costly fellow, whose being about him I verily fear the Lord God doth mislike and doth less bless your brother in credit and otherwise in his health – surely I am utterly discouraged and make a conscience further to undo myself to maintain such wretches as he is.

Our mother strikes with the dagger in one hand and the broadsword in the other, thinks Anthony; this is none too promising.

And then she plies her broadsword again. It is most certain, she says, that until first Enney – Essex? God's teeth, this handwriting! – a filthy wasteful knave, and his Welshmen one after another, for take one and they will still swarm ill-favouredly, did so lead him as in a train, Francis was a towardly young gentleman and a son of much good hope in godliness. But seeing he hath nourished most sinful proud villains wilfully, I know not what other answer to make. God bless you both with his grace and good health to serve him with truth of heart.

Anthony pauses. Our mother diagnoses the malady all too well, he reflects. But if she only knew what pains the Earl had taken to advance the interests of her sons! Why, even now he misses no opportunity to press the Queen, forcing her from their play at cards so that he may sing the merits of Francis for the Attorneyship, which, once granted, would secure his future.

But then Anthony turns the page of his mother's letter, and there is more.

If your brother, Lady Bacon says, desires a release to Mr Harvey, let him make and give me a true note of all his debts, and leave to me the whole order and receipt of all his money for his land, to Harvey, and the just payment of all his debts thereby. And by the mercy and grace of God it shall be performed by me to his quiet discharge without cumbering him and to his credit. For I will not have his cormorant seducers and instruments of Satan to him committing foul sin by his countenance, to the displeasing of God and his godly true fear. Otherwise I will not *pro certo*.

Little is hidden between the two brothers. But Anthony does not for a moment yield to his mother's demand, and he never mentions it to Francis. So he returns his mother's harsh words with gentle, knowing that with her there is nothing *pro certo* except her love of God and of her sons, and that where these two loves come into conflict then, like the lapping tides, a mild persistence may wear away even an adamantine heart.

And so it does. Lady Bacon sells the Marks estate, Mr Harvey is paid off and Francis has no need of the moneylenders. For the present.

24

THE LOPEZ TREASON, JANUARY 1594: I

'You have heard the news, my friend? About Master Bacon?'
Coke snorts.

'Indeed, I have not. I could never wish for a time which paid so ill that it paid me to think about Bacon. They say he is a great scholar, but I have ever found him empty in his profession. He prateth on about maxims of law as though they were some new thing. Had he read Plowden or the yearbooks and much else with care he had found all this there and more.

'Bacon seeketh the Attorneyship, he pretendeth to a great knowledge of the law, yet he is a stranger to the courts and I never see him at Westminster Hall. This is not a man to be taken seriously.'

'Easy, good Edward, this is my cousin of whom you speak. He hath not your experience of the law, 'tis true. But he is not so unserious as you say, for he hath the Earl of Essex and Egerton and my own brother behind him for the Attorneyship, and a host of others; and who knoweth where the Earl may end up after this latest business with Lopez has gone through?

'And the news doth bear me out, for I hear just a few days hence Bacon will plead his first case, for Sir Thomas Perrot in the King's Bench.'

Another snort.

'What, Bacon, pleading in a court of law, that he hath ever felt beneath him! Sooth, he must be desperate for office. Let us see what he maketh of his action. And it of him.'

But this is all by-play, for Coke and Cecil have business to attend to. The Earl of Essex has come forward with a sheaf of secret letters to denounce none other than Dr Lopez, the Queen's personal physician, on charges of conspiracy and intended murder. As Essex writes in great excitement to Anthony: I have discovered a most dangerous and desperate treason. The point of conspiracy was Her Majesty's death. The executioner should have been Dr Lopez, the manner poison. This I have so followed, as I will make it clear as noonday.

Burghley and Cecil had picked up Essex's interest some months before, but they have stayed away from the matter. The Queen will not hear of it. Doctor Lopez, poison her? Why, she has consulted him personally for thirteen years; he holds a position of extraordinary trust. She has liked and valued him enough to give him not merely her care but several years of monopoly on the importation of aniseed and sumac. He has attended Walsingham and Leicester and Burghley too. He is a Fellow of the Royal College of Physicians and has been house physician at St Bartholomew's Hospital; men know his colours.

Why should Burghley and his son give the Earl of Essex credit from this affair by taking it up? Does any man of gravity believe his wild claims? Chances are they will simply go away. If they do, he will look a fool. And if not, there is nothing lost.

But there is bad blood here, and Essex will not be deterred. Lopez had pressed the Queen into an expedition to put the pretender Don Antonio on the throne of Portugal. Leicester led it, Essex by his side, and it was an expensive failure. Essex has ever after suspected Lopez of playing a double game; but it is in the nature of such men that they can be turned, and so the Earl also sought to recruit the doctor as his intelligencer. Lopez assented, only then to pass the same secret information to Burghley, so that when Essex arrived with it at court the Queen laughed at him for proffering her such stale matter.

And there is worse, for in his cups Lopez has boasted to Don Antonio and the Spaniard Perez that he has cured the Earl of Essex of a painful and disabling venereal disease. Personal loyalty, a man's proper station in life, a promise, the duty of physician to patient: all have been betrayed. And hidden secrets of the Earl's own body parleyed and bantered with two of the indiscreetest men in London!

Essex thirsts for revenge against the doctor. Now he has what he needs: secret letters that tie Lopez to a plot to make peace with Spain, earlier testimony of a design to kill Don Antonio, a history of correspondence between him and the King of Spain, and what Essex now claims to be a most desperate treason to kill the Queen. To his great joy and satisfaction, Burghley and Cecil have had to acknowledge his leading role in discovery of the plot, and join themselves to it; still better, they must come in time to admit their own error before Her Majesty in doubting him. It is a pattern Essex has every intention to repeat, for these workaday men can learn from his example.

The three of them have summoned Lopez to Burghley's house in the Strand for questioning. The doctor's own house has been ransacked for papers, without result, and he then committed to the Tower. 'Digest me no digestions!' says Essex to Cecil as the two men return by carriage to Whitehall, in the heat of their dispute over whether Francis Bacon shall be made the Queen's Attorney. But in truth it is Dr Lopez's life and works that have been well digested, and they who have digested them, in their search for incriminating materials.

Yet if Burghley and his son have joined Essex, still they jostle for contention with him; the whole affair must be controlled and managed so that it does not touch Burghley's own extensive dealings with Lopez. Cecil rushes back to reach the Queen before the Earl, and even then to reassure her about the character of her doctor, so that when Essex arrives full of news she turns him away, publicly rebuking him as a rash and temerarious youth intent on the destruction of an innocent and faithful servant.

Essex retreats in mortification to his apartments, and will not stir for two days. And he adds this further slight to the list he keeps of those he has endured by Cecil's hand.

25

THE LOPEZ TREASON, JANUARY 1594: II

'I will make this conspiracy as clear as the noonday,' said Essex, and he has been good to his word. It seems he must. Given his former closeness to the doctor there must be no imputation of his own complicity.

Lopez himself has been let alone. There has been no rigorous usage or torments, much to the displeasure of Topcliffe, who plies his notorious trade with the rack and other instruments at the top of the Tower. But Topcliffe has been allowed to show the manacles to Tinoco, another witness, and nothing more is necessary. Tinoco and several others have confessed what was meet to confess, and much more. For in the face of such torments, a man with gentle hands will betray anything: his chattels, his wife, his family, his religion, even his own life.

The royal prerogative is limited by common law. Coke will have much to say on these matters in due course. As he insists, there is no law to warrant torture in this land... and there is no one opinion in our books, or judicial record for the maintenance of tortures or torments. It is against Magna Carta. Yet torture there is, most regularly, and all know it, not by common law but by the Queen's warrant and in the exercise of the prerogative right that attaches to her crown. Coke himself and Burghley, Cecil, Essex and many others have signed the Queen's torture warrants as her officers. For discovery rather than for evidence, it is true, but what is this nice distinction to a man dangling from the manacles for hours by his wrists till his shoulders dislocate and start to hang above him?

Yes, Coke will have much to say on these matters. But not now, when he must go down by boat every day to the Tower to question the conspirators. Not now, when as Solicitor General he takes command of the trial, his first great prosecution, and is thereby gifted a priceless opportunity to remind all those present of his credentials to be Attorney. Not now, as he rises before a special commission of fifteen men of rank chosen as judges, to indict Roderigo Lopez, sometimes known as Roger Lopez or Ruy Lopez, on eight charges ranging from the acceptance of a jewel from the King of Spain to trading secrets to compassing by plot the murder of the Queen to planning his final escape through Antwerp to Constantinople.

Francis watches the whole action from start to end. He has helped Essex to prepare the case, but there can be no question of him conducting the prosecution; as Cecil says, he hath not the age nor the experience nor the office for it.

Instead, he must sit at the back of the court and watch Coke at work in the full weight of his bombast, Coke as he arraigns and insults Lopez again and again for a perjured and murdering traitor who has received the *abracijo* or personal embrace of King Philip himself. 'He did conspire, imagine and fantasise the death and destruction of the Queen's Majesty,' Coke charges, 'and to stir rebellion and war, and to overthrow that state of whole common weal of this Realm.'

Francis sees Lopez protesting his innocence, his love of the Queen, his service of thirty years to his adopted Church and country. He sees how Coke carefully leads his audience away from any prior connection between Lopez and the Cecils, or any knowledge of Lopez's past service to the Queen, the Privy Council or to Councillors and other men of high office. He sees the inevitable conviction and condemnation of the conspirators to death, each to be dragged on a hurdle to the place of execution at Tyburn, and there to be emasculated, his entrails opened and burned, his body quartered and the parts taken to divers points around the city for the education and instruction of the people.

But Francis feels not elation at Essex's triumph, at the brilliant success of his master, or at the notice and preferment it must surely bring him, but sadness at what has happened and the violence of its remedy.

Yet not many weeks afterwards, while memories are fresh, he writes *A True Report of the Detestable Treason Intended by Dr Roderigo Lopez* at Essex's demand, in hope that it will please his Lordship, and Her Majesty.

26

THE PALACE OF WHITEHALL, APRIL 1594

The news has come at last: Edward Coke has been appointed Attorney General.

Francis flinches at the news, and Essex embraces him, full of apologies and remorse. He had encouraged hopes, raised spirits, yes, but only as merit allowed and in the noblest of causes. And though he wants and expects no thanks for his troubles, he says, the world can see how he has expended himself with the Queen to the uttermost of his credit, friendship and authority but without avail.

But Essex has set himself a new task: to secure the post of Solicitor General for his friend. Yes, it is inferior to the Attorney, but as Essex insists, this time the auguries are all fair. There is no evident successor, the field is clear of other candidates of any great achievement or repute. There is no ordered opposition. And see who has already been mustered on their own side! For Francis's declared supporters include not merely Essex himself but Burghley, the Lord Keeper, the new Master of the Rolls, the Vice-Chamberlain and senior judges, plus a dozen other men of quality. Even Leonidas and his Spartan hoplites could not withstand such a mass of sentiment and influence. This prize will show the yield of all their efforts hitherto.

Francis accedes, and dares to believe it may be so, for how else to progress? But, as he writes to Greville, my matter is an endless question. Her Majesty had by set speech more than once assured me of her intention to call me to her service; which I could not understand but of the place I had been named to; but Her Majesty is not ready to dispatch it. And though the Master of the Rolls, and my Lord of Essex, and yourself and others think my case without doubt, yet in the meantime I have a hard condition, for whatsoever service I do to Her Majesty, it shall be thought to be but to place myself; and so I shall have envy, not thanks. This is a course to quench all good spirits, and to corrupt every man's nature.

For, Francis adds, to be like a child following a bird, which when he is nearest flieth away and lighteth a little before, and then the child after it again, and so *in infinitum*, I am weary of it; as also of wearying my good friends, of whom nevertheless I hope in one course or other gratefully to deserve.

It was on the secret testimony of the Spaniard Antonio Perez that Dr Lopez incurred the undying hatred of Essex for his disloyalty and indiscretion.

This Perez is a nobleman, formerly close to King Philip but since 1591 a fugitive. He had sought sanctuary with Catherine of Navarre in Pau, then journeyed from France to England with intelligence said to be fit only for the eyes of the Queen. As is her way, Her Majesty has refused to see his papers; for if he has betrayed one monarch, who is to say he may not seek to deceive another? But she grants him audience, gives her consent for his intelligence to be shared with Essex, and makes him a grant of money by means of the Earl.

Now Perez is staying at Essex House, bringing with him his chest of strange potions and medicaments, charming the servants and dallying with man and woman alike. A generation older than the Earl, he comes garlanded in rumour: that Philip has put a price on his head, that he had a love affair with the King's mistress, that he has been tortured and imprisoned, helped foment an uprising in Aragon against Madrid, and been charged as a sodomite by the Inquisition.

Far from dispelling these suggestions, however, Perez delights in them, adding detail and decoration to them like a skilled goldsmith on each retelling. He has even coined names for those he despises, so that Robert Cecil is *Microgibbus* or *Robertus Diabolus*, names Francis dislikes but cannot help but laugh at. And as Perez tells it, the history of his escape from Spain alone – setting out one November evening from the far north of Aragon to cross the Pyrenees disguised as a shepherd, wading for days through thick snow with but a few companions and pack animals, sleeping in long-vacated mountain huts before making an exhausted but triumphant arrival at the court in Pau – has the household enraptured.

For Anthony, Perez's arrival has been a godsend. Their personal connection through the Kingdom of Navarre gives Anthony a hostly status, one supported by the local knowledge and languages they share. Like Anthony, the Spaniard is much given to physic, in which he professes great expertise. But Perez is also a notable scholar, who has translated *The Odyssey* into Spanish. His aphorisms are much admired, and his delight is palpable when Anthony agrees to edit an English translation of his book *Fragments of History*. His knowledge of Spain and the diplomacy of states and princes across Europe is a rich seam of ore to be mined for nuggets of insight and intelligence, and there is wisdom as well as honour in the Queen's choice of host: Essex will ever be hostile to Spain, but his friends have a certain warmth for the old religion, and he allows Perez to hold mass, quietly, in his house.

So Anthony is well satisfied. But for Francis, matters are not so clear. Like the others, he is intoxicated by Perez's warmth and energy. But he himself is neither patron nor partner in business with the older man. So what is he to him? And Perez, for all his flamboyance and outward display, has other facets to his character. When he and Francis talk, there is none of the foolish swordplay of the court, where men come with their blades of raillery and dismissal polished through the long nights in hope they may disport themselves and dispatch each other.

No, no: from the start Francis loves the Spaniard's sense of risk and adventure, his apparent scorn for the opinions of others, the spirit in him that gives life to all it touches. But for Francis, and it seems for him alone, there is an unexpected inner seriousness of address.

To meet with Perez is to feel the force of his intelligence, be it from a distance or hot upon the face. To converse with him is to enter on a long dance, in which each man is ever aware of the proximity of the other to the hairsbreadth: the approach, the set, the touch, the clasp. And if it start with the distant formality of the galliard, yet it may end with the rapture of the volt. Though as Antonio remarks, 'Francis, you dance like a camel. Where is your *duende*? If we were in Aragon, I would show you the *jota* they dance in the villages late into the hot nights. That comes not from the memory, but from the body.'

No man can live without his mask, thinks Francis. For Perez, the mask is the urbanity of the traveller, of the *roué* come to rest. In company, he provokes, he teases, he has a story for every occasion, yet you must quarry hard to find the man within. But as for Francis, it is the exact reverse: from first meeting, it is as though every aspect of his life and person were laid out naked on the surgeon's table. Indeed, not merely naked, but without even the covering of a human skin.

Soon after that first meeting, Perez takes Francis aside after dinner one evening and says, looking direct into his eyes, 'My friend, you have greatness locked in your soul. But how to set it free?'

No one has ever spoken to Francis like that. A channel has been opened between them, and Francis feels ravished and exalted by the Spaniard's attention. Difference of age or birth or history they do not know. There is no work of art or literature they cannot discuss, no idea they cannot debate, no feeling or passion or desire they cannot share, and rarely do two or three days pass without their meeting.

A letter, from Antonio Perez to Anthony Bacon, January 1595: Your brother invited me to dinner. He has wounded me in writing – his pen being the most rabid and biting of teeth. As if he himself were above blame – some kind of vestal virgin. You can tell immediately what this imagined modesty of his is all about. For I am just the same. Those who claim to love modesty are in fact the most bold of men, and submit to force, and enjoy the excuse of being taken by force, like the Roman matron in Tacitus who consented to be raped by her lover.

27

TWICKENHAM PARK, OCTOBER 1595

He is at the landing place by the water at Twickenham when Essex arrives.

'Francis, Francis, by all that I hold dear I wish it were not so, but Her Majesty hath declared her choice for Solicitor, and it is Serjeant Fleming. As God is my witness you will know the depth and extent of my pleading on your behalf.'

Of course, Francis knew it, had known it for many months and long suspected it would be in vain. It is failure, public and confessed failure yet again.

The Queen had refused him access to her, and reproved him for his presumption in asking leave to travel before she had made her decision for Solicitor. But, but… she let him hope, too. She engaged him on Star Chamber business, and there had been other signs of movement, of returning favour; fair words to Essex, to Egerton and, on one unforgettable occasion, his own glance returned full on by her at court one morning, with a smile. That smile alone had carried him for weeks.

Time was when to have heard this news would be to feel the crush of masonry upon his head, and all the more for knowing Fleming's limitations. But not now. It has been too long. He has had sickness, melancholy, overwhelming lassitude, despair. He has long endured ridicule and mockery at court, even in the Earl of Essex's house. He is wiser now.

'My Lord, I had expected it. I am sorry the merits of my suit were not sufficient to your pleading.'

Essex looks at him, eyes flashing hot. Then he smiles.

'Nay, nay, my friend, do not scold me. Your talents shine like the comet in Cassiopeia, have I not ever said so? But a man's merit has ever been but one cause of his preferment, if it were even that.

'We have had Monsieur le Bossu and his father to contend with, and the old man's zeal to lodge his placemen in every nook and corner of the state is unabated. He had promised me his support on this matter, at least till Her Majesty rebuffed us both, saying our joint petition undermined her princely authority. Then Burghley turned away from me. Great evil will come of all this, mark my words. The Queen has desperate need of new counsellors to invigorate and guide her court.'

'She wanteth them, my Lord, yet she wanteth them not. She doth not want me, and I shall not be among them. I will never have a position while she reigns. No, for me it must be the *via contemplativa*. I will retire and spend my remaining days here. But I had thought to serve her and to serve you, as the fittest instrument she hath to do good to the state.'

'Francis, the Queen hath denied me yon place for you, and hath placed another. I know you are the least part in your own matter, but you fare ill because you have chosen me for your mean and dependence; you have spent your time and thoughts in my matters. I die if I do not somewhat towards your fortune: you shall not deny to accept a piece of land which I will bestow upon you.'

They are walking in Francis's gardens at Twickenham. Essex has been at the court in Richmond but crossed the river to break the news. Francis remembers every word of their exchanges, and much more besides: the earnestness of the Earl's manner, the hands that clasp his own. Essex's friendship, his sense of honour, are not to be doubted.

Yet matters are not quite as they were. Every man must be a double man if he would succeed at court. It is a theatre where the players must profess an outer show of loyalty and wit, of amity and comfort, whatever their inward beliefs or dreams or debts may be. Yet, through his mind and station Francis perhaps feels the clash between these warring interests more than any other.

He is the victim of thought. And as he reflects on Essex's words, Francis cannot prevent other and more disobliging ideas from insinuating their way into his mind. That he himself has no special merit to Essex, and has been but a minor piece in a grand game of chess waged across the court, the Council, Parliament, the law and the carriage of arms. That Essex uses his charm and patronage, his chivalry and gifts, the language of loving regard as weapons in that contest; yet take these things to Eastcheap, try to negotiate them for cash with the moneylenders of Leadenhall and you will find what they are really worth, while Francis and Anthony receive no stipend for their work and stay forever locked in correspondence with their creditors.

This offer of a packet of land may be something, or it may not; there have been other such words. And, most painfully, there lurks in Francis's mind the idea that throughout this endless difficult courtship the Queen has been rebuffing not Francis himself, but the Earl.

If the Earl had not been so loud, so sharp with her in his pursuit of the Attorneyship, yet I might have had it.

He recalls a letter lately from his mother, bemoaning the fact that you, Francis and your brother, but especially you, be still occupied and entangled with state and worldly matters above your calling, to make you the more unfit to be employed and your gifts appear to your own credit. Exercise your self in the knowledge of holy and profitable things to please God and then men.

Lady Anne had also said that though the Earl showed great affection, yet he marred all with violent courses. These are harsh words, but who is Francis to say they are untrue? What has he to offer against them as reply?

So, no, he cannot petition further. Essex must fight his own battles, and if good comes of them, then so be it. As always Francis feels himself drifting, carried on some vast swelling sea, to no end, no purpose and no reward yet desperate for the power to shape his own destiny. And still the questions nag at him. Where am I to go? How can I act to fill the vacant hours? And, with no less anxiety: How does the Earl of Essex fare with Her Majesty? What does he fear, that he presses her so hard?

28

ESSEX HOUSE, SPRING 1596

For, make no mistake, the Earl is pressing ever onwards, and he will take the brothers with him.

So Anthony can plainly see, for he has been resident now at Essex House for some months. He had briefly lodged in Bishopsgate, to the consternation of his mother, who deplored his departure from the Christian community of Gray's Inn and denounced his new parish as nothing more than a plague spot close to the theatres, its minister ignorant and careless, its people given to voluptuousness and infected with corrupt and lewd dispositions by their proximity to the notorious Bull Inn tavern.

For Anthony, The Bull has been a fine place and all else about it rather to the good. But his health is weakening; it tells upon him, and gout and the stone leave him ill-matched to the growing business of the Earl. Why not come to Essex House, the Earl insists, and live alongside their joint enterprise? Perez has left his chambers to go abroad, so there is logic to the move. Essex House lies outside the city walls, near the Strand, and its greatness will keep the creditors away.

Yet the move ruffles feathers. Again, Lady Bacon does not miss her chance. Having dismissed the house in Bishopsgate, now she sings its praises: so well agreed and most necessary, she says, whereas your new situation must bring you envy, emulation, continual and unseasonable disquiet to increase your gout. Peradventure not so well liked yourself there, as in your own house. Some increase of suspicion and disagreement, which may hurt you privately, if not publicly, or both by all likelihood in these so fickle times. You have hitherto been esteemed as a worthy friend to the Earl. Now you shall be accounted his follower.

And so it falls out. The secretaries resent the burden of Anthony's supervision, while the young noblemen despise his circumstances and begrudge his access. He is not fish, nor fowl. He is the 'special friend' of Essex and a guest, yet he must pay – or rather, Lady Bacon must pay – the cost of the coal in his grate.

He is not sound of limb or wind, he cannot hunt, he affects a carriage, yet when the young men chaff him he turns their scorn aside with ease and wit. They cannot bear the private jokes he shares with the Earl, the stories of his travels, the costly beaver hats he buys and gives his friends, his network of foreign advertisers and intelligencers, the hours he spends advising his master before a visit to the court. And, they know well, the Earl will not bear to hear intriguing rumours against his friend.

Besides, Anthony and his master have work to do. Essex continues hot, and he advances his business ever on in diverse directions. One is to the north, where Scotland still rejoices in the recent birth of King James's son Prince Henry.

Henry! Now that is a name which carries implications, and aspirations. Men are not slow to see them, nor to draw the contrast between the King his father and the heirless barren spinster Queen of England, whose fits of ill temper and indisposition grow more frequent.

Surely the Tudor dynasty must die with her. Yet she still refuses to name a successor, indeed forbids all mention of it, to the frustration and despair of Burghley, who feels the structures of her power start to fracture and split apart. Look at Philip II of Spain, couched on his velvet sickbed in the Escorial. He too must surely be near his end, but there will be order and continuity, for he has a son to inherit. There will be no loss of menace in the threat Spain offers to true religion in England.

But there is opportunity for others here, and Essex takes it. Anthony has long been close to David Foulis, James's confidant and ambassador in England, and through him the Earl opens a private correspondence with the King. The language is French, and names are coded or numbered. The Earl is Plato, or the number twenty-eight. His Majesty is Tacitus, or ten.

Letters are sent, replies received. To King James, Lord Burghley is nothing less than the despised intriguer against his mother Queen Mary, the adviser who dripped poison against her into Elizabeth's ear for so many years, the direct cause and agent of her murder. Essex plays upon his hatred, trading secret information for future position. When Elizabeth dies there must be a smooth succession for the King, and he is the man to make it so.

But if that is so, and James succeeds by Essex's hand, it must surely spell ruin for Lord Burghley and his son. These men are playing for their lands and fortunes, perhaps their heads; and they know it.

Essex cannot hide his excitement at the prospect of James as King. He is apt now to strike a pose at court designed to flatter his appearance and power: legs apart, head thrown back, arms on hips, codpiece up, a great straddle in the style of King Henry VIII.

And with the Queen too it seems Essex's luck has turned. Even disaster begets triumph. Anthony has lately picked up news from Antwerp of a scurrilous volume discussing and debating the succession, as though it were fit topic for tavern chat. Worse, that book is dedicated to the Earl of Essex, and has the temerity to hint at his own claims to the throne through his nobility, favour with the Queen and high liking of the people.

Her Majesty will be ablaze with anger when she sees it. Yet instead of bringing the book forward and denouncing it before her, the Earl does nothing, and he has no defence to offer when she peremptorily summons him to the Privy Council Chamber and taxes him in the harshest terms with his treachery for conniving in the work.

But once the libel becomes clear, once her error is plain, then bitter remorse sets in and relations are restored. The Queen and the Earl seem more dear to each than ever, and she decrees that letters from abroad are to be sent to my Lord of Essex, and he to answer them. That is another step upward for Essex, another frustration for Sir Robert Cecil and his father.

❧

So Anthony and the secretaries are busy now at Essex House as they deal with the daily flood of correspondence from ambassadors, travellers, agents, advertisers and officers abroad, much of which must be translated and then replied to in translation.

Across all Europe, it seems events are on the move again. As the century draws to a close, so you would think the stars move faster in their courses, and time itself to quicken.

Henry of France has declared war on Spain, and rumours abound that King Philip is assembling a new Armada. But the Queen is in two minds, and takes counsel where she can. Lord Admiral Howard and Sir Francis Drake press for an expeditionary voyage over the high seas, to intercept a supply of Spanish gold at its embarkation point in Panama. Burghley supports it, Essex opposes. A compromise plan sends Drake and Sir John Hawkins to capture a Spanish treasure ship in Puerto Rico, but the operation is a costly failure and both men's lives are taken by disease.

Now the Spanish have seized the port of Calais after a huge bombardment and stand ready to use it as a base to supply their Armada in an attack on England. Calais, for so long an English possession, that used to send burgesses of its own to Parliament! Calais, lost to France in 1558 and now to Spain. This is a double indignity.

But what quickens the pace of work at Essex House still further is that the Queen has at last accepted the Earl's proposal to attack the Spanish mainland itself. Howard has planned it and, though Essex abhors the prospect, the Queen's instructions in March make clear that the two men are to share the high command. Beneath them, Sir Francis Vere, fresh from campaigning in the Netherlands, will direct an army of over seven thousand men, and Raleigh a fleet of one hundred and twenty ships. Security is paramount, with the nature and target of the operation kept secret from all but a few officers.

On 3 June, the fleet sets sail from Plymouth. Its destination: Cadiz.

29

TWICKENHAM PARK, SUMMER 1596

Then man is a world; in which, officers
Are the vast ravishing seas; and suitors,
Springs; now full, now shallow, now dry; which, to
That which drowns them, run: These self reasons do
Prove the world a man, in which, officers
Are the devouring stomach, and suitors
Th'excrements, which they void. All men are dust;
How much worse are suitors, who to men's lust
Are made preys? O worse then dust, or worms meat,
For they do eat you now, whose selves worms shall eat.

Yet as Anthony is pulled closer and closer to the Earl of Essex, Francis starts to feel ever more adrift. He sees his brother at the centre of a whirring mechanism of planning and information, he sees the secretaries hard at work, Essex swinging from exultance to melancholy and back again.

For Francis, however, there is only the growth of his own misgivings, about his patron's restless yearning for primacy over his fellows, his conduct towards the Queen, his military capacity. Francis dares not comment on the Cadiz project. He is by it, among it, owned by it, but not of it.

It is now fifteen years or so since Francis wrote that long, hopeful letter to his uncle setting out his plans for a new college to rival the ancient Lyceum. Since that time, he has written letters for Walsingham, pamphlets for the Earl, for Burghley and others, papers for the Queen, a notable reading for the Inn, parts for masques and revels, legal notes, and even a few briefs.

Yet there has been little enough in his own name for men to read and hear. His speech on the subsidies in Parliament was one heartfelt exception, and if he still flinches at the memory of it, still he does not disavow the act or its meaning.

To what purpose all these writings for others? They have served him not. *I have vast contemplative ends, for I have taken all knowledge to be my province.* So he had said, so he has always believed, but where are the fruits of that contemplation? What sets him apart from any other jobbing clerk or seeker after place? If his time were suddenly ended today, with perhaps half his adult life gone, what would he have to show for it? His dreams of a sinecure place are come to naught, so surely he can have naught to fear and naught to wait for now.

So Francis writes, in his own name, on his own behalf, but for the eyes of others, ten *Essays*. In name, they draw on the *Essais* of Michel de Montaigne, his brother Anthony's celebrated friend from Bordeaux. But in style they owe more to Aristotle and Seneca, and in content to Machiavelli. Montaigne was personal, confessional, expansive, a subtle loose assembler of anecdote and insight. Francis admires the Frenchman's essays; who could not? And his own titles echo those of Montaigne: *Of Expense, Of Regiment of Health, Of Faction, Of Studies, Of Followers and Friends, Of Discourse, Of Negotiating, Of Suitors, Of Ceremonies and Respect, Of Honour and Reputation.*

Yet Francis's own intention is quite different: not to show mankind in all its colours, its strengths and weaknesses, its vanity and foibles, but to instruct the reader in the ways of advancement. The titles tell the tale: to progress, a man must manage his income and expense, keep in good health, harness the love of friends and the ambition of supporters, win over superiors, conciliate enemies, transact his business, build reputation and recognition. These are all so many sheaves of grain, to be sown and gathered, reseeded and multiplied, grown and harvested. The man who can do these things with skill can fill his barns and augment his fortunes.

And their style is unlike any other. This is not the closed fist of logic, that punches a man into submission, but nor yet is it the open hand of rhetoric, that woos him into assent. There are no softening proems, no easy introductions, no misplaced or needless words. Every essay seems to draw directly on Francis's own experience, from above and underneath, as master or as mastered, as observer or subject of princes and high counsellors and men of business. Each shows the delicacy of his observation, and bears the imprint of his anxieties and fears. Each is written as though first in Latin, and then translated.

Yet Francis himself is hardly to be found in these *Essays*, and they are not structured to convey single meanings. Instead the sentences pile up on top of one another, like so many stones in a wall with no mortar between them. There are lists, enumerations, categories culled from his notebooks. The style is lapidary and disjointed, the tone mosaic in its patterns and authority. The *Essays* are brief, yet any of them could become a treatise.

This, then, is a handbook for the effective exercise of power, a handbook that deals in practical advantage not dreamy aspiration, writ in the spirit of Tacitus not of Cicero. Here is Francis on how to use men:

> *In choice of instruments, it is better to choose men of a plainer sort, that are like to do that that is committed to them, and to report back again faithfully the success, than those that are cunning, to contrive, out of other men's business, somewhat to grace themselves, and will help the matter in report for satisfaction's sake.*
>
> *Use also such persons as affect the business, wherein they are*

employed; for that quickeneth much; and such, as are fit for the matter; as bold men for expostulation, fair-spoken men for persuasion, crafty for inquiry and observation, froward and absurd men for business that doth not well bear out itself.

It is better dealing with men in appetite, than with those that are where they would be. If you would work any man, you must either know his nature and fashions, and so lead him; or his ends, and so persuade him; or his weakness and disadvantages, and so awe him or those that have interest in him, and so govern him.

Francis can turn a phrase like no other, as every page attests.

Mean men, in their rising, must adhere; but great men, that have strength in themselves, were better to maintain themselves indifferent, and neutral.

To spend too much time in studies is sloth; to use them too much for ornament, is affectation; to make judgment wholly by their rules, is the humour of a scholar.

Reading making a full man, conference a ready man, and writing an exact man.

Some books are to be tasted, others to be swallowed, and some few to be chewed and digested.

So the aphorisms proceed, each more memorable than the last.

Yet copies have been quickly made by others. So to protect his authorship Francis gathers the ten essays together with a few brief homilies in Latin that he calls sacred meditations, has them copied, and circulates them: to Anthony, to the Earl, to his friend Fulke Greville, to uncle Burghley and Robert Cecil, and to the Queen.

When they are published, in January 1597, it is with a dedication to Anthony, his loving and beloved brother, saying I have preferred them to you, that are next myself, dedicating them, such as they are, to our love; in the depth whereof I sometimes wish your infirmities translated upon me, that Her Majesty might have the service of so active and able a mind, and I might be with excuse confined to these contemplations and studies, for which I am fittest.

But after they are published, Anthony quickly writes to the Earl of Essex, to yield to him the dedication, saying I am bold to present the first sight and taste unto you of such fruit as my brother was constrained to gather before they were ripe, to prevent stealing, and humbly to crave your honourable acceptance and most worthy protection, to whose disposition and commandment I have entirely and inviolably vowed my poor self, and whatever appertaineth unto me, either in possession or right.

Thus Francis has not needed to dedicate the *Essays* to the Earl himself, for the Earl to feel the honour of a dedication. It is handsomely done.

Yet still Francis sees the cormorants wheel and dive in search of prey.

Harvey has been paid off. Other creditors – Mills, Alderman Spencer – have been assuaged and numerous petty bills part-paid or postponed. This is a moment of respite, of calm, for the brothers, though Lady Bacon warns Anthony they can expect no help from Robert Cecil or his father, since both are joined in power and policy, and be it emulation or suspicion you know what terms Robert standeth in toward yourself.

Throughout, one true friend has been Nicholas Trott, but now even he is turning against them. Trott is a Yorkshireman, who has come to know Francis through the Inn, but has of late grown close to Anthony. He has been open-handed to them both in times of need, and as the sums have grown, so have the pledges. He has helped Anthony to sell properties in Hertfordshire, and had receipts from marshlands in Woolwich. And Anthony has much reassured him regarding Francis: the post of Attorney General brings with it fees, gifts of thanks, acknowledgements, anticipations. Once Francis has the prize, as he surely must, these will be more than enough to settle the debt.

But now the Attorneyship has gone, and the brothers' plans lie in ruins. Pursued by creditors of his own, Trott is almost unhinged by loss of prospects. He turns in despair upon Francis.

Somehow, with Anthony's help, drawing on his mother and the help of others, Francis is able to cobble together enough money to meet his friend's immediate needs. The lease on a parsonage in Redbourne is sold, as is a manor at Burstone. For a moment it seemed he must sacrifice the value of his reversion to the clerkship of Star Chamber, the last great thing he has. In the event he makes do, but only by mortgaging his beloved property in Twickenham.

And now even Francis, who despises the moneylenders and hates the sordid and ungentle pettiness of debt; Francis, who averts his eyes and blocks his ears, must come to see an awful truth.

Not only is his own credit near exhausted, but so is that of his brother and of his mother too. And what is worse: the sums are now so large that he struggles even to pay the interest on them. For a man to have to borrow to pay the interest on his debts: from this vice there can be no escape.

30

CADIZ, AUTUMN 1596

Meanwhile, the expedition to Cadiz has been a triumph; less so the sequel.

Arriving on 20 June, the English fleet attacks at dawn the following day. It finds an undefended Spanish fleet of some seventy ships, including thirty-four merchant vessels loaded with arms, bullion, wine, silks and treasure, ready to set their sails for the West Indies. In a desperate effort to regroup, the Spanish withdraw towards the inner harbour, sheltering behind a defensive line of warships, which the English engage in a prolonged gun battle. Two Spanish ships are grounded by an ebbing tide, another is set on fire, till all in the line are finally destroyed. As the tide returns, the English press the fight to the inner harbour, capturing, burning or sinking Spanish galleons as they go.

But here the Earl of Essex makes a fatal error. Overruling the advice of Raleigh, he ignores the merchantmen with their priceless cargoes. Instead, he disembarks two thousand soldiers, takes the city of Cadiz by storm and spends the next day negotiating ransoms with the leading Spanish families, who have retreated into the castle, while his troops ransack the place for booty. The Spanish see their chance and set on fire and scuttle most of their merchantmen rather than have them fall into enemy hands. Other galleys are dragged secretly overland to safety.

On its face it is a glorious victory, and the name of Essex is celebrated across all England. But the Queen is enraged. She had given explicit instructions to the Lords General: to seize enemy warships, of course, but also to spare lives where possible, to take any and all treasure ships with their cargoes and not to garrison the city. She is furious now to hear that Essex is pressing the Privy Council to disobey her orders and allow him to settle troops in Cadiz. Taking advantage of his absence, Burghley and Cecil denounce the scheme, and though she has prevaricated for years and promised Essex she would make no such appointment while he is away, she immediately elevates Cecil to be her Principal Secretary.

On the Earl of Essex's return, the Queen's anger is further magnified when she learns not only that he has failed to capture the Spanish merchantmen, but that despite the plundering of Cadiz she, the Queen of England, she who paid for the whole expedition, has been left with booty that is scarce more than the dregs from the bottom of the barrel. And what a barrel! Twelve million ducats of treasure lost, they say. It is a sum almost beyond calculation.

Where has it all gone? Who has benefitted? Why have her claims been ignored, claims that should by every right predominate? By Burghley and Cecil's arrangement, she publicly takes the Earl of Essex to task at court for his inability to account for the lost spoils of war. In vain does he complain and protest at the inadequacy of others to match his vision, and urge the scale of his personal expenditures on the expedition.

And worse still for the Earl, in light of the losses to the Exchequer, Burghley has persuaded the Queen that she must make out no more warrants for grants of money to individuals on her own cognisance, but have them counter-signed by three or four members of the Privy Council.

In form this is a general measure, to be applied to all, for the better scrutiny of public expenditure. But it is one more mechanism of control, and as Burghley well knows, its effect will fall hardest on the Queen's favourite.

31

THE SEQUEL TO CADIZ, AUTUMN 1596

Through the chambers of his great house the Earl of Essex rages, thwarted and humiliated in his hour of triumph. But as Anthony discerns, this is not all that ails him, for Essex is increasingly impecunious as well. He has vast debts and vast expenses, still vaster after Cadiz, which are in no way met from his lands and benefices. His monopoly of the income of sweet wines keeps him alive, but barely so. Without special grants of money from the Queen, he must retrench.

Yet this is only part of what disturbs the brothers. What is worse is Essex's conduct, which is becoming ever more ambitious and irregular. He has set himself to be in competition with the Cecils for the Queen's favour, so much is clear. He grew a beard on the voyage to Cadiz, a beard not pointed in the court fashion but clipped square, and wears it now as the visible manifestation of his triumph, as well as of his maturity of counsel. His image is everywhere, in miniature and in grand, thanks to the artists Oliver and Gheeraerts whom he patronises. Yet his sudden marriage, his bastard child Walter, borne of him by one of the Queen's maids of honour, and his dalliances over the years have lost him many friends and much influence. All these actions point the same way.

The plain fact is this: led by Anthony's love for Essex and their own desperation for advancement, the brothers have taken sides, reluctantly but unmistakably, in his developing contest with the

Cecils. They have placed their bets, on the man and on his success, and they cannot afford him to fail.

If Anthony does not yet appreciate the danger, Francis does; and Francis is filled with a dreadful foreboding.

To offer advice is always a matter of the utmost delicacy. It is to presume, if not an equality, then at least a right of audience and a power of judgement that may be superior to that of the receiver. Still more is it delicate when the advice is given unbidden to a patron. What can be the result? The patron falls under some obligation to give an account of their action, which is not usually a pleasant thing to one in authority. And whether the advice be heeded or no, the adviser is rarely thanked; often they are secretly despised.

Francis knows all this when he writes a letter of advice to Essex in October 1596. His topic is of equal tenderness and timeliness, for it is nothing less than how to please Her Majesty the Queen. As he says, I humbly desire your Lordship, before you hear my poor advice, to consider, first, whether I have not reason to think that your fortune comprehends mine, and whether you have received injury by my advice.

Then Francis goes straight to the point, saying Win the Queen; if this be not the beginning, I see no end of another course. But how is it now? The Queen has little choice but to see you as A man of nature not to be ruled, that has the advantage of my affection, and knows it, of an estate not grounded to his greatness, of a popular reputation, of a military dependence. I ask whether there can be a more dangerous image than this represented to any monarch living, much more to a lady, and of Her Majesty's apprehension?

He continues, the excellence of the Queen's nature is not in question. But bad impressions breed great troubles.

Is it not evident, Francis says, that whilst this impression continues in Her Majesty's breast, you must ever face invented falsehoods by others to keep your estate bare and low; crossing and disgracing your actions; extenuating and blasting your merit; carping with contempt at your nature and fashions; breeding, nourishing, and fortifying those as are most factious against you, and yet also the repulses and scorns of your friends and dependents, that are true and steadfast; winning and inveigling away from you those as are flexible and wavering; thrusting you into odious employments and offices, to supplant your reputation… and perhaps venturing you in dangerous and desperate enterprises.

The message is unmistakable. Essex's high-handedness, military zeal and insistence on superiority at court are fit to lose him the Queen, Francis intimates, and to unite his growing number of enemies against him.

What is to be done? Francis is as direct in his remedy as in his diagnosis. Essex is at present unbending, dissatisfied and formal with the Queen; let him instead be pliable, courteous and sincere. He is ever apt to advertise the inadequacy of his estate to his greatness; if he must keep to this principle, let him at least abolish it in shows to the Queen. For till Her Majesty finds him careful of his estate, she will not only fear his continuing cost to her but also conceive that he has still higher ambitions.

So: Essex must confound the Queen's expectations. He now appears to seek a great popular reputation, so let him speak against popularity and popular courses vehemently to the Queen. But above all, let him controvert the impression of greatest prejudice: that he is only, and ever must be, a soldier.

Francis continues, You say that wars are your occupation, my Lord, and go on in that course; whereas you should have left that person at Plymouth. A military dependence maketh a suspected greatness. I heard your Lordship designing to yourself the Earl

Marshal's place, or the place of the Master of the Ordnance; but I would name you to the place of Lord Privy Seal, and bring in some military man such as Lord Mountjoy to the Council, to divert Her Majesty from this impression of martial greatness. For first Her Majesty loveth peace. Next, she loves not charge and expense.

Both in its tone and in its substance, the letter bespeaks the close relationship between Francis and his great patron. But will Essex heed his advice? That is the question.

32

ESSEX HOUSE, MARCH 1597

The starry heavens revolve, and all is still above. But on Earth, it is all change and chance, chance and change. And now, a new opportunity for Francis.

Fulke Greville has brought information to the Earl of Essex, which sets his table to furious talk. Sir William Hatton has died; a man of no great consequence in himself, but the nephew of the Queen's old favourite and Lord Chancellor, Christopher Hatton. The Chancellor had been rich indeed, with great estates in Northamptonshire. It was said he moved a village to improve the view from one of the windows at his house at Holdenby.

Sir William Hatton inherited these estates, and further magnified them by marrying Elizabeth, daughter of Thomas Cecil and so granddaughter of Lord Burghley. Now she is left as Hatton's widow. She is very rich, very beautiful and in her nineteenth year. Her connections are of the highest rank, reaching into the Presence Chamber and Privy Council alike.

Lady Hatton comes with a stepdaughter from Sir William's first marriage, but that is no matter since the girl has already been amply provided for. She has no children of her own, but will surely breed. With such a prize in prospect, little wonder there is talk. And all the more because this is no foreign maiden come to be wed in England. Essex has known her since birth, when he was a ward of her grandfather.

Greville will be hot in pursuit of Lady Hatton, that is for sure. To Francis, however, she is not Lady Hatton, not even Elizabeth, but cousin Eliza. Her father Thomas Cecil has long been his friend and supporter, her brother Richard his guest at Twickenham Park. And as for him and Eliza? Well, they have always been oddly close. She is quick and clever, funny and spirited and passionate. She sees the absurdity in things, be they men's manners or the tattle of the court, and she has long been happy to share them through a glance or a play of wit with her older cousin. With eight older brothers and sisters, she has yet made her own way in the family. She can tell that Francis too stands somehow to the side of things, and that pleases and amuses her.

But could she, would she? Come to that, could he? The thought of wooing her, of seeking her as his wife, comes instantly to his mind. And just as quickly he dismisses it. He has seen the rise of expectations for his brother Anthony with the Paget girl, and seen them come to naught. He understands the value of a marriage, of course, its power to transform a man's situation, and he has regularly thought of it as an idea, a project to be weighed for its gains and losses.

Yes, but for himself? And with a live, breathing woman of flesh and blood, let alone one like Eliza? A wife would bring property, her person, lands and goods and chattels, as prescribed by law and contract. Would he want to be her Lord, her keeper, head and sovereign as the law requires? Would she allow it?

She is yet childless, and would want children of her own.

But yes, he reflects, such a marriage would be the answer to all my prayers for wealth and connection. It must surely lead to a high position. Thomas Cecil her father may like the match.

As for uncle Burghley, how would it fall with him? He has not spent a lifetime gently keeping me from the ramparts of preferment only to welcome me through the palace gates! But, as he would surely see, it would bind me into the family and weaken my tie to Essex, and it would assist and not impede the progression of my cousin Robert.

These are not small things. And the Queen? Might not such an alliance please her?

33

HATTON HOUSE, LONDON, JULY 1597

'So, dear Francis, are you come to woo me? I hope so, for I have endured a most dreary procession of knights and nobles these past weeks, each less to be borne than the last. Truly, the Queen knows her business, never to be married.'

Eliza and he are walking among the magnificent arbours and alleys of Hatton House, her London residence.

'I am come to see you, fair cousin. But you must woo yourself if we are ever to be wed. I cannot think but you must have greater men than me spread out their cloth of gold at your feet.'

'I' faith I can hardly move for the silks, or breathe for the jewels they would place about my neck. And yet... hath not the Earl of Essex writ to my father in your cause? That soundeth most like wooing to me. Indeed, I swear I heard men say it *is* wooing.'

'He may have done, but it was secretly and in the warmth of friendship.'

'Secretly, you say? And yet do I not have here a letter in his own hand to my father? Let me find it... ah, yes, (*deep voice*) "what his virtues and excellent parts are, you are not ignorant. What advantages you may give yourself and to your house by having a son-in-law so qualified, and so likely to rise in his profession, you may easily judge."'

'This is nothing, cousin. A mere courtesy to me.'

'Well, it is a most loquacious courtesy. For he has also writ separately to my mother.'

'God's blood!'

'Easy, good Francis. Indeed, I hear of other great men who have spoken in your behalf. Is this not wooing? I say it is. Nay, I put it to you, it is a campaign of wooing.'

'Dearest Eliza, you mock me like a man in the stocks. Yes, yes, I confess it all. I would wed you and take you for my wife. Do I not delight you, and you me? Did my book of essays and prayers fail to please you? Have we not known and loved each other since your childhood?'

'Loved? Yes, in a way.'

'But Eliza, or may I say, my love…'

'No, no! Do not say that, for you cannot mean it, or mean it as I would want. Or if you do, then kiss me now, full on my lips and hold me to your body… but see, dear Francis, you cannot. You shrink from me inside, I feel it. There is no disguising.'

He cannot speak.

'Francis, Francis, I would have no man in the world before you as a friend. But marriage is not for friendship, or if it is, it is for much more besides. I loved my darling husband William very dearly. But that was luck, cousin, for I was bought and sold him by my father like so much cloth at the draper's market, and his father watching on in turn to see the deal were good.

'And, dear Francis, you are well away, for the truth is this: that you are the Pacific Sea and I the furious Adriatic. If we wooed in spring and married in summer, yet we would be stormy by Christmas. Love me, and be my friend, as I will always be yours. But let us have no more talk of marriage.'

After his visit to Eliza, Francis writes her a sonnet, saying I send this forasmuch as poems are as prime numbers, basic, indivisible, a part of the universe. It is not quite the proper form, but the spirit moved me in a rush, and I could not fight it.

To Lady H
Sweet love, 'tis true I was not made for love
With you; e'en Euclid could not make more plain.
Yet our twin natures nature's laws must move
As one, and human custom thus disdain
Thou Castor, I as Polydeuces, stay;
But as a comet if thou soar above
And join another body for a day
Hie thee then back in spirit to my love.
As older wine doth e'er mature the best
When divers grapes it brings in cask together
So shall our ancient love still stand the test
When rougher winds conspire to strain its tether.
For love commingled none can separate
Nor part a friendship so intrinsicate.

She keeps it in a special drawer in her closet, with her jewels.

34

THE CITY OF LONDON, SEPTEMBER 1598

'**M**aster Bacon, is it, sir?'

It is September, and Francis is walking back from the Tower to Gray's Inn in company with William Wade, Clerk of the Privy Council. They have been examining conspirators in the latest Popish plot.

'Yes, I am Bacon; and you, sir?'

'I am Williams, sir, authorised to serve you with this warrant of execution for the sum of £300 owed to Master Sympson of Lombard Street.'

And so Francis finds himself held by Sheriff More in a house on Coleman Street, while he casts around for money and writes to Secretary Cecil and Lord Keeper Egerton to express his indignation at the slight.

This Sympson is a goldsmith and, yes, a creditor; he had sued Francis for payment in Trinity term and agreed to bide till the start of Michaelmas, and that is yet two weeks away. So why does he press now, and in such a public manner? And how can it be that he, the first man named to be the Queen's Counsel extraordinary, can be detained while on Her Majesty's business, *eundo et redeundo*, going and returning, nay just a few steps from the Tower itself?

None can say. But one thing is for sure. The whole of London, the court, the Inns, the Commons, all now know of Francis Bacon's debts. It is an abject humiliation.

35

HATTON HOUSE, OCTOBER 1598

It is the scandal of the year. Edward Coke and Elizabeth, Lady Hatton, have been suddenly married, and not as it should be, with the Queen's foreknowledge and consent, in a church between eight and twelve of a morning and with the banns of marriage read in the accustomed way; but secretly, in a private house and in defiance of Church law.

At court, the chatterers rejoice. It cannot be chance that they have married only weeks after the death of the bride's grandfather. Lord Burghley's coffin was attended at his funeral by more than five hundred black-clad mourners, among them the greatest figures in the land. The Queen had visited him on his deathbed and fed him broth by her own hand. Now she weeps openly at his death.

Burghley would surely never have stood for such an illicit proceeding. Yet they say Coke made his offer of marriage at the funeral.

What can be its meaning? Coke has been nowhere among the suitors, but his wife is newly dead these past few weeks. He is neither knight nor nobleman, forty-six years of age and a widower with ten children already. How can Lady Hatton have stooped to accept such a man, near fifteen years older than her late husband, amid so many bounteous and honourable offers? Is she already with child? Who can have officiated at the ceremony, in defiance of the Church? It is a mystery.

But for Francis, there is no mystery. All the world knows that

Coke had £30,000 from his dead wife and has used it to accumulate estates and income, while Thomas Cecil would welcome an alliance with his friend. The pity of it is that now the world is doubly confirmed in the opinion that Francis is a man of little credit, who can bring neither money nor position nor prospects to a marriage even with his own cousin. No need of any Babylonian arithmetic to make that calculation.

It is yet one more deep wound to the body from Edward Coke. For Francis, there has never been great respect for that man, but there has at least been toleration. He has had to watch Coke ascend by degrees from lawyer to Member of Parliament, to Solicitor, to Speaker, to Attorney General, while he himself must ever scrape and crawl like a reptile along the ground. He has watched while Coke ingratiated himself by degrees with Burghley and his son and, through them, with the Queen.

And what has been the harvest? Simply this, that Francis has failed at every turn against him. He was beaten to the Attorneyship, and failed even to gain the Solicitorship that Coke left behind. And he has had to bear Coke's scorn and condescension throughout, and keep silent even as he saw Coke bark and bully his way through the prosecution of Dr Lopez.

Now this. It is Burghley's last bequest, assisted by his son no doubt: Coke winning Francis's beloved cousin Eliza, taking her over, taking her and all she has, all her revenue, her land and property for himself and away from Francis. Who can think she will fare well in the embrace of this brute? Francis could have endured it with any man but Coke, never Coke.

Everything is different now. Hatred overflows the jealousy in his heart. He sweats with rage to entertain the very name of Coke, and swears by any means he can to bring about his fall.

36

THE PALACE OF WHITEHALL, MARCH 1599

The Earl of Essex has been made Earl Marshal and peace restored between him and the Queen. He could not abide that she had elevated Lord Howard to Earl of Nottingham, but this new title restores his precedence. Essex's fortunes yet remain unrepaired, however; indeed, his expenses are much magnified by the cost of his campaigning. They say he owes £10,000, and now there is not the old flow of gifts and warrants from Her Majesty to help him meet these bills.

As Essex notes, the prospect abroad is a mixed one. France is cooler than she was. King Henry has treated with Spain, and calmed his Huguenots with a new edict of toleration at Nantes. Yet against England Spain is once more on the rise. Philip II is dead, but his son Philip III has sworn to avenge the Armada against the bastard heretic Queen of England. This is more promising to the man who has pledged himself to be the heir of Philip Sidney and the scourge of the Spanish.

Ireland, it appears, is to be Philip's means of vengeance. King Henry VIII had raised it to a kingdom and given it a true Parliament, but he had never fully subdued it. Many Englishmen that have gone there have huddled in the Pale of Dublin; others have been planters and taken land in the centre and south of the island, while old resentments simmer across Ulster in the north. Its religion remains unreformed, and it has monasteries that evaded even the reach of Vicar General Cromwell. And it has been in rebellion now these four years. Thwarted in his hopes to be made Lord President, the Earl of Tyrone has raised an army, spread revolt across the country, taken the Blackwater Fort and destroyed a relieving English army, with nigh on two thousand dead. Tyrone is fortified by mercenaries and feared to be in league both with the Spanish and with James of Scotland.

The Lord Deputy, Lord Burgh, is dead of typhus. Who is to replace him? It is a question that the previous year brought relations between the Queen and Essex to their lowest point. She had named Sir William Knollys to the post, whereupon Essex in a fit of anger turned his back upon his sovereign. Damning him for an ingrate and a fool, she boxed him on the ear, whereon he reached towards his sword and was taken away under compulsion by guards from the Privy Chamber, calling her as crooked in her conditions as in her carcass, and saying he neither could nor would put up with so great an affront and indignity, neither would he have taken it at King Henry VIII his hands.

And afterwards, when his friend Lord Keeper Egerton seeks to placate Essex, the Earl replies in the most intemperate terms, saying nay, when the vilest of all indignities is done unto me, doth religion enforce me to sue? Doth God require it? Is it impiety not to do it? Why, cannot princes err? Cannot subjects receive wrong? Is an earthly power or authority infinite? Pardon me, pardon me, my good Lord, I can never subscribe to these principles.

Yet now, once more, all seems mended between the Queen and her favourite. They have a compact, for she must be rid of the rebellious Earl of Tyrone, and Essex thirsts again for military glory.

For Sir Robert Cecil, who is Secretary of State and the Queen's leading minister, but who has no father now to protect and advise him, to have Essex gone away from court is nothing bad; the man has long been a distraction and an impediment to business. For Essex himself, there is a personal debt of honour to be settled as well: to avenge his father, the first Earl of Essex, who campaigned to subdue and settle Ulster for the plantations, and died on the Queen's service in Ireland.

But Burghley's death has made a deeper difference. While he lived, he commanded a son's love from Robert and a ward's respect from Essex. Now he is gone, there is nothing to control their rivalry.

For all his appetite for battle, Essex has set demanding terms. Letters patent release him from the debts still owing from his father's Irish campaign. The commission which the Queen signs at last gives Essex almost plenipotentiary powers; as she says, to prosecute or end the war as he sees fit, and to appoint a deputy so that he may return to England, as well to see our person as to inform us of such things as may be to our important service.

When he leaves in March it is at the head of twenty thousand troops and two thousand cavalry. Never before has such an army been sent to Ireland, never before a commander with such powers.

As for Francis, the Earl of Essex is now less wont than of old to seek his advice. Perhaps his thinking has been too regularly adverse, for men of power like adverse advice as they like salt: some not at all, some to season their meat, none to overwhelm it.

Essex had shown brief signs of moderating his behaviour, only to give in again to anger and injured pride. There is a reversion in his conduct, which grows wilder with the passage of time, thinks Francis. He must ever play the man of war, not the councillor of peace; but so long as he maintains the Queen's favour, all can be well. Yet he has heard Essex say that the Queen cannot be met well on terms; she must be mastered. Take that another way, and it could be treason.

Looking back on these times some years later, Francis likes to paint a rosy picture of his actions. He ever loved the Earl of Essex, he insists, stayed faithful to him in adversity, gave honest counsel and true: that Ireland was like to prove a place of utmost trouble.

For I was not called nor advised with, he says, for some year and a half before his Lordship's going into Ireland. At which time, I did not only dissuade but protest against his going; telling him, with as much vehemence and asseveration as I could, that absence in that kind would exulcerate the Queen's mind. And because I would omit no argument, I remember I stood also upon the difficulty of the action; setting before him out of history, that the Irish was such an enemy as the ancient Gauls, or Britons, or Germans were.

Yet, as he must know full well, this is not at all how it really was. In fact, when the Ireland campaign was first mooted, Francis had urged Essex to seize the opportunity for glory, Cecil being away from court in France.

He had written to Essex, saying that *this is the utmost occasion of honour, a means to pay due respect to the noble works of your father, and all the more since Irish causes have of late been much neglected.* In sum, it is one of the aptest particulars that hath come, or can come upon the stage, for your Lordship to purchase honour upon. If your Lordship doubt to put your sickle in other men's harvests, yet consider you have these advantages. First, time being fit to you in Mr Secretary's absence; next, *vis unita fortior*, force brought together is the stronger for it; thirdly, the business being mixed with matters of war, it is fittest for you. Lastly, I know your Lordship will carry it with that modesty and respect towards aged dignity as no inconvenience may grow that way.

In a second letter, Francis had gone further still, saying A treaty with Tyrone on suitable terms were not impossible. But because variableness is never restrained but with fear, I hold it necessary for him to be menaced with a strong war; not by words, but by musters and preparations of forces here, in case the accord proceed not. *And I think if your Lordship lent your reputation in this case, that if not a defensive war, as in times past, but a full re-conquest of those parts of the country be resolved on, you would accept the charge, I think it would help to settle him, and win you a great deal of honour gratis.*

HUBRIS

Then there is but silence. A year later, on the eve of his departure
to Ireland, Essex taxes Francis with that silence and asks his advice
once more. This time, however, Francis replies not with the same
clear words but with a letter of Daedalian complexity. On its face,
it echoes his earlier arguments, saying that the cause is one the
goodness and justice whereof can hardly be matched in any example. Of its honour your Lordship is in no small possession. Its
design doth descend from your noble father who lost his life.

There is frankness in his words, wisdom and dispassion. But
every line is limned and shaded with caveat and proviso. Francis
hopes his Lordship shall be as fatal a captain to this war as Afri-
canus was to the war in Carthage, yet notes that both his uncle and
father had lost their lives in the same war.

Time and again he lights upon the dangers to be faced, saying
that your Lordship goeth against three of the unluckiest vices of
all, disloyalty, ingratitude, and insolence; which three offences in
all examples have seldom their doom adjourned to the world to
come. And he sums up with a passage full of meanings, that your
Lordship is designed to a service of great merit and great peril; and
as the greatness of the peril must needs include no small consequence of peril, if it be not temperately governed; so all immoder-
ate success extinguisheth merit, and stirreth up distaste and envy,
the assured forerunner of whole changes of peril.

What is this florid nonsense of a letter, thinks the Earl, just as
I am about to set forth on this great and hazardous expedition?
Where are the clarity and wisdom I desire? This is not counsel. It
is yea and nay at the same time, it is coming and going at once, by
a man who lacks the spirit to put his thought to the purpose. It is
hiding before the battle.

37

NONSUCH PALACE, SEPTEMBER 1599

The Earl of Essex has marched into Dublin, then moved south to draw out the enemy, in vain. On its return his force is caught at Arklow and takes heavy losses. His ambition to establish a garrison in Lough Foyle in the far north behind the enemy cannot be sustained, especially now that the Privy Council led by Cecil has – from necessity, or perhaps for some other reason – chosen to reinforce Dublin instead.

The Dublin Council advises him against a march on Ulster, yet the Queen demands it. Essex's elaborate ceremonials and knighting of dozens of followers speak to his princely ambitions and his desire to mend morale and keep his troops attendant. But, though he marches hither and yon, he makes no headway against the foe.

All these things enrage Her Majesty. Ever since he turned his back on her, Essex has not been what he was; gone is the almost mystical connection he bore to her beloved Earl of Leicester.

The Queen has already made plain her personal displeasure by awarding the immensely lucrative Mastership of the Wards to Secretary Cecil, despite her undertaking to Essex before he left that she would make no such dispensation. Now she countermands Essex's appointment of the Earl of Southampton as General of the Horse, revokes his licence to return to England and instructs him in terms by letter to engage the enemy to the north.

The expedition to Ireland is turning into a disaster.

By July Essex has lost three-quarters of his men, more of whom have deserted or died of disease than have perished by the enemy's hand. But worse is to follow. For it is revealed that Essex has met in person with Tyrone, conversing with him from the banks of the river at Ballaclinch Ford, privately and without the presence of others. And a second meeting follows, with six attendants on each side, at which it is agreed to negotiate a peace settlement and call a truce, but Essex says that this is not to be written down and can only be transmitted by him directly to the Queen.

So many men and so much treasure lost, and every one of his requests for arms and troops granted! And now comes the humiliation of a truce with rebels whom Essex had promised to extirpate only months before. Why make such terms? Who knows what else has been privately agreed between the two men? Essex has long been in correspondence with King James. Perhaps Tyrone is part of some complex plot across England, Scotland and Ireland for James to win the Crown?

And now Essex has disobeyed the Queen's direct command. He has come back without notice to England and confronted her in her privy chamber before she has dressed, denouncing his enemies on the Council for their treachery. Is this revolution? Have others struck against her elsewhere?

She cannot know. So she receives him carefully, with tender kindness. But once the danger is past she condemns him utterly, saying by God's son, I am no queen! That man is above me! Essex is committed to the custody of Lord Keeper Egerton. There is to be a hearing on his conduct in Star Chamber.

38

YORK HOUSE, SPRING–SUMMER 1600

The Earl of Essex is kept almost in custody at York House and is forbidden all guests, including his wife and their new-born child. When at last he is allowed to return to his own great house near the Strand, he finds it empty. His wife the Countess, Southampton and his lady, Fulke Greville, Anthony Bacon, who struggles with disabling illness; all have been removed. In place of Essex's thriving group of secretaries, the sheaves of correspondence arriving every day from points abroad, the regular clutch of private letters and secret messages, there is nothing.

For her part, the Queen has summoned Francis Bacon regularly to her presence since the Earl's detention and, a signal mark of favour, she has dined at Twickenham Park. She demands advice from Francis, and in reply he urges delay and a private reconciliation with Essex, for he can do no other.

But her true purpose is to sound him, for his information and for his allegiance.

Is Francis loyal to the Earl of Essex, or to the Queen? The question is inescapable, and already rumours start to spread that Francis has betrayed his patron. Essex is a celebrated figure, the victor of Cadiz, and much vaunted in the taverns and theatres. There is perplexity as to why and how he has been brought down. So great a man must have been betrayed, that is certain. But by whom?

Whether from kindness or to turn the screw a little, Secretary Cecil writes to say, Cousin, I hear, but I believe it not, that you should do some ill office to my Lord of Essex. Surely a gent so well born, a wise gent so well levelled, and a gent so highly valued by a person of his virtue, worth and quality, would rather have sought after all occasions of expressing thankfulness than either omit opportunity or increase indignation.

For his part, Lord Henry Howard writes to Francis that he cannot believe the giddy malice of the world. He notes the travail of that worthy gentleman the Earl in your behalf, when you stood for a place of credit, the delight he hath ever taken in your company, his grief that he could not seal up assurance of his love by fruits, effects and offices, proportionable to an infinity, his study to engage your love by the best means he could devise.

So wherefore thou? The reproach is unspoken but as plain as the day. Francis twists and turns on its point, in an agony of conflict and indecision.

There is no formal contradiction here, he tells himself. To the Earl of Essex, he readily avows that I confess I love some things much better than I love your Lordship, as the Queen's service, her honour, her favour, the good of my country. Yet he has also written to Essex that I am as much yours as any man's, and as much yours as any man.

And to Her Majesty, he is still more blunt: I am like a hawk, that bates, when I see occasion of service, but cannot fly because I am tied to another's fist.

Tied to another's fist.

Francis had written to Essex as well, saying that for as I was ever sorry that your Lordship should fly with waxen wings, doubting Icarus's fortune, so for the growing up of your own feathers, be they ostrich's or other kind, no man shall be more glad.

To this, he receives an answer that mingles dignity with lyric, Essex saying I am a stranger to all poetical conceits, or else I should say somewhat of your poetical example. But this I must say, that I never flew with other wings than desire to merit, and confidence in my sovereign's favour; and when one of these wings failed me, I would light nowhere but at my sovereign's feet, though she suffered me to be bruised with my fall.

And where, the Earl of Essex seems to ask, have Francis Bacon's wings taken him?

The proceeding against the Earl of Essex has been moved from Star Chamber to York House, for early June. It is not to be a public hearing, yet even so it has a large audience: an arraignment on charges before a grand commission of eighteen high notables, Privy Councillors and others, the prosecution to be led by Attorney General Coke, Essex to speak in his own defence. There is to be no charge of perfidy or disloyalty to the Queen; the topic is not to be raised at trial.

Francis does not begrudge Coke his leading role. To the contrary, he welcomes it. Francis missed a private hearing on the Essex case earlier in Star Chamber, pleading illness, and the Queen has noted it.

This time, wriggle though he may, there is no escape. Let Bacon speak, the Queen says, that men may see where he stands.

Francis begs Her Majesty that if she would be pleased to spare me in my Lord of Essex's cause, out of the consideration she took of my obligation towards the Earl, I should reckon it for one of her highest favours. But to the contrary, though he is not a sworn law officer, though he is not experienced in such trials, though the Queen has other more senior lawyers near her hand, it has pleased her, or perhaps it has pleased Secretary Cecil, to give him a place of some importance in the trial: the task of admonishing Essex for his letters to the Lord Keeper, and for his part in the production of a recent history by John Hayward.

Hayward's book dwells upon the corruptions and faction of the court of Richard II and his earlier failure in Ireland; among a public greedy for scandal it has sold like none other. To the Queen, however, the book is nothing less than a narrative of the overthrow and murder of an anointed Christian Prince, and an open invitation to popular rebellion... and it has been dedicated to the Earl of Essex in the most fulsome terms. Essex must be made to disown and disavow the book and its seditious teachings. Who better to do this, and make clear where his own loyalties lie, than Master Bacon?

Coke opens for the Crown, and presses the charges with so much vituperation and heat as to raise the forbidden question of disloyalty. When the Commissioners make clear that Essex's loyalty is not in question, Coke becomes caught up in detailed explanation and rebuttal.

At last Coke sits, and Francis rises to speak. There is absolute silence in the court: will Bacon tread softly from tender feelings for the Earl of Essex, men wonder, or will he do justice to Her Majesty?

The answer comes at once: Francis is more courteous than Coke, but there is no quarter given. He tasks Essex directly on the language of the letters, written by his own hand to Egerton: *Why, cannot princes err? Cannot subjects receive wrong? Is an earthly power or authority infinite? Pardon me, pardon me, my good Lord, I can never subscribe to these principles.*

Did Essex esteem the Queen as but an impotent? Did he think, Francis asks, that she in her imperial Majesty cared nothing any longer for truth and justice? Did Essex not owe her not merely his fidelity, but also his obedience and thankfulness?

To this there can be no answer: as with Hayward's book, the imputation of sedition is there for all to see. But Francis so frames his examination as to leave two dreadful further questions hanging in his audience's minds: Does the Earl of Essex deny the authority of Kings, though this is authority granted, given and endowed by God Almighty? Or is Essex an atheist, who would deny outright the divinity of God himself?

Francis has had his private doubts about the Earl of Essex for many months. Yet memories of their long alliance remain, and there are other questions the Commissioners may also ask themselves. Does past friendship count for nothing? Does Master Bacon not owe the Earl not merely his fidelity, but also his obedience and thankfulness?

By the close the Earl has ceased to contest the charges and thrown himself on the Queen's mercy and clemency. He is dismissed from the Privy Council and from his posts as Earl Marshal and Master of the Ordnance and is ordered to be detained in custody at the Queen's pleasure.

Yet she expressly stipulates that he is not to be removed as Master of the Horse. As for so many others before him, there is a path back to her favour, if he will take it.

39

THE TOWER OF LONDON, FEBRUARY 1601

It is 25 February in the forty-third year of the reign of Elizabeth. Ash Wednesday, on which Christians mark the start of Lent, a day of penitence and prayer, of sin acknowledged and forgiveness sought.

A cold day today, made colder still for being a day of execution.

The Earl of Essex leaves his cell at seven o'clock of the morning and walks to the scaffold. By the Queen's special grace this is to be a private execution within the precinct of the Tower itself, not a public one on Tower Hill. The Earl is dressed in black with a black felt hat, and is attended by three priests and sixteen guards, led by the Lieutenant of the Tower. A hundred or so others stand by. It is said that Sir Walter Raleigh looks on from a window in the armoury, weeping, yet determined to watch the death of the man who was both his rival and his friend.

'Know ye all that I do freely confess and acknowledge the evil that I have done, and pray forgiveness for this last bloody, crying and contagious sin,' Essex proclaims, in a steady voice that rings out across the silence of the courtyard.

'Yet I solemnly swear I meant no violence to the Queen, whose love hath ever been my grace and benediction.'

To the executioner he says, 'Thou art welcome to me, I forgive thee; thou art the minister of true justice.' And, removing his hat and bowing his head, he prays, 'Almighty God, lift my soul above all earthly cogitations, and when my soul and body shall part, send thy blessed angels to be near unto me, which may convey it to the joys of heaven.'

He removes his doublet to reveal a scarlet waistcoat and scarlet shirt, sleeves billowed down to the cuff. There is an audible inward breath from the crowd at this last display of dash and colour. Then Essex lies down upon the boards, smoothes his beard, lays his head upon the block, arranges his golden-brown hair to either side to expose his neck, murmurs, 'Oh Lord, into thy hands I commend my spirit,' and stretches out his arms. That is the signal.

It is not pretty. The executioner takes three strokes, such is his anxiety. But there is no movement after the first.

So, too, is it all over for the brothers. Anthony lies abed, grievously sick and full of physic. Banished from Essex House and its protection against his creditors, long separated from the Earl yet still in touch by letter, he had arranged for all but the most vital documents to be burned. Now these last papers too are destroyed. But they are as nothing to the destruction of his heart, as grief consumes him for the loss of his friend and patron. Soon he too will be dead.

After the hearing at York House the previous June, Essex had remained in custody. But, over time, the close restrictions about him were gradually relaxed. All expected him to retire for a period, to be among family, to mend friendships, to give assistance where he could to the state, and by degrees to work his passage back into the Queen's favour. He remained Master of the Horse; she had not dismissed him from her service.

For several weeks Essex stayed in retirement in Putney, while ceaselessly writing to placate the Queen through declarations of loyalty and service. Francis was even moved on his behalf to draw up a fabricated exchange of letters between Essex and Anthony, to be shown to Her Majesty, in which his Lordship might plead his case and by indirect means move her to greater mercies.

In October, the Earl moved back to Essex House, yet he kept himself very private. But this was a man who could not be alone with his ambition, or live with his debts. His freedom now regained, he was fired with anger at his ill treatment, with indignation at the fools of the court and ingrates of the Council, and with lust to recover his old position, or exceed it. In this, the flame of his feelings was fanned by the sly words and flattery of his secretary Cuffe, his steward Meyrick and his father-in-law, Sir Christopher Blunt.

Thanks to Anthony Bacon, Essex had remained in correspondence with King James. But Essex had also kept open his private channel to Lord Mountjoy, his close friend, his sister's lover and his successor as Lord Deputy in Ireland. They had started to form a secret idea: for Mountjoy to cross over with the bulk of the army to England, join with Essex and march to London, ridding Elizabeth of her cankerous advisers and assuring the succession of James to the throne.

With James installed as King, the way would be clear for Essex and his allies to take over the Privy Council; Cecil and those around him, Raleigh, Cobham, Coke and others, would be crushed.

For both sides, the stakes were of the highest. The Scottish King kept himself carefully at a distance. But Essex was undaunted, and through intermediaries began to summon meetings of friends and allies, and to plot his way back to power. His own house being under constant watch, he called a secret group of friends and allies together in Drury House, the Earl of Southampton's residence, some way away on the Strand, in order to allay suspicion.

Essex had counted upon receiving the Mastership of the Wards after Burghley's death, in vain. All now depended on his keeping the immensely valuable farm of customs revenue from the importation of sweet wines, set to expire imminently. The Earl had enjoyed the lease for more than a decade. Its renewal would be a sign of the Queen's continuing favour, and point the way to his return. Without it he would be ruined.

For weeks, he heard little but occasional reports that she must first see what value it was of, and that benefits were not to be bestowed blindfold. Then at last, the Queen gave out that it was ended. She said privately that an unruly horse must be abated of his provender, that he may be the better brought to managing. And she commended the aphorism of the physicians, that corrupt bodies the more thou feedest them, the more thou hurtest them.

40

THE TOWER OF LONDON, FEBRUARY 1601

So, fired with indignation, and with financial ruin set to fall upon him, the Earl of Essex was resolved to act. Early in January 1601 his great friend Southampton had been attacked in the street, yet the assailant had been but lightly punished. Rumours flew that the Privy Council was examining prisoners in the Tower, to prove Essex's complicity in treason.

There was no time to waste. The plot had been to gather men and march directly to petition the Queen at the Palace of Whitehall. Sir Christopher Blunt at the head of a band of men would seize the gate, Sir John Davies the Hall, Sir Charles Danvers the Great Chamber and the Presence Chamber, and then Essex would come forward, kneel before the Queen and beseech her to put her evil counsellors on trial and change her government.

The preparations were in place, men notified. To raise spirits and bring old friends together, Essex's steward Meyrick had even paid Master Shakespeare's company, the Lord Chamberlain's Men, to put on his *Richard II*, with its story of corrupt government, rebellion and regicide. The players had grumbled at the need to bring back a play so old and so long out of the theatre, but Sir Charles Percy had insisted upon it, and stopped their mouths with an extra payment of forty shillings.

However, there had been many comings and goings at Essex House, and suspicions had been aroused. On Saturday 7 February, the same day as the play was performed, the Earl was sent an order to appear that evening before the Privy Council at the Lord Treasurer's house.

Fearful of a trap, and with private information that Raleigh and his guardsmen were planning to kill him if he went, Essex refused. Quickly he and his confederates brought forward their plans; rather than advance on the court and face cries of treachery and sedition, the Earl would go first to the City of London, to play upon his huge popularity there and among the people, and then proceed to Whitehall to petition the Queen for change, but at the head of a wider body of citizens.

Perhaps it was not Shakespeare's *Richard II* but his recent *Henry V* that Essex had dwelt on:

> *But now behold*
> *In the quick forge and working-house of thought,*
> *How London doth pour out her citizens!*
> *The mayor and all his brethren in best sort,*
> *Like to the senators of the antique Rome,*
> *With the plebeians swarming at their heels,*
> *Go forth and fetch their conquering Caesar in.*
> *As, by a lower but loving likelihood,*
> *Were now the general of our gracious empress,*
> *As in good time he may, from Ireland coming,*
> *Bringing rebellion broached on his sword,*
> *How many would the peaceful city quit,*
> *To welcome him!*

But again, bad luck or his enemies ran against Essex. On Sunday morning, a delegation of Privy Councillors, led by the Lord Keeper and with the Lord Chief Justice in attendance, arrived at Essex House to test the Earl and his intentions. To their surprise and horror they found several-score men and horses assembled there, horror redoubled when the courtyard resounded with cries of

'Let them be slain!' and 'Let that great seal be thrown away!' Essex motioned the visitors inside, but instead of conferring with them he locked them in the great chamber of the house, put guards on the doors and hastened with a hundred or so men to London, shouting 'For the Queen, for the Queen! A plot is laid for my life!'

Yet Sir Robert Cecil had already sent a message in the Queen's name to the Lord Mayor of London, enjoining him to be cautious and do his duty. So when Essex arrived at St Paul's he was met not with acclamation but with prevarication and delay, the Aldermen all dispersed and men looking not to any loyalty or enthusiasm but to their wealth and prudence.

Then the tide of opinion quickly turned. Essex and his accomplices found themselves being publicly denounced as traitors to the Queen in every ward of the city. Seeing their return blocked, the Earl drew his sword and ordered Blunt and his men to attack, which they did, Blunt being wounded, and another man killed. They then made their way back to Essex House by boat, and Essex frantically started to burn a casket of private papers, as well as the contents of a little black bag he kept around his neck, thought to contain his secret correspondence with King James, saying that they should tell no tales to hurt his friends.

The house was soon surrounded by the troops of the Lord Admiral. The women were suffered to leave unharmed. Essex swore he would not be taken alive, yet soon thereafter he sought to negotiate. The Lord Admiral instructed that cannon should be brought to bear and would grant no conditions, except safety of person and due process of law. At ten o'clock at night the Earl of Essex and his men surrendered.

41

WESTMINSTER HALL, FEBRUARY 1601

A nd now, eleven days after these events, there is a second hearing. But this one will be very different from that at York House the previous June. This is a trial in Westminster Hall of the Earls of Essex and Southampton for their lives.

The charges are of high treason: that they have plotted to deprive the Queen of her Crown and life, having entered into counsel to surprise the Queen in the court, and broken forth into open rebellion by imprisoning the counsellors of the realm, by stirring up Londoners to rebellion by feigned tales, by setting upon the faithful subjects in the City and by defending the house against the Queen's forces. Lord Buckhurst as Lord Steward presides, with a body of no fewer than twenty-five Lords and other eminent men to try them, including friends and connections of the accused.

For Secretary Cecil and his followers, as for Essex, there can be no going back now. To fail of a conviction is unthinkable. But, more, there must be no doubt remaining, either in the minds of those present or in the streets outside. The Earl of Essex, his reputation, his rank, his history as a soldier, his status as object of the people's love: this trial must be the destruction of them all.

Once again, Attorney Coke leads for the prosecution. Again, the Queen has passed over other more senior lawyers and insisted that Francis Bacon follow him.

Coke had risked censure in the previous proceeding by questioning Essex's loyalty, hinting at sedition and conspiracy. Now he repeats and magnifies these claims with impunity, indeed with a swagger; the facts have borne him out.

The Earl of Essex is a Catiline come among us, he says. Catiline had plotted treason in ancient Rome and drawn together men of the lowest sort behind him; just so has Essex gathered atheists, papists and criminous persons about him, his intention nothing less than to take away the Prince from the people. He has plotted to surprise the court, seize possession of Her Majesty's sacred person and call a parliament.

Essex would make himself King of England, Coke insists, and he would make his scheming confederate Tyrone King of Ireland, amid a general toleration of the Catholics. And this is no recent or adventitious enterprise but a plot of long gestation, like to the whelp of an elephant that they say is many years in breeding before it be brought forth. Hayward's history of the overthrow of Richard II by Henry IV readily attests the fact, with its seditious language and usurping dedication to the Earl of Essex.

There follows simple, moving testimony from the Lord Chief Justice, who tells the story of his imprisonment at Essex House; then comes the evidence of witnesses and others implicated in the plot. Essex's defence, that he had been given cause to fear his murder by Raleigh and the Queen's guardsmen, is shown to be without foundation. Essex is forced to admit the meeting at Drury House, but insists it was only to procure an interview with Her Majesty, and even that not merely for the redress of private wrongs but to cure many foreign practices and broils in neighbour states.

Indeed, in his own testimony Essex goes further, alleging that the Queen's councillors, nay Secretary Cecil himself, had acknowledged the superior title of the Infanta of Spain to the succession… only for him to be utterly confounded when Cecil himself suddenly emerges from behind a curtain, and begs the court that he may clear himself of this slander.

Cecil's testimony is quickly vindicated by the evidence of Sir William Knollys. And Knollys is uncle to the Earl of Essex, which makes his words still more telling. It must be true, for why else should Sir William incriminate his own kin?

But in other respects Essex makes some progress. He is granted leave to question witnesses, and defends himself with eloquence and force. What he yields, he yields cheerfully. As he says, the art of oratory is proper to advocates, who count it their glory to oppress the innocent by an aggravating speech. But he is a man of plain words. He had ever intended to present his case and place himself directly under the command of the Queen, to whom all access and communication had been denied him. There was no perfidious intent, only the violence of Cobham, Cecil and Raleigh had driven him to his necessary defence of self. Again and again he declares his loyalty and sincerity.

The day drags on, with repeated delays to the proceedings. The judges' assistants must be consulted on points of law. Witnesses must be sent for, and their testimony heard and weighed.

Essex does not miss his chances to raise a question or plead a mitigation. There are even signs that the audience is losing the thread of the evidence, even perhaps starting to entertain doubts as to the merits of the case against him.

Above all this must not happen, Secretary Cecil thinks. Or we are all done for.

42

WESTMINSTER HALL, 19 FEBRUARY 1601

For Francis Bacon, the past weeks have been a tumult of emotion. But it is for his brother Anthony, and not the Earl of Essex, that he chiefly feels.

It is Anthony who cannot leave his rooms, who daily drugs his pain away with physic. It is Anthony who had found himself cut out of Essex's deliberations, as pride and insolence and the cooing words of Cuffe, Blunt and Meyrick led his Lordship to his last mad throw of the dice. And it is Anthony whose moderating counsel and wider information might have saved the Earl from ultimate disaster.

Beloved brother Anthony! Who from childhood has been his own soul's other half, *animae dimidium meae*, who has always given what he has without stint or complaint; Anthony whom the world, the Queen and men of power have ever ill esteemed. He cannot be long to live. He too is mired in debt. Yet the cause of death will not be his illness or his want of money. It will not be this or any trial. It will – who can doubt it? – be a heart broken by grief and the loss of hope and friendship.

For the Earl of Essex, however, in what must surely be his own life's last days, Francis now feels nothing. Yes, they had been close. No, more than close: the Earl had been not just his patron, his ally and support, but his friend in mind and feeling. He had fought for Francis again and again, had battled for him to be Attorney, then Solicitor, with the Queen, Burghley and Robert Cecil. He had pressed

Francis's suit in marriage to Eliza Hatton. He had made connections for him with the great, lent him money, given him a handsome parcel of land at Twickenham Park. Innumerable were the evenings when Francis and the Earl had sat like Heraclitus the sage and Callimachus the bard and set the sun in their talk, be it of the court or foreign matters or natural philosophy, poetry or history.

It has ever been part of Francis Bacon's nature that he must explore, almost come to inhabit, both sides of any case. His cleverness is no sure friend to his honesty.

So it is now. All these doings are ancient business, he tells himself, and not to the point. The Earl of Essex used me as he wanted, and got good service by my works; these were like exchanges of gifts, which leave both sides the better. Yes, I sought advancement, but only for the public weal, never for myself alone. For years I did little else but devise and ruminate of anything that might advance his Lordship's honour, fortune or service. I esteemed him for his abilities, to be sure, but still more as the fittest instrument to do good to the state. He was ever but a means by which I might serve the Queen.

The Queen decided to test my loyalty at York House; today she will do the same. I can best serve her by making the Earl's misdeeds manifest beyond any cavil or possibility of question. And thereby I may preserve my chance to serve her in future. That is all I seek.

So Francis says to himself. Yet who would not misgive himself in such a circumstance?

In the courtroom, Coke has exhausted his questions, and perhaps himself, such has been the violence of his attack on the Earl of Essex. It is now Francis's turn to address the court. As if to draw a contrast with the late harangue, he goes straight to the point:

'No man can be ignorant, that knows matters of former ages, and all history makes it plain, that there was never any traitor heard of that durst directly attempt the seat of his liege Prince, but he always coloured his practices with some plausible pretence.

'Thus the Earl made his colour the severing of some great men and councillors from Her Majesty's favour, and the fear he stood in of his pretended enemies lest they should murder him in his house. Therefore he sayeth he was compelled to fly into the City for succour and assistance; not much unlike Pisistratus...'

There is a murmur from some among the audience. Pisistratus! The tyrant of Athens, who seized power by conciliating the mob and directing it to overthrow the established government.

Francis continues, '... Pisistratus, of whom it was so anciently written how he gashed and wounded himself, and in that sort ran crying into Athens that his life was sought and like to have been taken away; thinking to have moved the people to have pitied him and taken his part by such counterfeited harm and danger; whereas his aim and drift was to take the government of the city into his hands and alter the form thereof.'

'With like pretences and dangers and assaults, the Earl of Essex entered the City of London and passed through the bowels thereof, blanching rumours that he should have been murdered and that the State was sold, whereas he had no such enemies, no such dangers, persuading themselves that if they could prevail all would have done well.'

And then he turns to address the Earl of Essex directly:

'But you, my Lord, should know that though princes give their subjects cause of discontent, though they take away the honours they have heaped upon them, though they bring them to a lower estate than they raised them from, yet ought they not to be so forgetful of their allegiance that they should enter into any undutiful act; much less upon rebellion as you, my Lord, have done. All whatsoever you have or can say in answer hereof are but shadows. And therefore methinks it were best for you to confess, not to justify.'

Yet ought they not to be so forgetful of their allegiance that they should enter into any undutiful act. Coming after ten years of friendship between them, this is too much for Essex. He rises instantly and cries out, in a voice shaking with bitterness and anger:

'Nay, sir! I call forth Master Bacon against Master Bacon. You are then to know that Master Francis Bacon hath written two letters, the one of which hath been artificially framed in my name, after he had framed that other in Master Anthony Bacon's name to provoke me. In the latter of these two, he lays down the grounds of my discontentment and the reasons I pretend against mine enemies, pleading as orderly for me as I could do myself.'

Essex continues, 'If those reasons were then just and true, not counterfeit, how can it be that now my pretences are false and injurious? For then Master Bacon joined with me in mine opinion, and pointed out those to be mine enemies and to hold me in disgrace with Her Majesty, whom he seems now to clear of such mind towards me. And therefore I leave the truth of what I say and he opposeth unto your Lordships' consideration.'

These words are *ad hominem, non ad causam*. Formally, they are nothing to the case, yet they are a direct attack on Francis's own honour, his sense of loyalty and gratitude. And they show the familiar association of the two men, accuser and accused. All present knew that the Earl of Essex and Bacon were close, but not all knew how close they were. Only for Essex to be betrayed in such a way! Such is the evident sincerity and indignation of the outburst that a shiver of interest ripples across the chamber.

Francis hastily rises, to repair the damage and move matters on.

'Those letters, if they were there, would not blush to be seen for anything contained in them. I have spent more time in vain in studying how to make the Earl a good servant to the Queen and state than I have done in anything else.'

But, as he looks round the court, he sees to his dismay that men are frowning, whispering, uncertain. They will remember Essex's words long after the case is closed.

More evidence is given, depositions read. The confessions are heard of the other leading conspirators, Davies, Danvers and Blunt. They admit the visit to see *Richard II*, in a specially commissioned performance for the Earl of Essex's men, and Coke ties it in as a damning part of the wider conspiracy by these secret papists to foment sedition and compass the Queen's demise.

Then attention shifts to the case against the Earl of Southampton. Southampton protests that he was taken in by Essex's apparent fears of murder, and meant no malice or injury himself. Against this Coke argues at length that the conspirators must have known they would face resistance to their plans, and therefore intended violence against any opponents. But the cases and precedents he cites are mystifying to the jurors in their complexity and law French; again the thread of the case is being lost.

Francis rises to speak once more. This time his aim is to dispatch the Earl outright.

'I have never yet seen in any case such favour shown to any prisoner,' he says. 'So many digressions, such delivering of evidence by fractions, and so silly a defence of such great and notorious treasons. May it please your Grace, you have seen how weakly the Earl of Essex hath shadowed his purpose, and how slenderly he hath answered the objections against him.

'Now put the case that the Earl of Essex's intent were, as he would have it believed, to go only as a suppliant to Her Majesty. Shall their petitions be presented by armed petitioners? This must needs bring loss of liberty to the Prince. Neither is it any point of law, as my Lord of Southampton would have it believed, that condemns them of treason. To take secret counsel, to execute it, to run together in numbers armed with weapons: what can be the excuse? Warned by the Lord Keeper, by a herald, and yet persist! Will any simple man take this to be less than treason?'

The Earl tries to contest the detail, but the point is unanswerable. The conspirators had plotted to take control of the Queen. That is high treason.

43

WESTMINSTER HALL, 19 FEBRUARY 1601

At the end of the day, the Lords retire to consider their verdict. They return within an hour to announce they find the Earl of Essex and the Earl of Southampton guilty as charged.

Essex is sentenced to death.

It is only then, faced with God's imminent and everlasting judgment, that Essex finally makes confession to the Privy Council. He seeks an audience with Secretary Cecil and others, begs forgiveness for his calumnious slander against him as to the Infanta, and tells how he had considered bringing his army back from Ireland, had been in secret correspondence with King James of Scotland, and now cannot in all conscience but admit that if he had gained access to the Queen, others might have exploited it for their own purposes.

Essex implicates Sir Henry Neville, a former ambassador to France, and others who had hitherto escaped the prosecutors' attention, some of whom he names on the slightest grounds. But he denounces his secretary Cuffe as the chiefest instigator of all the disloyal courses into which had fallen; and he begs God's forgiveness for his sin, his leprosy that has infected far and near.

Southampton is sent to the Tower; he will be spared. The other main conspirators are tried, convicted and sentenced to death. Cuffe and Meyrick are hung, drawn and quartered at Tyburn. Blunt and Danvers are executed on Tower Hill. The others are punished as is meet. No indictment is made of Anthony Bacon; some say he has been saved by the actions of his brother.

Some days afterwards, Francis is summoned to see Sir Robert Cecil in his great chamber at Whitehall. The little man scuttles over to him, more like a crab than ever. The smile is welcoming, but the eye is cool. His burdens as Secretary of State have aged him, and his hair turned grey after the death of his beloved wife. But inwardly Cecil rejoices, for now he has no rival.

'Good cousin, the Queen desireth there be a published account of this dreadful business,' he says. 'A narrative of the treason, fit to be printed and circulated in the taverns, but also to include the trial proceedings and the damning confessions and repentance of the conspirators. Something to quell seditious rumours and enlighten the common people. It must be brief, and compelling. There can be no place for doubt, either of the case or of Her Majesty's gracious but inevitable justice.'

Cecil hesitates, before he goes on.

'The Queen was not quite certain whether you were the man for the task, given your former... closeness to the Earl. I assured her you were. Pray, do not prove me wrong.'

'I shall not, Mr Secretary.'

'And Francis...'

'Yes?'

'You will know that there are aspects of the case that must not be made public. Mountjoy doth most valuable work in Ireland; there can be no suggestion that he was part of the conspiracy. The confessions must be tidied up, the sequence of events made to hang together, contradictory possibilities excluded. There is a particularly scurrilous suggestion that I myself was paid ten thousand crowns after my necessary engagement in France. The King of Scots must not appear... you understand me.'

'So too have they libelled my dear brother Anthony.'

'Omit mention of him also. A draft by Thursday fortnight, if it pleaseth you.'

Francis's narrative condemns the Earl as a traitor with force and energy. As required, it includes the conspiracy, the trial proceedings and the confessions of the guilty with their damning incriminations. It has been shown to members of the Privy Council, perused, weighed, censured, altered and thereby made almost a new writing. And it has been read closely by the Queen, who has made alterations of her own, commanding in particular that all references to my Lord of Essex be reduced to just Essex, or the Earl of Essex.

A Declaration of the Practices and Treasons Attempted and Committed by Robert Late Earl of Essex and his Complices against Her Majesty and her Kingdoms is printed in London and published in the Queen's name by Robert Barker for the Society of Stationers, and widely circulated.

To many people in and around the court, the work is all the sweeter for being written by a man who was once the Earl's friend, councillor and intimate, indeed who it seems but for circumstance might even himself have been counted among the Earl's accomplices. These are claims which, scurrilous or no, they are careful to make widely known.

In August 1601, the fines levied from those implicated in the treason are divided among the deserving servants of Her Majesty. Francis Bacon receives £1,200 for his service. The Queen hath done something for me, he writes to a creditor, though not in the proportion I had hoped.

Francis is now forty years of age. His beloved Anthony has at last passed from this world to the life everlasting, leaving warm memories but also great debts. Their mother Lady Bacon rests at Gorhambury, but grows demented over time.

As for Francis himself, his own prospects have been and gone, if they ever were. He has no money and no close family. His public reputation has been destroyed. He has been forced to watch as his cousin Cecil has overtaken him, been made Knight and Secretary of State. Now it seems he must do the same while Cecil's wagtail Edward Coke, who is Francis's inferior in birth and intellect and imagination, flies ever higher.

Who now could ever contemplate that Francis Bacon could be Lord Chancellor?

III

NEMESIS: 1601–1608

44

STOKE HOUSE, SUMMER 1603

It is evening. As Edward Coke gazes out over the spreading parkland before him, he feels a deep sense of accomplishment. He will always love Huntingfield, that handsome corner of Suffolk where he and Bridget raised their family. But this new estate at Stoke is something greater still: a thousand acres of prime farming and woodland, wonderful hunting and hawking, a large house newly rebuilt in brick with gables and chimneys and many glassed windows, and all of it scarce thirty miles from the courts and Parliament of Westminster.

It has been less than two years since the Queen herself came there on her autumn progress, bringing a vast train of courtiers and ladies in waiting and musicians, trumpets blaring at her approach to the gates. The house had been weeks in preparation, provisions bought in by the sackful from miles around or brought down at prodigious cost by wagon from London.

The tapestries had been dusted, the thick Persian carpets relaid, the younger children called together and clad in splendid clothes, his eldest daughter Anne and her new husband Ralph Sadleir to hand. Coke himself had arranged, on careful advice, for an array of jewels and gowns and suitable other gifts to be presented to Her Majesty. And through all the festivities like a thread of gold wove his young wife Elizabeth, long familiar to the court, delighting their guests with her vital spirits, her charm and beauty. And at the end the Queen had left well pleased. Truly, that was a time!

Yet he has other reasons for satisfaction. He was but ten when his father Robert Coke died. But he was lucky in his parents, for Robert was an attorney, a Lincoln's Inn man of fine reputation, his mother Winifred from a good Northamptonshire family, a woman interested in the law herself so that she even had some of her own law books, and he, Edward, favoured from birth as the only boy among seven sisters.

He is fifty-one now, almost an old man, but his health has always been good, sustained by many hours in the saddle. His figure is fuller than it was, but strong, his moustaches and beard still brown, though flecked with grey. He takes pride in his exterior, seeing the outward neatness of men's bodies as a monitor of purity to their souls. He dresses finely, but soberly, to mark his respect for the dead Queen and all she stood for; he will have none of the strut of the young men he sees peacocking about the new King her successor.

Coke has grown his legal practice till it gives him several thousands of pounds a year in income. He has bought many wardships, the deeds of custody which entitle their owner to all the profits from a ward's estate during his minority; bought them from Burghley while his Lordship was alive, and from his son Cecil when he was dead, and they have paid him well. Coke now owns dozens of estates, rectories, mills and benefices, and not just in Stoke and Huntingfield, but dotted around Tittleshall and Holkham in Norfolk. Add in his fees as Attorney General, and he must be one of the richest commoners in the kingdom.

He has hundreds of books in his library, more there he fancies than in the libraries of all four Inns of Court combined, many of his volumes stamped on the leather with his quartered coat of arms. Coke reads more for purpose and profit than for pleasure. Some say his learning is but insular, and begins and ends with the English common law. But the book dealers of London know better. They know the breadth of his interests – religion, history, the classical authors, translations of great continental writers, tracts and discourses, architecture and agriculture, dictionaries, heraldry, pedigrees, even some rhetoric, grammar, poetry, natural philosophy, mathematics and cosmography, works in Italian and French as well as Latin, a growing collection of works by recusants, who silently refuse the services and rituals of the reformed Church.

Yes, the book dealers of London know better, true enough: they have long gathered volumes in for him from Paris, Amsterdam and Frankfurt. When Elizabeth married Coke she brought many handsome books from Lord Chancellor Hatton, and they too have been made welcome in his library.

Many of these books are working volumes. Coke has the habit of writing brief notes in their margins. Sometimes he draws in a dagger, sometimes he makes careful little drawings of hands, each with a finger pointed towards a passage of text he wishes to mark out. Most precious of all to him are his notebooks, in which he takes down the details of cases he has seen: hundreds of pages written and overwritten in his tiny writing, till they are so black with ink a man could study them for years and not make them out. These are his lifeblood, and he guards them close.

At the front of many of his books is his signature: *Edw. Coke.* This is the product of much practice, with a great *E* at the head, its bottom line a slash across the page, its top line extended to the right, the *d* and *w* two upward sweeps of the pen in parallel. Then a *C* equal to the *E*: dropping below the line, with a swirl of ink back and forth beneath. A signature of authority and force, fit for the Queen herself to admire if she should ever see it. Some men who read his name and do not know him pronounce it Coak, not Cook; they do not make the same mistake twice.

No great man should be without a motto, and Coke has one: *prudens qui patiens etenim durissima coquit*, the prudent man is patient, for he can digest the hardest things, with its play on Coke in the final word. His father had adopted the turkeycock as his crest, the fat game bird of Christmas from the New World. But his son has gone one better. He has cast it away and chosen the image of an ostrich with a horseshoe in its mouth. Give it time, and even iron itself can be digested.

Not bad, for the only son of a middling provincial lawyer.

And with Coke's wealth, so has there been a rapid rise in his standing. He has been Member of Parliament and Speaker, but also Recorder of London, Justice of the Peace and Treasurer of the Inner Temple. He has won the glory of the successful prosecution of that foul and scheming traitor, Essex. But he does not omit his other prosecutions from mind; of Dr Lopez, of Squire the poisoner, of Walpole, Smyth and the rest of them.

Coke retains a private respect only for that papist Father Gerard, the Jesuit equivocator and supporter of Mary of Scots, whom he had examined in the Tower in '97 alongside Bacon and Wade and others. John Gerard: a big man, a countryman almost like a squire, who had lived five years in Norfolk and was known with some affection to friends and neighbours of Coke's. Gerard, who when locked in the Tower had constantly asked for oranges that, as it proved, he might make rosaries out of their peel and send secret messages writ with the orange juice on the wrapping papers; a man who fainted nine times from pain when put to the manacles but could not be broken; and who then managed to escape, climbing out across the prison walls and down by rope despite his mutilated hands.

Coke likes none of this, but he can respect it.

He recalls the string of successful legal suits that have made his name: *Shelley's Case*, and *Chudleigh's Case*; and just recently *Slade's Case*, five years of toil in which he, abetted by old Popham, had finally got a special assembly of judges in the Exchequer Chamber to supersede the old treatment of debt in common law and put in place a swifter and fairer remedy.

A great reformation – and if that were not enough, he had bested Master Bacon in the process! The man will ever be on the losing side, Coke thinks, except when he is joined with me as counsel… and he should have declared an interest in the trial, given how deep in debt he is. He smiles to himself. The fool! Bacon must be in fear of his livelihood now that the field is so open to plaintiffs who might sue him for recovery. That too is not an unpleasing prospect.

So the law has been good to him. But these courtroom victories did not come *ex nihilo*, from nothing, as Coke knows only too well. They did not spring like Minerva, full grown and armed from the cleft head of Jupiter. No, they came slowly, by degrees and from grinding labour. Even now he remembers every detail: not just the readings and mooting and the law French that says *la reine le veult* and *la comen ley*, or the Latin which Coke loves for its accuracy and sometimes uses to vaunt his scholarship, but twenty-five years of tenures and uses, of what lawyers call hereditaments and socage and feoffments and advowsons, up at three of the clock every morning and his eyes grown short-sighted with the toil, though he can never bring himself to the weakness of wearing spectacles in front of others.

That is why he has taken such pleasure just recently in the printing of his *Reports*: three volumes of his personal notes on cases that go back nearly thirty years, to his earliest days as an utter barrister learning his trade at Clifford's Inn.

His *Reports* are already proving their worth as a resource, a trove of precedents, for practising lawyers, but they do more than that. They elicit what is systematic in the law and make its reasoning more plain, so that justice be not merely done but seen to be done – though not so plain as to destroy the mystery of the courtroom, for that were to weaken the authority of the law and, worse, the fees. The *Reports* help to curb abuses, which are manifold. Between the lines, far from being insular and confined, they reflect no small understanding of the civil law. And they give Coke himself a public status as an expositor of law, perhaps once even to rank in time with Plowden himself. If others mislike them or dispute what he writes, let them publish.

And there is much more to come. Coke has a fourth *Report* in preparation, and it is a matter of some delicacy, since there are many who would say this foreign-born Scottish King means to amend, nay abolish, the English common law, and the English Parliament with it. For take his plan for a single kingdom, a consolidation to be called Great Britain, the names of England and Scotland no more persisting: what can this mean, but the drawing together of English and Scots law into one common whole, codified like the Roman law, and the abolition of all the great offices of state of England, and the dissolution of the great court of Parliament itself? This would be, not an inheritance, but a conquest.

So, when he writes the Preface to this new *Report*, Coke is careful to honour the King, but also to place the guiding hand of the common law gently upon the royal shoulder. The King, he notes, whose commandment, being to me *suprema lex*, supreme law, hath both encouraged and imposed a necessity upon me to publish... for the laws of England are indeed so called *iura coronae*, or *iura regalia*, laws of the Crown, kingly laws... because, as Bracton saith, the King is under no man, but under God and the law, for the law maketh the King.

The King is under no man, but under God and the law, for the law maketh the King. Now there is a thought.

All this law work, and for what? Let there be no feign or figuring. It was for the fees, yes always, and the rank to be gained; and the *Reports* have done nothing but good for the name and authority of Edward Coke. But most of all for the power: the power of legal reasoning, rooted in the common law as the law of the land, of the earth, of property.

For what is the law? To some it is adjustment, compromise,

agreement. To Coke it is violence and its remedy in one. But *violentia per regulam*, by rules, not disordered.

It is duelling in the library, with words not swords, and Coke glories in it: it is the power that has allowed him over the years to clear adverse titles on dozens of his estates, dismissing some claimants and beating down others by threats of court action, till he owns the properties free and clear and in his own name of Edward Coke, Esq. But that is just one part of the gigantic force that the law can put into a single man's hands, to bend others to his will, to humble the rich and send traitors to the block; and who knows, perhaps to reach still higher...

But also for passion. For knowledge of the law is like a deep well, Coke says, out of which each man draweth according to the strength of his understanding. He that reachest deepest, he seeth the amiable and admirable secrets of the law. These secrets are vouchsafed only to a few, and only by unremitting effort. Coke himself has sat and listened intently to Bendlowes and Dyer and Plowden. He has devoted many painstaking years to studying Littleton's *Treatise on Tenures*, a work he venerates not just for its learning but for its science, carefully taking the reader through different forms of the law of property, setting out the leading principles in each case and then drawing out variations, in the Roman style, as modes or accidents of a single substance. Building up a single common understanding out of the shared experience of many thousands of people bartering, trading, disputing, resolving what they own and what they want, over hundreds of years.

Even the great invasion of William of Normandy was no true conquest, Coke is sure of it. There had been English law and custom before it, as there were much of the same law and custom afterwards. All of which goes to show that even Kings are not superior to law.

No man can spend such efforts without a passion for the law. But for those that do, there are riches of the intellect and of the world. The Queen knew it, and favoured Coke. King James has done the same, and took little time on arriving in London to make him Knight. *Sir Edward Coke*: what a thing of glory and beauty is that!

And how much better it was, Coke reflects, for him to receive it from the King in a small and personal ceremony, among six men, with special words of favour. Unlike Master Bacon, who was elevated by His Majesty but only on the day of the coronation, and that amid a motley throng of three hundred other little plump piglets all scrambling over each other to suckle at the royal teat, and every one of them baubled by the end.

45

STOKE HOUSE, SUMMER 1603

For now it is a different world, Coke reflects. The old Queen is dead, and King James is on his throne, surrounded by Scotchmen whose speech and peculiar ways no Englishman can readily understand.

The Queen died of melancholy, they say, her body of firm constitution to the end, but she unable to sleep and unwilling to go to bed, simply lying on her cushions and then stalking the corridors of the court at night in silence. And never to her last hour to name a successor, though when King James's name was mentioned near the end they say she made the sign of a crown above her head.

Few knew of her last decline, for that was a moment of utmost public danger, against which Secretary Cecil had prepared for many months. The King of Scots had been in secret correspondence with him, and took advice from the son of the man who killed his mother, so he believed; yet Cecil had won his trust.

There had been talk of challenge from Lady Arabella Stuart, who like James is descended from Margaret, the sister of great King Henry. But she had no party, no supporters. As for the Infanta of Spain, there are still plenty of quiet papists who would gladly see her on the throne, but it is clear that the young King Philip has neither the funds nor the stomach to attempt another invasion.

So it was, it would be, it must be, James. This was not the time or place to dissolve the Privy Council, as was meet. Even as the old Queen departed this life did Cecil send the message north, and set in motion the passage of power to her successor. The new King came to London; came slowly and in a great progress, scattering his bounty like rose petals at a wedding, filling men's mouths with gold and loading their backs with peerages and titles.

To him has fallen the joy of deciding who shall prosper, who shall not... and who shall be brought low. The towns and cities have prostrated themselves before him in greeting: an inspection of seventy teams of horse and plough at Godmanchester, a hundred men on stilts in Lincolnshire.

The King is strange to look at: he has bulging, expressive eyes, a slobbering mouth and an awkward gait. He dresses finely, yet somehow contrives to look ill-kempt. He speaks Scots with an accent, loves to drink ardent alcoholic spirits and swears like a tavern brawler.

The terrors of his early life were unabating, men say, and they have left their mark, for the King has a nervous disposition, a hatred of loud noises and any talk of war, a suspicion of manly courtiers, a distrust of strangers, and a fear of violence to his person so strong that he must wear thick-quilted doublets to protect his sides against a knife. But His Majesty loves to display his learning with a classical or biblical line, and there is no doubt that he is clever and well read, thanks to Buchanan, his tutor. His wife Queen Anna, Princess of Denmark – our own Queen Anne, they call her – is much admired, and they have three young children, including two boys, so the succession is assured.

Yet the King's true affections lie elsewhere. They say he has three addictions: to disputation, to hunting and to Frenchified young men, and the great families of England are already ransacking their junior relatives to the uttermost, knowing that the King will never turn away a fair youth with a nice turn of phrase and a couple or two of good hounds.

There is a sour hexameter that does the rounds: *Rex fuit Eliz-abeth, nunc est regina Jacobus.* Elizabeth was a King; now we have James as our Queenie.

And there are signs of danger as well. They took a cutpurse working the crowds at Newark, and the King had him hanged on the spot, without process of law; this has given the lawyers, the judges and Parliament men a severe chill. There is the matter of religion; how will James, son of the Catholic Queen of Scots, treat the Catholics?

There is the extravagance of the new court; such a relief after the old Queen's parsimony but ruinous to the Exchequer if unchecked. And then there is the King's attitude to Parliament. He has long had the mastery of the Scottish legislature, but the English? English parliaments are a different thing entirely. The House of Commons is more than twice the size of its Scottish counterpart, full of querulous voices and malcontents, easy when stroked but ready to turn at a moment's notice. It will not lightly brook his interventions.

The Queen had the measure of her parliaments, as Coke well recalls from his time as Speaker. She knew when to cosset and when to scold. But where are the old men of business? The Privy Council is grown small and aristocratic. There are many from the Inns who are now Members of Parliament, and these are men of much more independent temper; they will need careful and expert marshalling.

46

STOKE HOUSE, SUMMER 1603

Yet as night falls that evening, as Coke works late at his desk, straining to see his papers in the candlelight, he cannot be content. And the cause is as plain to him as the face that stares back, fractured and unblinking, from the glass. For a man in his position, with so much achieved and so much surely yet to come, for a man so dedicated to his work, his home should always be a source of the greatest felicity and joy.

Fifteen years and more, it had been so. Ah, Bridget! Now, there was a wife without equal. Married at twenty and bore him ten children, seven of whom grew to adulthood and marriage, yet she managed the household in Norfolk and London, travelled with him and without him, advised him, welcomed the great figures of London and the county, and never a cross word between them till she was taken up to heaven. He still has her account books, with the expenses for each day carefully written out with the words Discharged the XXII December by me Bridget Coke, or some such, and signed by her own hand.

When she died, he wrote of her as My most beloved and most excellent wife – who well and happily lived – the true handmaiden of the Lord – fell asleep in the Lord – now lives and reigns in heaven. He buried her in the parish church he loves in Tittleshall, the church where he had honoured his mother with an engraved tablet, and near the altar he put up a monument to Bridget in alabaster, with an inscription from the Book of Proverbs: *Many daughters have done virtuously, but thou surmountest them all.*

Yet these days there is discord in his house, rancour and, worse, disobedience. And it comes from that same wondrous, laughing creature that delighted the old Queen and has already started to entrance Queen Anne: his new wife Elizabeth. Hard to imagine there could be so much trouble encased in such a beauteous frame! He had attended her from the first with fond hopes and expectations, had struck the bargain quickly with her father, and she had warmed to him, that much was clear. Indeed, after such a flurry of suitors she seemed ready, waiting for a real man, a man of experience and command.

It would be a brilliant match for him, of course: to take such a wife, to join the Cecils, with Thomas and Robert in accord, a match to move him on from grieving after Bridget's death. And as Bridget had brought a great dowry, so too did Elizabeth come, like a merchant ship from the Indies, richly laden. Rank and fortune would be joined, and of course he would not begrudge her offspring of their own, if she could bear them. Far from it! For the sap rises in his veins even to think of her face and body.

Yet, did he but see them, the signs were there from the beginning. He had wanted a wedding that men would remember, feasting and celebration and finery to mark the moment, the families come together as one; but she would not hear of it. He dealt politely with her on the matter, then found himself treating, nay entreating her father to put the girl in order forthwith, but to no good.

So they must be married at night, without banns or a licence, in a private house, the Queen none the wiser: a shameful proceeding. And then he, Coke, must bear the lash of the royal tongue for his contempt, and suffer the indignity of being haled before the Archbishop, none other than his old tutor Whitgift, to be threatened with a fine and imprisonment and forced to plead that Her Majesty's Attorney General, no less, was ignorant of Church laws so well known, so recently advertised in Parliament, that any common tailor or cobbler would abide by them.

Truly, they said, there is no fool like an old fool addled by youth and beauty. How men laughed at him!

🌱

But that was just the start of it. Elizabeth insisted on keeping her name; she would be Lady Hatton, not Mistress Coke. The reason? Some bequests from Sir William Hatton's will to his friends and servants, which Elizabeth wanted Coke to pay out of her share or jointure, when in fact they should have been paid by the estate itself. The law was clear, the sums were not small and naturally enough Coke had refused, whereupon she had flown into a rage and declared she would never willingly style herself by his name till he buried her first husband according to his directions. But the law was the law; and of course he could not waiver in the face of such insults.

Even so, they had quickly had two daughters, Elizabeth and Frances; she seemed only fit to breed girls. Had their mother been another Bridget, all would have been well. Yet more and more Coke has seen in Elizabeth not a true wife, not a womanly helpmeet to ease his troubles and share his glories, but a female of vexatious and equalising spirit. He fancied she had fomented a marriage between one of her gentlewomen and a ward of his, keeping it secret without his knowledge or permission. Of course when he heard of it he had the marriage annulled – and if he was so angry as to pull the very ruff off his wife's neck on discovering this deception, well so much the better, for she deserved it.

But the worst came with her stepdaughter, Frances. Not his own dear little daughter Frances, born just the previous year, but Hatton's girl, whom Elizabeth had brought to the marriage. Coke had been foolish enough to write a paper at the start, promising that he would give any profits from her wardship to Elizabeth. He had got the paper back and destroyed it – and why not? In law it was his property as her husband, after all, to dispose of as he saw fit – but such had been her anger that Elizabeth had packed herself and the girls up and moved back to her father's house. It had taken a year, many hours of negotiation and much loss of money before she would return.

Try as he may, Coke can never make his wife out; her mood seems to change with the winds. At one moment she is playful and alluring, beckoning him out to embrace in the rose gardens at her house, or daring him to swim at night with her in the lake at Stoke; at another, she is sombre and wistful; at yet another, cutting in her words, or gentle, or jealous, or kind, or disputatious. It is too much!

Another man might match her mood for mood. But as for him, Coke has neither the time nor trouble for it. They are now married. In law, control of much of her land and possessions has passed to him, at least during his life. He is her master, and no man living knows more about the common law than he does. He will put the bit between the teeth of this troublous mare and bring her to the curb.

His work remains without limit or respite. Indeed, its pace has quickened. The latest is with Raleigh.

Sir Walter used to sponsor privateering raids with Robert Cecil but has since fallen foul of him, and Cecil has spoken against Raleigh in his secret correspondence with James. The King has no liking for free thinkers, let alone men of swagger and virility who would make war on Spain. Still less can he abide the person of Raleigh himself, whom he ever sees as the father and sponsor of tobacco, which James calls that malodorous and unsavoury supposed antidote for the corrupted and execrable malady of the pox, the stinking suffumigation whereof they yet use against that disease, making so one canker or venom to eat out another.

All the world has heard how when Raleigh went forth to meet the King at Burghley House, James received him by punning sharply on his name with the words 'I have heard *rawly* of thee'. And was it not Raleigh who advised, when the old Queen died, that England should not be subject to the needy, beggarly nation of Scotland?

So Raleigh has long been a marked man. He could bear his dismissal as Captain of the Guard on the King's accession, for his debts were forgiven and more besides. What is intolerable is his summary eviction from his home at Durham House; as he says, now to cast out my hay and oat into the street at an hour's warning, and to remove my family and stuff in fourteen days after, is such a severe expulsion as has not been offered to any man before this day.

But there is worse to come for Raleigh, for he has been detected that same summer in a colluded treason with Lords Cobham and Grey and others against the King, and in the autumn Coke prosecuted him in Winchester. A difficult business: the case was circumstantial at best, and Coke found himself haranguing and bullying to make the difference. Raleigh had a silver tongue, which he did not fail to use to humble Coke and to flatter and persuade those in the courtroom.

Men told how they had hated Raleigh when the trial began, and loved him when it ended. He had been reviled by the mob at the start, but his name was celebrated and songs sung of him at the close. And Coke had somehow made it so, calling Raleigh a viper, a spider of hell, the rankest traitor in all England.

Coke had in hand a signed confession from Cobham, but little knew what the man might say if called to give evidence. Who knows, but he might have recanted all that he had written! Since the case rested upon that confession, it would have had to be given up. They say the King was in Winchester to hear the case. Think of the embarrassment if it had collapsed.

Coke decided not to call Cobham to give evidence. It was a stratagem, yes, but it was not against the law, and it succeeded.

Yet by the end, it mattered not, he tells himself. There were so many lies, slanders, allegations and retractions between them that no one much doubted the guilt of the defendants. Coke had secured their conviction; and their execution too but for His Majesty's grace, which instead had seen the lesser conspirators banished from the kingdom and Raleigh and their Lordships sent to the Tower.

Yet this is but the prelude, for there will shortly be revealed the foulest and most damnable treason of all: a plot long concerted by papist conspirators at home, in league and at the direction of their masters in Rome, to lay charges beneath the House of Commons, thirty-six barrels of gunpowder, and destroy the monarchy, the first flower and genius of the nation's aristocracy and the whole of Parliament, in one gigantic and all-consuming fiery detonation.

47

GORHAMBURY, JULY 1603

With the new King has come a rain of gold. But though others have been drenched through the length and breadth of England, barely a drop has fallen on Francis Bacon.

Anthony's debts have been added to his own. In all, they make a round £5,000, a vast sum. Francis has had no choice but to borrow from Sir Robert Cecil, or Baron Cecil of Essendon, as he must now refer to his younger cousin. But now it is his debts to Cecil that are coming due, and it is to Cecil that he must write for relief and help.

Here is another puzzle. Ever since he can remember, Francis has believed in the power of a man to advance himself, to create his life for himself. As he is wont to say, *quisque faber fortunae suae*: every man is maker of his own fortune. But not just man: men, a nation, a people. And as if to bear this out, all around him today he sees advance, progression: in warfare, in men's skills, in the arts of production, in knowledge of other lands. The silks he buys are of far better quality now than those of his father's time, new houses sprout up like asparagus shoots around London, and each successive year brings new reports of voyages made and treasure gained. It is all matter for his philosophy, and that too continues to grow.

Progression is everywhere. Everywhere, that is, but in his own circumstances, where there is no change but merely repetition. It is more than a decade since Francis wrote to uncle Burghley that *I wax now somewhat ancient: one-and-thirty is a great deal of sand in the hour-glass*; yet nothing has been done for him. His mother still

174

lives, witless and decrepit amid a few last servants, so Gorhambury
is not his. He is now counted among the King's learned counsel,
but it is not a sworn position, and he has not a brief to show for it,
so to what purpose?

Francis has kept his creditors away from his claim on the clerkship of Star Chamber, but still the fees have not reverted to him,
so it does not pay. His papers remain in disarray, only to them are
now added those of Anthony. He writes continuously, about law,
about natural philosophy and the interpretation of nature, except
for when a melancholy overcomes his mood. His reputation is not
much mended, for men still din against him as false friend and
betrayer of Essex. Fame hath swift wings, as he says, specially that
which hath black feathers.

And as to preferment? Well, as it was with old Burghley, so now
it is with his son; there is amity, but no amelioration. One generation passeth away, another cometh; but the Earth, and Francis's
debts, abideth still.

Still, Cecil has hinted at a knighthood, so there is nothing lost
if Francis's letter touches upon that too. He takes up his pen. For
my estate, he writes, I shall be able by selling the skirts of my living
in Hertfordshire to preserve the body. For my purpose or course, I
desire to meddle as little as I can in the King's causes, His Majesty now abounding in counsel; and to follow my private thrift and
practice, and to marry with some convenient advancement. For as
for any ambition, I do assure your Honour mine is quenched. My
ambition now I shall only put upon my pen, whereby I shall be able
to maintain memory and merit of the times succeeding.

He continues, For this divulged and almost prostituted title of
knighthood, I could without charge, by your Honour's mean, be
content to have it, both because of this late disgrace, and because I
have three new knights in my mess in Gray's Inn's commons; and
because I have found out an Alderman's daughter, an handsome
maiden to my liking. So as if your Honour will find the time, I will
come to the court from Gorhambury upon any warning.

For Robert Cecil, there is much to savour in this letter. He had taken over the papers of the Earl of Essex after his execution, including the letters to and from Francis Bacon, so there is little about his cousin's relations with Essex that is hidden to him.

Now, as he reads, Cecil is pleased to note Francis saying *I desire to follow my private thrift and practice*, but he is not rash enough to believe it. As for … *and to marry with some convenient advancement*, well, this is unexpected indeed. And *As for any ambition, I do assure your Honour mine is quenched. My ambition now I shall only put upon my pen*, how often has Cecil read these words before!

No one can dress a demand in the clothes of humility and soft reason like Bacon, no one more elegantly disclaim a yearning for worldly preferment that manifestly still burns within him like a furnace. And Cecil smiles still more when a letter of reminder arrives not two weeks later, Francis saying for my knighthood, I wish the manner might be such as might grace me, since the matter will not; I mean, that I might not be merely gregarious in a troop. The coronation is at hand. It may please your Lordship to let me hear from you speedily.

The coronation comes, and with it at last the longed-for knighthood. The King grants Francis's wish, but only after his usual jocular fashion. For Francis is not gregarious at the ceremony in a troop, as he feared; nothing so choice. No, he is just one head, just one capped poll among a thronging, petitioning, exulting multitude dragged into the Royal Gardens at Whitehall, men many of whom have paid good money in hope of getting this almost prostituted title, gathered on a hot July day from every vulgar corner of the land, a riot of favours received and to come the like of which has never been seen, and will never be seen again.

If the manner fails, yet the matter succeeds; that is something. But it rankles with Francis that Coke has been knighted privately and with great respect, while he himself must join with such a crowd.

And worse, it rankles that some around the King have intimated that this honour and the trifling pension that came with it are not Francis's due. No, they say, these are merely a gift of thanks made in recognition of his brother Anthony, who had supported the Earl of Essex to the end, and kept and sustained communications with the Scottish court in those uncertain days of the late Queen's reign. The King still holds the memory of Essex in his esteem. His men may have set aside Francis's treatment of the Earl, but they have not forgotten it.

And as for Coke, even to think of the man torments him! The Attorney General has moved smoothly into favour with the new court, always protected by Cecil, and the Raleigh case will make him unassailable with the King. Even now Francis has heard how Coke speaks ill of him with Cecil.

And there had been a moment, in that spring of 1601, between Essex's execution and his own brother's death, when the curtain of polite manners was suddenly pulled aside. A moment when he and Coke had confronted each other face to face like a pair of birds in the cockpit. When time stopped for an instant, and Francis saw how matters truly lay between them.

It was in the Court of Exchequer. Francis had moved for a reseizure of the lands of one Moore, a relapsed recusant, a fugitive and traitor. It was routine business, the work of a few minutes before the court moved on. But suddenly the Attorney had kindled at him and said loudly, 'Master Bacon, if you have any tooth against me pluck it out; for it will do you more hurt than all the teeth in your head will do you good.'

Francis answered, 'Master Attorney, I respect you; I fear you not; and the less you speak of your own greatness, the more I will think of it.'

Coke said, 'I think scorn to stand upon terms of greatness towards you, who are less than little; less than the least.'

'Master Attorney, do not depress me so far; for I have been your better, and may be again, when it please the Queen.'

'That is nothing to it, sir. Pray do not touch upon the Queen's business, but keep you to your own. These are not matters for one such as you who are unsworn in the law, for all your imagined expectations.'

Francis replied, 'Master Attorney, sworn or unsworn is all one to an honest man. I have ever set my service first, and myself second; and I would wish to God that you would do the like.'

It was coolly done, to be sure. And it must have goaded Coke beyond endurance, for he said, 'Do you deny my service, sir? Do you chaff my office? It were good to clap a *caput legatum* upon your back, that you feel the law of debtors on your neck.'

'Nay sir, you are the one at fault, for you hunt upon an old scent.'

In his anger and his insults, Coke had come off worse in the duel, as all could see. Yet it is Francis who still feels the pain. He had written at once with unsuppressed indignation to cousin Cecil, in hope he would put this errant and ambitious office-holder nearer his duties.

But even that was not enough. So Francis confronted Coke directly in a letter, saying Mr Attorney, I thought best, once for all, to let you know in plainness what I find of you, and what you shall find of me. You take to yourself a liberty to disgrace and disable my law, my experience, my discretion.

But, he says, I am one that knows both mine own wants and other men's, and it may be, perchance, that mine mend, others stand at a stay... You are great, and therefore have the more enviers, which would be glad to have you paid at another's cost. Since the time I missed the Solicitor's place, the rather, I think, by your means, I cannot expect that you and I shall ever serve as Attorney and Solicitor together, but either to serve with another, upon your remove, or to step into some other course.

You are great, and therefore have the more enviers, which would be glad to have you paid at another's cost. Yes, but enviers are fickle, and every cost must have its recompense. Who can say, but in time Coke may wobble on his eminence.

Upon your remove; well, that is something for the future.

48

THE STRAND, SEPTEMBER 1603

The visitor is announced, and Lady Pakington is all graciousness.
'*Sir* Francis! I must confess, I *do* like the sound of that. It hath
a lovely ring to it. Can it be that our sweet Alice hath brought you
back to our little house in town? We are honoured. I will have her
brought to you now.'

Francis is in pursuit of a wife. Alice is Alice Barnham, daughter of the late Benedict Barnham, Alderman and then Sheriff of
London, himself the son of Alderman and Sheriff Francis Barnham. A draper, married to Dorothy, daughter of the Queen's silk
man, and the drapers and mercers two of the richest livery com-
panies in London. But Benedict Barnham died suddenly five years
ago, leaving a large fortune to his wife and daughters, and the wife
has since married Sir John Pakington. And as Lady Pakington well
knows, her house is far from little. It stands over against the Savoy,
and it is dressed and bedizened inside with silks and velvet, from
curtains to coverings, as fits her family.

So Francis fancies he is on the right trail. Barnham he knew
slightly for a sober, sensible merchant, the Member for Yarmouth
in Parliament a few years before. But 'Lusty' Pakington is a quite
different matter. His nickname was given him by the Queen. He
cut a dash at court when Francis was a lad, captured Her Majesty's
attention for his handsome looks and his shapely calves, kept it
with his wit, and never lost it. His finances were broken with the
effort to keep up at court, but marriage to Barnham's widow has

mended them. They have had children of their own, but she has also brought four older daughters, and Lusty wants them married off, and well.

Francis has taxed Robert Cecil for his help in finding a wife of means, and now Robert has obliged with a recommendation to Sir John. The suitor and his potential father-in-law met over dinner that spring and struck the deal: Alice is to come with £6,000 and leases on estates in Essex. Since that time Francis has only met her once, briefly. Now he has returned in order to make her better acquaintance.

The birds sing, the bees buzz, the trees rustle in the slanting sunlight of a glorious late September day. They walk in the gardens behind the house, Lady Pakington hovering behind.

'Alice, I hope you are well?'

'I am, sir.' 'Oh, she is wondrous well, Sir Francis. Truly, she cometh on day by day. Almost to say blooming, I would venture… as you may see for yourself.'

'And do you study well?'

'Yes I do, sir, every day.' 'Study, Sir Francis? Why, Alice is a veritable bookworm. I hear you are fond of books yourself, and I commend you for it. Now as for Sir John, he is not so much of a bookworm as a malt worm, if I may say! He doth not hold with studies for young ladies, saying it spoileth them for marriage, but that was never my late husband's view, and nor is it mine. Nor is it mine.

'And when', she continues, 'Sir John is on his estates in Worcestershire, I must have my way. Sewing, embroidery, music, of course, but also what you might call *letters*. We have a Master Collins, an Oxford man, to teach her. Under my close supervision, of course. Nothing that is not seemly.'

And so it continues, till they have been full five times around the gardens.

Then Francis says, 'And Alice, is there anything you should like to ask me?'

'Yes, sir. When we are married, will we live in a house like this one, with servants and a coach and four, and will I have dresses and jewels and fine draperies, so that I may attend Her Majesty the Queen at court?'

There is a pause. The birds cease to sing, the bees to buzz, the trees to rustle. Lady Pakington cranes her head forward, indecorously, to hear the answer. But Francis does not miss a step.

'Yes, Alice, you shall have all that and more.'

The singing, buzzing and rustling resume.

'Oh thank you! Mother, that will be wonderful! I cannot *wait* to be married!'

Alice is eleven years old. She will be married at thirteen, when Francis will be forty-five.

49

INNER TEMPLE, MICHAELMAS TERM 1604

In the country, it is Stoke House; in London, Hatton House. But for concentrated work, free from the interruptions of state business, the King's Attorney keeps his lodgings at the Inner Temple as a retreat. Edward Coke has many of his books and papers there. He has the library of the Inn to hand, there is youthful company and, when he needs the sights and smells of the open air, there are the long gardens stretching down to the river.

But now he is full of discontent and wants time and space to think. Only a few weeks earlier, he had to deal with Lord Zouche, Lord President of the Council of the Marches, which is charged with the government of Wales and the Marches.

For Coke, Lord Zouche is an overweening and presumptuous man, who would play *rex* in Wales and extend his Council's jurisdiction to take cases in law and make men prisoners from the English counties nearby. He has been rebuffed by the Court of Common Pleas, only to refer the matter to the Privy Council in the King's name.

The men of the Privy Council would not usually be apt to take Lord Zouche in any serious way, but his Lordship has brought in that devious dolt Bacon to advise him. And Bacon, ever a friend to the royal prerogative, has submitted a memorandum which argues that the authority of the Council of the Marches derives directly from the absolute power of the King; for, as he says, the King holdeth not his prerogatives of this kind mediately from the law, but immediately from God.

Prerogative! Aye, there's a word much abused, thinks Coke. It is supposed to be a special right or privilege belonging to the King in his own person. Not the product of any statute or legislation, that might be done and so undone by a parliament, not requiring or permitting any further ground or justification for it, but possessed of the force of law. Yet a right to do what, to what extent, in what circumstances, and how? These matters are not well defined, and they are more and more being questioned.

Bacon's memorandum continues, saying It is His Majesty's prerogative right to establish courts as he may see fit, as other Kings have done before him. Besides, the King has a prerogative power whereby he is the supreme judge both in Parliament and all other courts, and hath power to stay suits at the common law. And this inherent power of his is therefore free from control by any court of law, and this free jurisdiction the King exerciseth by his Councils.

The argument will go nowhere, in part because it would put the Council of the Marches on a level with the Privy Council itself, which to the Privy Councillors is unthinkable. To Coke, it is a nonsense. But it is a dangerous nonsense, which would expand the power of the Crown without scrutiny from the courts, and so it demands rebuttal. That is why he burns the candle now at four and five of the morning, his usual time of private work, in researches and reflection.

What results is nothing much in size: some pages in his notebooks on a few words of Latin. Yet what words are these! He has read them, learned them, parsed and construed them as he would construe a passage of Virgil in Latin for Mr Hawe when he was a boy in the grammar school in Norwich. He could recite them in his sleep:

Nullus liber homo capiatur, vel imprisonetur, aut disseisiatur, de aliquo libero tenemento suo vel libertatibus vel liberis consuetudinibus suis, aut utlagetur, aut exuletur, aut aliquo modo destruatur, nec

super eum ibimus, nec super eum mittemus, nisi per legale judicium
parium suorum vel per legem terrae.

No free man shall be taken or imprisoned or dispossessed of his
freehold, liberties or free customs, or outlawed or exiled or destroyed
in any other way, neither will we go against him, nor send against him,
except by the lawful judgment of his peers or by the law of the land.

It is Chapter 29 of Magna Carta 1225. Not the bargain at Runnymede
made ten years before, for that was struck by King John under compulsion from the barons, and repudiated by him thereafter as swiftly as
he were able, with the blessing of Pope Innocent to confirm the deed.

No, that document of 1215 was no statute, enacted as any statute
must be by the King on the advice of the peers and commons in
Parliament assembled.

But matters were very different in 1225, for the Charter then was
granted by King Henry III of his own free will and discretion, in return
for a subsidy that had itself to be authorised by the bishops, peers and
commons in a great assembly. That assembly of 1225 was a parliament,
and the Charter of 1225 was then confirmed by Edward I and confirmed again more than thirty times thereafter. It is from 1225 that the
authority of Magna Carta as statute derives, of that Coke is sure.

Magna Carta, the Great Charter, the taproot of our English liberties.
Coke writes that inasmuch as everything that anyone has in this world,
or that concerns the freedom and liberty of his body or his freehold, or
the benefit of the law to which he is inheritable, or his native country
in which he was born, or the preservation of his reputation or goods, or
his life, blood and posterity: to all these things this Act extends.

A statute can hardly be of wider application than this, from a
man's property real and inherited, his rights to deal without infringement or monopoly, his own life and limb and those of his
heirs. To take a man and deprive him of his liberty without due
process... there can be no more fundamental oppression.

But though it has the form of a grant from the King and has been
given the force of statute, yet that does not mean the Charter can

be cancelled by the King, or even by another statute, of that Coke is also sure. For it is part of the English common law, *lex terrae*, the law of the land, arising not from any conquest but from custom and usage since time immemorial; time out of mind, as some say. It is declaratory of law, a confirmation and restitution grounded in a steady accumulation of law proven through particular cases over hundreds of years, constantly fined and refined so as to be a body of wisdom and human experience greater than any individual could ever possess, not to be changed without much hazard and danger.

Coke loves to echo the lines of Chaucer: out of the old fields must spring and grow the new corn. So it is with law.

How strange to reflect, he thinks, that just a generation ago the Charter lay neglected in our statute books, barely referred to, barely pleaded in our courts and cases! Much has changed since then. Old Snagge had given a reading on Chapter 29 in the Middle Temple thirty years before, but he was a querulous Puritan apt to offend the benchers and was almost stopped, if Burghley had not intervened.

But then Burghley was always a friend to the Great Charter. He cited the statute in Star Chamber as the basis of our English freedoms, and the lawyers were not slow to take the hint from the Queen's leading minister. Since then the use of Magna Carta has spread with speed through men such as Fleetwood and Lambarde, Tanfield and Popham. It has become almost a fashion.

Coke has long known of Snagge's reading, and took it in even in those days, when he was arguing a hundred cases a year, almost a new case a day, as a rising young barrister. He gave it prominence in his second *Reports* and has used the Charter on many an occasion in the courts himself.

Yet he saw what even these others had not: that this was a sword that, though it be of ancient origin and had lain rusty in its scabbard for three centuries, could still be drawn forth by some new Arthur and used to devastating effect in the law.

But for that the blade must be sharpened.

50

INNER TEMPLE, MICHAELMAS TERM 1604

Edward Coke has the text of Magna Carta before him. Now he brings the full powers of his mind to bear upon it.

He takes Chapter 29 carefully apart, eight vital words, word by word: 'taken', 'imprisoned', 'disseised', or dispossessed; 'outlawed', 'exiled', 'destroyed', 'go' or 'send' against a man. He drafts a little treatise, couched in law French for propriety and accuracy, written and then in time so overwritten with later thoughts and references in his usual cramped and tiny hand that in parts it is all but impossible to read.

Some say there is no use for Magna Carta because it lacks enforcement, but Coke will not truck with that. For though no express remedies are mentioned, yet Magna Carta is a statute, and every statute made against some injury, mischief or grievance implies a remedy.

And the common law may afford remedies of its own besides. So if a man is taken and sent to prison without lawful warrant, or detained, he has three remedies, at least: he may bring suit in his own name, as party against party; he may procure an indictment in the name of the King; and he may approach the judges of the Court of King's Bench and obtain a writ, a direct command from the court, of *habeas corpus cum causa*.

Such a writ of *habeas corpus* requires by law that the petitioner's body be returned to the court, and if he was imprisoned contrary to the statute of Magna Carta, then the judges must discharge him from his unlawful imprisonment. It comes to the King's Bench as the highest court of common law, and just as that court is the highest so it is the most wide-reaching court, for it may direct a *habeas corpus* into any of the King's dominions, even though they are not parcel of England. By this means it may reach even outside the English nation itself.

Habeas corpus: this is the blade to which the stone of Magna Carta gives its edge, the device that ensures that no free man shall be imprisoned under English law except by lawful judgment of his peers, or by the law of the land. It is hard to imagine the writ of *habeas corpus* was so little seen till the time of Henry VIII. But Coke has been gathering the precedents since 1587, and more; that is seventeen years now. And there are other writs that may be used as well, when a senior court so decides: such as writs of prohibition, which prevent upstarts such as my Lord Zouche from exercising unlawful jurisdiction over a case.

All this may serve as a rebuttal to his Lordship and the Marches Council, but Coke wants something more: a refutation. So he gives these eight words a reading designed to confute Lord Zouche outright.

His Lordship has claimed a right in exercise of the King's prerogative right; but, Coke argues, in fact he would destroy the prerogative. For Magna Carta does not merely protect the subject, but the King himself.

Quel chose est pluis pur le honor del roy et del common profitt del roy et son realme que ses subjectes serront free de tout oppression? What is more to the honour of the King, and for the common profit of the King and his realm, than that his subjects should be free from all oppression? No need of any manual of law French to translate these words!

But there cannot be a greater oppression than loss of their liberty by unlawful imprisonment, so that people cannot in their callings serve the King or the public weal. And precisely because they themselves are subject to the Crown of England, Lord Zouche and his Council of the Marches must yield their claim to jurisdiction in the face of a *habeas corpus* issued out of the King's Bench.

So, then, Lord Zouche, and that man Bacon who serves him, are in grievous error. To imprison a man unlawfully is not to confirm but to damage the royal prerogative. The King's true friends are not the jurisdictions of these far-removed councils, but the common law and the courts of common law.

For the benefit of the law is not to be taken away from anyone, Coke insists, unless it is for his contempt or contumacy. Every subject is inheritable to the laws of the land, which are to be esteemed worthier of respect than his goods or lands, and dearer and more precious to him than his wife or children, for the laws preserve and protect not only all of these things but also his body and his life itself in peace and tranquillity.

But there are words too in the shadows of the text, words that Coke does not and may never say. The common law derives from countless minds, from time unknown. It is, like nature, an almost infinite distinction of particular cases, that may be traced back to a unity and consent proceeding from God himself.

Is it therefore superior to the judgement of a single mind... even the mind of a King?

If at least in parts it cannot be overturned by statute, is it thereby made superior law, and may it bind a parliament? Is there any matter, whether spiritual or temporal, which might not fall within its scope? Is the common law an empire?

51

GRAY'S INN, NOVEMBER 1605

hear you are fond of books yourself. Lady Pakington little knew the truth of her words. Francis sometimes thinks back to that moment in the garden.

He has spent the time since then as he did the time before: periodically afflicted by rheums and fevers, barely occupied with matters of the law or of the Inn, fending off his creditors, and prisoner always to his ambitions. There had been more plague in London; Parliament was prorogued, and he has used the time among his books and notebooks, writing, writing.

The result is a new work, *Of the Proficience and Advancement of Learning, Divine and Human*, printed by Henry Tomes and sold from his shop in Gray's Inn Gate. A book, Francis reflects, unlike any other. For what prior book could be the plan or predecessor in design to a work that aspires to chart – nay, and reclassify – all human knowledge existing and projected, and within a single span? It is a writing out, but also a gathering in, nothing less than the digest and abstraction of a lifetime's reading, from the ancients to those of his own day.

But the whole has one guiding purpose. It is not merely the same purpose as in his great letter to Burghley of – can it be near twenty-five years before? Dear God, how a man can age, and so little done! – that letter where Francis made the case for a new college of learning.

No, this book goes far beyond that. Its design is nothing less than to urge King James to a total reformation of learning and re-searches across the kingdom that he has so recently gained: a refor-mation in men's understanding both of natural and of civil science, and a reformation in policy and in the arts of the statesman.

To that end, Francis says, a platform is needed. It is meet to have new institutions, for the great foundations across Europe are ded-icated to the professions, and there are none as yet devoted to the arts and sciences at large. But great new institutions of learning must in their turn have able and sufficient men, and the public lectures of those men must be properly rewarded. They must have instruments for the pursuit of natural philosophy, for testing and experiments: furnaces and engines and spheres, globes, astrolabes, maps, gardens of physic, dead bodies for anatomies.

There must be regular visitations to them by the monarch or his delegates, he says, that they may be examined and held to proper account for what they have done or failed to do. There must be more intercourse and mutual intelligence between them and the universities of Europe than there now is. And there must be public designation of inquirers, to give them standing and inducement to venture into regions of knowledge as yet unknown.

For why should a few received authors stand up like Hercules' col-umns, beyond which there should be no sailing or discovering, since we have so bright and benign a star as your Majesty to conduct and pros-per us?

As with science, so with policy, Francis continues. Does not Aris-totle himself say that the legislation of the true statesman must be directed more to reason than to appetite, and more to ends than to means?

Yet, he writes, the great *organon*, the canon of the teachings of Aristotle, contains not just gold, but fool's gold withal. Its arid and empty logic must be set aside in favour of a new experimental method of inquiry in natural philosophy. Learning itself must be delivered from the discredits and disgraces which it hath received, all from ignorance, but ignorance severally disguised; appearing sometimes in the zeal of divines, sometimes in the arrogance of politics, and sometimes in the errors of learned men themselves.

For the present it is as if, he says, there were sought in knowledge a couch whereupon to rest a searching and restless spirit; or a terrace for a wandering and variable mind to walk up and down with a fair prospect; or a tower of state, for a proud mind to raise itself upon; or a fort or commanding ground, for strife and contention; or a shop, for profit or sale; and not, as there should be, a rich storehouse for the glory of the Creator and the relief of man's estate.

But this ambition points to practical education, to new instruments by which to test and examine nature, to great new public places of higher learning and research. These things are the future.

Latin, not English, is the language of natural philosophy, civil law and religion, the means by which knowledge may be shared across Europe. But *The Advancement of Learning* is written in English.

Francis intends it to have a domestic audience, for a total reformation requires both direction from above and reception from below. States may be made great and their laws more perfect by means of policy, and such policy must be based on learning. This is a novel gospel indeed.

The King must lead, he says, but the men around him, and those in the universities, the cathedrals and the Inns, must all be made ready for the change. And as for the work's title, it plays on the idea of advancement: advancement in the state of knowledge, advancement in the means of procuring knowledge, and advancement in the standing among men of knowledge itself.

Perhaps too, Francis prays, the book will bring him advancement in his own fortunes. Certainly, it cannot be for want of trying. There is some delicacy in the subject: he cannot presume to advise the King, and too forward an address will surely turn His Majesty away. Yet the King is a most learned man, possessed of a rigorous education, and he is the author of renowned works on kingship and its origin in divine law.

So in composing a prefatory letter to the King, Francis adopts the mood obsequious, saying Your Majesty I have been touched – yea, and possessed – with an extreme wonder at those your virtues and faculties, which the philosophers call intellectual; the largeness of your capacity, the faithfulness of your memory, the swiftness of your apprehension, the penetration of your judgment, and the facility and order of your elocution: and I have often thought that of all the persons living that I have known, your Majesty were the best instance to make a man of Plato's opinion, that all knowledge is but remembrance.

As for speech, he says, your Majesty's manner of speech is, indeed, Prince-like, flowing as from a fountain, and yet streaming and branching itself into nature's order, full of facility and felicity, imitating none, and inimitable by any.

Hard indeed must be the heart of a man, not to melt in the heat of such flattery! But though Francis has few equals at court for sweetness of tongue, yet there are many rivals who would ply their tongues in hope.

At such a moment, it will not do to have any stint in the matter.

So he pushes on, gathering his argument to say outright that I am well assured that this which I shall say is no amplification at all, but a positive and measured truth; which is, that there hath not been since Christ's time any King or temporal monarch which hath been so learned in all literature and erudition, divine and human.

It is sent. It takes but a few days for Francis to learn, yet again, how vain his letter is. For this is early November 1605, and the hideous revelation of the Powder Treason now sweeps all things before it, including his unhappy book.

52

THE NORWICH ASSIZES, AUGUST 1606

For Coke and for Norwich alike, this is the homecoming of a favoured son. He rides through the city gates, past the ancient walls and towers and into the centre in a great train, attended by the Sheriffs of the county and dozens of clerks in livery, trumpets blaring, pikemen behind, and met with great pomp by the mayor, Aldermen and a host of local people, burghers, county notables, shopkeepers, townsfolk high and low accompanying.

Coke is a local boy, after all. Over the years Norfolk people have followed his progression in the law through excited glimpses and gossips, and by his regular visits to attend clients and do legal business. But today is another thing entirely. For these are the Assizes, and come to preside over them for the first time, to do right by local people in the name of the King, is not Edward Coke, nor even Sir Edward Coke, but Coke who is now Chief Justice of the Court of Common Pleas.

It is forty years and more since Coke first made the journey into Norwich, from the family home in Mileham parish twenty-five miles west, to attend the grammar school. Four decades of years since he stood in the vaulted schoolroom upstairs to recite the ancient authors, since he walked the few yards round to the cathedral to hear the weekly sermon and then write it all out in Latin as best he could the following day. Queen Mary had been dead but three years, and a Protestant spirit breathed hard again upon the icons, the relics and the coloured glass of popery. This was a small and serious world, hard by the North Sea; a place of long memory.

Now Coke's head is held high, and his heart is racing as the train processes in behind him. The city fathers have long since determined that an occasion such as this is too large for the Shire House. When the Assizes convene, it is in the great hall of Norwich Castle, atop the mound, the square block of the keep ghostly at night but gleaming white now in the summer sun. There is a lively bustle as nigh on a hundred jurors and fifty justices of the peace are added to the hubbub of clerks, with constables and beadles set to keep good order. The Bishop and his Chancellor are in attendance, as the duties of ecclesiastical law require.

The preferment had been long coming; it is twelve years since Coke was made Attorney, and no one can doubt his eminence in the common law. Indeed, he has perhaps been too useful to the King and to Cecil, too much the effective man of business, both in the courtroom and without, for them to let him go. Edmund Anderson had been Chief Justice more than twenty years, and when he died the previous August Coke had pressed Cecil as hard as he dared for the job, and by every right might have had it. But something stayed the King's hand, and he gave the place to Francis Gawdy instead, though Gawdy was just five years younger than his predecessor, and more respected than admired as a lawyer.

But Gawdy was in post just a few weeks, and absent all the winter term, before he died of an apoplexy. This time Coke was not to be thwarted, and Cecil agreed. Coke even went so far as to draft a minute setting out the procedure, saying that first, I must be made Serjeant, which may be on Saturday next, and the Chief Justice on Monday. There must be a writ (for which my Lord Chancellor will have warrant) returnable on Saturday to call me to be a Serjeant, and a warrant for the patent of the office of Chief Justice of the Common Pleas. Hereof I presume to inform you, lest if other should complain, blame might be imputed on me.

Cecil was not deterred to receive such an instruction; the two men know each other too well, and, consumed as he was with mending the royal finances and dealing with a Commons to which he no longer belonged, Cecil hardly had time to do otherwise.

Yet that was February, and it was not till June that Sir John Popham, Chief Justice of King's Bench, placed the Serjeant's robe on Coke's shoulders; and some days afterward, as Coke's minute prescribed, he was created Chief Justice of Common Pleas, entitled to wear what is called the golden chain of esses, the meaning of its SS links lost to time, but signifying Sapience and Science, as Coke likes to think.

That evening Coke holds a huge feast at Hatton House for his friends in celebration. He and they are in festive mood, for he has given many of them a gold posy ring with the inscription *lex est tutissima cassis*, law is the safest helmet, as symbol of the moment. There is some wit to the phrase, for Lord Chancellor Hatton's motto was that virtue is the safest shield. Coke has stripped away what is personal, as if to say that you cannot trust a man as you can trust the proper process of law.

Yet may that not be true of the King himself? May the law be trusted more even than the King? None thinks that thought amid the toasts to His Majesty that evening, but on the rings it is *lex*, not *rex*, that is inscribed.

To all outward appearance, this is but the normal succession by which one man gives way to another.

But, steeped in history and legal practice as he is, Coke feels it as a momentous change. To be an attorney and a judge are two different things. He must give up the connections of the bar, formally depart the Inner Temple, his brothers in the law and his favourite lodgings by the river, and move to Serjeants' Inn. He must doff the black wool of the barrister, and don robes of fine scarlet cloth faced with miniver: the robes of the President of the court. He must cease to be an agent, whether of a private client or the King himself, and speak only as a servant of the law.

When he takes the oath of his office, with his hand on the Bible, as administered by the Lord Chancellor in solemn ceremony, the words declare what he now must be:

'You shall swear that well and lawfully you shall serve our Lord the King and his people in the office of Justice, and that you shall lawfully counsel the King in his business; ... and that you shall do equal law and execution of right to all his subjects, rich and poor, without having regard to any person; and that you shall not take by yourself, or by another, privily or openly, a gift or reward of gold, silver, or anything else which may bring about your profit, unless it be meat or drink (and that of small value), from any person who shall have any plea or process pending before you, as long as the same process shall be so pending, nor thereafter for the same cause; and that as long as you shall be justice you shall take no fee or robes from any person great or small, but only from the King him-self... and you shall deny to no person common right by the King's letters, or of any person, or for any other cause... and in case you shall hereafter be found in default in any of the points aforesaid, you shall be at the King's will in respect of your body, lands, and goods, to be done therein as shall please him: as God you help and all his saints.'

'I do; so help me God.'

53

THE NORWICH ASSIZES, AUGUST 1606

And you shall deny to no person common right by the King's letters,
or of any person, or for any other cause. Few men outside the law
know Magna Carta in these days, Coke reflects, and there's the
pity of it. But as he settles down in his judicial seat at the Norwich
Assizes, he recalls its words, with their echo of his oath: *To no one*
will we sell, to no one deny or delay right or justice. And they are in his
mind as he rises to address the assembled company.

Yes, this is a homecoming. But the Chief Justice has a purpose,
and he purposes to teach these men present, and many other men
beyond them, a lesson they will long remember.

It starts with a paradox, that he has come among them to take
his leave of them. 'For in the manner of judgment,' he says, 'no
acquaintance, no griefs, no friends, no remembrance of present, or
hope of future friendship must direct the thoughts of him that is a
judge. All that on judgment's seat is done, must be, because justice
commands the doing thereof, and that with no other affection, but
only because it is just.'

A judge must dedicate his labours solely to the public benefit, he
says. And so he must bid them all farewell.

'It is true that I purpose, as I must,' he says, 'to take my leave
of you all, and to be a stranger to my dearest friends, and nearest
allies: I must depart from you, and yet continue amongst you, for I
am appointed to be a judge, and in the seat of Justice I must forget
the remembrance of your former friendships and acquaintance, and

only in the person of a judge, with respect to keep my conscience clear, I must with equity and uprightness, justly administer justice unto you all.'

It is the same speech as he gave to his brothers of the Inner Temple, and it is cunningly done. By this tale Coke announces himself in a new garb to his kith and kin, yet he also explains and excuses what is to come.

For this is just the prologue; the honey before the wormwood. Coke now declares he will address them under five words, each bearing on his commission and appointment as judge: *Quis, Quibus, Quid, Quomodo* and *de Quibus*.

Quis, who? This commission comes from the imperial Majesty of Great Britain's monarchy, our dread Lord and sovereign, King James.

Quibus, to whom? It is directed to us His Majesty's justices of assize, to whom is given such power, as that in the administration of justice we do represent the person of our King.

Quid, what? We have authority, as in the person of our sovereign, to judge in causes, that do concern the life and death of the subject.

Quomodo, how? Not according to our own will, conceit or opinion, but according to the law, custom, and manner of England, which must be executed with knowledge, judgement, understanding, and equity.

It is a familiar form of argument, but it sounds out across the great hall like a catechism. Coke puts these questions in order to educate his listeners. They see a great priest, swathed in scarlet, come to lift and exalt their spirits with his incantations.

'For justice is a silver current,' Coke says, his voice rising, 'and with what just proportion she doth disperse her streams, without betraying any little rage of intemperate violence. But if the passage of that stream be stopped; then how like a raging sea she overflows her banks; and then the meadows, humble valleys, weak and low-grown shrubs are drowned up, whilst hills and mountains stand safe from fear of harm.

'Even so it fareth with us,' he continues. 'The equal course of justice being stayed, the poor and meaner sort of people are overwhelmed with wrong's oppression, whilst great and wealthy men, like hills and mountains, build their stations sure, being freed from any cause of grief. Justice withheld, only the poorer sort are those that smart for it. Justice unto all estates doth measure an even proportion to rich and poor.'

Nor does Coke spare those who sit in judgment. 'Partiality in a judge, is a turpitude, which doth soil and stain all the actions done by him. Bribes and partial dealing doth defile the purity of Justice, with great suspected evil. For a judge, if but in some things he be known to take a bribe, or be approved partial, he leaveth no one action done by him free from the like suspect.'

Now, like the current of justice itself when it overflows, he is in full spate, lecturing, hectoring those about him.

Finally, he asks, *de Quibus*, concerning whom must a man act as judge? Those by whom our King is most disobeyed, his state disturbed, and kingdoms threatened.

That is, Popish recusants, Jesuits, seminarians, traitors fomenting sedition and rebellion. Men such as Ridolfi, Campion, Parsons and their like, who conspired with excommunicating Popes against our late sovereign Queen of virtue over thirty years to work her ruin and her kingdom's overthrow, secretly planning how on a sudden they might bring upon us destructions, spoil and general desolation, till by God's deliverance she did utterly disperse and overthrow, that surnamed invincible Spanish navy, so that not any Spaniards float, unless brought captive could arrive, upon her England's shore.

'Then, latterly, Garnet, Catesby and his fellows,' Coke says, 'the Powder Treason by inhuman savages plotted: I know not what to speak, because I want words to describe the traitorous, detestable, tyrannical bloody, murderous villainy of so vile an action.'

His mind goes briefly back to his interrogation of 'John Johnson', as the depraved and wicked Guido Fawkes had called himself. King James was not new to torture, for Scottish law permitted it, and His Majesty had written his instructions on the warrant with care and precision: that the gentler tortures are to be first used unto him *et sic per gradus ad ima tenditur*, thus in stages proceed to the worst. If the manacles be not availing, let him be racked.

Back to the matter in hand. Though these men be the worst, Coke says, they are but one canker among many that afflict the kingdom. He will proceed to others.

But first, he says, he has heard a general complaint against the multiplicity of ecclesiastical courts, by means whereof His Majesty's good subjects do receive loss, and are much hindered, by their so often constrained attendance; and he reminds the magistrates, the Lord Bishop and the Chancellor present of their authority to effect badly needed reforms of the Church courts.

Reformation of the Church courts! It is a favourite theme. Coke notes with relish much muffled expostulation and glaring from the seated clerics. This, surely, will be reported. And it will not go unnoticed.

But as to these Assizes, he continues, they must deal with such as are escheaters, who try to seize men's lands by tainting their inheritance in law, or clerks of the market or purveyors, who will purvey money out of your purses if you will suffer them, or concealers, promoters, monopolitans and alchemists.

A particular blight is the monopolitan, who will spend his money in purchasing a monopoly such as in starch, vinegar or *aqua vitae*, thereby to annoy and hinder the whole public weal for his own private benefit. There has been much trouble on that account in Parliament of late. But the magistrates will do well to have an eye also to others: vagrants, stage players, young gallants, tradesmen, artificers and the company that frequent taverns, inns, alehouses, bowling alleys and such like thriftless places of resort.

Coke's speech is coming to an end. But he unleashes one final great shout of reprimand and warning to the assembled company.

'As touching all the abuses last recited,' he says, 'do you have great respect to punish one abuse, in which all our idle gallants and disordered dissolutes do desire to swim, until themselves and their whole estate do sink in the slimy dregs of swinelike drunkenness. To drunkards therefore have especial heed. Whence as from Hell's mouth flames forth riots, murders, manslaughters, quarrels, fightings, whoredoms and presumptuous blasphemies, all proceeding from that sink of sin, in whose sick healths is drunk the body's surfeiting and the soul's damnation.

'In this, as in all the rest of the abuses specified, use your best endeavours for the furtherance of a settled reformation, according to the laws established. For you must know, that *vita et vigor juris in executione consistit*, the life and strength of the laws consisteth in the execution of them. For in vain are just laws enacted, if not justly executed.'

This is his solemn declaration.

54

LAMBETH PALACE, OCTOBER 1607

'**W**ell?! Where stand you on this matter, my Lord?'
The questions are not so much asked as grunted. Now they hang, poised in the still air between the two men. While he waits, Bancroft turns, brushes the sleeves of his cassock and looks out of the window and across the river. It is low tide; men and birds are picking carefully among the mudflats.

'Why, Archbishop, I stand where I have always stood, with the King. And with the Queen before him.'

The words are calm, but Lord Chancellor Ellesmere is not by nature a calm man, and he has come down to Lambeth, at short notice and despite his rank, not to swap pleasantries but to do business. He and Bancroft stand each of them atop a great hierarchy. Except the King himself, they are the living embodiments of state and Church.

Ellesmere has held almost every great temporal office: as plain Thomas Egerton, he has been Solicitor General and Attorney; as Sir Thomas, Master of the Rolls and Lord Keeper to Queen Elizabeth; as she rightly said, 'the last that I shall have'. At the King's accession, he was raised to the peerage as Baron Ellesmere and made Lord Chancellor, presiding over the House of Lords, and as well the Court of Chancery – the conscience of the King, where matters of equity and justice of law are decided.

That is one peak. Looking over at him from the other stands

Archbishop Bancroft, who in turn commands the vast panoply of the ecclesiastical courts. The Court of Arches, the Courts of Archbishops, of Convocation, of Delegates and Appeals, the Consistory Courts beneath, and above them all the High Commission; these courts all active, all busy with the care of men's souls, he at their head charged with the maintenance of the spiritual health of the realm. And now steering the King's great project of a new Bible to its conclusion.

'The question is rather,' Ellesmere goes on, 'where standeth Coke.'

'Coke!' Bancroft spits the word out in distaste. 'They talk of brethren in the law, my Lord Chancellor, and brethren there may be, but I bear no fraternal feeling towards him.

'Nay, sir, to me he is a dangerous wanton. And he has been Chief Justice barely a year! I will tell you where he stands. Today it is against the High Commission and the Church, but his next target will be the Court of Chancery.

'And where will that lead? In time it will be to the King's prerogative itself, mark my words. For this judge maketh the law as he goeth, as though the Church courts in these days were still held tight to the see of Rome and Lord Cromwell himself had sent Coke to break them. Even Cromwell had more respect!'

Bancroft continues. 'And let me ask you, Lord Chancellor: how have matters come to this? Do I not recall Coke when he was the Attorney? Was he not ever hot for the prerogative, laying about him against one and all who would contest it? The King had no halberdier more stout. And now see him! Pah!'

Ellesmere holds his temper.

He says, 'It may be so, Bancroft. Coke has done good work for the King as Chief Justice, when we needed manors for Prince Henry in the Duchy, and in many other matters. The King doth not forget that.

'But now perhaps the man is turning proud. As if His Majesty had not enough to deal with! These Parliament men snap round his heels like curs, with their commissions and petitions, every one of them a lawyer, or a would-be. They thwart him on the union, on his rights of purveyance of goods to the royal household, on subsidies.

'It is our duty,' Ellesmere adds, 'you and I in our different ways and different domains, to protect the King. We need the Common Pleas four square behind His Majesty. So let us talk further, and see if we may not trim our Chief Justice a little in his powers and his ambitions.'

In truth, neither Ellesmere nor Bancroft has any great reason to love Edward Coke. For Ellesmere, there is respect, for theirs has been a working relationship of long standing, since 1592 when he was made Attorney General, and Coke Solicitor, with Coke succeeding him as Attorney two years later. They had fought corruptions in the courts together, sought to moderate the increase in litigation and to control the rise in lawyers' fees, as contrary to justice.

Yet Ellesmere is cut from a different cloth to Coke. He had dallied with Roman Catholicism in his youth, and that indulgence cost him. He had been slow to progress in the law at the start, and the twelve years' difference in their age is itself a source of jealousy of the younger man. So is the difference in their birth and wealth. Ellesmere was born the wrong side of the bed, from his father Sir Richard's dalliance with a servant girl, and he does not forget it. He has always valued the pennies, and in his deep heart he begrudges Coke's rapid ascent to great riches.

Ellesmere was never one of Burghley's men, and the Queen liked him the more for it. He admired the Earl of Essex for his easy grace and energy, and he supported him. But he paid dearly for the privilege, for his own son died of wounds sustained in the Earl's service in Ireland.

Even Ellesmere's friendship and sober judgement could not save Essex from his final folly of rebellion. For Ellesmere too found himself imprisoned with the others at Essex House on that fateful day. He too condemned Essex for his sedition and treachery. But, in that curious way of humankind, that only reinforced the bond between them; he will not forgive Coke at the trial for his words of denunciation of Essex, who was Ellesmere's friend.

And then there is Francis Bacon. Bacon, whom Ellesmere support-ed for Attorney all those years ago, and when that failed, for Solic-itor; Bacon who, knowing Ellesmere's appetites once offered in all seriousness to trade his reversion to the clerkship of Star Chamber for an offer of the Mastership of the Rolls, such was his ambition.

That was an act of insolence, which Ellesmere quickly refused. But it was an act of intimacy too, and Ellesmere did not disdain to be patron to the younger man. For his part, Bacon had once con-fessed that I do find in an extraordinary manner that his Lordship doth succeed my father almost in his fatherly care of me and love towards me. They have stayed close since then.

For Bancroft, the mislike of Coke is of more recent vintage. Ban-croft made his name as Whitgift's man, sworn to conform men to the true Church in the face of papists, recusants and Puritans and to defend the bishops against the congregators who would abolish them. Indeed, if anything Bancroft has been harsher than Whit-gift in rounding up and penning clerical sheep who have wandered from the fold, to bring them into the Church courts.

But religion is not the point of difference here. No, what has incensed Bancroft is the challenge to his authority and power from the steady stream of writs of prohibition that has issued from the Court of Common Pleas since Coke became Chief Justice.

These writs are nothing less than judicial orders, which require that cases deemed to be on temporal matters be transferred from Bancroft's own ecclesiastical courts to those of the common law. To Bancroft and his officials, they are an insult and a provocation; nothing less than an attack on the Church itself.

He as Archbishop must keep good order, maintain men in their morals, hunt out error and destroy heretics; and it seems the Court and its new Chief Justice would thwart him in his duties.

55

THE COURT OF COMMON PLEAS, WESTMINSTER HALL, WINTER 1607

If Coke hears of the meeting between Archbishop and Lord Chancellor, he is not much troubled by it. He has stated his purpose, at the Norwich Assizes and in many other places. He has professed his commitment to the common law, to Magna Carta and to the silver current of justice, whose equal course must benefit high and low, rich and poor alike.

The King has seen fit in the exercise of his prerogative to appoint him Chief Justice of Common Pleas, and has done so in thanks for his service and recognition of his pre-eminence in the law. Now it is for him, Coke, to discharge the duties not merely of that office but of justice, and he will pursue justice wherever it leads him. This is, he insists, the sum and total of the matter.

But there is also the authority and jurisdiction of the Court of Common Pleas to be considered. For Coke has inherited a court, indeed a conception of law, that he sees as under grave threat.

Early in Queen Elizabeth's reign there had been established an Ecclesiastical High Commission, charged by Act of Parliament to keep order through and within the established Church. The Church had long governed family and household matters, of course: baptisms, marriage and divorce, burials, wills and the like. When men broke the commandments in their private, moral aspect, by fornication or adultery or perjury, or when they fell into dissipation and drunkenness, then it stood to the Church to correct these sins. But over time, and especially after the accession of King James, so the Commission has grown. Now it numbers more than eighty men and calls itself a Court of High Commission. In pursuit of justice, and as a body of the Established Church, it professes to act in the discharge of the royal prerogative itself.

To no one will we sell, to no one deny or delay right or justice. To Coke's eye, the High Commission is an ecclesiastical court established to try enormities, as the most serious cases are called. It has no special or particular status, and no special rights over the courts of common law. The Commission was established by exercise of the Queen's prerogative as supreme head of the Church, and by Act of Parliament with the Lords and Commons assembled, and by Parliament it may be amended or abolished.

First, there is the serious question of encroachment: the Court of Common Pleas is the senior court of common law for actions between one subject and another, inferior only to the Court of King's Bench, which hears actions to which the King is party. By what right may the High Commission treat of temporal matters properly reserved to the Common Pleas?

But, second, there is also the question of procedure: does the procedure of this High Commission truly serve justice? For there is in the High Commission no trial by jury, but trial by cross-examination under the oath *ex officio*. In the courts of Roman law, in Chancery, in Star Chamber, trials are held as to matters of fact by this procedure, and no one much complains, for it is quick, inexpensive and equitable. No need of juries; there is a bill at the outset stating the charges to be answered, and many men are glad to have the chance to give direct answers under oath.

But in the High Commission, matters are otherwise. In such cases there is no bill of charges, and the oath *ex officio* is not the simple trial oath to tell the whole truth and nothing but the truth as to the charges put. No, it is a general oath that demands a man tell the truth whatever questions may be asked. Meanwhile the accused has no sight of the charges to be answered, but must sit while the court treats of potential shame and infamy, such as adultery, incontinence, usury, simony or the sale of Church offices, the hearing of mass, and heresy.

To pursue papists and conspirators by such means is one thing. But to use the oath to test and question a man on his private beliefs in a temporal matter, every word noted down carefully by the clerks for further use, comparison and re-questioning... well, that is something else.

Little wonder the common lawyers detest the use of these general oaths, and denounce them as against Magna Carta itself; for what are these oaths but a means to deprive a man of his liberties without judgment of his peers or process of law? Little wonder, too, that there has been such great concern among Members of Parliament.

Now Parliament has voted to consult the two common law Chief Justices, Popham of King's Bench and Coke of Common Pleas, as to the question in what cases a bishop may examine any person *ex officio* upon oath. The Justices have deliberated, and their opinion is clear: a bishop or Church judge cannot constrain any man, ecclesiastical or temporal, to swear generally to answer to such interrogatories as shall be administered unto him, but ought to deliver to him the articles upon which he is to be examined, that he may know whether he ought by the law to answer to them.

But, as if this were not rebuff enough, Coke and Popham also stated the general principle that no man ecclesiastical or temporal shall be examined upon secret thoughts of his heart, or of his secret opinion, but something ought to be objected against him what he hath spoken or done. Except in two special causes, no layman may be examined *ex officio* ... for laymen for the most part are not lettered, wherefore they may easily be inveigled and entrapped, and principally in heresy and error.

It is the old doctrine of Elizabeth restated, that we do not make windows into men's souls.

Not long after, a conference of judges and senior lawyers at Serjeants' Inn concludes that the powers of the High Commission, including the power of imprisonment, as conferred by Act of Parliament can extend to ecclesiastical cases only. They cannot be enlarged by the Commissioners, or even by the King by means of letters patent, but only by Parliament itself. And after nearly two years of legal wrangling, the case of that querulous barrister, Nicholas Fuller, who represents Puritans against the Church and who has abused the High Commissioners in open court, is finally brought to judgment in the Court of King's Bench.

Fuller is convicted of slander and sent to the Fleet prison. But, slander being a temporal and not a spiritual offence, the principle is established that the boundaries of the ecclesiastical courts as to what cases shall be taken and what shall not, are not to be set by the High Commission, but by the judges of the common law. Where they so decide, the same judges may by issuance of writs of prohibition require that cases are removed from the ecclesiastical courts to the common law courts for trial by jury on known charges according to the usual oath.

It is good law, and it is good business, for the fees will not be small.

All these changes betray the motive force of Coke behind them. They are not developments fit to please Bancroft; or Ellesmere come to that, or Francis Bacon, who is Ellesmere's man, if they do not please the King. But how do they please the King?

56

GORHAMBURY, JULY 1608

Francis Bacon and Alice Barnham are now two years married. The wedding is a decorous one, at Marybourne Chapel, on the way up to Hampstead, not two miles or so from the Strand. As that great tattler Dudley Carleton recounts, the groom is clad from top to toe in purple, and hath made himself and his wife such store of fine raiments of cloth of silver and gold that it draws deep into her portion.

The dinner is held at the Pakington house by the Savoy, Lady Pakington presiding, with due magnificence and three knights in attendance. Sir Robert Cecil, who is now the Earl of Salisbury, cannot be present, and there's a pity since he had originally commended Francis to the father of the bride, but at least they have his Lordship's leading councillors to represent him. Of Lady Bacon, Francis's mother, now in her dotage but to whom the proceedings would have brought a great measure of joy, there is no sign.

It has taken many months, much to and fro and the intervention of friends to bring the marriage negotiations to a satisfactory conclusion, for the Barnham estates are complex and jealously guarded, and Francis seeks to bring some order to his own affairs at the same time. Salisbury lent a hand at one point, Ellesmere's wife Lady Derby at another.

The result is that, at the age of thirteen, Alice Bacon enjoys settled title through trustees to real property in three manors, including three mills, twelve gardens, 1,200 acres of land, 100 acres of meadow, 500 acres of pasture, 400 acres of wood, in all a life interest of £300 per year. There is more if her husband should predecease her. Friends of the bridegroom murmur at the mention of offspring to whom the property may in time descend.

But the rest of Alice's capital now belongs to Francis, as her lawful wedded husband. Now, at the age of forty-seven, for the first time in a life burdened with debt, Francis Bacon has money of his own to spend. As he had put it to Salisbury, he has married with some convenient advancement.

Quisque faber fortunae suae. Of what he has, Alice's estates or no, Francis has been the ultimate director and creator, of that he is sure. Yet there is also luck; and when good luck comes, in a rush as is sometimes the way, he takes it at the flood. His hopes of preferment had been dashed yet again in 1604 when Doddridge was made Solicitor General, but now the tides are changing. Ellesmere presses his case, and Salisbury is fully taken up by the desperate state of the Exchequer. The King is not averse, and he needs able men to do his business.

Francis writes letters to each of them touching the matter, letters that are steady, deferential, not overly familiar, yet all of them quietly beseeching. But what finally makes the difference is not his letters, not his skill in the law, not his position among the King's learned counsel, not his many pamphlets, not his elaborate plans for the reform of learning and natural philosophy, let alone his *Essays*: it is the work Francis does in Parliament, where he has with vigour pressed the case for an Act of Union between England and Scotland. This is a matter close indeed to the heart of the monarch, who demands to be called King of Great Britain, and has ordered vessels English and Scottish alike to fly a new Union flag which draws together the red Cross of St George with the blue of St Andrew.

So it is not much more than a year from his marriage, in June 1607, that Francis is at last made Solicitor General, with an income of £1,000 or so a year. And not much more than a year after that, on 16 July 1608, William Mill, Clerk of Star Chamber, finally expires. Whereupon the post reverts to Francis, and he is immediately sworn in as Clerk. That is a further £2,000 a year.

᛭

Francis Bacon has always had rich tastes. Now he is a rich man. But exultation quickly yields to dissatisfaction.

He had written soon after his marriage to his cousin Sir Thomas Posthumous Hoby, to say that *your loving congratulation for my doubled life, as you call it, I thank you for. No man may better conceive the joys of a good wife than yourself, with whom I dare not compare. But I thank God I have not taken a thorn out of my foot to put it into my side. For as my state is somewhat amended, so I have no other circumstance of complaint.*

Yet, in the months that follow, Francis has cause to doubt these words. For Alice's mother Lady Pakington is becoming the very thorn in his side that he thought to have avoided.

Her Ladyship's situation is not helped by the foul terms into which she has fallen with her husband. Thanks to her money, for years now Lusty Pakington has floated joyously on the tide of his recovered fortunes, and they have led him to undertake a bold new house at Westwood, atop a hill barely a mile from the family seat in Worcestershire.

Lusty calls it a mere 'lodge', but no one who has seen it is deceived, for it has a tower of four floors, which at each corner gives on to a wing so that the whole in plan is a cruciform. Having entertained the King lavishly a few years earlier in his parliamentary seat at Aylesbury, Lusty's dream is that he may welcome James once more to hunt the chases and drives of the forests at Westwood. From this can only come new glory.

But after nine years of marriage, years in which his wife has borne him two daughters and a son, and even as he has depleted her capital on this vast construction, so the jovial Lusty has tired of her. This is a source of deep vexation, and some danger, to Lady Pakington. What has moved her beyond vexation and to mortification is the conduct of her new son by marriage.

For Francis, the Barnham connection began with Alice, but its possibilities have not by any means ended with her. No, it presents new vistas of possibility, to strengthen a connection and soothe a creditor of his own at a single stroke.

After the wedding he moves quickly to procure the marriage of his friend and fellow Gray's Inn man John Constable to Alice's sister Dorothy, twelve years old, ignoring the loud protests of the girl's mother at the unsuitability of the groom, the girl's young age and the absence of a proper settlement to support her in the event of his death.

What right has this violent little lady to object? Francis is indignant. The thorn pricks ever deeper in his side. He thinks to have assuaged her when, in October 1607, he is able to secure a knighthood for Constable from the King. Yet still the letters of reproach pour in. Lady Pakington will not be satisfied. She asks Why doth Sir Francis extend himself for this impecunious wretch, and not his own family?

The answer is simple: a sum of £600, which Francis owes to Constable. But worse is to come to Lady Pakington, for Francis intends to make the same play again, to procure the marriage of Alice's youngest sister, eleven-year-old Bridget, to one Master Smith. This will further aid his purse and credit.

57

GORHAMBURY, JULY 1608

To some perhaps my name is odious;
But such as love me, guard me from their tongues,
And let them know that I am Machiavel,
And weigh not men, and therefore not men's words.
Admired I am of those that hate me most:
Though some speak openly against my books,
Yet will they read me, and thereby attain
To Peter's chair; and, when they cast me off,
Are poisoned by my climbing followers.
I count religion but a childish toy,
And hold there is no sin but ignorance.

Yet even Lady Pakington is not the deep cause of Francis Bacon's melancholy.

It has been fifteen years since Francis first set his hopes on becoming Attorney General, near nineteen since he received the reversion, and twenty-nine since that moment after his father's death when he first wrote to his uncle to seek his help.

In that time he reckons perhaps a dozen men have been directly preferred for office to him; that is, he has been weighed in the balance a dozen times and found wanting. There are many other positions he could have got, had the will been there in others. His ideas and schemes have been ignored, his family and connections unavailing or even at times obstructive to his hopes, for all the warm words of his supposed friends and sponsors. The late Queen called him her young Lord Keeper, gave him access to her presence other men might have dreamed of, yet all this aided him not.

And so much time lost. Think what he might have achieved if they had trusted his youthful energy and imagination! A great new college of the practical arts, a reforming system of laws, the very basis of knowledge itself transformed among men for human betterment.

Now, however, all is changed. There is a new dispensation, a new King upon the throne, Francis has had preferment at last, and his fortunes are much improved. Yet he remains restless and full of discontent. Who at court has not seen how the King has taken up with his new young favourite, Robert Carr, how he leans on his arm, pinches his cheek, smoothes his ruffled garment? Riches and place are sure to follow.

Francis cannot keep himself from melancholy at the injustice, the waste and frustration of it all. Now, just when he should be rejoicing, these dark reflections crowd in upon him and he takes to his bed. His mind is cloudy, his limbs leaden with fatigue. Full of fever, he will not eat, and when he does, he is struck down with pain. Days pass, the servants mutter their concern. His new wife feels but cannot fully grasp what is amiss, and blames herself.

A week goes by before he stirs, and then it is to give himself a task. This is the moment to make an assessment, he thinks, an inventory of what I have and could have. And so, over several days, he sits at his desk and writes. Before him are the piles of his books and papers: composition books, sheaves of legal and professional papers, household and office notebooks, personal notes. He copies out needed items from the notebooks, and adds new thoughts and resolutions of the moment, topic by topic but as they come to him, in no particular order, while his mind is full.

These things are not the planning. They are but the materials of the planning. The planning will come later.

First, ready money and credit: what he has, and to whom he could apply if more were quickly needed. He is old enough to know his weaknesses, knows he has no head for commercial business and loves to spend. He has felt the bailiff's challenge, and he will never forget Coke's taunt that he would clap a *caput legatum* on his back.

So Francis must have sources of ready money. Then, he must have favour: with the King, with Salisbury, and with many other men, and some women, who may help him to ascend, and further his projects, and himself. He must make himself inward with Lady Dorset, recently widowed of the old Lord Treasurer, that she may remember him in her will. With the young Prince Henry, now four-teen, to whom the aspirants around the court are already turning. With the little-known but essential men, so easy to miss, who run the household and who have direct access to the King. Sir Thomas Chaloner is an old acquaintance, but what of Sir David Murray, who keeps the Privy Purse? Francis does not know Murray, but he knows Russell, who knows him: perhaps that is a way in.

And there are others. The Scots, Dunbar, Lenox, Daubiny, who wield such influence; perhaps Francis may succeed Salisbury as the King's channel to them. The Earl of Northumberland is a great patron of learning and supports Harriot the mathematician; both may be of use. The Archbishop, who is now Chancellor of Oxford, yes, and Bishop Andrewes, but also Sir Walter Raleigh.

Raleigh is still kept prisoner in the Tower, where he complains about the damp, tends the little physic garden he has created, and distils the Balsam of Guiana whose curative properties he extols. He is down at present, but who knows what may come? The Ex-chequer is empty; one voyage to the New World could bring him back to favour. Francis will see him. It is well to be prepared.

All these things are carefully noted down.

Francis follows where his mind will take him, and for a day it takes him to natural philosophy, and meditations on different forms of motion and change, of emission, evaporation, exhalation, coagulation, liquefaction, fractionation, congelation, of rusting and moulding, of bodily infection, generation and defecation. Perhaps these will become the subject of a new work? Then it is back to power and purpose, purpose and power. How to enhance and protect the King's finances, better management of the Commons, equalling of the laws of Scotland and England into one codified whole, the handling of recusants, restoration of the true glory of the Church, the need to keep courts to their proper jurisdictions, the defence of the King's prerogative powers.

Another day, and Francis turns another half-circle, returning to himself. A complete inventory of his personal property and debts. His personal regimen and the effects of a familiar cooling clyster, which four or five days without intermission is of good success. The ease and relaxation to be had from a slight anointing of my sides and the region of my belly under the navel with some oil appropriate to corroborate the nerves and membraneous parts. My desire to make a place of pleasure at Gorhambury, with gardens, lakes and islands: one island with a grotto, another where the fair hornbeam stands, a third with an arbour of musk roses, set all with double violets for scent in autumn. And in the middle thereof to build a house for freshness with an upper gallery open upon the water, a terrace above that and a supping room open under that; a dining room, a bedchamber, a cabinet and a room for music, a garden.

Finally it is back to great matters of state, and his own advancement. Francis has withheld little from this private inventory of thoughts, but when they touch his secret interests and desires his notes become so elliptical and coded that even he sometimes struggles to understand them. Yet their meaning lies not merely in the words themselves, but in their recurrence and their intent.

For a man to succeed Salisbury or Ellesmere, wealth and credit are requisite; but also favour, above all with the King; regular access through presence at court, and on particular occasions, fit and grateful and continual, to have private speeches with great people, sometimes drawing more than one of them together.

But if Francis is ever to follow Salisbury as Lord Treasurer or Ellesmere as Lord Chancellor, even these things are not enough. He must also overtake others, for the King is ill-served by rivals at the table.

Attorney Hobart Francis anatomises on the page: good of speech but weak in the law and in his own authority. He is no threat. But Coke? There is no disguising it: this is a man with the ambition and ability to ascend to the Privy Council, nay to the very highest office in the land, for it is evident he has an eye to be Lord Chancellor. He is well protected, too: intimate with Salisbury, close to Queen Anne, much respected and admired for his learning by the King. It may be disease will take him, but Coke seems the picture of good health.

Coke cannot be relied upon to fail; but perhaps he may be brought low. For that, time and care will be needed. As Francis says, death comes to young men, but old men go to death. And Coke is not yet old.

For Francis himself, there can be no rising save by a commixture of good and evil. He must proceed like the crab, which goeth sideways to progress. He must ascend by a stair that, if it is upwards, ever winds its way. And he must moderate his speech so that it is always temperate and light; no one must know what anger lingers in his heart.

His brother Anthony used to quote an adage of the old French Kings: *qui nescit dissimulare, nescit regnare.* He who cannot feign, cannot reign. Would that Essex had lived by such a maxim.

No, Francis has not forgotten Edward Coke; not just the preferment he has gained so often at Francis's own expense, but his arrogance, and the indignities and slights Coke has heaped upon him.

He blames Coke as the preferred instrument of Burghley, blames him for poisoning Salisbury, his own cousin, against him, and the

Queen and many others too; for belittling his knowledge of the law, his character, his range and facility. Coke! He can barely bring himself to scrawl the name. The thought of him hangs ugly and unbidden over the freshly written pages of his notes.

But now everything is different. Men ever yield to what they do not know, and despise what they think they understand. When Coke was the Attorney, he was the King's man. The King did not know him, but he relied upon him, and Coke used all his breadth of cases and depth of precedents on the King's behalf. But now Coke is a judge, and who knows where that path may lead him? He vaunts his independence, and fidelity to the law, yet the law is the King's law, the courts are the King's courts, the judges are the King's judges.

Still, these writs of prohibition that Coke is so fond of, they say something. They speak not merely to his reforming zeal, but to his pride.

This is a man who will not bend, and those who will not bend can be broken. That is promising material to work on.

As for Francis himself: before, he was a nothing, a petitioner, a mendicant about the court without even the status of a family retainer, for all he was a Member of Parliament and had the rank of Knight and the title of learned counsel.

Now, however, Francis is Solicitor General. He holds an office. He speaks not for his own account, but in the name of the King and the prerogative. He does not merely advise others; he acts. Others attend him for his status. He may address himself directly to the King, if need be. And he may go about his business without eliciting the suspicion of the needy. Speaking always lightly to others, lightly always… in friendship, or its likeness.

For the first time in his life, Francis has real power. And then, as he reflects, it suddenly comes to him, not the knowledge itself, but the sense of it: how he may at once advance himself, and bring his rival low.

IV

KRISIS: 1608–1617

58

YORK HOUSE, 13 NOVEMBER 1608

A most miraculous work in this good King;
Which often, since my here-remain in England,
I have seen him do. How he solicits heaven,
Himself best knows: but strangely-visited people,
All swoln and ulcerous, pitiful to the eye,
The mere despair of surgery, he cures,
Hanging a golden stamp about their necks,
Put on with holy prayers: and 'tis spoken,
To the succeeding royalty he leaves
The healing benediction. With this strange virtue,
He hath a heavenly gift of prophecy,
And sundry blessings hang about his throne,
That speak him full of grace.

Archbishop Bancroft has had his way at last. Three years before, he had issued his *Articuli cleri*, a list of Church grievances against the depredations of the common lawyers, and demanded the judges respond. Yet the damnable stream of writs of prohibition, writs issued by Chief Justice Coke that remove cases from the ecclesiastical courts to those of the common law, has not been stemmed. On the contrary, it has expanded, both in number and in breadth of subject. It is a provocation and a scandal to the Archbishop, one that, for him, brings into question the King's very right to govern through his Church.

Now, with the support of Lord Chancellor Ellesmere, Bancroft has moved the King to call the judges and the bishops together in conference. Ellesmere will play the host; it is to be at his residence, York House. This is Francis Bacon's childhood home, and in these matters Bacon is rarely far from Ellesmere's side.

The King relishes such occasions. He loves learned debate, the play of the intellect on points of nice consideration. He loves to hold the ring among these exquisitely polite men of the Church or the law who would, with great delicacy, rip the throats out from each others' necks. He loves the theatre of it, the speeches, the display, the finery of each man's garb and address; above all he loves to sit in judgment and deliver his own verdict at the close, and know that it will be obeyed.

James has ever seen himself as *Rex legifer*, the lawgiver, but is he not also *Pater nutricius*, the nourishing father, and *Rex pacificus*, the peacemaker, beloved of Jesus and come among men to unify and prosper them? Let men never forget that he it was who calmed the brawling factions when he reigned in Scotland, and he who brought peace at last to the war with Spain. Bancroft's scholars seek to remake the Bible; they will do well to improve on the words of the old Bishop's Bible, where it says, 'Blessed are the peacemakers: for they shall be called the children of God.'

Yet James's mind is more to rule than to make peace this morning. Part of him begrudges any day spent away from his hunting, and the past weeks have been a torment of official business. He is well pleased to have gained a judges' opinion restricting the jurisdiction of the stannary courts in Devon and Cornwall. When Prince Henry becomes Duke of Cornwall he will need revenue, and this will inhibit the use of local courts against him by his tenants who would thwart and frustrate the collection of that revenue.

But Wales is a different matter. There too the interests of the young Prince Henry are at issue, and the sense of acting for his son and his posterity quickens the King's spirits. Earlier in the year he had asked the judges in Westminster whether he could appoint judges to the Court of Great Session in Wales by royal commission, as Henry VIII had done. They have responded that Henry acted under an Act of Parliament 1543, which invested him with a temporary and personal authority that does not extend to his heirs and successors.

That is a rebuff. But nothing daunted, James has put the judges a second question, whether the jurisdiction of the Council of the Marches may extend outside the principality of Wales itself to include the four next counties of Gloucestershire, Herefordshire, Shropshire and Cheshire. It is the matter of Lord Zouche revisited. The question drags on for months without result, till the King in frustration calls the judges together with the Privy Council in conference at the Council table to decide the matter.

But his frustration only grows at what takes place, for the judges decline to give an opinion on the issue outside a court of law. When the Lord Chancellor tells them this is a matter of state and their oaths require them to render advice when it is sought by the King, they remain silent. Then the King himself enters with Prince Henry, sits the lad on a stool and presses the judges again, implying that they will cost the Prince dearly, and set dangerous precedents elsewhere, through an adverse decision. Again receiving no response, he raises his voice and rebukes the judges for their obstinacy and unwillingness to assist their King, from whom, lest they forget, their own powers and authority derive.

But even as he speaks, the King detects the guiding influence of Sir Edward Coke among them. For the eyes of the Lord Chief Justice and the Chief Baron weep welling tears of frustration in the face of his criticisms, while those of the Chief Justice of Common Pleas are dry.

The King hates to be crossed, hates it all the more with others there to witness it. And he is everywhere sensitive to matters that touch his prerogative right. The matter is common currency among all who have seen him: has he not written books of his own on these matters? Indeed in *The True Law of Free Monarchies* James has given a whole argument for kingship, setting out its basis in scripture and drawing out his conclusions each in turn, in the manner of the geometers. He says there that the Kings in Scotland were before any estates or ranks of men within the same, before any parliaments were holden, or laws made; and by them was the land distributed, states erected and discerned, and forms of government devised and established. And so it follows of necessity, that the Kings were the authors and makers of the laws, and not the laws of the Kings.

It flows from this that the King is above parliaments. For, James says, albeit the King makes daily statutes and ordinances, enjoining such pains thereto as he thinks meet, without any advice of Parliament or estates; yet it lies in the power of no parliament to make any kind of law or statute without his sceptre be to it, for giving it the force of a law.

And, he says, while the King should act lawfully as a father to his people, yet out of the law of God, the duty and allegiance of the people to their lawful King ought to be to him, as to God's lieutenant in Earth, obeying his commands in all things, acknowledging him a judge set by God over them, having power to judge them, but to be judged only by God, whom to only he must give count of his judgment; fearing him as their judge, loving him as their father; praying for him as their protector, following and obeying his lawful commands, eschewing and flying his fury in his unlawful, without resistance but by sobs and tears to God.

And now do these judges dare to give him, their own King and judge, who is accountable only to God himself as judge, no answer?

59

YORK HOUSE, 13 NOVEMBER 1608

That was less than a week ago. Now it is early on a cool morning, a Sunday morning, at York House. The King sits at the centre of the great hall, flanked by the Lord Chancellor and by the Earl of Salisbury, bishops and judges arrayed on either side. Those who have come to dispute must stand before him, a useful tonic against long-windedness. The whole is a mass of red and white and purple and gold.

Once all have settled, the King speaks briskly and to the point. He has come not to make or hear orations. He expects an answer from the judges after last Tuesday touching the four shires, as to whether they lie in the jurisdiction of the Marches of Wales. This for him, he makes clear, is no less a matter than robbing the Prince of Wales of his right and patrimony, if the four shires be denied to belong thereunto. But he has also a grave care to the security and wellbeing of his Church, and so requires answer in the matter of writs of prohibition and the oath *ex officio*.

Before the King turns to the judges, Archbishop Bancroft speaks to these latter issues, and it is as though he has James's own *True Law* open at the desk in front of him.

'When the question was made,' Bancroft says, 'of what matters the ecclesiastical judges have cognisance, either upon the exposition of the statutes, or any other thing ecclesiastical, or upon the statute of the first year of Elizabeth concerning the High Commission, or in any other case in which there is not express authority in law, the King himself may decide it in his royal person.

'For the judges are but the delegates of the King,' he continues, 'and the King may take what causes he shall please to determine from the determination of the judges, and may determine them himself. These things are clear in divinity, that such authority belongs to the King by the word of God in the scripture.'

Bancroft gives a last portentous glare around him and is seated. Coke looks ahead and sees the King nodding judiciously, as though already called to give a verdict. Ellesmere sits impassive, but there can be little doubt that his sympathies lie in the same direction. Salisbury is silent and withdrawn.

The judges of the other common law courts of King's Bench and Exchequer are in attendance, alongside those of Common Pleas. Sir Thomas Fleming, as Chief Justice of King's Bench, is the most senior of them all. But all know that it is Coke who is making all this trouble. It has been put that Coke should lead in reply to Bancroft, and the others have been only too happy to agree.

The King abruptly turns to Coke. 'What say you, Chief Justice?' It comes out as 'Wha' say ye?' – raw Scots, a sure sign of his agitation.

Coke begins gently, for the occasion and the message will not prove a pleasing one to the King, of that he is sure. His colleagues are careful scholars of the law, Judges Walmsley, Daniel, Warburton and the others. But they are not brave men. They have been brave these past weeks, but they have quailed in private at the King's rebuke. Now he must protect them, and for that he must address James's argument to its face.

'Your Majesty,' he says, 'I speak not *in propria persona*, in my own behalf, but from custom and practice, in character of a judge and from a careful review of our laws and statutes.' He lists some of the leading statutes by name.

'As precedent maketh clear, the King in his own person cannot adjudge any case, either criminal such as treason or felony, or betwixt party and party concerning his inheritance, chattels or goods.

Any such case ought to be determined and adjudged in some court of justice, according to the law and custom of England; and always judgments are given, *ideo consideratum est per curiam*, thus it is decided by the court, so that the court gives the judgment.

'And the King hath his court,' Coke continues, 'that is in the upper house of Parliament, in which he with his Lords is the supreme judge over all other judges. For if error be in the Common Pleas, that may be reversed in the King's Bench, and if the Court of King's Bench err, that may be reversed in the upper house of Parliament, by the King, with the assent of the Lords Spiritual and Temporal, without the Commons.'

Now Coke is in full flow. 'The King may sit in the Star Chamber; but this is to consult with the justices upon certain questions proposed to them, and not *in judicio*. So in the King's Bench he may sit, but the court gives the judgment. Judgments are always given *per curiam*, by the court; and the judges are sworn to execute justice according to law and the custom of England.'

A cloud passes over the visage of the King. These are lawyer's words, and they directly controvert his speech given of but a few days ago, and the beliefs of a lifetime. He, James, first of England and sixth of Scotland, is God's lieutenant on Earth. He has been anointed so at the coronation, has taken the coronation oath. Being the author of the law, he is the interpreter of the law, the supreme judge, and these inferior judges are but his shadows and ministers. He needs no judge to set limits to his power, no court for him to give judgment, no Lords to give their assent. Nor in God's name may any do so, except he will it.

Still, he is the peacemaker. He feels his anger rising, but swallows it: it will not do to use harsh words.

Instead, the King says, mildly, 'I had thought the law was founded on reason? Do not others have reason as well as the judges, Sir Edward? Do not I' – and here he makes an effort at jocularity, looking around the room – 'Do not I have reason enough as your King?' There are smiles, of relief and flattery, and a murmur of assent.

Coke says, 'True it is, that God has endowed your Majesty with excellent science and great endowments of nature, but your Majesty is not learned in the laws of your realm of England and the causes which concern the life, or inheritance, or goods, or fortunes of your subjects.'

The skies are darkening, for the King is very tender as to his learning, and in particular as to his knowledge of English law. The failure of his recent project to unite England and Scotland into a single British nation bears full witness to it.

Again, however, he swallows his anger. Coke proceeds.

'These causes are not to be decided by natural reason, but by the artificial reason and judgment of law, which law is an act which requires long study and experience, before that a man can attain to the cognisance of it.'

Artificial reason? Artificial treason, more like! Coke would reserve judgment in law to himself and the judges. But if that is so, what need of Kings?

Coke goes on, 'The law is the golden metwand and measure by which to try the causes of your subjects; and it protecteth your Majesty in safety and peace.'

There must be a stop to this talk.

'Nae saw!' The King is much agitated. 'Not so! For if that were true, then the King himself should be under the law, which it is treason to affirm. Nay, the King will ever protect the common law.'

'The common law protecteth the King, your Majesty.'

Now the King is shouting. 'A traitorous speech! The King protecteth the law, and not the law the King! The King maketh judges and bishops. If the judges interpret the laws themselves and suffer none else to interpret, they may easily make of the laws, shipmen's hose!'

'Bracton saith of old, *Quod Rex non debet esse sub homine, sed sub Deo et Lege*. The King should not be under any man, but under God and the law.'

At this the King leaps up and raises his arm, incoherent with anger, hand clenched into a fist, as though to strike Coke in the face. Coke stops and instantly throws himself to the floor, exclaiming, 'Your Majesty, I humbly beseech you take pity on me! And pardon me if I have in any way offended, or zeal taken me beyond my duty and allegiance.'

There is absolute silence across the hall, all stunned by what has happened. The King is thwarted, raging and in no way satisfied, Coke spread headlong before him. Nothing good can come of this.

60

SALISBURY HOUSE, 13 NOVEMBER 1608

'**M**y dear friend, but that was close. I cannot thank you enough.'
'In truth I thought you were for the Tower, and perhaps me also.'

It is not wise to talk of matters of state, let alone of the King, except in the most private company. Even now, some hours afterward, Coke cannot say for certain how he and Salisbury came away from York House, or what transpired after the King's sudden outburst.

It must be reconstructed, step by step: he, prone before them all on the cold flagstones, Salisbury darting down to kneel beside him and beg the King's forgiveness with the words 'I pray you my Liege and Majesty show pity on this man, show him the light of your favour', the King's blunt question 'What hast thou to do to entreat for him?', answered by the most modest and gentle 'In regard he hath married my nearest kinswoman', Coke still silent.

Perhaps it is the Chief Justice's self-abasement, his own Lord Treasurer on his knees, or the sight of this little halt and hunchback figure coming to the aid of his friend. Perhaps it is the movement towards the two men by the other judges, or simply that this sheer, sudden demonstration of a king's power is enough. But James's mood again changes. He gathers himself, bids them rise, calls for a seat for Coke, nay seats for all those standing, and invites them to parley.

No one can recall what is said; it is not even noted down by Sir Julius Caesar, a lawyer and judge who is punctilious about such things. But it does not matter. Any words will do, to smooth over such a moment.

The two men are able to make a more or less dignified exit, to Salisbury's magnificent new brick-and-timber house close by. Yet, as they share a bottle afterwards, Coke does not regret what has occurred. He has shown himself, and his fellow judges, that a man can speak a painful truth unto a king, and live to speak again. There will be no lessening in the flow of prohibitions from the Court of Common Pleas.

Let the incident be brushed aside, effaced from any official record. It has not gone unnoticed by the Solicitor General, Sir Francis Bacon.

61

SALISBURY HOUSE, MARCH 1609

The King's anger with Coke is no small thing. But to Salisbury, now charged as Lord Treasurer with the need to replenish the Exchequer, it is just one item among many dozens with which he must deal.

The King has not shied from loading my shoulders with business. He must think they are broader than they are, Salisbury ruefully reflects.

Yet, as befits a great man, he has much else to occupy him. The King fell in love with Salisbury's house Theobalds some while back on a visit, and pressed him to exchange it for some properties, including the royal residence at Hatfield. The trade was made, and now Salisbury is much extending his new home. But he is also building at Salisbury House on the Strand, at his Cranborne estate in Dorset, and in the Strand with the New Exchange, an arcade for shops by which he seeks to lure trade away from the City of London nearby. All this expense is the despair of his household staff.

And then there is a family matter that has dogged Salisbury for some years; a matter of considerable delicacy and potential embarrassment, which concerns his cousin, Francis Bacon.

Lady Pakington had approached both Lord Salisbury and Lord Ellesmere in a state of some desperation, and begged for their intervention and the protection of the Privy Council itself for her daughters. And their Lordships did justice by her. At their insistence, Francis Bacon's friend Constable has been obliged to put in place a jointure or settlement of £400 a year for his young bride Dorothy when he comes into his estate.

But Constable adds, or perhaps it is Francis the lawyer who slyly attaches, a condition to the legal instrument saying that, as Francis puts it, those her friends which have so intolerably slandered and wronged me, shall have no intermeddling at all either in the assurance or in the allowance of these articles.

The effect of this is to require the trustees to ignore any further efforts by Lady Pakington to assist her daughter. And when she approaches Francis directly to express her concerns and seek his help, he shuts and bolts the door on her, writing that Madam, You shall with right good will be made acquainted with anything which concerneth your daughters, if you bear a mind of love and concord: otherwise you must be content to be a stranger unto us. For I may not be so unwise as to suffer you to be an author or occasion of dissension between your daughters and their husbands, having seen so much misery of that kind in yourself.

And, Francis goes on, above all things I will turn back your kindness, in which you say you will receive my wife if she be cast off. For it is much more likely we have occasion to receive you being cast off, if you remember what is passed. But it is time to make an end of those follies. And you shall at this time pardon me this one fault of writing to you. For I mean to do it no more till you use me and respect me as you ought. So wishing you better than it seemeth you will draw upon yourself, I rest, Yours, etc.

For it is much more likely we have occasion to receive you being cast off, if you remember what is passed. Cruel words indeed to a woman who has borne children and given her fortune to support the feckless Lusty Pakington!

But again, Francis has badly misjudged his mother-in-law. Lady Pakington immediately applies again to the Earl of Salisbury. She names Francis for contracting her daughter to Constable, and casting her away with a very careless and slender provision.

Nor in her boldness does Lady Pakington spare Salisbury a reminder of his own originating hand in the affair, saying My very good Lord... forasmuch as I have endeavoured by sending unto the said Bacon to know what is done for my little daughter Dorothy, and instead of satisfaction, have received an insolent letter of contempt, penned after his proud manner of writing – my husband nor my brother knowing nothing, as being secluded and thrust out from all privity of dealing therein – I am forced to beseech your Lordship to let me know what order is taken for her.

And, she goes on, thus being sorry I have such cause to complain of his bad dealing whom your Lordship heretofore recommended to me, and whose folly hath lately more abounded in procuring the said Constable to be knighted, being of himself a man of very mean estate – whereby he has taken all ordinary means of thriving from him – craving pardon for my boldness, I humbly take my leave. From Drury Lane, this 28 November 1607. Dorothy Pakington.

That was more than a year before, yet still the matter lingers. Private and public matters alike combine to burden Lord Treasurer Salisbury. Caught between the exigencies of the King and the wrath of Lady Pakington, he hardly knows which to prefer between them.

62

WESTMINSTER, SPRING 1610

But it is, it must ever be, the King's business that predominates with Lord Salisbury. The 1604 parliament is now in its fourth session, six years after it was first begun, and hitherto it has been preoccupied with His Majesty's ardent desire to enact a Bill of Union with Scotland, a Bill repeatedly thwarted by the Members, to the King's deep frustration.

Now, however, the issue is money. Salisbury's commission as Lord Treasurer since 1608 has been to fill the yawning void in the Exchequer. It has taken all his energies, wits and financial understanding even to make a start.

The ancient sources of Crown revenue, the King's rights and royalties, licences and tenures, are worth less and less with time. To supplement them Salisbury has tapped old streams, with a huge sale of Crown lands. He has found new flows of income where there were few or none before, in impositions (as such taxes are called) on the import and export trades that now yield a handsome £70,000 a year.

Salisbury has urged the King to the limits of persuasion itself to make economies in his expenditure; but without success, since James affects an ignorance amounting to disdain about such matters. These things are for others. Yet still the debts come in, piling one upon another, accruing still more in interest due. Salisbury reckons the total at £300,000, with an excess of spending over income of £160,000 a year. And now the King seeks a separate establishment for the young Prince, and there is talk of war in Cleves. He seems to feel, not only that there is no limit to his spending, but that there must not be.

It cannot be borne. Some way, a way more durable, must be found to relieve the King's necessity, and with other avenues now closed, the way must pass through Parliament. With new revenue in prospect, the moneymen, the merchants of the City, can be held at bay. But the old subsidies from Parliament too bring in ever less, when they are given, and after a decade of peace there are voices among the Members calling for the King to mind his own establishment, as Kings were wont to do.

Wherefore all this new money, the Commons ask, if it is simply to be sucked up by the King's favourites? These impositions may have been found good in law, some add, but they are yet extra duties, and levied by the prerogative of the Crown, without the sanction of Parliament. And if this were not bad enough, every thought of subsidy leads to petitions that anger and dismay the King.

Yet there is also cause for hope, for spirits rise with thoughts of the young Prince Henry. And did not Parliament grant a handsome settlement in 1606, after the Gunpowder Treason?

Salisbury resolves to take a direct approach. He will put the matter squarely before Parliament, not from any pressing urgency of war but as a matter of prerogative right: the King has opened a new session of Parliament so that it may authorise and ratify the creation of Prince Henry as Prince of Wales and Earl of Chester, for which is requisite some supply of treasure. It is the duty of Parliament so to provide.

To that end, Salisbury seeks a new kind of settlement, in two parts, which he calls *supply* and *support*: supply, a sum of £600,000 to pay off the King's debts; support, an annual payment of £200,000 to maintain the royal household and estates. At a conference convened between the Lords and Commons in February 1610, he sets out the case. The money is plainly needed, he says, for the monarch must have a revenue, to maintain his state and sustain his family, to resist his enemies, to help his friends and, if need arises, to make diversions of war. For if the late Queen had not given aid to the low countries and the French King, what a neighbour might we have had ere this? The coffers were empty at King James's accession, there has been great expense in Ireland and the low countries; even Queen Elizabeth's funeral was no small matter.

But Salisbury then goes further still, and takes those assembled into his confidence. For the first time, he discloses the outline of the King's debts and revenues. It then falls to Sir Francis Bacon, Solicitor General, Member of Parliament since 1581, that eloquent upholder of the royal prerogative, to present these matters to the conference in detail. And if Sir Francis is aware of the contrast between the manager of the Commons he is now, and the independent younger self who had had the audacity to question the burden of the Queen's subsidy in 1593, he shows no sign of it.

Is it high-mindedness that moves Lord Salisbury to make these revelations? Is it simple force of circumstance, or a lack of caution, being too long away from the House of Commons? Whichever is the cause, or all of them perhaps, it is not hard to divine what happens next. The matter is taken under advisement by the Members of Parliament and cast in terms of a bargain. If they are to vote for a contribution, what recompense – they call it retribution – may they expect from His Majesty in exchange? The noble Lord has mentioned the redress of all just grievances, but to what do these amount?

The matter is referred to a Committee of Grievance. Now the Commons is in its element. The King has shown his hand: he is in dire need of funds, and there is little to be lost, and much perhaps to be gained, by delay and further inquiry.

Yet there is interest in the proposal among the Commons, even so. To the Members of Parliament, there are three potential prizes on offer, for it seems the King would give up his rights to rents from his tenured lands, to the proceeds of the sale of wardships, and to the subsidies from purveyance of goods to the royal household at less than market prices, in exchange for a regular income.

These are not small things. As Francis says in a further conference with the Lords, this tree of tenures was planted into the prerogative by the ancient common law of this land; it hath been fenced in and preserved by many statutes; and it yieldeth at this day to the King the fruit of a great revenue. But yet notwithstanding, if upon the stem of this tree may be raised a pillar of support to the Crown permanent and durable as the marble, by investing the Crown with a more ample, more certain and more loving dowry, than this of tenures; we hope we propound no matter of disservice.

As for the trade in wardships, the King has always enjoyed the use and benefit of his wards' estates. But their value is much more than monetary: there is a vast array of office-holders who benefit from wardship income, and so its disposition carries with it the power to dispose of men's fortunes and shape their rank and status. It is not to be easily renounced by His Majesty, and must be the more valuable for that. And purveyance has never had friends in Parliament, which sees the King's right to buy goods at less than market price as at once illegal, a source of abusive profit for his agents, and a burden on the poor. So let the abolition of purveyance too be part of this Great Contract, as it is becoming known.

For months, there is little advancement in the business, which nearly gives up its life's breath when the true magnitude of Salisbury's demands becomes clear. The Commons willingly offers £100,000 for the abolition of tenures and wardships, only to profess itself astonished that Salisbury expects an additional £200,000 a year. But, the Lord Treasurer insists, of what use is it to the King to replace one revenue with another, when he must have a clear surplus?

The blood is quickened on both sides by the news in May that Henri IV of France has been murdered, stabbed in his carriage by a

Catholic assassin in the centre of Paris. Always anxious for his own safety, and mindful of the many attempts on the old Queen's life, the King immediately publishes a proclamation requiring every subject to take the oath of allegiance. At the same time, his courtiers calculate what extra revenue may be extracted from the general alarm.

But by early July, with the summer recess nearly upon them, the Great Contract is still not yet made. The King has run out of patience, and announces that he will prorogue Parliament in eight days. Whereupon, the Commons responds immediately: it will give £180,000 annually, not a penny more to be offered, with £40,000 each for the loss of wardships and purveyance, and a further £100,000 for other matters.

Salisbury rides out to his old family home of Theobalds, now a favourite residence of the King, to consult with His Majesty, and returns with a demand of £200,000, which the Commons accepts. A few days later, he has secured the assent of the Lords as well. After all his long endeavours, this is a triumph.

63

WESTMINSTER, SPRING 1610

From his place on the bench of Common Pleas, a few dozen yards from the Chamber of the Commons, Chief Justice Coke sees all this activity.

He sees the Members of Parliament making their way through the great North Door and down the length of Westminster Hall: those from the shires walking slowly and with dignity, those from the boroughs in a chatter, the great figures alert against importuners, men with dogs, shops and stalls, clerks scuttling back and forth, the occasional halloo against a cutpurse. He sees the thrust and jostle of it all, and feels his loss that he is no longer part of it.

Edward Coke retains many friends in Parliament, and through them he is aware of the happenings, the plots and counterplots, the subterfuges and stratagems that fill the stuffy, crowded chapel of the Commons. And though the minds of men are turned to Salisbury's Contract now, yet there are other matters here to which Coke must attend.

In March, the King had opened the new session of Parliament with a speech that was pregnant with meaning and purpose.

In His Majesty's mind, the words he speaks are a work of grace made still more gracious by reason of his Highness, as he rarely fails to remind his auditors. But he does not stand upon his grace: it is his duty to explain it. He wants, he will have, that supply of treasure from the Commons. But he will have it on his own terms, and will not spare to discourse on other matters of import.

The state of monarchy is the supremest thing upon Earth, he says to the assembled men of Parliament. For Kings are not only God's lieutenants upon Earth, and sit upon God's throne, but even by God himself they are called Gods. They make and unmake their subjects; they have power of raising, and casting down; of life, and of death: judges over all their subjects and in all causes, and yet accountable to none but God only. They have power to exalt low things, and abase high things, and make of their subjects like men at the chess; a pawn to take a bishop or a knight, and to cry up, or down any of their subjects, as they do their money.

This is familiar ground, such as few common lawyers can imbibe without dilution. And so dilution there is, in the King's gracious concession of the divine to the temporal.

For how soon kingdoms began to be settled in civility and policy, James says, then did Kings set down their minds by laws, which are properly made by the King only. And so the King came to be *lex loquens*, the law itself in speech, after a sort, binding himself by a double oath to the observation of the fundamental laws of his kingdom; tacitly, as by being a king, and expressly, by his oath at his coronation… Therefore all Kings that are not tyrants, or perjured, will be glad to bind themselves within the limits of their laws; and they that persuade them the contrary, are vipers, and pests, both against them and the Commonwealth.

But now the King takes a different turn, to consider the law itself, and the law courts.

The other branch of this, he says, is concerning the common law, being concerned by some, that I condemned it, and preferred the civil law thereunto. As a king, I have least cause of any man to dislike the common law. For no law can be more favourable and advantageous for a king, and extendeth further his prerogative, than it doth; and for a king of England to despise the common law, it is to neglect his own Crown.

It is true, James goes on, that I do greatly esteem the civil law, the profession thereof serving more for general learning, and being most necessary for matters of treaty with all foreign nations... My meaning therefore is not to prefer the civil law before the common law; but only that it should not be extinguished, and yet so bounded to such courts and causes as have been in ancient use.

Nay, I am so far from disallowing the common law, as I protest, that if it were in my hand to choose a new law for this kingdom, I would not only prefer it before any other national law, but even before the very judicial law of Moses... As for example, if the law of hanging for theft were turned here to restitution of treble or quadruple, as it was in the law of Moses, what would become of all the middle shires, and all the Irishry and Highlanders?

Irishry and Highlanders? The King's mind is surely wandering. Yet, as he continues to speak, his meaning starts to become clearer to his audience. He is watering the roots of the common law, that he may prune the trunk the harder.

Yet in another respect, he says, both our law and all laws else are far inferior to that judicial law of God. And therefore I could wish some three things specially to be purged and cleared in the common law.

First, I could wish that it were written in our vulgar language: for now it is in an old, mixed and corrupt language, only understood by lawyers; whereas every subject ought to understand the law under which he lives.

Next, our common law hath not a settled text in all cases, being chiefly grounded either upon old customs, or else upon the reports and cases of judges, which ye call *responsa prudentium*, responses of the wise. But though it be true, that no text of law can be so certain, wherein the circumstances will not make a variation in the case – for in this age, there are so many doctors that comment upon the text, and never one agrees with another – yet could I wish that some more certainty were set down in this case by Parliament.

For since the very reports themselves are not always so binding, he goes on, it were good, that upon a mature deliberation, the exposition of the law were set down by Act of Parliament, and such reports therein confirmed, as were thought fit to serve for law in all times hereafter, and so the people should not depend upon the bare opinions of judges, and uncertain reports.

And lastly, the King says, there be in the common law diverse contrary reports, and precedents; and this corruption doth likewise concern the Statutes and Acts of Parliament. And therefore would I wish both those Statutes and Reports, as well in the Parliament as common law, to be once maturely reviewed, and reconciled, and all contrarieties should be scraped out of our books.

The King says much else, notably on the excessive use of writs of prohibition. But this is enough. On its face, this is a reforming speech, and Edward Coke is no enemy to gentle reformation in the law. How could he be, with so many cases lying in the many courts, and the High Commission and Chancery both exceeding their proper limits and encroaching on the courts of common law?

Yet the speech cuts against so much that Coke holds dear: the use of law French, in which the fine detail of the law books, the maxims, moots and readings is couched; the old reports, on which he has so deeply drawn himself; the diversity and depth of precedents, each capturing some moment of judgment, of decision, of application of law to circumstance, the whole amounting to a vast mass of intricate thought, an artificial reason which it is the judge's task to gather, separate and explicate. For reason, as he likes to say, is the life of the law.

To seek to codify this, to trap this multiform diversity, this inherited wisdom, this reason of the law in a statute is a thing nigh impossible to do. Under cover of the language of reformation, it is an erasure, an abolition of history, only to be undertaken for compelling cause and under pain of the utmost care. Once begun, there is no limit to which it might not go, even to Magna Carta, confirmed thirty times and more by successive Kings in Parliament, from which so much else derives.

This is no gently reforming speech, Coke thinks. The King is like a child: he will not be still, he wants everything at once, he has an absolute desire for power and he hates any rules to bind him. Here he would set up an ideal of the law as an unchanging commandment, his own commandment to serve as a bed of Procrustes against which men's cases must be judged, rather than understand it as the nurturing tree it is; a tree that grows every day a little more, and sustains life amid its enfolding branches.

But there is something else. As Coke reviews the King's words, he cannot but see them as aimed at his own person.

There is the suggestion, mischievous to him, that the common law must ever be friend to the prerogative… the questioning of the settled practice of the courts… the subtle undermining of the status of the judges, and of law reports… the deliberate conflation of reform of statutes with consolidation of the common law… the protestation that the courts should know their boundaries, and prohibitions be restrained. No Parliament man could hear these things and be in doubt as to who is their main target.

Yet there is something here that even Coke does not see. A man more attuned to the shadows of politics might detect another animating power here in operation.

Working behind and between the King's words, a second mind… one skilled in the law, a friend to the codes of civil law, adept in counsel, allied to an eloquent and persuasive tongue. The mind of Francis Bacon.

64

YORK HOUSE, SUMMER 1610

The King's speech is something to ponder. But by itself it cannot explain Coke's growing sense of disquiet; his feeling that somehow the walls of his existence are starting to close in on him.

Though he would be the last to admit it, Coke has found the past two years far from easy. To be in open conflict with the King at York House was bad enough, but his disagreement with the Archbishop over prohibitions has also continued, so that Coke feels like a man caught up in a dance. Some stately pavane, perhaps, back and forth, in which every advancing step is followed by rebuff and retreat.

The February previous, that of 1609, Coke had been summoned by the King to explain fifty or sixty writs of prohibition he had issued against the court of the Lord President of York; summoned personally, no other judges being there, and Coke to be questioned in the presence of Lord Chancellor Ellesmere, Lord Treasurer Salisbury, the Lord Privy Seal, the Lord Chamberlain, the Archbishop of Canterbury and others.

These writs are fast becoming a Privy Council matter, he had noted, not without a glint of satisfaction.

The conference was unexpected, and Coke had had little time to prepare. But even so, he was able to take the King through the facts in several leading cases. In one, the suit was begun as a means to avoid paying the King a fine of £200 that would be due at common law; the prohibition prevented this stratagem, and removed the case to the common law court for judgment. There is a satisfying grunt of assent at this monstrosity from His Majesty.

In other cases, he had the pleasure of hearing the Lord Chancellor say 'This is good law.' And Coke did not shrink from saying plainly that the President and Council in York are not learned in the law, yet may make judgments and deny reliefs without appeal and remedy, which is contrary to law and not to be found in the King's courts.

It is the same point for which the King nearly struck him at York House; yet here Coke's command of law and quality of judgment were so evident that the King came away well pleased.

Then, in May of that year, Ellesmere had called together a further conference at York House on the matter of writs of prohibition, and pressed Coke to produce precedents that the King might review them. Over three days, Coke and his common law brethren were examined as to prohibition on certain tithes, the tenth parts of a man's income levied as taxes. The Church has a jurisdiction here, but there are cases of variant or wrongful tithing which the judges insist are to be tried not by Church courts but by jury according to immemorial custom and common law.

The case for the Church was argued by the King's law officers, Attorney Hobart, Solicitor Bacon and another junior, and Coke swiftly drew His Majesty's attention to this fact.

As Coke said, the judges have been called not to frame or devise new laws, but to inform your Majesty what your law of England is, and therefore it was never seen before, that when the question is of the law, that your judges of the law have been made disputants with those who are inferior to them, who day by day plead before them at their several courts at Westminster... your Majesty detesting novelties and innovations, we leave it to your Grace and princely consideration, whether your Majesty will permit our answering.

The King had bidden them all continue, but by the end of the third day His Majesty was evidently bored and tired, and he referred the matter back to the judges. Coke was told to write a further justification, which he did. And, after an interval, again the flow of prohibitions resumed from Chief Justice Coke and the Court of Common Pleas.

Advance, retreat, advance, retreat; so the pavane continues. But even for a man of Coke's formidable energy, these movements have been a drain and a distraction.

This matter of prohibitions on which he fights the Church is no small affair. It is to restrain the ecclesiastical courts from usurping the role and duties of the common law, to prevent them from incriminating any man on the vague and general oath *ex officio*, according to the ancient legal principle *nemo tenetur se ipsum prodere*, that no man should be brought to foreswear himself, and to stop the Church's High Commission from exercising any power to arrest men by warrant, or to send its pursuivants and warrant officers to break into men's homes, rifling all corners and secret custodies, as in cases of high treason.

These are not the debating points of scholars; they are powers that would control the life of every man, in his business and his bedchamber. And as Coke is apt to say, *domus sua cuique est tutissimum refugium*: a man's home is his castle.

65

WESTMINSTER, AUTUMN 1610

He that should search all glories of the gown,
And steps of all rais'd servants of the Crown
He could not find, than thee of all that store
Whom Fortune aided less, or virtue more,
Such, Coke, were thy beginnings, when thy good
In others evil best was understood:
When, being the stranger's help, the poor man's aide,
Thy just defences made th'oppressor afraid.

And still the walls seem to draw in ever closer to Chief Justice Coke.

For the contest with the High Commission is just one among many in which he is presently engaged. That with the Council of the Marches still endures. There is, too, a continuing dispute with the Court of Requests. The Requests was once the refuge of the poor seeking justice, but would now ape the Court of Chancery and grant men relief after a case has already received judgment in the Court of Common Pleas. Coke has no doubt that this is contrary to law.

Then there is the serious matter of proclamations. In recent years the King has grown fond of them, that is plain. He has published edicts on a host of matters such as grain, the use of the forests and timber, foreign trade, the control of piracy, new buildings in London, the production of starch and the oath of allegiance. The printing of them must have doubled or more in number; many more messengers are needed to carry them about the countryside than in the old Queen's time.

But are they good law? May the King make new law by his proclamation? Many common lawyers doubt it, and there are many of those in Parliament. They will not let the matter go away.

The Commons issues a Petition of Grievances to the King, an extensive document with nine counts elaborated, saying that there is nothing that they have accounted more dear and precious than to be guided and governed by the certain rule of the law... Out of this root hath grown that indubitable right of the people of this kingdom not to be made subject to any punishments that shall extend to their lives, lands, bodies or goods, other than such as are ordained by the common laws of this land, or the statutes made by their common consent in Parliament.

Proclamations are not statutes made by common consent in Parliament; no, they are a very different thing. Nevertheless, the Petition continues, it is apparent both that proclamations have been made of late years much more frequent than heretofore, and that they are extended not only to the liberty, but also to the goods, inheritances and livelihood of men... By reason whereof there is a general fear conceived and spread amongst your Majesty's people, that proclamations will by degrees grow up and increase to the strength and nature of laws, whereby not only that ancient happiness and freedom will be much blemished, if not quite taken away... but the same may also bring a new form of arbitrary government upon this realm.

Now the King wants to discuss the matter of proclamations with the judges, but within his Privy Council. That should help to discipline them, he thinks.

So it comes about that in September 1610 Edward Coke is again summoned at short notice to a conference with the Council. At issue are two questions: first, if the King by his proclamation may prohibit the construction of new buildings in and about London; and second, if the King may prohibit men from making starch, which is so widely used in the manufacture of ruffs and collars.

Alongside Attorney Hobart and the Recorder, Solicitor General Bacon is also present, as an Officer of the Crown.

'So, Chief Justice, the question comes to this: whether the King may use his power of proclamation to forbid or control these matters, on which the Commons have petitioned His Majesty.'

The speaker is Lord Treasurer Salisbury, friend to both sides. The matter is of great importance to him, for proclamations have shown themselves a swift route to new sources of royal revenue.

Coke replies with caution and humility. 'My Lord, these questions are of great importance, and the more since they concern the answer of the King to the Commons of the House of Parliament. I did not hear of them until this morning at nine of the clock, for the grievances were preferred, and the answer to them made by His Majesty, when I was travelling in my circuit.

'Moreover, both these proclamations were promulgated in the fifth year of His Majesty's reign, after my time of Attorneyship. For these reasons I do humbly desire you that I might have conference with my brethren the judges about the answer of the King, then to make an advised answer according to law and reason.'

'Come now, Sir Edward.' It is Ellesmere, playing the Cheshire man, bluff but not unfriendly. 'Let there be no delay, for every precedent has first a commencement. The duty of the judges is to maintain the power and prerogative of the King, who is the source of all our law.'

Ellesmere continues, 'In cases where there is no authority and precedent, the judges must needs leave to the King to order things according to his wisdom, and for the good of his subjects. Otherwise the King will be no more than the Duke of Venice! And so much restrained in his prerogative, that the bonds of it will be broken.'

The Earl of Northampton adds, gravely, 'The physician is not always bound to a precedent, but to apply his medicine according to the quality of the disease.'

There are nods of assent around the table. The Councillors are used to these pleas for consultation by Coke, and they are desirous of action. The other judges will follow the Chief Justice; let him now confirm the King's prerogative right in this matter of proclamations, so that the Council may proceed to other business.

Again, however, Coke will not be moved. 'True it is,' he says, 'that every precedent hath a commencement. But when authority and precedent is wanting, there is need of great consideration, before that any thing of novelty shall be established, and to provide that this be not against the law of the land.

'Tis long held that the King cannot change any part of the common law, nor create any offence by his proclamation, that was not an offence before, without Parliament. But at this time I only desire to have time of consideration and conference with my brothers, for *deliberandum est diu, quod statuendum est semel*, what is laid down once requireth long consideration.'

All eyes turn to the King, who does not look pleased. But now comes the mellifluous voice of the Solicitor General. The words are sweet, but the intent is deadly. He is doing what few dare to do: he would challenge the Chief Justice on the law itself.

'But Sir Edward,' says Francis Bacon, 'Permit me to say I do not understand your reasoning. Diverse sentences have been given in the Star Chamber upon the proclamation against building. Indeed, have not you yourself given sentence in cases, defending this proclamation? Did you not have the precedents then in mind when you defended it?'

This is a knife fight, Coke thinks: Ellesmere is sending his lackey-boy Bacon in again to do his work. Again, he is being questioned before the King by an inferior, in defiance of established custom. But he is not to be turned. 'No, Master Solicitor,' he replies carefully. 'Precedents must be seen, considered and discussed in conference with my brethren, for that *melius est recurrere, quam male currere*, it is better to run back than to run astray.

'Perhaps I may remind you', he adds, 'that the form of indictment concludes that a man be charged for an offence *contra leges et statuta*, against the laws and statutes. But I never heard an indictment to conclude, *contra regiam proclamationem*, against the proclamation of the King.'

Bacon has been silenced. The Council can make no further progress with the Chief Justice. He and the Chief Justice of King's Bench, and therewith Chief Baron Tanfield and Baron Altham of the Court of Exchequer, are appointed to have consideration of the question. Some weeks later, they return with their considered and collective view. Having scrutinised the law books, Coke announces, they find diverse precedents of proclamations which are utterly against law and reason, and so void; for whatever is brought in contrary to the reason of the law ought not to be treated as consequential.

They place some sugar at the cup's edge for the King, saying that where proclamations are lawfully made, the King's prohibition will aggravate the offence that may be afterwards committed. But otherwise it is as wormwood for His Majesty, for the judges repeat that the King by his proclamation, or other ways, cannot change any part of the common law, or statute law, or the customs of the realm, the three parts into which the law of England is divided; nor may he impeach any man by this means in his inheritance, goods, body or life. By his proclamation he cannot create any offence which was not an offence before, for then he may alter the law of the land by his proclamation in a high point; and upon the creation of an offence ensues fine and imprisonment.

In all, it was resolved by the judges, Coke says, that *the King hath no prerogative, but that which the law of the land allows him.*

This is not a resolution fit to please His Majesty. But, again, there the matter lies. It has been rendered not as a judgment in a court of law, but upon examination in the Privy Council, and privy it remains. It sets no precedent of case decided. No man outside the Council may hear of it, and though the King issues no more proclamations for a period, he does not end his use of them.

Yet, Coke notes proudly, following this resolution no proclamation imposing fine and imprisonment was afterwards made. As is his way, he makes a note of the matter, perhaps for some future volume of *Reports*.

What then does all this matter? What do all these writs and conferences, cases and judgments have in common? What is the thread of thought that ties them all together?

Coke need not even entertain such questions, for the answer is evident to the lowliest novice that ever took a yearbook to hand in his old haunts of Clifford's Inn. These matters all go to the royal prerogative. Shall the ecclesiastical courts imprison a man, shall the Court of the Lord President of York tax a man of a tenth of his income, without proper process of law? Shall the Court of Requests, even Chancery itself, issue decrees after judgment in a common law court, decrees against which there is no appeal, and so no remedy?

Shall a king make law in his own person, or levy fine and punishment, without the consent of Parliament?

But that is not an end of the questions. For if the King may not, if these things be against the law, then what law do they break, when law itself comes through the King from God? If they break the law, shall they then be stopped? And who, or what, shall stop them?

Even to frame these thoughts is sedition. There no man may go.

66

PARLIAMENT, DECEMBER 1610

And now it is back to politics, and the Chamber of the House of Commons. For many months the Earl of Salisbury has moved ceaselessly back and forth between the King, the Lords and the Commons, encouraging, persuading, counselling, trading the terms of his Great Contract to repair the Exchequer.

Salisbury had ridden away from the King at Theobalds that past July in high spirits, an agreement for £200,000 in his satchel. His purpose has always been to construct a great bridge to join the gap between the two sides, King and Commons. Once that is completed, he knows, it will bring further commerce between them, and even perhaps a measure of amity restored. How had Francis Bacon responded for the Commons to His Majesty? He described their grievances as *gemitus columbae*, the mourning of a dove, with that patience and humility of heart which appertained to loving and loyal subjects. Let it be so.

Salisbury's heart was further lifted by the prospect of the long vacation. Parliament would not sit now till October, and that is three months in which he may snatch some repose, and three months in which the Members can reflect on what they have achieved.

For, they may console themselves, has not His Majesty agreed to make no more impositions without consent of Parliament? Have they not granted such a revenue on conditions, that the Court of Wards be dissolved, that abuses of purveyance be taken away, that His Majesty pursue no old debts or claims to land more than threescore years out of his possession? As for the King, he may look forward to an easing of his present difficulties, and new sources of treasure and patronage.

Yet when Parliament reassembles, Salisbury quickly learns that the converse has happened. Far from being reinforced, or even standing firm, the two sides have moved apart.

The Members in the Commons fret at how little has been achieved; there is no removal of the present impositions, and of the King's speech, the rest is air. Three months of talk with local people in towns and taverns far from Westminster have driven home a simple question: how is this vast new royal revenue to be paid for? And another: if it be paid, if the King receive a standing grant of such a magnitude, then what need of parliaments?

The Lords say little, but send private warnings to the King. As for the King himself, he will yield nothing but out of his grace. He complains that he feels a loss of powers; even this new revenue will not mend his debts, and it will give but a temporary respite.

Now in desperate worry, Salisbury hastens again between the parties, but to no avail. In November, the King writes to lay out his message to the House of Lords, saying that His Highness wisheth your Lordships to call to mind that he hath now had patience with this assembly these seven years, and from them received more disgraces, censures, and ignominies, than ever Prince did endure. He followed your Lordships' advices in having patience, hoping for better issue. He cannot have asinine patience... For his part he is resolved, though now at their next meeting they would give him supply were it never so large, and sauce it with such taunts and disgraces as have been uttered of him and of those that appertain to him... nay though it were another kingdom, he will not accept it.

Finally, the King sends a message through the Speaker, saying that it was never his intention to proceed with the Contract, except his debts be paid, and though it will not be enough, he expects to receive £500,000 to that purpose.

It is a mortal blow. The Commons erupts in anger and passes a unanimous resolution not to proceed on these conditions. Himself in grave discontent, the King prorogues the Parliament at Christmastime, and then dissolves it in the spring.

Salisbury's Great Contract lies in ruins. Nothing has been gained for the King. In place of amity, the air is thick with mutual recrimination. Salisbury ruefully acknowledges the fact, saying that I have seen this parliament to an end, whereof the many vexations have so overtaken one another as I know not to what to resemble them so well as to the plagues of Job.

The King writes to him, that your greatest error hath been that ye ever expected to draw honey out of gall, being a little blinded with the self-love of your own counsel in holding together of this parliament, whereof all men were despaired (as I have oft told you) but yourself alone. The tone is friendly, and James still calls him my little beagle, as he was wont to do. But for counsel he starts to turn away to others, to the Earl of Northampton, as Henry Howard has become, and the Earls of Suffolk and Shrewsbury.

Francis Bacon watches all this with care. He has been closely involved throughout this sorry episode, and to him has fallen the duty of responding for the Commons on occasion to His Majesty. He has fought for Salisbury's Great Contract, and, when that failed, for a subsidy; and suffered the double indignity of seeing a motion made, and made by his own half-brother Sir Nathaniel Bacon, that unless the Contract proceeded the Commons would grant no supply of revenue. All these things are matters for dismay.

Yet Francis is not dismayed by them. Nor is he dismayed by the damage done to his cousin Salisbury, who has taken to his bed with illness and exhaustion. It is a rare man that can see the failure of a rival without rejoicing. Cousin Robert, like his father Burghley, hath ever professed his love for me, he thinks, but hath rarely shown it. Meanwhile he would succour and support men such as Coke, that regularly oppose the King.

So this adversity of fortune may do his cousin some good, and recall him to his friends. But if it do not, if fortune do his cousin down, well, that may be no bad thing either. For there are other men that rise, such as Sir Robert Carr, the King's new favourite, and with change cometh chance and opportunity.

67

GORHAMBURY, SPRING 1611

ap tap tap. Tap tap tap.
The masons have a shed set up in front of the stables, which they use as a workshop. But on a balmy day in April they are much happier to ply their trade outside. The local clunch stone is pleasing to the eye, and his father had used it within the house, but it does not weather well. So Francis has sent for stone from the isle of Portland in Dorset. The cost is excessive, but it is the best of its kind, and for the rebuilding of Gorhambury there can be no sparing of expense. He can well afford it, and he wants it badly.

With the masons has come an ever-changing throng of other craftsmen. Tilemakers led by Signor Belletti, a Florentine now established in London, glaziers from the Weald under Mr Tyzack, some of the younger ones still speaking the French of their birthplace, plasterers, joiners, carpenters, plumbers, painters, brickmen and paviors, smiths for the ironwork, leadmen for the gutters and water works. There will be twenty-three men and women employed about the gardens alone over the spring and summer months, and that is to say nothing of the orchardmen, sawyers and treemen and husbanders in the park.

Tap tap tap. Tap tap tap.
To split a block of Portland stone, you must find the bed lines, the grain of it. Then run a chisel along the length at the top, and strike it evenly at each point.

His mother Lady Bacon had died at last the previous August.

Francis brought Mr Fenton up from Gray's Inn to preach a last sermon for her, and had her buried in the churchyard at St Michael's close by. The old woman departed in her ninth decade. In her later years she had at last become quiet, the great vaults of her learning emptied out by time; her voice, her clarity of judgement gone. But, thinks Francis, see it for all in all, I have taken as much from her as from my father, and more from them than any other.

There was no money at the end, the old servants had died, the new ones did what they could, and the estate grew ever more wild. There were plants that sprung from the rooftops, shrubs untended, green mould along the marble facings. The courts were overgrown, and the western tower reeked from the occupation of bats. His father's Italian statues had been fouled by birds, and birds nested in the chimneys and even behind the statue of King Henry VIII in the cloister. And what Francis especially could not bear: some of the stained glass was broken, and the colours faded on the frescoes, and on the family coats of arms around the house.

But now all is changed. Thanks to his marriage, the fees from his position and his Star Chamber income, for two years now the gold has flowed like a river, and Francis loves to splash in it, and to drench others. He has long planned for this moment, and for the first time he has a free hand. Let others see what he makes of it!

First he thought to make the house new again, before directing himself to the other great works he has sketched: the water gardens, the island, the grotto. But when it comes to it, he cannot bear delay. The men are here, they cannot be left idle, he loves to see them work, so let them work. He has always admired the terraces above the gardens at Kenilworth, and visited them when the Earl of Leicester was in his pomp and bidding for the Queen's favour, so let there be elevated walks and streams beneath at Gorhambury. He can pay for it, pay for it all, with more left over for local works, and he did not miss the opportunity at his mother's funeral to make a donative to the church, for a new font and pulpit, and other works. He is a rich man now.

As for Alice, she has become a young woman of nearly eighteen, and she has grown up in the married state. Her husband is not everything he might be to her, she knows, but there is affection as well as respect between them. He has treated her well, and he has more than discharged the promise of their walk that day in the garden before their marriage.

She has the use of a coach and four, and the stables are filling rapidly with new geldings. She has draperies, cashmere from Paris, garments of silk and wool whose quality would make her mercer forebears weep with joy. She has new silver at her table, and by some miracle her steward in London has found a superb set of glasses from Murano to accompany them, something not to be had these days at any price. Jewels from her husband pour into her lap. The estate is filled with working men and women, and if she is not quite mistress of the house and able to direct them, yet she will be with time.

Tap tap tap. Tap tap tap.

The strike of the hammer must be firm but light. Too strong, and the mason loses control; the stone may splinter, or crack across the grain.

Because the breath of flowers is far sweeter in the air than in the hand, Francis says, the gardens have been replanted with flowers that do best perfume the air: the violet, most of all the white double violet that comes twice a year, musk roses, sweet briar, wall flowers, pinks and honeysuckles. He has had tulips, fritillaries and jonquils imported from Delft and Haarlem in the low countries, cherry and black mulberry trees. Every meal at Gorhambury sees the table strewn with scented herbs and flowers. There are red and white wines from France, Rhenish whites, sack, malmsey, hippocras and muscatel. The house is filled with music, and when Sir Francis and Lady Bacon entertain, as they do more and more now, it is like a royal banquet.

As Francis says, the mind languishes that is not sometimes spirited up by excess. But he knows himself too well not to be aware of other alterations that have taken place, alterations not of his life and possessions but of his soul. He had loved and reverenced his father, and been left grieving and friendless by his father's death. Now his mother's decease marks the loss of his last connection to the past: to her world, the world of the ancients, of piety and learning, and the world of his own golden youth betrayed.

He cannot forget what followed: his years of debt and despair, of promise unfulfilled and undischarged, of great projects ignored or passed over by others, of a young man desolate in his hopes.

But success brings its own costs. A man cannot ascend by virtue alone, that he knows; there must be vice in him as well, to give vigour to his virtue. And a mixture of a lie with the truth doth ever add pleasure. Dissembling has become a second nature over years to Francis Bacon; he knows it, he hates it, he rejoices in it, he cannot, he would, he will not escape it. He has learned to cast it like a cloak around his soul, and wear the mask of feigned courtesy.

So Gorhambury acts as his release. It is his privy domain, and with his golden treasure he is building a kingdom of glory and beauty. He need see no one, he need beg or plead with no one, he can act and feel and be exactly as he wishes. If the music of the virginals or the viol will please him, he has it. If he needs a new coat or doublet, he orders it. If he likes the curve of a young lad's back, he has the lad wait upon him.

I am a fallen man, he thinks. But I will rise by falling. I become closer to the Lord Chancellor, and His Majesty heeds my counsel ever more. As for Coke, three years ago his bond of service and respect with the King seemed all but indissoluble, he keeps close with Queen Anne… yet now the fissures are everywhere to be seen. Many notable men are discontented with him, for there is barely a court of law in England but that one of Sir Edward's prohibitions lies against it. Ellesmere stands against him, while Coke's protector Salisbury is surely losing ground.

Bancroft is recently dead, alas, but the new Archbishop, Abbot, is little better disposed than Bancroft ever was to Coke. Why, only the other day I caught a whisper in Whitehall that Coke would be replaced. Every time he is bidden to appear before the Council, and I to question him, he falls in dignity and I do rise.

And the King? The royal regard for Coke is still there, but His Majesty's love is like the sun, always in motion; it rises high at the noonday only to sink below the horizon at eve.

The King's patience is being tested again and again by the Chief Justice, who would curb the Church and fence the prerogative itself. Only a few months ago there was the case of Dr Bonham, wherein Coke had the temerity to remark that in many cases the common law doth control Acts of Parliament and sometimes shall adjudge them to be void, a statement many deem out of sorts with our law and fit to please neither Commons nor King. As at York House, as in the Council, the King was angered at this presumptuous speech. How long can it continue?

Tap tap tap.

The mason cannot know how long his chisel is needed. He simply works the stone from every direction, and listens for the single hollow sound that signifies the fracture within.

Attend, attend, ply the chisel, and the stone will split of itself, and fall apart.

68

LAMBETH PALACE, OCTOBER 1611

No sooner has Parliament been dissolved than new writs of prohibition issue from the Court of Common Pleas, each in the name of the Chief Justice. It is almost as though Coke deliberately seeks to affront His Majesty.

The King writes to Salisbury that these writs are of a nature extraordinary, and showing more the perverseness of his spirit than any other prohibitions, and his private secretary hints that the King will dismiss Coke and no longer be vexed with him. What to do? Coke's eminence in the law is without rival. His judgments have won him national renown and a huge following of admirers in the House of Commons.

George Abbot has been installed as Archbishop of Canterbury, successor to Bancroft, and he too will have none of this nonsense, which is fit to undermine the very foundations of the Church. He has but newly taken office when his allies the civil lawyers petition the King directly, calling on His Majesty to set bounds to the Court of Common Pleas.

Coke replies to the petition and is summoned yet again to the Privy Council to account for the writs and defend his views, which takes two long days. It is, he says, the first time that ever any judges of the realm have been questioned for delivering their opinions in matter of law according to their consciences in public and solemn arguments.

The Chief Justice is not to be bested in the law, nor cowed by examination in the Council, that much is clear. But then the King, advised by Ellesmere, sees a new way forward: a means by which to sustain his prerogative and have his way with this recalcitrant man. In July he announces that he intends to reform the High Commission, and thereby to reduce it to certain spiritual causes. There will be new letters patent, and Salisbury is expectant as to the changes.

But when the letters are published, it is seen that Coke has himself been named as a Commissioner. That is a source of rumour indeed. Will he accept his King's command and join his opponents? Or spurn the Commission and defy the King?

So it is that on a Thursday in October a vast flood, a swelling bore of dignified and notable men comes up the river from Westminster to sit in the Great Chamber of the Archbishop's palace at Lambeth. The Chief Justices, the Barons of the Exchequer, other Justices, all the Lords of the Council, Bishops, Deans and Doctors of the canon and civil laws, as well as the Attorney and Solicitor General. Ninety-two in all, larger than any court or council save for Parliament itself.

Arrayed beneath the hammer beams of the roof, with the autumn sun streaming through the high windows, they make a sea of scarlet and black, of lawn surplices and coifs, of ruffs and golden chains and miniver.

The intent is clear. It has been framed by the Archbishop and is pleasing to the King. Ellesmere supports it, Salisbury is willing. The Commissioners will be convened and sworn in, and they will then proceed immediately to try a chosen list of enormous crimes. No man can doubt that enormities lie within the jurisdiction of the High Commission, for has not Coke himself stated that it is so?

But in so acting they will join, all in all, across Church and state, all branches of the law, in affirmation of the new Commission, of its powers and competence, and of the discharge through it of the

King's prerogative right. This must surely tie the hands of the Chief Justice of Common Pleas. It is a moment Abbot has been eagerly awaiting; the moment when he accomplishes what Bancroft could not, quells this damnable court and establishes the legal authority of the Church in its full purview once again.

Yet at the very start there is a difficulty. All are commanded to sit, but Coke will not. Others take their seats, but the Chief Justice remains standing. It is an offence and an embarrassment. Coke is nearly sixty now, still upright and clear of eye, but thinner than he was. There is yet more grey in his beard, and under his cap his forehead has become more prominent with time. Now the eyes of all are upon him.

After a few moments, Lord Treasurer Salisbury comes over and seeks to persuade him to be seated, that they may proceed, but Coke refuses. He explains that the commandment to sit comes by force of the commission made, and neither he nor any of his common law brethren is acquainted with that document, though he notes pointedly that it appears the judges of King's Bench have seen it.

He has endeavoured to inform himself of it, he says, and sent for a copy to the Rolls, but it has not been enrolled. But without such knowledge, no judge can execute a commission with a good conscience, and if what they are instructed to do be against the law, they ought not to sit by virtue of it. Besides, there are other judges present who have read and perhaps advised as to the commission, so there is not any necessity that he should be there.

Coke has not raised his voice to say this, but he has not needed to, for the Great Chamber is utterly still, and all are straining to hear the words. There is whispering among the Barons and the Justices of King's Bench, as though to show their support, while Salisbury confers in private with the Archbishop. Abbot cannot conceal his anger at the interruption and delay. They have a bill of cases to be tried, heresy and incest and the like, and must move to business.

But all know they cannot do so with Coke still standing, for that would throw the whole proceeding into doubt. So eventually, with an ill grace, Abbot causes the commission to be read out, all the three great skins of parchment of it, and as they hear its terms the judges rejoice in their hearts that they will not sit by its force, for there are diverse points at which it contradicts the laws and statutes of England.

The reading has taken much time, and still more time is consumed when Coke insists on reading and considering the oath of supremacy and allegiance which they are bidden to swear. But eventually he and the other judges swear it. Then and only then may the business of the day begin. The Archbishop makes an opening oration, in commendation of the care and providence of the King, and for the peace and quiet of the Church, and he instructs the Commissioners as to their duties, to try enormous crimes and thereby to prevent heresy and schism in the Church. Then he produces a most blasphemous heretic, and then another, to show to all present the necessity of their work.

Coke has remained standing throughout all this, the reading, taking of oaths and the oration, and his brethren with him. Now the Archbishop approaches him and promises him a copy of the document, so that he may read and compare the new text with the old. The King has commanded the High Commission to convene regularly. But they do no business on that day, and Coke is not invited to sit on the High Commission again.

69

LONDON, 1611–12: THREE LETTERS

Francis ever works his chisel upon the stone. He had served the King diligently and well in Parliament during that difficult last year, when the Great Contract hung in the balance; advised on it, argued for it with the Lords in committee, defended it on the floor of the House of Commons, when many were remonstrating over impositions and purveyance. Such service deserves to be recognised.

But the King's mind, while an iron trap for the memory of slights and indignities received, is slippery over favours owed. It is well to remind him, and remind him again.

Hobart, the Attorney General, has not been well. Weeks have passed since he has sent word that he can do no business; the Inns are full of rumours that he may not survive. It is an opportunity.

The Earl of Salisbury is not, perhaps, the man to advance matters of such delicacy and dispatch. So Francis writes directly to the King, that It may please your Majesty, your great and princely favours towards me in advancing me to place, and that which is to me of no less comfort, your Majesty's benign and gracious acceptation from time to time of my poor services, much above the merit and value of them, hath almost brought me to an opinion, that I may sooner perchance be wanting to myself in not asking, than find your Majesty's goodness wanting to me in any of my reasonable and modest desires.

The style is Asiatic, the language folded, as his mother might say. Now it starts to unfold.

Francis says, And therefore perceiving how at this time

preferments of the law fly about mine ears, to some above me and to some below me, I did conceive your Majesty may think it rather a kind of dullness, or want of faith, than modesty, if I should not come with my pitcher to Jacob's well, as others do. Wherein I shall propound to your Majesty that which tendeth not so much to the raising of my fortune, as to the settling of my mind: being sometimes assailed with this cogitation, that I may *in fine dierum*, at the end of my days, be in danger to be neglected and forgotten.

If he is to be neglected and forgotten, deprived of outward ornaments and inward comforts, then so be it, he adds. He can endeavour to do the King some honour by his pen.

But if not, Francis says, not to hold your Majesty long, my humble suit to you is that I may obtain your assurance to succeed (if I live) into the Attorney's place, whensoever it shall be void; it being but the natural and immediate step and rise which the place I now hold hath ever in a sort made claim to, and almost never failed of. In this suit I make no friends to your Majesty, but rely upon no other motive than your Grace; resting your Majesty's most humble subject and servant.

And when he next sees the King, His Majesty gives him that assurance.

Yet months later, nothing has changed. Hobart still lies sick on his bed, while his papers pile up and the Solicitor must carry the Government's business in the courts himself.

Surely Hobart cannot last long in this enfeebled state. It is time to freshen the King's mind on this matter. So Francis writes again, that It may please your most excellent Majesty, I do understand by some of my good friends, to my great comfort, that your Majesty hath in mind your Majesty's royal promise (which to me is *anchora spei*, the anchor of my hope), touching the Attorney's place.

I hope Mr Attorney shall do well. I thank God I wish no man's death; nor much mine own life, more than to do your Majesty service. For I account my life the accident, and my duty the substance. But this I will be bold to say; if it please God that I ever serve your Majesty in the Attorney's place, I have known an Attorney Coke, and an Attorney Hobart, both worthy men and far above myself: but if I should not find a middle way between their two dispositions and carriage, I should not satisfy myself.

Which is to say, if explanation were needed, that he can bring together the acumen of Coke with the mild temper of Hobart, both surely to the liking of His Majesty.

✿

In January 1612, at the time of the New Year, Francis takes the moment of an exchange of gifts to register his unflagging loyalty to Lord Treasurer Salisbury.

Hobart has now at last recovered. Francis has the King's promise of his succession as Attorney, and he wants Salisbury's good will to make it certain.

So he writes, It may please your good Lordship – I would entreat the new year to answer for the old, in my humble thanks to your Lordship, both for many your favours, and chiefly that upon the occasion of Mr Attorney's infirmity I found your Lordship even as I would wish. This doth increase a desire in me to express my thankful mind to your Lordship; hoping that though I find age and decays grow upon me, yet I may have a flash or two of spirit left to do you service. And I do protest before God, without compliment or any light vein of mind, that if I knew in what course of life to do you best service, I would take it, and make my thoughts, which now fly to many pieces, be reduced to that centre.

And I do protest before God, without compliment or any light vein of mind, that if I knew in what course of life to do you best service, I would take it. A very handsome tribute; yet it will prove an empty one. For by now Salisbury knows what Francis does not; that he is not far from death's door.

70

THE WEST COUNTRY, MAY 1612

I, that am rudely stamped and want love's majesty
To strut before a wanton ambling nymph;
I, that am curtailed of this fair proportion,
Cheated of feature by dissembling nature,
Deformed, unfinished, sent before my time
Into this breathing world scarce half made up,
And that so lamely and unfashionable
That dogs bark at me as I halt by them –
Why, I, in this weak piping time of peace,
Have no delight to pass away the time,
Unless to see my shadow in the sun
And descant on mine own deformity.

Salisbury had not been right for months. Fatigued, yes, and to the point of exhaustion; who would not be so after the endless travails of the Great Contract? Yet there was something else as well, in the background: a profound lethargy, a deep aching in the joints such as he had not felt in twenty and more years of service to the late Queen and her successor.

In his disappointment at the failure of the Contract, the King had dealt roughly with him for a little; it is evident His Majesty's attentions lie ever more with his new favourite, Sir Robert Carr, now created Viscount Rochester. Yet the King renews Salisbury's farm of the silk trade, worth £7,000 a year, and within weeks the

Lord Treasurer is back in his old place, handling the King's business as could none other. He does a brisk trade in the new hereditary knighthoods called Baronetcies, sold at something over a thousand pounds apiece and especially attractive to Catholics seeking to prove their loyalty to His Majesty. The serried ranks of petitioners look elsewhere for patronage, find little to satisfy them, and return to Salisbury. His is still the principal pen of the kingdom.

But then there is more pain. Sores start to break out on his body, and his breath becomes fetid and disgusting. By August 1611 he can disguise these symptoms no longer; the royal doctor, Sir Theodore Mayerne, is in attendance and diagnoses scurvy, for which he recommends a moderate diet and regular exercise. By year's end, however, Salisbury can feel the tumours that have grown in his stomach, liver and neck. Now his sores have multiplied, they have ulcerated, are weeping a filthy scabrous froth and must be dressed daily. He is tormented, in and out of fevers, and his whole body reeks with the stench of a continual putrid sweating. The papers pile up, he sends his clerks away unsatisfied. His servants do not know where to look or how to breathe safely in his presence.

The King and Queen Anne send jewels, and sweet delicacies to comfort him, but what are these to a man who can barely think or move in his agony? Nothing, not doctors, nor physic, nor all his carefully accumulated wealth and power, can save him now; of that he is sure.

In desperation he journeys to Bath in April to seek relief in its waters, stopping on the journey to stay with his friend Edward Coke and Lady Hatton at Stoke. On his return a few weeks later, accompanied by his doctors, Poe and Atkins, he is struck down again by fever. His coach is halted in Marlborough, and he is carried to an inn, where, gripping Dr Poe hard by the hand, sinking down without a groan or a struggle, he is finally claimed by death.

His body, now little more than a grey and pustule-ridden bag of bones, is borne back to his new palace at Hatfield, where, such is his care and foresight, he has redecorated the chapel in the high ornate style, and designed a magnificent tomb in the parish church.

Above, his effigy lies in state on a great black marble slab, clad in his Garter robes, the staff of the Lord Treasurer in his hand, the whole held up by womanly figures of the Cardinal virtues of Justice, Temperance, Fortitude and Prudence. Below, there is the likeness of his skeleton, laid out on a mat. It is high and low, alpha and omega, human aspiration raised up and brought to dust at the end by God's almighty power.

After more than fifty years, the *regnum cecilianum* is over. Like his father Lord Burghley, Salisbury has been Lord Treasurer, Secretary of State and Master of the Court of Wards; unlike his father, he has been them all in one. So great a presence, once removed, must leave a great absence.

His innermost circle is distracted with grief, and Edward Coke keenly feels the loss of his friend, ally and kinsman by marriage. The Earl of Pembroke and his circle are disconsolate. Even Sir Walter Raleigh, still under arrest in the Tower, recalls with sadness a last visit from a much diminished Salisbury, his former friend and foe.

Yet otherwise few tears are shed. The King, who had bewailed Salisbury's impending death, scarcely seems to notice the fact of it. The University of Cambridge cannot bring itself to mourn its late Chancellor, or even to put out a message of thanks and commemoration. Few of the gentlemen of Hertfordshire attend his funeral; and anger still smoulders among the poorer sort at his enclosure of Hatfield Wood in his estate.

Unlike his father Burghley, Salisbury has left no heir to power, no guardian of his reputation. His son William lacks the years, the stomach and the capability. Even during his lifetime the Earl was much abused in the taverns and on the streets; now the field is clear for the tattlers and defamers. God has paid him off with an agonising death for his treatment of Essex, they say. Justice has come to him who ensnared Fawkes and the Catholic martyrs with cunning and deceit.

Those who flattered his magnificence and generosity in life now denounce him in death for his corruption. He is *volpone*, the fox, a Judas come again, Robin Crooktback, a dissembling smooth-faced spider-shapen dwarf, a new Richard III. Men say *Here lies great Salisbury, though little of stature / A monster of mischief, ambitious of nature.* Verses proliferate. *He stank while he lived and died of the pox.* You can libel the dead, and they have no remedy.

Meanwhile the gossips of the court wax more lyrical than ever. The death of Salisbury has left a huge void, and ambitious men, like nature, have a *horror vacui*. Who will be the new Lord Treasurer, and who Secretary of State? Northampton? Surely not: the King needs agents, practical men, not scholars, and besides, is the Earl not a papist like his Howard kinsfolk? So, then, Rochester? The King loves him, so much is plain, but he is little more than a Scotch boy whose cheek has barely lost its downy covering; a youth better fitted for the privy chamber than the Privy Council. The Earl of Suffolk? Hero of the Armada, and beloved of the old Queen, he has long been a great courtier and statesman. He too is a Howard, for good or ill, and a papist. Whether he has a head for numbers, and a taste for the press of business, is another matter.

But if not Suffolk, then who? All are circling about the prize, anxious to triumph, desperate to stop their enemies. And for the first time in fifty years, there is no Cecil to give counsel to the monarch.

71

GORHAMBURY, SUMMER 1612

Francis sits in his gardens, watches the birds as they wheel and dive, and revolves these matters in his mind. He hesitates, gropes, smiles. A *garruling* of starlings… yes, that is good.

The birds in their pleasure make a continuous succession of shapes before him: an arrowhead, a mushroom, a snake, a whale. So it is in nature as a whole, Francis reflects, for nature every day offers change, but change which has a shape and order to it. This is God's creation, so it must have a meaning. It is the literature of our experience, built up from its own ABC or spelling book.

Yet how to read it? Like the civil law, he muses, God's literature needs interpretation, by some mind that can find its underlying principles. And like the laws of man, the laws of nature are only to be judged by their works, by what results. Whence it follows that the improvement of man's mind and the improvement of his fortunes are one and the same thing. What do the scriptures say? *By their fruits shall ye know them.*

There is more. Take that last particular instant. No bird is like a whale, but many together can have a whale's shape. None of them knows it, none intends or desires it. Perhaps all they want is to feed and to mate, and not to be eaten.

Are we humans not the same? Yes, and no. To feed, to mate, and not to be eaten; that is the sum of many men's desires, true enough. But men can know what shapes they make, can direct themselves and be directed to make new and better ones. That is the art of government. And as with natural philosophy, as with the practice of the courts, good government too may be reduced to rules and maxims. That he knows, that he will prove.

Coke has the will and talent to follow Salisbury, little doubt of that. But why should Francis not press his own cause? He has served abroad, in his youth. He knows the King's finances, and Parliament too, few better, and the way to salvation for the finances must lie through Parliament. He is son of the late Lord Keeper. So, why not Bacon for Secretary, or even Lord Treasurer? He would overleap Coke at a single bound.

Francis did not weep at the failure of the Great Contract, and he does not weep at Salisbury's death. To die so horribly, and at such a young age, must ever be a source of pity. Yet time has eaten up Francis's pity and his friendship. His mind goes back to that moment by the ponds, barely a mile from where he sits now, Anthony choked and lain on the ground, desperately gasping, grasping for any breath he can take, Robert Cecil standing over him.

But, on reflection, Francis can forgive his cousin that. What he cannot forgive is what follows: the torturous, dragging years in which Cecil and his father Burghley, with courtesy and precision, blocked the means of his own and Anthony's advancement. Beloved Anthony, so generous of soul, who had freely spent his patrimony in France as intelligencer and spy for Her Majesty; first sent at Burghley's instance, yet denied a place of honour and reward by Burghley on his return, plead though their mother did for him.

And as for Francis himself, the great schemes and ideals of his youth were steadily ignored by the father, while the son munched his way like a woodworm through state papers and books of record till he sat at the centre of the court's administration. Francis's own repeated applications for a position, as Attorney, as Solicitor, denied, his patron Essex cornered and thwarted till his own desperate rebellion ensued.

Fine words and flattery, malice and deception! Yes, these men granted Francis a few crumbs even as they amassed a vast store of riches; crumbs enough to keep him at bay, but not to free him from debt, or do honour to his wit and his imagination. And not even crumbs to Anthony, who died ignored, unhappy and alone before his time.

And now he, Francis, is but a little further advanced, and in his sixth decade. Even in death Salisbury has thwarted him, or so it seems; for Francis petitioned the King in May to be made Master of the Wards, which is a font of patronage and personal reward. He even wrote some pages of *Directions*, that the King might know how he would do the work... only for His Majesty to appoint Sir George Carey instead! A man of meagre capacity but much self-insinuation, and Francis forced to attend his entrance and hear a formal oration that is nothing but his own words parroted by another.

So much time wasted, so much left undone, so much yet to do.

No, Francis is not sad. He used to be a man of feeling. No longer; the grim decades have left their mark. They have bleached the warm colours of his feeling out of him, till nothing is left but a cold white attention to the means of his ascent. He can feign feeling, can write it down on paper, share the idea of it with servants, clerks, his readers, even with Alice. What he cannot do is feel it. Surely that will be enough?

Open dealing is a weakness of mind. *Qui nescit dissimulare, nescit pugnare.*

Now he considers the draft before him. It is a letter to His Majesty, written as he says not out of presumption but of affection. For of the one I was never noted and for the other I could never show it hitherto to the full; having been as a hawk tied to another's fist, that might sometimes bait and proffer but could never fly...

That hawk again. Too poetic, perhaps, too preening? He discards the draft, and writes instead of Salisbury that Your Majesty hath lost a great subject and a great servant. But if I should praise him in propriety, I should say that he was a fit man to keep things from growing worse, but no very fit man to make things to be much better. For he loved to have the eyes of all Israel a little too much upon himself, and to have all business still under the hammer and like clay in the hands of the potter, to mould it as he thought good; so that he was more *in operatione* than *in opere*, devoted to the making than to the result. And though he had fine passages of action, yet the real conclusions came slowly on.

But Francis also aspires to place himself. The King must come to see him not as Solicitor General but as his counsellor; a man not merely to advise him of the law, but of matters of state. So then, a few weeks later, Francis finds a way to put the question itself directly before the King, saying If your Majesty find any aptness in me, or if you find any scarcity in others, whereby you may think it fit for your service to remove me to business of state... I will be ready as a chessman to be wherever your Majesty's royal hand shall set me.

Francis has damned Salisbury in death to the King, damned him carefully, sparingly, as it seems in pity more than in anger. But this was merely a private condemnation. He comes to feel that something more is needed.

The dissolution of Parliament has been good to him, for it has given time for writing. Late in that year of 1612, he publishes a new and much expanded edition of his *Essays*. Among them are new writings *Of Death*, *Of Youth and Age*, *Of Beauty*, *Of Seeming Wise*, *Of Friendship*, *Of Fortune*, *Of Nobility*, *Of Riches*, *Of Cunning*, and others. Each is finely wrought, the language twisted and implicated, layer upon layer, so as to hint at meanings unstated; yet on the whole the style is more connected and flowing than it was. Many of the essays bear a sense of Francis's greater project, from the earlier

Advancement, to chart the nature and limits of human knowledge, be it moral or civil. And concealed throughout the essays there is advice to the King, quietly urging him whom to trust, whom to disregard, how to use a man for action, how for contemplation.

Such topics! They might almost have been designed as a disquisition on the late Lord Treasurer, in all his aspects and accidents. What was Salisbury, after all, but the offspring of Welsh farmers, from the tiny hamlet of Allt yr Ynys in the Marches of Herefordshire? A politique grown to great riches by birth, cunning and fortune, unbeautiful but ever seeming wise? A man not yet aged, on whom an untimely death has been visited?

Yet one essay in particular catches the eye: *Of Deformity*. Here Francis writes that men devoid of the affection of nature commonly have their revenge upon it. So deformed persons may get even with nature through their discipline and virtue. Therefore it is good to consider deformity, not as a sign but as a cause, which seldom faileth of the effect. Whosoever hath any thing fixed in his person that doth induce contempt, hath also a perpetual spur in himself to rescue and deliver himself from scorn. Therefore all deformed persons are extreme bold. First, as in their own defence, as being exposed to scorn; but in process of time by a general habit. Also it stirreth in them industry, and especially of this kind, to watch and observe the weakness of others, that they may have somewhat to repay.

He continues, Again, in their superiors, deformity quencheth jealousy towards them, as persons that they think they may at pleasure despise; and it layeth their competitors and emulators asleep; as never believing they should be in possibility of advancement, till they see them in possession. So that upon the matter, in a great wit, deformity is an advantage to rising.

What is this?! Men have ever thought that deformity is the product of some ancient rot or canker in a family that has offended against nature or God. But, Francis argues, it is the other way round. Deformity is less a product than a cause, and it can be a cause of good. Far from resulting from corruption, it makes a man the more apt for greatness.

Does any man truly believe this delicate daisy chain of irony and paradox? It is a subtle degradation indeed to attribute the achievements of a great man to the mis-shape of his body. And, both at court and in the streets, the link to Salisbury is instantly made. As one fellow writes, the world takes notice that he paints out his little cousin to the life.

So be it: Francis is at last avenged on him. Now, onwards.

72

GORHAMBURY, AUGUST 1613

Francis is apt to say that no man prospers so suddenly as by the fault or failure of others. *Serpens nisi serpentem comederit non fit draco*; the serpent, unless he has eaten another serpent, can never become a dragon. When the moment of decision comes, there can be no squeamishness or delay.

Event has piled upon event of late. The previous November, barely six months after Salisbury was in his grave, there came a true catastrophe for the King, with the death of his first-born son and heir, Prince Henry. There was much talk of poison: the boy was just eighteen years of age, how else to explain so unnatural an outcome than by poison? Surely God cannot have willed it. Many still recall how the Prince had been the very picture of health at a great spectacle on Twelfth Night just two years before at the new Banqueting House, displaying his martial skills with the pike and the sword.

Prince Henry's appetites ranged from the arts and literature, to natural philosophy and the study of strange and exotic animals, of which he had a collection that contained ostriches, pheasants, parrots, chickens from the Americas, even a bird from India they call an emu. But it was known at court that he had been sick for months, with fevers, terrible headaches and a great lassitude of body. The sight of his eyes began to fail, till he could not bear even to see the candlelight in his privy chamber. The doctors were full of quack remedies that did the Prince no good as he slipped away. His parents were heartbroken; the Queen will never have it spoken of in her presence.

To Edward Coke, distraught at the loss of Salisbury, the death is a heavy further blow. He had made it his goal to become close to the Prince, and had laid out a first course of readings in the law to aid the young man's understanding of matters of state. And Coke loves the Queen, whom Eliza has long served as lady in waiting, and sees the intensity of her anguish.

But, though Coke has never been a man for idle prognostication or vague fears, yet he sees something else as well. Salisbury is gone, Prince Henry is gone. They were two of his protectors, Salisbury of the present, Henry of the future. Now they are no more.

There is still no successor to Salisbury in his great offices. The King has handed the Treasurership not to a single man but to a group of commissioners, and he has postponed the appointment of a new Secretary of State; so he is bereft of counsel. The candidates now throng the court. They strut and parade in public; and plead, bully and canvass in private.

Then, a third death, not untimely, but one that changes all. On 7 August, Thomas Fleming, Chief Justice of the Court of King's Bench, suddenly passes away in his sleep, at the age of sixty-nine.

This is the moment, the *kairos*, the time of decisive action; of that Francis is certain. The King has promised him the Attorney-ship, but when? The incumbent, Henry Hobart, has the heart of a mouse, and is ill suited indeed to be what the Attorney should be, the sword and shield of the King's prerogative. But Hobart is just a year older than Bacon himself; now that he has recovered from illness there is reason to think he will endure for many a year to come.

And yet... given Hobart's pacific temperament it would much better suit the King if Hobart were moved to succeed Fleming as

Chief Justice of the Court of King's Bench. That would in turn open up the position of Attorney for Francis himself. And if the King should choose otherwise, should decide at this great moment of uncertainty that it is to Francis himself instead that he should turn for a new Chief Justice, well, that is better still.

Francis waits a little while, so as not to be unseemly at a time of sadness, then writes to the King, saying it may please your most excellent Majesty, having understood of the death of the Chief Justice, I do ground in all humbleness an assured hope, that your Majesty will not think of any other but your poor servants, your Attorney and your Solicitor (one of them), for that place. Else we shall be like Noah's dove, not knowing where to rest our foot.

The Mastership of the Rolls, he continues, is blocked. My Lord Coke is like to outlive us both. So as, if this turn fail, I for my part know not whither to look. I have served your Majesty above a prenticehood, full seven years and more, as your Solicitor, which is, I think, one of the painfullest places in your kingdom, specially as my employments have been; and God hath brought mine own years to fifty-two, which I think is older than ever any solicitor continued unpreferred.

My suit is principally that you would remove Mr Attorney to the place; if he refuse, then I hope your Majesty will seek no further than myself, that I may at last, out of your Majesty's grace and favour, step forwards to a place either of more comfort or more ease. Besides, how necessary it is for your Majesty to strengthen your service amongst the judges by a Chief Justice which is sure to your prerogative, your Majesty knoweth.

Francis sends the letter. The idea of drawing the name of Hobart into the advancement of his own suit amuses him.

But then another idea presents itself to his agile, labile mind: a glorious, subtle idea, an idea far more cunning, far more advantageous to himself, far harder to refuse. Above all, a way for him not merely to ascend, but to ascend while damaging his rival.

So he composes a formal memorandum of advice to the King:

REASONS FOR THE REMOVE OF COKE

Reasons why it should be exceeding much for His Majesty's service to remove the Lord Coke from the place he now holdeth to be Chief Justice of England, and the Attorney to succeed him, and the Solicitor the Attorney.

First, it will strengthen the King's causes greatly amongst the judges. For my Lord Coke will think himself near a Privy Councillor's place, and thereupon turn obsequious.

Secondly, the Attorney sorteth not so well with his present place, being a man timid and scrupulous, whereas the now Solicitor going more roundly to work, and being of a quicker and more earnest temper, and more effectual in that he dealeth in, is like to recover that strength to the King's prerogative which it hath had in times past, and which is due unto it.

Thirdly, the King shall continue and add reputation to the Attorney's and Solicitor's place by this orderly advancement of them, which two places are the champion's places for his rights and prerogative. Besides, the remove of my Lord Coke to a place of less profit, though it be with his will, yet will be thought abroad a kind of discipline to him for opposing himself in the King's causes, the example whereof will contain others in more awe.

Lastly, whereas now it is voiced abroad touching the supply of places, as if it were a matter of labour and canvass and money, and other persons are chiefly spoken to be the men, and the great suitors; this will appear to be the King's own act, and is a course so natural and regular as it is without all suspicion of those by-courses, to the King's infinite honour.

For Francis, this is nothing less than a master-stroke. Coke can hardly refuse a place of greater honour, yet it will take him away from the Common Pleas, the court he loves, and there will be far less scope for him to wreak his legal mischief among the criminal cases that occupy the King's Bench. Indeed, since all its cases refer to the King, they will be apt to render His Majesty touchy, especially if Coke is tempted to make law as he has done.

All the world knows that Coke loves money, so he will keenly feel the loss of fees when he is moved, while Hobart at Common Pleas will be too timid to vaunt his office in the face of the King. The thorn of Coke's opposition, as it plainly is, will be plucked out from His Majesty's side. Men will see that the King has laid a discipline on his foremost judge, but conclude that he has acted of his own decision, in the normal course and without the sale of office; three things which will magnify the King in honour and respect.

Ellesmere will be delighted; the Archbishop will rejoice. And all this by a few simple moves on the chessboard of preferment. The elegance and irony of it all are delicious.

But there is something more. Coke longs to be a Privy Councillor, of that Francis has no doubt. But that is to be a courtier, a familiar of government. It requires, not a deep and expert knowledge of the law, but the gentle skills of ingratiation and conciliation, the arts of the dallyer and gossip. These are foreign to the Chief Justice, who loves conflict, direct speech and opposition, and he will surely struggle.

Above all, Coke will be mortified to discover that Francis has been the instrument of his removal; all the more that he has done so while himself becoming the Attorney, in one and the same action.

And as for him, Francis Bacon? He will at last succeed to the Attorneyship, the place he should have had in 1594, nearly twenty years before. But why should that be his resting place? He will be near the King. And, now more than ever, the King lacks men who can do his business.

73

YORK HOUSE, AUTUMN 1614

It is the Lord Chancellor's receiving chamber, at dusk. The man who enters is spare, his face narrow, bony and pallid, his eye modest but alert. This is John Selden, not quite thirty years of age but already recognised as a brilliant and wide-ranging antiquary of the law.

Ellesmere awaits him. But there is another man in the room, in the shadows, whom Selden cannot quite make out.

As is his way, the Lord Chancellor goes straight to the business. 'Master Selden, welcome. Before we begin, let me make myself plain. We seek your information and advice on a confidential matter. If you are questioned about this meeting hereafter, you will not disclose what was discussed. Otherwise, it is as though we never met. Is that understood?'

'We...?' Selden murmurs.

'You know the Attorney General?' Francis Bacon steps forward into the light. Selden eyes him carefully.

'Of course. I am doubly honoured. How may I assist you, sirs?'

'You will be familiar no doubt with the *Reports* of the Chief Justice of King's Bench. He seemeth to publish them every year. God knoweth the King hath read them, and with some distress.' Ellesmere pauses at the thought.

'The Attorney and I wish to ensure both that these *Reports* are accurate in themselves, and that they set out a true understanding of the law.'

'I am at your service, Lord Chancellor,' says Selden. 'But I have heard but a very few of these cases argued, and many of the *Reports* rely on the Chief Justice's own notes.'

Francis steps in. 'Perhaps that is too hasty, Master Selden. Since you know the *Reports*, you will know the prefaces to them. So you will know that the Chief Justice hath there set out his views of the common law. That it is immemorial and existeth time out of mind, that it had no beginning, that it preceded any kingship, and sundry other matters.'

How could Selden not know this? As chance would have it, he has directly followed Coke's own path into the law. Like Coke, he has studied at Clifford's Inn and then at the Inner Temple. He knows his writings, his reputation, he has heard the talk about him in this most chatterous of professions, he has seen him in court and at table at the Inn. So much of what he knows and believes of the common law is due to Coke. There can be no disguising it.

Selden says, 'Of course. He hath quoted Glanvill, Bracton, Fleta, Fortescue and many other authorities in support.'

Bacon goes on. 'Indeed. But take his Ninth *Reports*, which I have here. There he sayeth he will stay his foot and fix his staff a while, to discourse how the *Mirror of Justice* will show the great antiquity of the courts of common law, and particularly of the high court of Parliament since the time of King Arthur in the year 516. What think you, Master Selden, of this document they call the *Mirror of Justice*?'

'To speak frankly, I have severe doubts of it. To me it seems a work ridiculous.'

'What of the *Modus Tenendi Parliamentum*, that purporteth to survive from the time of the Confessor to instruct us how to hold a parliament?'

Selden says, 'In truth, I believe it to be a work of dubious origin and uncertain authority.'

'Coke sayeth that parliaments, the Courts of Chancery, King's Bench, Common Pleas, Exchequer, the Court of Admiralty, county and local courts, all these date from before the Conquest. What say you?'

'My researches would suggest that these are more complex matters than is supposed.'

Bacon: 'Is the common law an imperial realm, untouched by Roman law or other foreign influence, as he suggests?'

'No, Master Attorney, it is not, as you will know, perhaps far better than do I. But again the picture is not a simple one.'

'Come to the point, man!' Ellesmere breaks in. 'Coke setteth out these works as authorities, and they are specious.'

'Forgive me, Lord Chancellor; surely he speaketh as an advocate making his case, not as a scholar of the antiquities.'

'Maybe so. But nothing can follow from a false authority, whether in the law or elsewhere. He draweth conclusions, which are vicious. He scattereth his own conceits almost in every report, he soweth more novelties than corn in these old fields of his. He presumeth to act as the interpreter of law, the King's law, which is a usurpation in itself.

'And he claimeth that the common law is above the King,' Ellesmere is ranting now, 'as though God's grace and the Conquest of Duke William were as nothing. Coke purposely laboureth to disesteem and weaken the King in the ancient use of his prerogative and, he says, all in the name of the prerogative!'

There is danger here. Selden says nothing.

'And mark you where his actions tend, through prohibitions and the like. They tend towards the derogation of the rights of the Church. To the abolition of the High Commission. To the reduction of our ecclesiastical law to a rump of offences, or even to nothing. Even perhaps to an attack on Chancery itself. And there's an end of it, except there may be no end.'

74

WHITEHALL, FEBRUARY 1615

As wise men see, the past years have not been a thing of beauty for the King. The Exchequer is empty, yet he will not restrain his extravagance. His Majesty has not made good the deficit in knowledge and capability that has come from Salisbury's death, and plays at the role of Secretary himself, but he has not the application for it. Besides, even a king must have counsel, must have men who know Parliament, men to keep him at a distance from his petitioners.

James is still sore from the indignities of the Great Contract. If he could do so, he would rather rule personally, in his own name alone, than call another parliament. But time and want of money do their work, and in 1614 he is prevailed upon to do so.

And he has the occasion for it: the naturalisation of Count Frederick, the Elector Palatine of the Rhine, who is now married to the Princess Elizabeth. This offers good matter for a subsidy to be sought from Parliament. Careful preparations are made for the order of presentation of Bills, and the handling of different Members who may be querulous or discordant. At the urging of the new Attorney General, Sir Francis Bacon, the King is set to come to them benevolently and in the princely manner, not as a merchant ready to bargain.

Yet from the start the whole venture turns into a disaster that eclipses even its predecessor parliament of 1610. When the election returns finally come in, it is apparent that there is now a profusion of new Members who have few feelings of loyalty to the King. Barely a few days after the session opens in April, there are accusations of electoral misdemeanours and calls to revisit the issue of impositions, a subject sure to anger His Majesty. Rumours swirl of Catholic plots and the evil influence with the King of the new Spanish ambassador, Sarmiento, soon to be known as Count Gondomar; there is, too, the familiar denunciation of court extravagance and Scottish influences.

The Speaker is unable to maintain order. Nor is the King's cause helped by his recent choice as Secretary of State: Sir Ralph Winwood, a former diplomat who has no experience of parliaments and lacks the guileful and politic temperament needed to manage the House. In vain does James call this the parliament of love. The Commons seeks a conference with the Lords to enlist their support regarding impositions, only to be refused after an incendiary speech in the Lords by the Bishop of Lincoln. At this, the House descends into uproar.

Finally, after little more than two months, James dissolves the assembly. Let it be known, he says, not as the parliament of love but as *parliamentum inchoatum*. For there was never known a more disorderly House, many times more like a cockpit than a grave council of the state.

Now at last the King makes the Earl of Suffolk his new Lord Treasurer; and in so doing James does not miss the chance to damn the memory of Salisbury, saying he has chosen Suffolk not for his learning in Greek and Latin, or for that he could make epigrams and orations, but for his approved fidelity and integrity.

Yet it was not epigrams and orations that made Salisbury what he was, but his understanding of the finances of the realm and his unremitting application to business. Few reckon Suffolk his match, but he played the game hard and well to be appointed. He and his

Howard kin have long circled around the King, and each other. But what has been ingenious is to turn the King's devices to Suffolk's own benefit, as he has done.

The King has ever used marriage as a cure to faction; thus he arranged a match between Salisbury's boy William Cecil and Suffolk's daughter, Lady Catherine Howard, and then between her sister Lady Frances Howard and the orphaned Earl of Essex. But that latter marriage foundered amid some scandal and discontent, and Northampton and Suffolk saw their chance. The King's favourite, Rochester, had long been Lady Frances's paramour: to marry them off would make the couple orderly, and remove a potential rival.

The King was swiftly persuaded. When his special Church commission would not agree to nullify the existing match with Essex, His Majesty simply added two new members to it and they saw the matter through. Then Lady Frances swore an oath affirming that she never had carnal copulation with the Earl. She was examined by doctors and found to be unsullied by any consummation, to the surprise of many at court.

Lady Frances was married with her hair down in December 1613; and Rochester was created Earl of Somerset so that she could stay a Countess after they were wed. There was vast ceremonial. It was rumoured that the King spent £10,000 on the wedding. Rochester even had his new man Donne compose an epithalamion for the occasion:

> *Blessed pair of swans, oh may you interbring*
> *Daily new joys, and never sing,*
> *Live, till all grounds of wishes fail,*
> *Till honour, yea till wisdom grow so stale,*
> *That, new great heights to try,*
> *It must serve your ambition, to die;*
> *Raise heirs, and may here, to the world's end, live*
> *Heirs from this King, to take thanks, yours, to give,*

Nature and grace do all, and nothing art,
May never age, or error overthwart
With any west, these radiant eyes, with any north, this heart.

The poem is pretty, and it would be prettier still if men could understand it. What is certain is that they understand the power which this marriage has created for the new Lord Treasurer.

For Edward Coke, however, the past months have offered a mix of blessings.

To his delight, his son Robert makes a brilliant and remunerative marriage to Lady Theophila Berkeley, relative of the Howards and the de Veres, who had been bridesmaid to Princess Elizabeth. And Coke is further gratified to be elected by unanimous vote as High Steward of Cambridge University, his *alma mater*, second only in precedence to the Chancellor.

He rides the judicial circuit, as he has always done, twice a year, revelling in the opportunity to stretch his body and leave the rank and noisy capital behind. His family continues well. Between his work in court and her attendance with Queen Anne, he and his lady Elizabeth are often apart, but they have found their lives are more convenient and more congenial that way. Coke is abed at nine each evening, and up at three in the morning to work, and these are not conjugal hours.

Coke has reached a public apogee, in the law and in affairs of state. As Chief Justice of King's Bench, or Lord Chief Justice of England as it is sometimes known, he has no judicial superior under the King. He is a member of the Privy Council, the supreme governing body of the nation. Liverymen attend his every public movement. He is now often called Lord Coke, from courtesy.

So to outward appearance all is set fair. Yet inwardly, matters are different.

Coke still mourns the Court of Common Pleas. He fought the King's decision as long as he dared, stickled and fenced, canvassed friends in his support, pressed His Majesty that the Common Pleas was his element, where he could do most good. The King was friendly, but he was not to be turned. So it came about that on 25 October 1613, weeping openly and with his brethren and most of his clerks and functionaries also in tears, Coke took his leave of Common Pleas and walked the few dozen yards down Westminster Hall from the great North Door to the Court of King's Bench.

He misses the Common Pleas still: not so much the loss of fees, which he can afford though he begrudges it, but the loss of his natural home. Even his Privy Councillorship has had a sharp edge given to it, for after the failure of the parliament to provide supply of treasure, the Archbishop of Canterbury had come forward with the idea of a benevolence, a gift of plate or gold from every prominent citizen in the land. Coke had to warn the Council that this revenue could not be by way of a tax, according to law. Yet it is very near a tax, indeed one levied without the consent of Parliament, and though he gives the handsome sum of £200 himself, yet he hates to have his signature on such an authorising paper.

So Coke should be happy, but he is not; and he is sure he knows the cause of his distress. It is the new Attorney, who has poured poison about him into the King's ear. Poison doubly envenomed, since it was not only for Bacon's own advancement but for Coke's removal.

Bacon lay at the root of it all; Bacon of the viper eye.

Coke can feel the eye upon him. It seems to track his every movement. Coke is preferred in office; so is Bacon. Coke is honoured by his university; Bacon has been returned as the MP for Cambridge, and has feasted the city with venison at Christmas. Coke is raised to the Privy Council, and Bacon arranges and pays £2,000 to create a whole garden at the Banqueting House for the Somerset wedding, with flowing water and statuary and promenades and sporting nymphs at play. Bacon calls it a Masque of Flowers, set to honour the newlyweds and curry goodwill with the Howards, and he will take no gift from others that might seem to lessen the magnificence of his generosity.

Francis Bacon: this is a man Coke has ever held of little account. In normal times he would not dream of acknowledging the hurt. Yet afterwards, when they cross in Westminster Hall, he cannot forbear from accosting the wretch in public:

'Master Attorney, this is all your doing. It is you that have made this great stir!'

But far from slithering away, the viper turns on him, and instantly spits:

'Ah, my Lord! Your Lordship all this while hath grown in breadth. You must needs now grow in height, or else you would be a monster!'

How men will laugh at Coke when they hear of the exchange! And they will hear of it; of that Coke has no doubt.

75

A PRIVATE CONFERENCE, FEBRUARY 1615: I

There are three ways to kill a man. The first is by force, from the front in daylight, trying your strength against his. The second is by guile, from the back, under cover of darkness, that he does not know the weapon till the fatal wound be dealt.

What is the third, you ask? Why, that is simplicity itself. So to arrange matters that others kill him, or he kill himself. For this he must be isolated, cut off in his support from others, fenced in till he become desperate. Then there must be occasion for the deed itself. It need not be by a single blow.

And here comes Edmund Peacham, a foolish old parson out of the west country, full of empty threats and mad imaginings. A ranter, a pulpit-beating busybody, a plucker of elbows. Who might think he could be such a weapon?

Bacon himself has come to confer privately with Coke on Peacham's treason. It is his third visit, and he seeks an answer.

Three visits; more than enough for such a case, he thinks. Peacham had denounced the Bishop of Bath and Wells, and been brought up for libel before the High Commission. They searched his house and discovered papers full of violent and abusive language against the King, saying His Majesty might be stricken with death on a sudden, the King's officers put to the sword and the people rise against him for taxes and oppressions. The Privy Council saw the papers and committed Peacham to the Tower. The Council then issued a warrant against him for treason, that he be examined and, if found to be obstinate and perverse in his replies to the interrogatories, that he shall be put to the manacles.

The commission of interrogation is led by Winwood, as Secretary of State, but it is Attorney General Bacon who acts within it as its learned counsel. This is a role he has played many times before, from the time of the Armada. Now the commissioners put twelve interrogatories to the prisoner; questions upon which, on 19 January, Peacham is examined before torture, in torture, between tortures and after torture. But nothing of value can be drawn out of him.

The King is hot to pursue the charge of treason. But the case will come to the Court of King's Bench, and here Francis apprehends a potential difficulty. On the face of it, Peacham's guilt is manifest; but what if the judges, what if the Lord Chief Justice, do not see it that way? The matter is already such a source of rumour, and the King's displeasure so well known, that anything short of quick success will prove a source of embarrassment. Yet as Francis advises the King, St Paul said to the centurion, when some of the mariners had an eye to the cock-boat, *Except these stay in the ship ye cannot be safe*. So it is with the judges. They must be kept on board.

The Attorney has devised a means to deal with this matter, however. Has the King not seen how the judges cluster together for mutual warmth when the wind turns cold? They did it at York House, when they stayed silent in the matter of the jurisdiction of the Marches Council; they did it at Lambeth Palace, when Coke alone remained standing; and Coke himself refused to answer on the question of proclamations until he had consulted with his brethren. Show them danger, and these men are like sheep that huddle behind the ram.

Yet, Francis says, each of the judges is sworn by oath to advise and counsel His Majesty. Let each therefore be asked, one by one and in the King's name, to give his opinion on the case at issue, and on Peacham's guilt or nay. Then there can be no hiding or huddling, and Coke will not be able to protect his herd, or lead them awry.

It plays out as he has planned. When the matter comes before the Privy Council, the Lord Chief Justice at once rejects the proposal, calling the idea an auricular taking of opinions, like each man making private confession to a priest, which the judges will not bear. As all the lawyers know, there is a case of 1485, when the judges were asked by Henry VII to give their opinions in advance of judgment, and Chief Justice Hussey replied that they should not, since the case might yet come before them. Yet when Bacon replies that every judge is bound expressly by his oath to give the King counsel when he is called, and whether he should do it jointly or severally rests in His Majesty's good pleasure, the Council overrules Coke and concurs.

Thus has Francis put Coke and the King at odds with each other, in front of the Council. Now Coke must be made to comply.

So Francis has a Serjeant sent at once to each of the lesser judges, to ascertain that day his willingness, and agree when he will see the papers. And it is quickly clear that they will act as he anticipates. Judge Doddridge is very ready to give opinion in private; so too is Judge Croke. Judge Haughton wishes a little time, but he will opine. If the papers are provided and the judges' views sought betimes, then Francis has little doubt of their opinions.

And Coke? Francis dares not leave the Lord Chief Justice to any Serjeant, but has reserved him to himself. As he writes to inform the King, neither am I wholly out of hope, that my Lord Coke himself, when I have in some dark manner put him in doubt that he shall be left alone, will not continue singular.

76

A PRIVATE CONFERENCE, FEBRUARY 1615: II

Since then some weeks have passed. The King is with a few dozen retainers and attendants at his favourite lodgings at Royston, not far from Cambridge. He rides out every day to hunt, despite a winter that has turned bitterly cold.

The ice and snow do not deter His Majesty, nor do they serve to cool his indignation over the Peacham case. Indeed so hot does the King run that he has sent a paper of his own composition to the Privy Council, arguing for the poor parson's treason and destruction.

If the man had compiled a sermon on another ground, he says, or only powdered it here and there with some passages of reprehension of the King, or upbraided him two or three times either in drunkenness or in some fit of passion, it might yet have been some way excusable. But to heap up all the injuries that the hearts of men, or malice of the devil, can invent against the King, and not to do this hastily or rashly, but after long premeditation, first having made collections in scattered papers, and then reduced it to a method, in a formal treatise applying all his wits to bring out of that text what he could against the King – this, he says, is a plain proof that he intended to compass or imagine the King's destruction. And that is treason.

For his part, Francis has run the Lord Chief Justice like a big brown trout, gently; no need of force now the hook is in. He saw him first, so as to deliver the papers on the Peacham case, and then again some days later with a sheaf of carefully gathered precedents on the matter.

It was evident then that Coke was out of sorts, and his language was not that of the Council table.

'The whole procedure is improper,' he had insisted with asperity. 'The judges are not to give opinion by fractions, but entirely according to the vote whereupon they should settle in conference.

'This auricular taking of opinions, single and apart,' he said, 'is a thing new and dangerous, like to set judge against judge. It will fetter their deliberations and diminish the authority of the court and the common law. It is not justice to seek to prejudge a man before the case be considered, how much less when he is on trial for his life.'

Coke dresses these matters in the garb of high principle, thinks Francis, but this is all wriggling; it is the challenge to his own power that he cannot abide.

At their next meeting, Francis runs through the precedents with the Lord Chief Justice. These show that there are, as he sets out, four means whereby the death of the King may be compassed and imagined: the first, by some particular fact or plot; the second, by disabling his title, as by affirming that he is not lawful king, or an usurper, or a bastard, or the like; the third, by making his title subject to another, be it to Pope or people, so that he is not an absolute king but a conditional king; and the fourth, by disabling his regiment or rule, and making him appear to be incapable or unworthy to reign. It is plain that Peacham's treason falls within the last division.

Coke is taking careful note of these points, which it is pleasant to see. But Francis closes with some words of warning.

'My Lord, you say that in the end your brethren will shy from giving their opinions, and take advice with the others. I am sorry to hear you say this, for if it come to pass, some that love you not may make a construction that what you had foretold, you had wrought.

'The Serjeants will dispatch their parts with the other judges. I fear I will be behind with mine, and that His Majesty will impute this to your backwardness and not my negligence. Let it not be so.'

🌾

Now they are met a third time. Bacon is insistent.

'My Lord, I had word that you have at last delivered yourself of an opinion on Peacham's treason.'

'I have, writ these last days in my own hand.' Coke thrusts a bundle of papers into Bacon's hand.

There is something about him, something calm, that does not bode well. And as for the papers, there are more of them than Francis would like. Perhaps it was too much to hope that Coke could address the matter without complexity.

Francis opens the bundle and reads the concluding paragraphs, and his mouth drops open.

'You find for Peacham, and against the King!' He gasps.

'No, Master Attorney. I do not defend the man, and I do not find against the King, for the just application of law doth always redound to the King's honour. But there is no treason here.'

'But on the fourth charge, of disabling his regiment... It is as plain as daylight. How can you find otherwise?'

'You may read my opinion,' says Coke, abruptly. 'There are words of scandal and defamation here, to be sure. Yet the test of disablement is something more than wild words.

'This remote and silly man hath lacked any capacity, through himself or, it must appear, through others. There is no show of conspiracy, no evidence of a consolidated intrigue, nor any ready audience of fellow conspirators. So, no, this is not treason, whatever you may hold, Master Attorney.'

'But your fellows say it is! I have their opinions and they are for the King, without exception.'

'So it may be. Whether they would be so in conference, in the collective judgment of the King's Bench sitting in such a case, is a further matter.'

And that is all that can be done with him.

The King is angry beyond measure with Coke. Bacon proceeds with the case, for he can do no other. But there can be no great state trial now, for it is soon known that the Lord Chief Justice is against the prosecution.

Peacham is interrogated again, and tells a further story which no one believes. He is sent to the Assizes in Taunton and condemned for high treason. Yet he is not executed, but is allowed to live un-molested till he dies in jail some months later.

77

WESTMINSTER HALL, MAY 1616

*Besides, in their wisdom they understood that the affairs in court
were not long wheeled about one axle-tree; that there are periods of
hatred, love, suspicion, and clemency, though to us unknown. That no
man knoweth whether tomorrow he may be thought worthy of love or
hatred. That the purposes of Princes are close and secret. That they, to
redeem their own fame, are wont to sacrifice to the multitude the chief
of their ministers, repeating the examples of Empson, Dudley, Cardinal
Wolsey, Cromwell, etc. Such as men observe a Prince to be towards
others, such may they judge he will be toward themselves when occasion
shall be given.*

Back and forth, back and forth, the dance continues. Yet with
every movement Coke feels his freedom lessen, his feet in retreat, his power as a judge diminish.

There is a wall behind him, and soon he will have his back to
it. Then they will come for him, for his person, and where will he
turn? Even the thought bids to unstring him. Time was when he
had friends and allies for protection and advice, but a great eminence is a lonely place. Now, when he looks round the Council
table, he sees few who would shed a tear to lose him, and many
who would like little better.

But for Francis Bacon, this has become a time of joy. He knew
this moment would come, and he sees how the action must play
out. It is as though he has written a great masque, the greatest of

all he has ever written, in which the tableaux succeed one another until a climax be reached; or still better, a drama whose events propel each other towards a vast and inevitable outcome.

A comedy, a tragedy? Who can tell? Who cares? And the best part of it is that each particular turn has been set in motion by his own hand.

❧

So, then, he must hie him to Westminster Hall for the latest scandal to grip the public mind, perhaps the greatest since the fall of Essex: the trial of Lady Frances Howard, Countess of Somerset, charged with the murder of Sir Thomas Overbury.

Overbury had been boon companion to Robert Carr many years before, and had brought Carr to the court, where he beguiled His Majesty and became his favourite. When Carr was made Viscount Rochester and then Earl of Somerset, Overbury rose with him, as adviser, friend, some say master.

But now Somerset is Lady Frances's husband and Overbury is dead, killed they say by rosealgar, mercury, great spiders, powder of diamonds, cantharides, arsenical and other poisons procured and fed him in the Tower of London and administered by agents under the Countess's guiding hand.

Murder by poison! A foul and detestable crime, an Italian crime fit only for the Court of Rome. Rarely to be found in England, and all the worse that it was inflicted under colour of friendship on a man already in the Tower, and in the safe keeping of His Majesty. All London has been convulsed for months with the news of it.

The King hated that men said he was ruled by his favourite, and his favourite by Overbury. The Queen deplored the fellow's insolence. But all might have been well, if Overbury, whether from fear for his friend, hatred of the Howards or simple jealousy of person, had not quarrelled with Lady Frances. He even had the audacity to circulate a poem he had written, instructing Somerset as to good and bad in the duties and conduct of a wife. In it, he warned the Earl that

> *For wand'ring lust; I know 'tis infinite,*
> *It still begins, and adds not more to more:*
> *The guilt is everlasting, the delight,*
> *This instant doth not feel, of that before.*

Yet, he said, marriage can be a cure for human passion, for

> *Marriage our lust (as 'twere with fuel fire)*
> *Doth, with a medicine of the same, allay,*
> *And not forbid, but rectify desire.*
> *My self I cannot choose, my wife I may:*

And what matters great honour or high birth in a woman, if there is only virtue?

> *Birth, less than beauty, shall my reason blind,*
> *Her birth goes to my children, not to me:*
> *Rather had I that active gentry find,*
> *Virtue, than passive from her ancestry;*
> *Rather in her alive one virtue see,*
> *Than all the rest dead in her pedigree.*

This is the motive that men seek: that Lady Frances took mortal offence at the poem and vowed to have Overbury killed. It is said that she intrigued with her Howard relatives to have the King send Overbury away as ambassador to Muscovy; and when, on the Earl's advice, Overbury declined the commission, to put him in the Tower. Thus was he originally entrapped.

The previous months have seen a succession of trials at law to catch the little fishes: Sir Gervase Helwys, a weak man, whom Lady Frances had had installed as Lieutenant at the Tower, in place of honest Sir William Wade; Weston the gaoler, a man well acquainted with the use of drugs; Franklin the apothecary, who provided the poisons, enough to kill twenty men, and was paid by the Countess in gold; and Mistress Turner, who made the poisons into tarts and jellies to feed the prisoner over many weeks, and finally into a clyster or suppository which they told Overbury was for his good treatment, but which quickly killed him.

All these people have been taken, interrogated, convicted and executed, amid a mass of incriminating detail.

78

WESTMINSTER HALL, MAY 1616

A page, a Knight, a Viscount and an Earl
All those did love a lustful English girl
A match well made, for she was likewise four:
A wife, a witch, a poisoner and a whore.

Now it is the turn of the Earl and Countess of Somerset themselves. Westminster Hall is bedecked in the full panoply of a
great state trial, with the peers summoned who are to try the case,
all the senior judges present, the law officers engaged or otherwise
on hand.

A vast throng of notables has come to watch the festivities, with
crowds outside kept back by the guards. Such is the interest that
seats have been changing hands at monstrous cost: £10 for two, £50
for a corner or box fit for a group.

Lady Frances is summoned first, and, sobbing and in a low voice,
pleads guilty. Rising as the King's Attorney to address the assembled peers, Francis Bacon says he is glad to hear so free an acknowledgement of guilt, for confession is noble. This is the second
time since the King's coming that any peers have been arraigned,
and though at the first Lords Grey and Cobham were convicted,
yet execution followed not. In all this meantime, the King hath
reigned in his white robe, not sprinkled with any drop of blood of
his nobles of his kingdom.

The Countess is sentenced to death, but few doubt that she will be spared.

The next day it is the turn of the Earl of Somerset. If anything the hubbub is still greater than before. Yesterday was full of disappointment, and the poor throng of notables went away in sadness, starved of scandal, intrigue and spectacle. Today promises much better, for it comes yet nearer to the King and the case is more uncertain. There is a mass of incriminating detail, but little to link the Earl directly to the crime. He has continually affirmed his innocence, but how will he plead?

As for the King, closeted at Greenwich, he is in a mad fit of anxiety and cannot be still from nerves. He wants rid of his former favourite, yet he has warm feelings for him, he wants justice done, yet he will not shed blood. Above all, he is frantic that the Earl may reveal secrets of state, or worse, secrets of the bedchamber. Oh, why cannot Somerset simply plead guilty so they may all have done with it?

No man, not even a king, may treat for the outcome of a legal suit, but Francis has earlier sent ambassadors to the Earl, to hint and scout the possibilities if he will accept the charges. He will not.

Now Somerset stands before the court, to plead not guilty. He is dressed in black satin like a man mourning, and such is the King's panic that there are men placed near the defendant with blankets to muffle him if he starts to speak of things unspeakable. The Serjeant Crier calls loudly to all that have evidence to give to step forward, and Bacon opens for the Crown.

He says, 'As to the offence itself; it is of crimes, next unto high treason, the greatest; it is the foulest of felonies.

'And take this offence with the circumstances, it hath three degrees or stages; that it is murder; that it is murder by empoisonment; that it is murder committed upon the King's prisoner in the Tower. I might say, that it is murder under the colour of friendship, but that is a circumstance moral; I leave that to the evidence itself.'

By the end of the day it is all done. To the King's relief, there are few new details to delight the crowd. The Earl is found guilty and sentenced to death. As with the Countess, few doubt that he will be spared.

Under questioning, the gaoler Weston had said he hoped they would not make a net to catch the little fishes, and let the great ones go. Yet the little fishes all lie dead, while the great will be pardoned and live on to old age.

It was to Sir Edward Coke, as investigator, that Weston expressed that hope. In turn Coke had vowed to trap the great fishes; and he has done so. They have been found guilty of murder, before the highest tribunal, and for their later handling he bears no responsibility. The law has spoken, even if justice be not done.

Still, as the Lord Chief Justice watches the proceedings, he can feel nothing but a fatigue so deep it penetrates him to the marrow. This is a trial, not just of persons but of families; there are great honours and great fortunes at stake. There can be no room for error, as interrogatories are taken and the case is assembled.

How easy must it have been for Bacon to persuade the King to reach for the services of Coke, his oldest and sturdiest weapon, his incorruptible Excalibur of the law, the man who brought down Raleigh, the traitors of the Gunpowder Treason and so many others! This is no time for error or omission, your Majesty. It would be folly to turn elsewhere.

But for Coke the result is to pile Pelion and Ossa on his back. Over the previous months he has conducted over three hundred separate examinations, has questioned every person who might have had some bearing on the case, high and low, has compiled and compared their answers, re-examined them and then re-examined them again to address flaws and gaps in testimony. It has been a colossal task, young men's work, which he has approached with his usual painstaking care and diligence. And all this on top of his usual business at King's Bench, his writing of notes and reports, the management of his estates; and for a man who is sixty-four years of age, there is no turning back the burdens of time.

The worst of it is this: that Coke could never bring himself to turn from his course or soften his questioning, but it must remain blunt and harsh. He could not be softer even if he felt the need. The inevitable effect has been to anger and inflame those on every side of this dispute. The Howards are united in little but their family interest, and they are bitterly against him. Somerset and his lady and their friends will ever be implacable, while Overbury never had many supporters to feel grateful now for Coke's diligence. And Overbury is dead.

How easy, then, for Francis Bacon to foresee that Coke's appointment would divide him still further from men's opinions and loyalties.

And the King? For *Rex legifer*, the law must take its course. But he cannot abide the passage of secrets about him from one man to another; it is to place weapons into their hands. Who knows what Coke has heard? Any revelations, of state or bed, might have marred the trial entirely. At least James can now find consolation in the company of Sir George Villiers, his new and very lovely favourite.

79

KING'S BENCH AND CHANCERY, JUNE 1616

Yet all this trouble for Coke is but the first part of Francis Bacon's joy. For the Lord Chief Justice has also plunged into a public conflict with Lord Chancellor Ellesmere. And that must mean a further conflict with the King.

It is as Ellesmere foretold at their meeting with Selden, Francis thinks. After Coke's volleys of prohibitions against other courts, after his attacks on the jurisdiction of the High Commission and the provincial Councils, after his efforts in restraint of proclamations, now he has trained his fire upon the High Court of Chancery itself. The court sits just opposite the King's Bench, at the bottom of Westminster Hall, before the steps that run up to the Commons. There Ellesmere presides, served by his Master of the Rolls, his Masters of Chancery and clerks. As Lord Chancellor, whether speaking as judge or in the House of Lords, he stands next to the King himself.

But if the courts of Chancery and King's Bench are situated just a few yards apart, if their practice and procedures interpenetrate each other, yet they are at opposite poles of the English law.

As Ellesmere is apt to tell his fellow Councillors, Chancery is the leading court of equity, of relief to those oppressed by any harshness or insufficiency in the common law. It issues decrees to suit the particular facts of a case, not judgments of law that stand precedent to others. And it has a wider range of relieving powers and remedies than does the Court of Common Pleas: in a case for breach of contract, say, the common law courts may be limited to an award of damages; but Chancery can force the offending party to discharge their promise.

Where a plaintiff cannot have justice due to illness or poverty, he may turn for help to Chancery, and the use of its discretionary power in the exercise of mercy. As Ellesmere has told the King to his face, the Lord Chancellor is the Keeper of the King's conscience, and therefore whatsoever the King directed in any case, he would decree accordingly. And so Chancery is the very citadel of the King's prerogative right.

As lawyer, as Solicitor and Attorney and as judge, Coke has ever recognised the importance of equity. He has regularly used the Court of Chancery, in matters of state, in private practice and on his own behalf. He knows as well as any man that there can be cases where the law may be of unjust effect, or where the common law remedies do not suffice. He does not like, but does not question, its inquisitorial procedure, or the particular and personal nature of its judgments. As he has said, the Lord Chancellor is the sole judge in matters of equity, and the Chancery is the warehouse of justice, to which a party may have resort at any time. Wherever the Chancellor is, there is the Chancery.

Yet, as Coke insists, to say the Chancellor has a discretionary power in such matters is not to say he may act as he pleases. Chancery may not interfere with men's title to freehold property. It may not imprison a man without lawful cause.

Above all, Chancery is not a court of appeal. It may not be used to overturn a case decided at common law, or to prevent the enforcement of any action already decided in the King's courts. There is an ancient principle, set by statute in 1402, that judgments in courts of record, where the proceedings are noted down for perpetual memory and in case a judgment is appealed, must be final.

Only lately, in 1597, the question has been put to all the common law judges of England, and the principle upheld, with but one dissent, and no demur from the very same Sir Thomas Egerton who is now Lord Chancellor Ellesmere. It is thus to the Court of King's Bench as the monarch's highest ordinary court, Coke avers, and not to Chancery, that any authority under law must ultimately be subject, in the name of the King.

Yet Ellesmere has demurred if not in words then in his actions, and this is the point of contention between the Lord Chancellor and the Lord Chief Justice. They are like two vast, clashing empires. Each has his own expansive conception of the law: one tending to the prerogative, grace, discretion and the power of the King, the other for a spreading and consistent rule of the common law.

It is the same question as of old: is the King *lex loquens*, the law speaking in human form, or does he too come under the law? One way or the other, there must be an answer, soon.

As he has aged, Lord Chancellor Ellesmere has become less diligent and less politic. Only recently he had Sir Julius Caesar, a civil lawyer of no great industry, made Master of the Rolls; it is an open secret that the cases are piling up in Chancery for want of decisions.

For his part, a few years earlier Coke announced in open court that he had discovered a treatise from the time of King Henry VIII opining that a writ of prohibition could lie against the Chancery, to curtail its scope and limit its right to hear cases from the common law courts. Such a writ would be an ostentatious challenge to the authority of the Lord Chancellor. Yet Coke has never issued one.

What alters now in Coke? Is it impatience, a sudden change of heart, an act of arrogance and folly, a desire to correct abuses that have grown too great or stood too long? Whatever it may be, the Lord Chief Justice is given new opportunities to act, and he begins to take them.

The first is in the case of Ruswell, committed to the Fleet by order of the Chancery, for cause unspecified. Coke's view of such matters is well known; as he wrote of Magna Carta, the common law of England gives to every subject a remedy for his lands, his goods and his liberty; and just as it gives an action for his lands and goods when they are taken away, so it gives in some cases a writ of false imprisonment. The Court of King's Bench has power to write for the body of a man in any place in England, and may discharge him from the imprisonment if it finds the cause to be unlawful.

Even so, when the inevitable writ of *habeas corpus* comes to King's Bench, Coke acts with restraint. The court does not discharge the prisoner, but merely invites the return to be amended. This is a rumbling, but not an explosion.

Not so with the case of Glanvill. This man had been imprisoned by Chancery for failure to obey a decree. He was discharged by the King's Bench by writ of *habeas corpus*, only to be imprisoned once more by Lord Chancellor Ellesmere. Then he had sought his freedom again through a *habeas corpus*. But in contesting the writ, Ellesmere did not bother to specify any cause for the imprisonment. It is as though he says Chancery wills it, and need not specify the facts or cause: let it be so.

This is a provocation and a trap, and Coke walks into it. Instead of showing restraint, the Court of King's Bench rejects the decision of Chancery out of hand. Ellesmere then orders the arrest of Glanvill for a third time, only on this occasion using a pursuivant or officer to execute the warrant, in the belief that such a man unknown cannot be served a writ. While the case of Glanvill is pending, others come forward: the case of Allen, and the case of Googe, Master of Magdalene College, Cambridge, imprisoned by Chancery over a dispute about property and then bailed by King's Bench.

All this is bad enough. But it is the characters of Glanvill and Allen that make matters much worse. For Glanvill is a known rogue, a jeweller who had conspired with an accomplice to defraud a man in the sale of a topaz as a purported diamond.

Allen is of still worse repute, a man who had taken advantage of a bankrupt debtor to acquire considerable lands at a low price, then turned the wretched fellow's children out of their family home and into the frost and snow.

While in the Fleet these scheming and resourceful men have instructed other prisoners in the use of *habeas corpus* to obtain release, pointing to the protection of the Common Pleas as a legal weapon against the Chancery. But this is a mere prelude, for Glanvill has also launched actions for false imprisonment against the Warden of the Fleet. These threaten to bring the Court of Chancery into derision, and to terrify its officers from doing their service.

Now in their audacity the two men take a step yet further. In the Michaelmas of 1615 Glanvill frames a writ of *praemunire* against all attorneys, solicitors and counsellors who have helped to impeach judgments of record.

Praemunire is like a great cannon ball able to carry away all before it. It was first instituted to prevent papal influence in the English Church, but has long fallen into disuse. Yet every lawyer knows how *praemunire* was used by Henry VIII to destroy Cardinal Wolsey and bring the clergy to his heel. It is a most dangerous weapon, and carries with it penalties of fines, forfeiture of goods and imprisonment. And Glanvill seeks to wrest it into his hands.

80

KING'S BENCH AND CHANCERY, JUNE 1616

The indictments made by Glanvill are considered at King's Bench by a grand jury of nineteen men specially convened for the purpose, and it is as though the process has driven Coke mad.

Seeing the issues to be weighty and rare, and to touch the King, the jury seeks the advice of His Majesty's learned counsel, but Coke denies them this, saying the matter is clear enough.

Coke then presses them for a verdict, but the foreman of the jury says they are unwilling to uphold a charge against men of known honesty and credit, made by such a one as is reported to have neither honesty nor credit, but known rather to be a cheater and a cozener. The indictments are returned all with the word *ignoramus*, we know nothing of it, inscribed upon them.

Coke sends the jurors back, and when they return the same word, sends them back a third time, with a threat to commit them if they do not reach a verdict. Yet still they persist; and, in a rage, Coke dismisses them and instructs the Sheriff to return a wiser jury next time.

What drives the Lord Chief Justice to such extremities? Glanvill and Allen are known thieves and scoundrels. It is as though Coke is using that very fact to show the soundness of legal principles that pay no regard to men's honesty or station. Men say Coke even suggested the use of *praemunire* against these courts of equity himself!

Certainly, Coke insists that the Court of King's Bench is the school of the law and ought to correct the abuses of the other courts. It would tend, he says, to the overthrow of the common law if judgments in its courts should be suffered to be called into question in courts of equity. For then there must be no end of appeals short of the Chancery. What need of Common Pleas or King's Bench if theirs are not to be final judgments? Wherefore even the high court of Parliament itself?

Take this thought to its end and the law becomes, not *lex terrae*, a common wealth of reasoned rules sprung from English custom and tradition to guide men of every estate, but a matter of discretion and royal mercy vested in the King's person. The judgement and integrity of this Lord Chancellor are not in doubt, but who can say what his successors will be? Men are not all of a like consistency.

For his part, Lord Ellesmere has been gravely ill, but is recovering. He is well enough to be indignant when he hears what has transpired, not least at the rumour that he may himself be subject to a *praemunire* from the wretched Glanvill.

But the Lord Chancellor is hardly without resources. He has been readying his defences, and has already sent his clerks to collect precedents and arguments to be put before the King and Council when the moment comes. He sees the lines of attack, notes Coke's vehemence, and prepares a set of detailed and moderate rebuttals. The use of equity, he maintains, is in no way contrary to Magna Carta. It is of great antiquity, well attested in the records, and is not the subject of extravagance by judges in its courts. It does not, cannot, question the correctness of a judgment at law, but goes only to matters of good conscience that the common law does not touch. But on the question of precedence there can be no concession, for the courts are the King's courts, and of them Chancery is the court next the King and the prerogative.

Behind these preparations, both while Ellesmere is in health and while he is sick, lies the diligence of Francis Bacon, who still reveres him almost as a kind of father.

They have an understanding between them. Defeat Coke and, when the moment comes, Ellesmere will support Bacon to succeed to his office as Lord Chancellor, its honours and its duties.

81

GORHAMBURY, JUNE 1616

How much pain, how much trouble may a man endure? Can it be long before Coke succumbs?

Francis Bacon's joy in that summer of 1616 comes not singly or in a pair, but in four parts. The first derives from the Somerset trial. The writs of *praemunire* and their consequence form the second. And the third? It lies in his cultivation of Sir George Villiers, the King's new favourite.

His Majesty had taken leave of the Earl of Somerset at Royston with every token of affection and kindness. Yet he was heard to observe, as soon as the Earl were gone, that he should never see his face more.

The royal attentions are elsewhere, and they are more full of amorous passion than ever. In two short years the King has knighted Villiers, given him a great pension and made him a gentleman of the bedchamber. Now he grants him the post that Somerset long coveted, the Mastership of the Horse, makes him viscount and elevates him to the Garter.

To His Majesty, Villiers is 'Steenie', his own St Stephen, bearing the face of an angel. With the young man's sweet countenance comes an open and easy manner, able to conciliate the opposing and the undecided alike; on that, all are agreed. What is less pleasing is his desire to place himself next to the King in matters of state. There Somerset had never bid to go.

Francis has noted the rise of Villiers and the changing tide of the King's affections, and he has been quick to form a connection. When in January 1616 a valuable office in the Common Pleas was known to be set by the King for his favourite, Francis intervened to keep any objections from Coke at bay; and he made sure to tell Villiers so himself. There have since been other matters of state to be dealt with between the two men, especially touching the trial of Somerset.

Francis starts to feel the same intoxicating hopes for Villiers as he had entertained with the Earl of Essex. Soon they are in a regular correspondence. The older man offers wise counsel and encouragement as the younger ever rises, but he does not shy from directness. Early on, Francis writes that You are now the King's favourite, so esteemed by all... Remember then what your true condition is. The King himself is above the reach of his people, but cannot be above their censures, and you are his shadow if either he commit an error, and is loath to avow it, or you commit the fault, or have willingly permitted it. So perhaps you may be offered as a sacrifice to appease the multitude.

You are as a continual sentinel, he continues. If you flatter the King, you betray him. If you conceal the truth of those things from him, which concern his justice or his honour... you are as dangerous a traitor to his state, as he that riseth in arms against him. A false friend is more dangerous than an open enemy.

And finally: The whole kingdom hath cast their eye upon you as the new rising star, and no man thinks his business can prosper at court, unless he hath you for his good angel, or at least that you be not a *malus genius* or evil spirit against him. This you cannot now avoid unless you will adventure a precipice, to fall down faster than you rose. Opinion is a master wheel in these cases.

But almost from the first Francis has also pressed his own claims to preferment, whether it be to the Privy Council or the Lord

Chancellorship itself, which had been almost promised him when it should be vacant.

The times, the secrets he shares, the actions of which he is a part, all these things demand his elevation. Francis writes in February to Villiers with broken thanks, for, as they speak of the turquoise stone in a ring, I will break into twenty pieces, before you have the least fall. God keep you ever.

Then follows another letter, saying I would be glad you went on with my first motion, my swearing Privy Councillor... My Lord Chancellor told me yesterday in plain terms, that if the King would ask his opinion touching the person that he would commend to succeed him upon death or disability, he would name me for the fittest man. You may advise whether use may not be made of this offer.

Barely a week later, Francis renews his suit to Villiers, saying I humbly pray you not to think me over-hasty or much in appetite, if I put you in remembrance of my motion of strengthening me with the oath and trust of a Privy Councillor; not for my own strength (for as to that, I thank God, I am armed within) but for the strength of my service.

And in another letter, lest his pledge and meaning be in any way unclear, I am yours surer to you than to my own life.

Francis is afraid for his own prospects, and Lord Ellesmere's grave sickness has fed those fears. Though they are delicately dressed in words, they extend to the King's intentions. Perhaps he will choose another man to succeed as Lord Chancellor? At the height of the disease, when the doctors had pronounced Ellesmere out of all human help, Francis had composed a long letter to the King, saying your worthy Chancellor, I fear, goes his last day. Upon this heavy accident I pray your Majesty in all humbleness and sincerity to give me leave to use a few words.

I must never forget, Francis had continued, that when I moved your Majesty for the Attorney's place, it was your own sole act. I shall now again make oblation to your Majesty, first of my heart, then of my service, thirdly of my place of Attorney. I hope I may be acquitted of presumption if I think of it, both because my father had the place, and chiefly because since the Chancellor's place went to the law, it was ever conferred upon some of the learned counsel, and never upon a judge.

It was ever conferred upon some of the learned counsel, and never upon a judge. Whom, pray, might the Attorney have in mind?

As far as he can, Francis seeks to disable rivals and remove doubts about himself. He writes, now I beseech your Majesty let me put you the present case truly. If you take my Lord Coke, this will follow; first your Majesty shall put an over-ruling nature into an over-ruling place, which may breed an extreme. Next you shall blunt his industries. And lastly, popular men are no sure mounters for your Majesty's saddle. If you take my Lord Hobart, he is no statesman but an economist wholly for himself. If you take my Lord of Canterbury, I will say no more but the Chancellor's place requires an whole man; and to have both jurisdictions, spiritual and temporal, in that height, is fit but for a king.

For myself, I can only present your Majesty with *gloria in obsequio*, renown in my obedience.

In May, a few months on, the matter is still not decided. But with the Somerset trial past, Francis decides to press again in the quest for great place and power. And now at last Villiers puts his own shoulder to the wheel, and the King responds, to offer to Francis a choice: the Council forthwith, or the Lord Chancellorship when it shall be vacant.

As Francis writes to Villiers in thanks: you are the man my heart ever told me you were.

In truth it is no choice, for the one is badly wanted now, and it will surely lead to the other. And so it is that on 9 June 1616 Sir Francis Bacon is made a Privy Councillor, swearing an oath that, among much else, he will not know or understand of any manner of thing to be attempted, done or spoken against His Majesty's Person, Honour, Crown or Dignity Royal, but he will let and withstand the same to the uttermost of his power.

It is, Francis notes, the first time in a century that this honour has been accorded to a serving Attorney General. Legal and political power have been joined in him.

Now is the moment to take full measure of the fourth and final part of his joy: the ruin of Sir Edward Coke, Lord Chief Justice of King's Bench.

82

THE PALACE OF WHITEHALL, JUNE 1616

For this fourth part, Francis does not need a new weapon. No, an old weapon far better suits his purpose.

Francis has long entertained the expectation that, take him and Coke for all in all, posterity will judge him to be the greater lawyer. Was it not he whose advocacy secured the victory in *Calvin's Case*, when a full court in the Exchequer Chamber found that a child born in Scotland after the Union of Crowns and James's accession as King of England is an English subject, entitled to the benefits of English law? That was a famous victory, one for the annals, and most pleasing to His Majesty.

Yet, even so, Francis has always envied Coke his knowledge of the common law. Coke has ventured further into the labyrinth, has read more deeply, more carefully and with more systematic compilation than any man alive into the precedents, the readings and arguments, the yearbooks, the digests and ancient treatises of the law. His recall of detail is quite out of the ordinary.

Whether *ex tempore* in the court or in the quiet of his own study, Coke can cite cases at will that it would take other men weeks to research, if they were able. He can quote the original law French or Latin as may be needed, and regularly corrects the quotations of others; he has won cases on the meaning of a single word. This profundity of learning is the ultimate source of Coke's legal power. Little wonder that even in his private career at the bar he was said to be an oracle of the law.

For all his own distinction in the common law, Francis knows he cannot match Coke case for case. He has tried to do so before the Council on more than one occasion, and has never bested him. Besides, his own taste runs more to maxims and the codes of the civil lawyers than to the dry and dusty manuscripts of common law precedent.

But here is a thought: what would it be to have a legal device of great antiquity to his own hand, in the struggle against his adversary? It would be two things in one. It would be to use Coke's own weapons, but to turn them against him, and in the public arena. Victory would mean not merely defeat but humiliation for the Lord Chief Justice.

Now Francis has such a device: the writ of *non procedendo rege inconsulto*. It requires that a case that touches the King may not go forward until it has been brought before His Majesty for discussion and consultation, after which it may then be removed to Chancery. As Francis writes to the King, it is a means provided by the ancient law of England to bring any case that may concern your Majesty in profit or power from the ordinary benches to be tried and judged before the Chancellor of England by the ordinary and legal part of this power.

He does not say what all men know, that Chancery is likely to prove a kinder place of judgment for the King.

But every lever, to have effect, must have a point of application. Here, that point is a case in which two men, Colt and Glover, have fought with the Bishop of Coventry over the income from a Church appointment that had lapsed and been granted anew by the Archbishop under the King's power of dispensation. In the course of it the plaintiffs have dared to argue that the King has no power in law to authorise such *commendam* awards, as they are known. The case is considered at Common Pleas, but it raises difficult issues and is referred for definitive sentence by a general council of judges in the Exchequer Chamber.

When James hears of the case, he is angered and alarmed. This is a proceeding directly contrary to his declared will, nay to God's will, which says that men shall not question the royal power in its absolute prerogative. The King has written privately to Coke to express his concern, lest being handled in haste some inconvenience might thereby unawares come to our prerogative.

What disturbs His Majesty still further is that there has recently has been another case in which Brownlow, the prothonotary or Chief Clerk of Common Pleas, had sued for loss of income when the King created a new office for a royal favourite. The case had come before the King's Bench, where counsel for the plaintiff argued that the establishment of the new office required an Act of Parliament, was thus illegal as it stood, and that any delay of justice would be contrary to Magna Carta.

Sir Francis Bacon had then laid a writ of *non procedendo rege inconsulto* in the King's name, demanding that the case be referred to His Majesty for consultation and discussion. In so doing, the Attorney gave what even Coke acknowledged was a famous speech in support. Yet even so it was held that the writ might have been refused and the King's power of establishment denied, had not the parties abruptly settled the matter.

The King sees great danger here, and will not suffer another such threat to his prerogative, that is clear.

Now, however, the case of Colt and Glover bids fair to reopen this tender matter. Francis has long kept the King informed of its progress.

Tap, tap, tap. I have you not yet, my Lord Coke, yet I shall have you.

In April, Francis wrote to put the Lord Chief Justice on notice, saying that it is the King's express pleasure that His Majesty be first consulted with, ere there be any further proceeding by argument of any of the judges, or otherwise; therefore that the day appointed for the further proceeding by argument of the judges in that case be put off, till His Majesty's further pleasure be known upon consulting with him. And to that end, that your Lordship forthwith signify his commandment to the rest of the Judges, whereof your Lordship may not fail.

But Coke does not do as instructed. Rather, he replies that it is fit the rest of his brethren should understand His Majesty's pleasure immediately by letters from the Attorney to the judges of the several benches. Francis must therefore write letters to each of the judges to that effect, as he does.

There is then a delay, a period in which the judges do something quite out of the ordinary: they assemble and confer, they convene in the Exchequer Chamber and they decide the case.

After that, they write a joint letter to the King as follows: Most dread and most gracious Sovereign, we are and ever will be ready with all faithful and true hearts, according to our bounden duties, to serve and obey your Majesty, and think ourselves most happy to spend our lives and abilities to do your Majesty true and faithful service.

The judges say, We have advisedly considered of the letter of Mr Attorney, and with one consent do hold the same to be contrary to law, and such as we could not yield to the same by our oath; assuredly persuading ourselves that your Majesty being truly informed, that it standeth not with your royal and just pleasure to give way to them. And therefore knowing your Majesty's zeal to justice, and to be most renowned therefor, we have, according to our oaths and duties, proceeded and thereof certified your Majesty, and shall ever pray to the Almighty for your Majesty in all honour, health and happiness long to reign over us. Signed, Edw. Coke, Henry Hobart, Law. Tanfield, P. Warburton, Geo. Snigge, Ja. Altham, Ed. Bromley, Jo. Croke, Hump. Winch, Jo. Doddridge, Augustine Nicolls, Rob. Houghton. Serjeants' Inn.

To this letter the King now replies, addressing all the judges, but Coke first. His words begin most mildly, but by the end they are like thunder.

He says, Trusty and well-beloved councillor, and trusty and well beloved, we greet you well. We perceive by your letter, that you conceive the commandment given you by our Attorney General in our name to have proceeded upon wrong information. Ye might very well have spared your labour in informing us of the nature of your oath. For although we never studied the common law of England, yet are we not ignorant of any points which belong to a king to know. We are therefore to inform you hereby, that we are far from crossing or delaying anything which may belong to the interest of any private parties in this case. But we cannot be contented to suffer the prerogative royal of our Crown to be wounded through the sides of a private person.

We are therefore to admonish you, the King continues, that since the prerogative of our Crown hath been more boldly dealt withal in Westminster Hall during the time of our reign, than ever it was before in the reigns of divers princes immediately preceding us, that we will no longer endure that popular and unlawful liberty; and therefore were we justly moved to send you that direction to forbear to meddle in a case of so tender a nature, till we had further thought upon it.

He says, *Our pleasure therefore is, who are the head and fountain of justice under God in our dominions, and we out of our absolute power and authority royal do command you, that you forbear to meddle any further in this plea till our coming to town, and that out of our own mouth you may hear our pleasure in this business.*

83

THE PALACE OF WHITEHALL, JUNE 1616

The King wishes it all to be handled just so. There can be no place for anger. There may yet be redemption.

His Majesty has fallen upon a happy conceit: the whole undertaking must resemble a geometrical proof. It must be a continuous passage of thought from its first axioms and postulates, through the design and construction of the procedure to the final demonstration. Each step must follow in an orderly way from the previous one, so that what results is perfectly clear and compelling.

Its spirit must be calm, balanced, free of favour or ill temper. Only, this is not geometry, but justice.

If it is justice, it is also a masque. Francis is expert in each, and has advised His Majesty some months before as to how the action is to be managed.

His words are measured, judicious, those of the councillor who proffers advice as to matters at whose sad outcome he feels some personal pain, but nothing more. For my opinion, he says, I am infinitely sorry that your Majesty is thus put to salve and cure not only accidents of time but errors of servants; for I account this a kind of sickness of my Lord Coke's, that comes almost in as ill a time as the sickness of my Lord Chancellor.

He continues, but for that which may concern your service, first, my opinion is plainly, that my Lord Coke at this time is not to be disgraced. On the other side, this great and public affront, not only to the reverend and well deserving person of your Chancellor (and at a time when he was thought to lie on dying, which was barbarous), but to your High Court of Chancery, which is the court of your absolute power, may not in my opinion pass lightly, nor end only in some formal atonement; but use is to be made thereof for the settling of your authority and strengthening of your prerogative according to the true rules of monarchy.

The true rules of monarchy; here is a man with the minstrel's touch to play upon the King's heartstrings!

Francis has not forgotten James's own *True Law of Monarchies*, with its ringing justification of his absolute power. There is opportunity here. To reaffirm the prerogative, to bring peace to these quarrelsome judges, and clarity to the law, to curb his turbulent Lord Chief Justice, and all at one time, these are things very pleasing to the King. Thanks to his Attorney, all is prepared.

So it is that the Privy Council meets on 6 June 1616, with His Majesty in the chair. There is a full Council at the table, with the Archbishop, the Lord Chancellor, the Treasurer, the Privy Seal, the Steward, the Chamberlain, their other Lordships, Secretaries Winwood and Lake, the Chancellor of the Exchequer, the Master of the Rolls. The Attorney and the Solicitor are in attendance, with clerks and others.

The twelve senior judges process in, Coke at their head, and are placed at the end of the chamber opposite the table. Coke looks at the faces in front of him. *These men are not my friends, save only Winwood; I am a Daniel come among lions.* He can sense what is to come, and he has sought to ready himself for it.

The King opens the assembly by saying that he has called them together on a question that has relation to no private person, but concerneth God and the King, the power of the Crown, and the state of his Church whereof he is Protector, and that there is no fitter place to handle it than at the head of his Council table. This question arose from the suit over *commendams*, into which he had commanded the Lord Bishop of Winchester and Secretary Winwood to inquire; and the Lord Bishop now stands to report that counsel for the plaintiff in that case had maintained diverse positions and assertions very prejudicial to His Majesty's prerogative royal.

The King then proceeds through the chain of events that followed. He had commanded the Attorney to write to the Lord Chief Justice of King's Bench seeking a delay. The letter is now read out, and the Council notes Coke's response by way of a servant that the Attorney should write to all the judges, as he duly did. Then the clerk reads out the letter of reply from all the judges to the King, saying that they held the Attorney's letters to be contrary to law, and such as they could not yield to the same by their oath; and that thereupon they had proceeded with the case, and did now certify His Majesty thereof. Finally, the King's reply is read aloud.

Thus the stage is set. Then the King steps into the character of prosecuting counsel, and with every successive word his passion grows stronger and more fervent.

'Ye judges have erred both in commission and in omission. As for omission, it is a grave fault that when you have heard a counsellor at the bar presume to argue against the prerogative right of a king, which is in effect his supremacy, you did not interrupt and reprove sharply that loose and bold course of disaffirming or impeaching things of so high a nature.

'Especially since I have observed that ever since my coming to the Crown, the popular sort of lawyers have been the men that most affrontedly in all Parliaments have trodden upon my prerogative.'

The words flow still faster, as they come nearer his deepest beliefs.

'Know ye not that a king has a double prerogative? Whereof the one is ordinary and has relation to his private interest, which may be and is every day disputed in Westminster Hall. The other is of a higher nature, referring to his supreme and imperial power and sovereignty, which ought not to be disputed or handled in vulgar argument.

'But of late,' James goes on, 'the courts of common law have grown so vast and transcendent, as they do both meddle with my prerogative absolute, and encroach upon all other courts of justice; as the High Commission, the councils established in Wales and at York, the Court of Requests.'

Men are silent. No one can doubt whom the King has in mind. But now he has moved on, to the judges' errors of commission.

'To put off proceeding upon a just and necessary cause, is no denying or delay of justice, but wisdom and maturity. There cannot be a more just and necessary cause of stay than consulting with the King, where the cause concerns the Crown. The judges do it daily upon lighter occasions. And there can have been no doubt that this case was one where the King's prerogative was directly and plainly disputed at the bar.'

Now the King is spitting in his anger. His eyes bulge, there is foam on his lips, his tongue rolls in his mouth.

'This is nothing but pretence! As for the judges' letter, it is a new thing, and very undecent and unfit, for subjects to disobey their King's commandment.

'Most of all, to proceed in the meantime, and to return to me a bare certificate! Ye ought to have concluded with the laying down of your reasons modestly unto my lawful Majesty; so to have submitted the same to my princely judgment, expecting to know from me whether you had given satisfaction.'

There is an instant of absolute, impenetrable silence. Then, as if by a sign, the judges rise from their seats and fall down upon their knees, acknowledging their error and humbly craving His Majesty's gracious favour and pardon for the same.

84

THE PALACE OF WHITEHALL, JUNE 1616

So far the proof has proceeded as expected; but now is the point of decision, whether it runs through to its conclusion or takes a new course.

Throughout the proceedings the King has enjoined himself to keep an open mind. He knows of his Attorney's hostility to Coke, of course; it is not a thing well hidden. But conflict between his councillors does not displease him, for conflict puts these men on their mettle, and brings to the fore their need for steady government and control by his own hand. Far better that, than have his own advisers machinating against him!

And, James knows, the Attorney's advice has assisted him, especially of late, just as it has smoothed the path of his beloved Steenie. What did Bacon say before? *My Lord Coke at this time is not to be disgraced.* Now there's a double meaning! Not at that time, or not ever?

As for Coke, what is to be made of him? The King respects his Lord Chief Justice. He had long hoped to cure the man of this spreading malady of opposition; that was his purpose in moving him from the Common Pleas and elevating him to the Council. And yes, Coke has done good work in bringing order to, and much new income from, the royal tenures. But a presence at the Council table has failed to assuage his turbulent spirit; if anything it has magnified it.

Yet the King still hesitates. He is the lawgiver; it is within his grace to grant redemption to those who seek it. Let him seek it who will.

And now here is Coke, Lord Chief Justice of King's Bench, who rises with some difficulty from his knees to address him. A moment of confession, of abject recognition of error, of apology, and all may be well again between them.

'Your Majesty, I and my brethren do beg to acknowledge your kingly power and authority, and have in no wise or to any degree sought to disobey you. But...'

But? Is this to be a defence of disobedience and insubordination?

'But for the matter of the letter, if I may offer, its effect was as of a stay of justice, which is contrary both to law and to our own judges' oath.

'We judges knew well amongst ourselves,' Coke says, 'that the case, as we meant to handle it, did not concern your Majesty's pre-rogative grant of *commendams*. If the case had been delayed, then the suit would have been discontinued. We could not adjourn it, because Mr Attorney's letter mentioned no day certain, and the law is clear that an adjournment must always be to a day certain.'

This man wants no redemption, thinks the King; and I will give him none.

'This is mere sophistry!' he shouts. 'That ye should take upon yourselves peremptorily to discern whether the case concerned my supreme prerogative, without consulting with me first, and inform-ing my princely judgement, is a thing preposterous.

'As for contravening the oath, what say you, Lord Chancellor?'

The masque proceeds. Now, before he offers his own opinion Ellesmere rises to ask for that of learned counsel to be heard; and all men's eyes turn to the Attorney General.

In his careful way, Bacon has long rehearsed for this moment. No haste, no zeal. 'My opinion is this,' he says, 'that putting off the day was without all scruple no delay of justice, nor did it endanger the judges' oath. Mine was no imperious letter to the judges. His

Majesty had important business, and required a stay till they might conveniently speak with him, which they knew could not be long.'

He has slipped the dagger in, between the ribs. Now he thrusts it harder.

'But I would wish the judges seriously to consider with themselves, whether they were not in greater danger of breach of their oath by their proceeding than they could have been by their stay. For it is part of their oath that they counsel His Majesty when they are called; and if they will proceed first in a business whereupon they are called to counsel, and will counsel him when the matter is past, it is more than a simple refusal to give him counsel.'

There is a muttering of assent from the other learned men. Now Coke interjects, in exasperation:

'Your Majesty will know well, what I have had cause to note in times past, that it is not in any way in order for your learned counsel to dispute with the judges, but to plead the facts of a matter before them and to seek their judgment.'

It is as I expected, thinks Francis: the same pettifogging, lawyerly point. Coke has lost the ears of all. What is all this to the King, when such matters of state are in the balance?

Then, smoothly, keeping any sense of superiority from his voice, he goes on, 'I must say I find this exception strange.

'For the Lord Chief Justice was himself Attorney in his own time, and he will surely not have forgot that the King's learned counsel are, by oath and office, and without fear of any man's face, to proceed or declare against any the greatest peer or subject of the kingdom; and not only any subject in particular, but any body of subjects or persons, be they judges or be they an upper or a lower house of Parliament, in case that they exceed the limits of their authority, or take anything from His Majesty's royal power or prerogative.'

Francis continues, 'So I would name this challenge for what it is: a wrong, and in His Majesty's presence, a wrong to our places, mine own and those of other learned counsel, for which I and my fellows do appeal to His Majesty for reparation.'

'Yea, Mr Attorney,' says the King, on his cue. 'This is so: I do affirm it. It is your duty so to do, and I shall maintain you in it.'

Coke has been trapped again into a direct public opposition to the King, before the full Privy Council and the judges. He attempts to recover himself by averring that he will not dispute with His Majesty, but the King waves this aside.

The final blow remains to be delivered. What had Ellesmere's words been to the judges more than ten years before? That 'the King's Majesty, as it were inheritable and descended from God, hath absolute monarchical power annexed inseparably to his crown and diadem, not by common law nor statute law, but more anciently than either of them.' Now the Lord Chancellor rises, and gives his opinion clearly and plainly, that the stay required by His Majesty is not against law, or any breach of a judge's oath. He demands that the oath itself is read out of the statute; which is done by the King's Solicitor, Sir Henry Yelverton.

This is the moment for Bacon to twist the dagger in the wound.

Each judge is questioned in the open, separately and in person, as to his counsel to the King: whether at any time in a case depending where the King required to consult with them, they ought not to stay proceedings. One by one, Houghton, Nicolls, Doddridge, Winch, Croke, Bromley, Altham, Snigge, Warburton, Tanfield, Hobart, they all yield that such is their duty.

But when it comes to Coke and he is put the question, he says, 'When that case shall be, I will do what it should be fit for a judge to do. And I will ever trust the justness of His Majesty's commandment.'

It must surely seal his fate.

85

THE PALACE OF PLACENTIA, 30 JUNE 1616

It is a glorious Sunday morning by the water's edge in Greenwich. The King has lately come out to Henry VIII's old Palace of Placentia, for rest and repair and, of course, for hunting; but also to be consulted about a new building, a house for Queen Anne, to be built in the Italian style.

The Surveyor of the King's Works, Mr Inigo Jones, has long been a particular favourite of the Queen, who loves his masques and his scenery and stage designs. Now he has returned from a tour of Italy loaded with drawings and sketches, and has filled their Majesties' heads with ideas of a building to rival the great *palazzi* of Florence and Rome. Mr Jones thinks of architecture as akin to rhetoric, in its style and sense of occasion. In part, this new house will be an act of persuasion, showing the greatness, longevity and grace of James's royal power; with, let it be noted, no hint of Popish ornament.

It is, then, an irritation for the King that he must attend to business that Sunday morning. But not an irritation without its pleasures, for he loves to give judgment, and to do justice. Kneeling before him now is Sir Edward Coke, who was Solicitor and Attorney to the late Queen and Attorney to himself, a man whom he has raised to the rank of Knight, made Chief Justice of Common Pleas and then of King's Bench, and elevated to the Privy Council.

To the sides are the other members of the Council. Behind

Coke stands his wife, Lady Hatton, who has come to plead for her husband, lest his fate sweep her and their children and all that they have and own away with him.

It is but four days since the Council met to discuss the Lord Chief Justice. The King had decided to proceed with a tribunal against him *ad hominem*, singling him out from the body of the judges as their leader and instigator. Yelverton, the Solicitor General, laid three charges. First, that Coke had deliberately arranged that a debt due to His Majesty for £12,000 should not be discharged by Sir Christopher Hatton, the offence compounded by Coke's later denials and protestations.

Secondly, that he had given heart and encouragement to Glanvill and Allen in their infamous *praemunire* suit, had vexed and constantly directed the jury, and remarked that if they failed to reach a verdict the common law of England would be overthrown and the light of the law so obscured that the judges would have little to do at the Assizes. Finally, that Coke had behaved undecently of late before the King, the King's Council and judges, wherein he took exception to learned counsel for speaking by the King's command, and that when the judges submitted themselves to His Majesty in the matter of *commendams*, he alone dissented.

There is great danger here for Coke; it would not do for him to dispute every item, especially when the King's mind was evidently so made up. So he had yielded on some points with meekness and contrition, had argued others, and pleaded mitigations to yet more. He should not have reproved learned counsel, he accepted; yet his was no dissent, but merely a judge's care for the proprieties of pleading. He had, it was true, uttered words about the overthrow of the law, but these were in another case; as for Glanvill and Allen, this charge was testimony on only one side.

If he had erred as to the undermining effects of Chancery on the common law courts, yet, he said, *erravimus cum patribus*, he had done so in accordance with the precedents, which he cited. As for the circumstances of the Hatton debt, these were *elephantini libri*, matters of great mass and complexity, which had happened twelve years before. At that time, he had been much occupied with the priests' treason, and afterward with the treason of Lord Cobham, and then the Powder Treason; and if anything had slipped him amid this multitude of business, then let these services blot out his errors.

There the tribunal had ended, to await the King's further consideration and final judgment. It is seen that both before and after it, in private and in public, at the Council table and at her house, with all the wit and charm and pity she can muster, Eliza Hatton pleads in desperation for her husband, and refuses to separate her state and her cause from his, resolving and publishing that she will run the same fortune with him.

Thanks to the Attorney General, this business too has been arranged in its proper order. The Privy Council tribunal settled the facts of the matter, but the law too must be settled. So at Bacon's urging the King came for the first time to Star Chamber, in defiance of near a century of precedent, to sit beneath its blue ceiling spangled with golden stars, in the chair last occupied by Henry VIII.

That thought strikes a chill among the Parliament men and common lawyers who have gathered to hear him. But why should he not come? This is the King's prerogative court of courts, it is of the prerogative that he wishes to speak. To do so from the chair itself, *ex cathedra*, as any Romanist might say, can only add to his authority.

Looking out across the Chamber and upon the Privy Councillors and the judges, the peers of the realm and bishops there convened, the King wishes to make law, of that there can be no mistake. As he says, *out of my own mouth I declare unto you, which being in this place is equal to a proclamation.* The speech itself is rambling and repetitious, as though the King were the owner of a great house who must show his guests the same rooms on every visit. He denounces bad justices of the peace as idle slowbellies, or busybodies, and gentlemen of great worth in their own conceit that give a snatch against monarchy through their puritanical itching after popularity. He distinguishes what he calls the polypragmatic papist from the still more to be despised Popish recusant, whom you may find out as a fox by the foul smell a great way round about his hole.

Yet His Majesty's speech has point and purpose; it is carefully fitted to denounce and refute the Lord Chief Justice of the King's Bench at every point.

The King, as he reminds his auditors, is *lex loquens*, and the law can have no life, and the judges no authority, apart from Kings. For Kings are properly judges, and judgment properly belongs to them from God; Kings sit in the throne of God, and thence all judgment is derived. As Kings borrow their power from God, so judges do from Kings; and as Kings are to account to God, so are judges unto God and Kings.

These are familiar strains. All wait patiently through the speech, in case a new melody shall be heard. Meanwhile, the King proceeds.

It is atheism and blasphemy, he says, to dispute what God can do; good Christians content themselves with His will revealed in His word. So, it is presumption and high contempt in a subject, to dispute what a king can do, or say that a king cannot do this, or that; but rest in that which is the King's revealed will in his law. As for what Coke has called a judge's artificial reason, the King remarks, I will never trust any interpretation that agreeth not with my common sense and reason, and true logic.

As for the common law judges? Keep your selves within your own benches, the King says, not to invade other jurisdictions, which is unfit and an unlawful thing. The prerogative? Encroach not... if there fall out a question that concerns my prerogative, deal not with it till you consult with the King or his Council, or both.

The Court of Chancery? The Chancery is independent of any other court, and is only under the King... from that court there is no appeal. Writs of prohibition? They are a cause why pleas are turned from court to court in an endless circular motion, like Ixion's wheel.

And then a moment comes when the King looks directly across at Coke, and fixes him with his gaze, and none can be in any doubt as to the force and target of his words. It is, he intones, the duty of judges to punish those that seek to deprave the proceedings of any of the King's Courts, and not to encourage them any way. And I must confess I thought it an odious and inept speech, and it grieved me very much, that it should be said in Westminster Hall, that a *praemunire* lay against the Court of the Chancery and officers there. How can the King grant a *praemunire* against himself?

No, says James. It was a foolish, inept, and presumptuous attempt, and fitter for the time of some unworthy King. And, therefore, sitting here in a seat of judgment, I declare and command that no man hereafter presume to sue a *praemunire* against the Chancery; which I may the more easily do, because no *praemunire* can be sued but at my suit. And I may justly bar myself at mine own pleasure.

Coke listens intently. He is impassive to look at, but inwardly aghast. In its practice and in its principles, his life's work is being systematically unmade before his eyes.

86

PRIVY COUNCIL, 30 JUNE 1616

Yet must not we put the strong law on him.
He's lov'd of the distracted multitude,
Who like not in their judgement but their eyes,
And where 'tis so, th' offender's scourge is weigh'd,
But never the offence. To bear all smooth and even,
This sudden sending him away must seem
Deliberate pause. Diseases desperate grown
By desperate appliance are reliev'd,
Or not at all.

That was two weeks before. Now the King's proof proceeds to the person of the Lord Chief Justice himself, and so to the court at Greenwich that Sunday, and Coke on his knees before His Majesty.

It is Coke's friend and neighbour Sir Ralph Winwood, Secretary of State, who reads aloud the finding of the tribunal. Their lordships have made report to His Majesty of that which passed on Wednesday last at Whitehall, where the Lord Chief Justice was charged by His Majesty's Solicitor with certain things; which being delivered in writing, and in his princely judgement duly weighed and considered of, His Majesty was no way satisfied with his answers to any of those points, wherewith he stood charged. Nevertheless, such is His Majesty's clemency and goodness, as he is pleased not to proceed heavily against him, but rather to look upon the merit of his former services; and accordingly hath decreed...

Coke is removed from the Privy Council, pending His Majesty's further pleasure, and forbidden to ride on his judicial summer circuit, though all has been prepared for him. It is an exquisite humiliation, at once to be suspended from office and publicly declared unfit to sit as judge even at the Assizes. The news will be round the court in a few minutes; the taverns and counting houses of London will resound with it. It will be the instant talk of the common lawyers in the Inns, and the Members at Westminster. And at every point on Coke's judicial circuit, the circuit he has ridden twice a year for so long, explanations must be offered and new arrangements hurriedly made to cover the fact that England's highest jurist will not be sitting.

His humiliation is all the more exquisite for being temporary. Coke has not been relieved of his judicial office. He is merely in a suspension, held there by the grace of the King. But for how long?

Ellesmere's men have already seen how the wind is blowing. Now they turn away from the Lord Chief Justice, do not remove their hats or give any other sign of regard for him. But for Francis, the best is yet to come, for at his suggestion the King has set Coke a task to fill the empty hours of the summer vacation. Coke is to review his books of *Reports*, wherein there be many exorbitant and extravagant opinions set down and published for positive and good law. Amongst other things, His Majesty was not well pleased with the title of those books, wherein he styled himself Lord Chief Justice of England, whereas he could challenge no more than Chief Justice of the King's Bench.

And, once Coke has corrected what in his discretion he finds meet in those *Reports*, His Majesty's pleasure is that he should bring the same privately to him, that he might consider thereof, as in his princely judgment shall be found expedient. Whereby Coke may hope that His Majesty in time will receive him again to his gracious and princely favour.

Thus may Coke restore himself, his rank and his fortunes: by a diligent review, recantation and correction of his own past errors, and by no other means.

Finally, the courts themselves must be fully set in order. Now that Coke has been removed, this may proceed without trouble or opposition.

So on 18 July 1616, King James issues under the Privy Seal a decree, which Bacon has drafted with extreme care. It laboriously rehearses the case Ellesmere has made for the superiority of the Court of Chancery. This is certified as in accordance with precedent and law by the Law Officers, the statutes are reviewed and the court is declared exempt from any writ of *praemunire*.

Then the King declares, that We in our princely judgment having well weighed and with mature deliberation considered of the several reports of our learned Counsel and all the parts of them, do approve ratify and confirm as well the practice of our Court of Chancery… and do will and command that our Chancellor or Keeper of the Great Seal for the time being shall not hereafter desist to give unto our subjects such relief in equity (notwithstanding any former proceedings at the common law against them) as shall stand with the true merits and justice of their cases, and with the former ancient and continued practice and precedency of our Chancery.

For Ellesmere, who had feared this day might never be while he was alive, the decree marks a final triumph over Coke. For Francis Bacon, the pleasure is sweet indeed. But this is not quite final triumph; that is yet to come.

87

THE PALACE OF WHITEHALL, 2 OCTOBER 1616

It is three months later, in the Lord Chancellor's chambers. And his Lordship is not happy.

'THIS is the result, Francis?' Ellesmere is incredulous; the fall of Coke has given him new life, and age adds extra force to his contempt.

'This is the product of his months of review and cogitation? It is derisory, a mockery of His Majesty, in his person and in his procedure. The man shall pay for it.'

'There can be no going back for him now, my Lord. That is for certain.'

Coke has at last responded to the task required of him by the King. Francis had not known what to expect, for His Majesty had set ambition against self-righteousness in the heart of the Chief Justice. A titanic struggle, to be sure! If ambition be uppermost, there was time over the summer for retraction, time enough for Coke to correct and perfect his *Reports*; perhaps at length, given the many ways in which they have been found wanting. If, however, self-righteousness should triumph, if Coke remains wise in his own conceits, then he may remit but a few sheets.

But this?! A single, solitary paper with a handful of scrawled notations on it?

The King being absent, they had summoned Coke that morning, Ellesmere as Lord Chancellor presiding, learned counsel in attendance. Coke had opened by referring those present to the eleven volumes of his published *Reports*, containing some five hundred cases. Yet, Coke said, he was bound to note that even in so esteemed an authority as Plowden, there had been found nevertheless errors which the wisdom of time had discovered and later judgments controlled. He himself had found four cases in Plowden's exquisite and elaborate *Commentaries* that were erroneous, cases that he proceeded to discuss at some length, the other men listening in silence.

There had then followed a brief homily from the Chief Justice on the commonplace dictum, that it was sin for a man to go against his own conscience, though erroneous, except his conscience be first informed and satisfied. After which, he had produced a paper with just four cases listed from his own researches, a few trifling corrections to them noted in his tiny handwriting. He expressed a measure of satisfaction that his own defaults had not exceeded those of the great Plowden.

This performance was met by those present with uncertainty at first, yielding to open astonishment by the end. There was nothing for them to say or do, however, but to receive Coke's paper and remit it to the King. Till the King's pleasure be known, the Lord Chancellor reminded Coke that he should forebear from sitting at Westminster, and from any other public exercise of his office as Chief Justice.

But, as Bacon reminds Ellesmere when they have withdrawn, the rights and liberties of the Church, the jurisdiction of the courts, the King's own royal prerogative, all these great and weighty matters have been ignored by Coke in reviewing his list of offences.

Coke has offered no recognition of error, no defence, no contrition, no remorse, no request for pardon, no repair. Rather, he has acted to disesteem the prerogative of the King and weaken the Church. They must press His Majesty for a further Privy Council proceeding, to confront the Chief Justice in his actions.

The King has seen enough, and resolves to act directly and in his own right. For Francis, this is the time to drive the dagger in to the hilt.

He prepares a legal memorandum to declare that His Majesty might, upon the grounds of deceit, contempt and slander of his government, very justly have proceeded, not only to have put Coke from his place of Chief Justice but to have brought him in question in the Star Chamber, subject to criminal proceedings.

Moreover, Francis invites His Majesty to affirm that he hath noted in Coke a perpetual turbulent carriage, and in his princely wisdom hath made two special observations of him. The one, that he having in his nature not one part of those things which are popular in men, being neither liberal, nor affable, nor magnificent, he hath made himself popular by design only, in pulling down government. The other, that whereas His Majesty might have expected a change in him, when he made him his own by taking him to be of his Council, it made no change at all, but to the worse.

To the sheet of charges against Coke is thus added the sin of disloyalty.

On 10 November, the King at last informs the Privy Council that Coke is to be removed from the bench. Not with discourtesy – the Queen has been very earnest on Coke's behalf – but with so many good words, as if he means to hang him with a silken halter.

Fine words or no, this is a public death. The Oracle of the Law, cashiered! Has Coke committed some unknown crime, to be treated so? No Chief Justice has suffered this fate for at least three centuries, maybe more.

The news quickly trickles out and fills the court with rumour, to Coke's added shame and humiliation. It falls to Francis Bacon to play the executioner; he prepares a writ of *mandamus* for the King, saying May it please your excellent Majesty, I send your Majesty a form of discharge for my Lord Coke from his place of Chief Justice of your Bench. I send also a warrant to the Lord Chancellor for making forth a writ for a new Chief Justice, leaving a blank for the name to be supplied by your Majesty.

Mandamus is a direct command from the King. This writ is brutal in its simplicity, and gives no reasons for the dismissal, simply saying Now for certain causes moving us, wishing you no longer to be Chief Justice to hold pleas before ourself, we command you that you no longer fulfil that office, and… we remove and utterly discharge you therefrom. It is signed and sealed on 16 November.

When it is delivered to Coke by Sir George Coppin, it leaves Coke weeping and desolate. He has been dismissed from office and publicly disgraced. The streets are full of the scandal, and the common talk is that four Ps have overthrown and put him down, that is PRIDE, PROHIBITIONS, PRAEMUNIRE, and PREROGATIVE.

The new Chief Justice, Sir Henry Montagu, has been commended to His Majesty by Francis Bacon. Montagu immediately sends to Coke to buy from him the golden chain of esses that is the mark of his office. Coke rebuffs him, saying he would not part with it, but leave it to his posterity, that they might one day know they had a Chief Justice as their ancestor.

Montagu is installed on 18 November, in great pomp, and at the ceremony he at once humbly and basely petitions the Lord Chancellor that he will do nothing unseemly. By this he signifies that no one need fear he will act in any way in opposition to the King. He has already agreed to yield the Chief Clerkship and its revenues to Villiers, as Coke had not.

For his part, Ellesmere rouses himself from his sickbed to attend, and gives a bitter little invective that slights and defames the departed Coke for his many errors and vanities, but specially for his ambitious popularity. Coke disbands his household in

London, keeps or handsomely pays off his servants, and retires to the country.

Throughout all this, Francis Bacon has watched and acted in a kind of rapture. It is as if fortune herself has reached out to place her guiding hand upon the course of events. Perhaps she has made the journey arduous, that to reach the final destination may satisfy still more.

As for Francis himself, he has played the game with a degree of skill, he grants it, but as every man is maker of his own fortune, so men must say that he deserves all that he has achieved.

Honour, rank, wealth, a wife of means, a great household. Above all, victory, sweet victory, complete and final victory over his enemy. Coke long rode high on his connections with the Cecils, he took more value from book learning and from his private study than any could have contemplated, more than he deserved. His empty bombast served him well in the courtroom, too.

Yet so full was his conceit that he never foresaw what would befall him. He thought himself immortal, and now like Icarus has fallen to earth. As Francis is wont to say, he doth like the ape that the higher he climbs the more he shows his arse. So it has happened.

But was not Coke, too, in his way, maker of his own ill fortune? And if Francis helped that ill fortune along, if, as often late at night he sees with piercing clarity, he made that ill fortune what it proved to be, scheming with Ellesmere, flattering Villiers – or as Villiers soon becomes, the Earl of Buckingham – ceaselessly working like a smith to shape and make adverse the opinion of the King, then Coke himself gave Francis all the material he needed.

Time was when Francis Bacon would have quailed and shrunk even from the thought of such acts, in terror for the soul of a man who could perform them. Not now. Not with Coke.

On 5 March 1617, the King finally accepts the resignation of the ailing Ellesmere. On the 6th the Great Seal is delivered up. On the 7th, the Seal is given, with the title of Lord Keeper, as both had been given by Queen Elizabeth to his father, to Sir Francis Bacon.

Francis knows whom he must thank. He writes to Buckingham, that *in this day's work you are the truest and perfectest mirror and example of firm and generous friendship that ever was in court. And I shall count every day lost, wherein I shall not either study your well doing in thought, or do your name honour in speech, or perform you service in deed. Good my Lord, account and accept me, Your most bounden and devoted friend and servant of all men living.*

On that same 7 May, the first day of the legal term, Sir Francis Bacon takes his seat in the Court of Chancery. The King is absent, on a royal progress in Scotland accompanied by Buckingham and other courtiers, from which he will not return till the autumn. He has left much of the business of government in Bacon's hands, and for this and other reasons there is a more than full attendance at the ceremony.

As it is noted, the new Lord Keeper *exceeds all his predecessors in the bravery and multitude of his servants*. He appeared in his greatest glory; for to the Hall, besides his own retinue, did accompany him all the Lords of His Majesty's Council and others, with all knights and gentlemen that could get horses, *more than two hundred horses*. All those present are amazed at its magnificence.

V

TESIS: 1617–1621

88

LONDON, YORK HOUSE, JULY 1617

'**L**ORD KEEPER!!' The woman is shouting, screaming, slapping the oak door of the inner chamber in her grief, her face streaked with tears, her exquisite garments spattered with dust and mud stains.

The servants of the house are in a quandary, whether to lay hand on her or let her be. Edwardes the doorkeeper is more used to ruffians than to high-born ladies. Davies the butler has a softer manner, but his efforts to quieten her are vain.

'My Lady, the Master hath retired to bed in some sickness. It were not good to wake him. If you will wait but a short time, I am sure...'

Again she cries, 'Good Lord Keeper, Francis, Francis, please awaken! It is your cousin Elizabeth, and I stand in desperate need of your assistance. Pardon my boldness, I pray you, for I am like a cow that has lost her calf.'

There are noises from within, and the door is slowly opened for the gentlemen of the bedchamber to emerge. Pushing them aside, Lady Hatton strides in, to find a vast room richly adorned, a bed dressed with silks and taffeta, and beside it a frankly bewildered and unnerved Francis Bacon, clad only in his undergarments.

For Elizabeth, the years of her marriage to Edward Coke have been long and troubled. In appearance, she is little changed; not yet forty, she retains the figure of her youth, and if anything a still deeper beauty, which she sets off to great advantage with bright dresses and finely sewn gowns. But in her inner self she feels old, her soul weathered and hardened by experience.

With my first most faithful and dear husband William, my transitory happiness expired, she is apt to say. But how could she have known it would? She was then so young, and all she had had was happiness; the happiness of family, of a life of ease and plenty, of a kind and loving spouse. Her new husband Coke was not a man of rank, but he too had had these things, ten children and a wife he doted on.

Why should a marriage between two people thus favoured be any different? Edward Coke was unlike all the others who made their way to Hatton House that spring and summer of '98; the aged, the callow, the querulous, and all of them burdened with debts and in quest of a dowry.

Yes, Edward was of another stamp; a man of wealth not of debts, who had no need of what she brought; a man of formidable reputation in the law, but yet also a man of action, not of shrivelled scholarship; a fine figure, well dressed, yet who still had a rough Norfolk way about him; a man of a man, not some fop or reed who needed another to plead for him. Someone she could admire and respect.

And there had been a spark between them from the start. Most men were made timid by her presence; not he. Indeed, he seemed to relish her vivacity. She had looked forward to being his wife, and to bringing her portion – not merely of land and jewels, but of influence and advice and connections, and of children too – to their marriage. It would be a union of intellect and beauty.

The early signs promised well. He had driven a stiff bargain with her father, it seemed, and his expectations as to her own wealth were clear, but so would they be for any man thus placed. And he had accepted her demands for the marriage itself, though all knew how out of the ordinary they were. But everything had been altered after the ceremony of marriage. He had refused to pay her dear dead William's household debts, and on a hundred smaller matters revealed a strand of bitter meanness. How could she take the name of a man who had behaved in such a way? It would be a double dishonour, to William and to herself, even though she knew her resolve would enrage her new husband.

As for him, at times it was as though a captious, avaricious demon had inhabited an often wise and generous spirit. Coke would spend lavishly on her, surround her with seamstresses, haberdashers and silkmen, for he wished his wife, like his houses, to be shown to her best – and would then refuse her access to her own money when she needed it.

He worked without cease, at hours forbidding human society, early to bed and rising before dawn. He seemed to delight in the birth of their first daughter, Elizabeth, but then to forget about her. Any rebuff, in the law or at court, would send him home in a furious silence. Above all, whether in private or in public, he could not bear to be contested or opposed in any matter. At all times, in all things, he must be the master, and all must know it. From a wife, he demanded what Elizabeth could never give, an unquestioning obedience and deference to his wishes.

Did he trick me, she asks, and hide his true nature until after their marriage? No. He wished to ingratiate, but he is too proud to deceive me. Why bother to deceive me, whom he holds of so little account? What she misses so deeply in him, what dear William had in abundance, is kindness: the recognition of her wants, the anticipation of her pleasures, a thousand small attentions to her self and soul.

Of these qualities Coke has but small measure. Catch him in his moment, and he will show you all the wit and good humour and courtesy you could want. But cross him, and he may fly into so violent a passion it would take ten men to master him. He has struck her, pulled the ruff off her neck, threatened to beat her on occasion till she had to lock herself away with her ladies. She has heard tales of wives being harmed, even killed, by their husbands, with never any need for the ruffians to answer for it. She cannot, will not, bear even the thought of it. But why should she endure its consequence, the subjection of herself and her daughters to a man unwilling to maintain them? It is insult to them and dishonour to her family.

After barely two years of marriage, she had first determined to make a stand against her husband, and had gathered up her daughters and moved back to the house of her father. Coke was furious, but he had no choice but to bargain with her; and, thanks to her father and uncle Robert Cecil, the matter was patched up, though it took many months to do it. Husband and wife were reconciled, and their second daughter Frances born soon after.

On the surface at least, all was restored. But in truth Edward ever treated them all like his property, marrying off her stepdaughter Frances Hatton to Robert Rich a few years afterwards.

Must it have come to this? Did not the Cecils nurture Edward Coke? Did they not pluck him from the ranks of the common lawyers and make him what he is? Oh that her family should be thus repaid!

Some of Elizabeth's fondest memories have been to play parts in the great masques of Queen Anne. The Queen casts herself in these productions, and often her ladies of the court as well. She loves to play the warrior queen – an Amazon one year, in another war-like Pallas Athene, in her helmet clad – women of strength and violence and beauty able to dominate and defeat Kings, and all while her husband the King sits watching.

Elizabeth herself has played Makaria the Blessed in the masque called *The Vision of the Twelve Goddesses*. Why should she grow up in the court of the old Queen Elizabeth, the one for whom her own name was given, why should she see such great female figures, and play them on the stage in front of royalty and peers, and yet fawn obeisance to her husband from the moment his foot first touches home?

Over the years Elizabeth Hatton has taught herself not to ask what might have been. There is no profit in it. She might have married Pembroke's boy, or Fulke Greville, or even her cousin Francis Bacon, and none make her happy.

Her daughters have been a source of joy. She is often at court, though she has never quite been an intimate of Queen Anne's. She has given many lavish entertainments; and she has enjoyed the rise of her husband, from Queen's to King's Attorney, to a knighthood, to Chief Justice of Common Pleas. It has helped that the two of them are often in different places.

That was a happy decade of years. But of late matters have again become more difficult. Edward was much affected by the death of her uncle Robert, Earl of Salisbury. He hated to be moved to the King's Bench, even though he was made a Privy Councillor as well. His spirits have become more quarrelsome, as he finds himself in opposition to the King; the names of Ellesmere and Bacon fill him with anger and suspicion. Now he faces what he most fears, a loss of all control, and public humiliation, and perhaps his ruin. And his ruin must surely also be hers.

At first he met it all in his usual way, with silent anger, so as to leave Elizabeth bereft and yet incapable of assistance. But then the rumours became so rife and the burden on him so heavy that he was at last persuaded to tell the detail of what had happened and seek his wife's support.

To confide in her, to share his troubles, to rely on her good offices for his help! He hated it, that was clear, but for one in her sad state, these things are sweet balm. They are all she has wanted and needed since that day she and Coke first met, and throughout the summer and autumn of 1616 she had thrown herself body and soul into the fight on his behalf. She had gone to court, and prayed the Queen's assistance. She had sought an audience with the young Prince Charles. She had petitioned the Council, and deployed every device and charm she knew to cajole and woo the courtiers of highest rank.

But then formal charges were preferred against Coke by Solicitor Yelverton in June, and his manner grew still more urgent and oppressive. One of the charges related to the old debts of Christopher Hatton to the King, and Coke threatened Elizabeth that if she so much as touched upon them he would make her pay double and treble what they were worth. She was indignant, but she loyally kept her silence.

So she did too, when the news of Coke's dismissal was made known in November. What else was left to her? Her husband could have repented and retracted, but he had spurned the proffered path back to favour, and had been disgraced. Though she had won men's admiration for her defence of him, and was still close to the court, she must share his fate. It might cost them dearly, and all the more if the King pursued the old debts on Hatton properties.

She and her husband must therefore retire to the country, gather themselves and the family together, weather the storm, and find a way for him to make a return to public life.

So Elizabeth is taken aback to hear that her husband has been with the King only a few weeks later, at Newmarket. And it shocks her to the very core to learn what he proposes: nothing less than the marriage of their fourteen-year-old daughter Frances to Sir John Villiers, the weak-brained brother of the Earl of Buckingham.

89

LONDON, YORK HOUSE, JULY 1617

They have moved from the bedchamber to the parlour. Francis Bacon has recovered his clothes, his composure and his dignity. Food and drink have been found for Lady Hatton. In a few words she tells him what has occurred.

'Dear Francis, much you may know already,' she says, 'and if so I am sorry for it. But I am so stricken that I must tell it in my own words. You will know my husband' – she cannot bring herself to name him – 'my husband resolved to offer our daughter Frances to Sir John Villiers last wintertime, to win favour from the King and the Earl.

'But the family and he could not agree terms, and while he was at Newmarket I had no choice but to take Frances away with many of my possessions. My husband was very angry, and kept from me money I was due, and he was still more angry when I took the matter last May before the Privy Council, of which you will have seen the consequence.

'The Council required us to agree terms,' she goes on, 'much to my husband's distress. I thought then that all would be well. But the matter of our daughter was not resolved. It was plain that Sir John and his family still wished to pursue the match. Much of the settlement on her would be paid for out of my own moneys, directly and by inheritance, and I had good cause not to trust my husband. So I raised the match directly with Sir John's mother, Lady Compton.'

Francis interjects, 'But cousin, did not Secretary Winwood approach the Earl directly with a renewed offer from your husband?'

'Yes! My husband hath offered £30,000 for the match, and been accepted. He informed me of it but two days ago.'

'But why, then, are you here and in such distress?'

'Francis, think of it! He is about to sell my daughter to a man she neither knows nor cares for, for a vast price of which I should bear the larger part, without any notice or consideration of me or her, but just for his own ends. You know me, dear cousin, you know how I care for little Frances and cannot bear for her or me to be trampled under foot, yet that is exactly what he proposes!'

'So that same evening,' Elizabeth continues, 'I waited till my husband had gone to bed, then gathered up Frances and took her away to lodge with my relative Withipole, who lives on the road to Weybridge. When my husband awoke yesterday, he must have gathered a group of men and searched for us. Somehow' – she gasps – 'somehow they found out where Frances was, and he secured a warrant from Winwood...'

'Ah!' Francis exclaims. 'They sought a warrant from me, but I would not grant it. So they went to his friend Winwood, who hath acted ill indeed.'

'... and came out to the house. I had been in London. When I returned last evening, I found his son Robert already there. I tried to block the gate but my husband arrived and they all got a great beam of wood, broke the gate down and searched the house. Frances was hiding but I saw them dragging her out in terror.'

She breaks off, to compose herself.

'Then today I came to your house, but such was my hurry that the coach overturned and cast me out of it into the muck and dust of the street. But I would not be deterred and pressed on to see you regardless.'

Now Elizabeth clasps his hand in hers and looks him full in the face.

'Francis, dear cousin, please, please, you know what I may have been to you, may still be; know that I keep that lovely sonnet safe in my home, and in my heart. I beg you, help me and my daughter. This is a monstrous injustice, and you are our only hope. It is all too much!'

And with that she is overcome with weeping.

It is later that day. Lady Hatton is somewhat recovered in spirits and has been escorted home. But she has left Francis deep in thought, turning the whole affair over in his mind. He has been much moved by her situation, and still more by her distress. He knew Coke was capable of cruelty, but this exceeds all bounds. It is a further matter for the Privy Council, of that he is sure, and he will make it so; he convenes a meeting of the Council for the following morning.

But there is also the wisdom of the marriage of the girl to Villiers to be considered. Here Francis sees an opportunity to his own advantage.

Taking his pen in hand, he writes a letter to Buckingham, who is still with the King in Scotland, saying My very good Lord, It seemeth Secretary Winwood hath officiously busied himself to make a match between your brother and Sir Edward Coke's daughter; and, as we hear, he doth it rather to make a faction, than out of any great affection to your Lordship. It is true, he hath the consent of Sir Edward Coke upon reasonable conditions for your brother. But the mother's consent is not had, nor the young gentlewoman's, who expecteth a great fortune from her mother, which without her consent is endangered.

This match, Francis continues, out of my faith and freedom towards your Lordship, I hold very inconvenient both for your brother and yourself. First, he shall marry into a disgraced house, which in reason of state is never held good. Next, he shall marry into a troubled house of man and wife, which in religion and Christian discretion is disliked. Thirdly, your Lordship will go near to lose all such your friends as are adverse to Sir Edward Coke; myself only except, who out of a pure love and thankfulness shall ever be firm to you. And lastly and chiefly, it will greatly weaken and distract the King's service; for opinion will do a great deal of harm, and cast the King back, and make him relapse into those inconveniences which are now well on to be recovered.

Francis continues, therefore my advice is, and your Lordship shall do yourself a great deal of honour, if, according to religion and the law of God, your Lordship will signify unto my Lady your mother, that your desire is that the marriage be not pressed or proceeded in without the consent of both parents; and so either break it altogether, or defer any further dealing in it, till your Lordship's return: and this the rather, for that it hath been carried so harshly and inconsiderately by Secretary Winwood. Thus hoping your Lordship will not only accept well, but believe my faithful advice, who by my great experience in the world must needs see further than your Lordship can, I ever rest your Lordship's true and most devoted servant, Francis Bacon.

The letter is sent. But there is still a vital question that remains: Coke obtained a warrant to search Withipole's house, but that warrant made no mention of breaking and entering the house.

On what basis of law, then, did Coke and his men break down the gate and enter? That could be a criminal offence, something to bring Coke to Star Chamber. Now there is a thought to excite the heart of Francis Bacon.

Thereafter, events move with great speed. On the next day, Sunday 13 July, the Privy Council meets to consider the matter of Frances Coke, and resolves to question Sir Edward on the Tuesday. But then Lady Hatton arrives, begs and is granted leave by Bacon to address the Council, and petitions that her daughter be immediately sent for, as undoubtedly weakened by the violence and fright of her removal, and be brought to London that night where she might have such help from physic and attendance as were requisite for her recovery.

If her last performance before the Council were worthy of a Burbage, this is no less than an Alleyn, and it quickly accedes to her request.

Under Bacon's guidance, the Council then writes to Coke to that effect, and receives a reply: that it is late in the evening, his daughter is in no such extremity, and that he will deliver her the following morning. Thinking its original order neglected, and filled with a concern that Coke may not keep his promise, at Bacon's urging the Council now issues a further warrant for the girl's delivery, with an added writ of assistance which gives powers to other officers and loyal citizens to help in bringing this about. However, she arrives safely on the Monday morning and the warrant is never served.

On Tuesday Coke himself appears before the Council. He pleads a fear that Lady Hatton intended to take their daughter away to France rather than see her married. But when he is asked for any evidence for this, he can produce none. When the Council turns to tax him with his use of riot and force, Coke points not to the warrant, but to a father's general discretion in law to use force to secure a fugitive daughter. This is a legal question and, guided by Bacon, the Council then refers the charge for prosecution against Sir Edward Coke to the Court of Star Chamber.

If the King will not destroy Coke for deceit, contempt and slander of his government, thinks Francis, then perhaps the courts may do so. That would be an irony indeed.

90

GORHAMBURY, JULY 1617

A letter has come from the royal court, now in the later stages of the King's Scottish progress. Francis reads it, then again, then a third time.

A friend writes, *But the King's ears be wide and long, and he seeth with many eyes. I pray God nothing be soiled heated or cooled in the carriage. Envy sometimes attends virtues and not for good; and these bore certain proprieties and circumstances inherent to your Lordship's mind, which men may admire, I cannot express. But I will wade no further herein lest I should seem eloquent.*

Folded writing indeed! This is veiled, almost disjointed in places. The flow of official business is unceasing, and the letter might refer to one of a dozen matters or more. But there is foreboding in it, and Francis feels himself a little unnerved. Who are these people, whose envy attends their virtues? Or is it his virtues that they envy? It is too unclear. Secretary Winwood, perhaps? He is no friend, and he is in constant correspondence from Whitehall with Secretary Lake, who is with the King. But Winwood's letters would not be soiled, heated or cooled in the carriage; they would leave him in that condition. So what does the letter mean?

Winwood and he had clashed only just now, over the case of Coke's daughter. After Francis had refused Coke a warrant, Coke must have procured one from Winwood, so much was clear; the two men are friends and allies, with lands that adjoin each other at Stoke.

But the Secretary should not go scot free for such an act, and Bacon in his anger had criticised him for it in the Council, even threatened him with a *praemunire* for giving Coke a warrant... only for Winwood to stand up and brandish a letter from the King himself in his support! A letter saying that His Majesty could see nothing wrong in what Coke had done, that the thefteous stealing away of a daughter from her own father was the true offence, and that what followed was but a redress of the former violence.

It was a great and unexpected reversal, which left all open-mouthed. For a moment, Francis had not known how to respond. Then he gathered himself. The Council cannot act against the King's wishes, and there can evidently be no prosecution now against Coke for the abuse of his warrant in the King's own Court of Star Chamber. The girl is sent home to her mother at Hatton House, and Lady Compton is given leave to proceed with the marriage to her son.

Once more, Francis has plotted the ruin of Coke, and once more Coke has escaped.

That is pain enough, but over those hot, wet July days Francis torments himself with further questions. The words of the letter are clear enough, but what do they mean? No one understands better than he how far he depends for favour on the King – and perhaps still more on the Earl of Buckingham. Take that favour away, and everything else must crumble. Yet Francis has put the full weight of his authority behind Lady Hatton, has granted her a warrant and denied Coke one, and even thrust the possibility of a *praemunire* at Winwood for doing so. All this may give offence.

Does the King now incline to favour Coke? May he in fact *support* this ill-starred, ill-advised marriage? It cannot be. But which way it is, Francis must know. He has heard nothing from Buckingham, and cannot abide to remain in ignorance.

So Francis writes to Scotland, this time not to Buckingham but directly to His Majesty: a cunning, careful letter which pretends that he is not hostile to the marriage, while condemning Coke for his behaviour. If there is any merit in drawing on that match, he says, let your Majesty bestow the thanks not on the zeal to please of Sir Edward Coke, nor on the eloquent persuasions and pragmaticals of Winwood, but upon them carrying your commandments and directions with strength and justice. Your state is at this time not only in good quiet and obedience, but in good affection and disposition. But let Coke come back into favour, and it will give a turn and relapse in men's minds unto the former state of things, hardly to be helped, to the great weakening of your Majesty's service.

Time passes, and there is still no letter from the Earl of Buckingham. If Buckingham sees the danger in the marriage, he may yet shape and shade His Majesty in his opinions. What did Francis write? *Hoping your Lordship will not only accept well, but believe my faithful advice, who by my great experience in the world must needs see further than your Lordship can, I ever rest your Lordship's true and most devoted servant...* Was that presumptuous? Surely not; the Earl is still but twenty-four years old. Has he not received his letter? Francis cannot leave the matter at rest, cannot prevent himself from writing further. He must know.

A further week passes with no response, the days drag on and Francis is almost beside himself with worry. Then at last a letter arrives from the Earl. He breaks it open in haste, and its words stop his heart with alarm.

My Lord, it goes, if your man had been addressed only to me, I should have been careful to have procured him a more speedy dispatch. But now you have found another way of address through the King my master, I am excused; and since you are grown weary of employing me, I can be no otherwise in being employed. In this business of my brother's that you overtrouble yourself with, I understand from London by some of my friends that you have carried yourself with much scorn and neglect both toward myself and friends; which if it prove true I blame not you but myself, who was ever your Lordship's assured friend, G. Buckingham.

The more courteous the words, the more hostile the intent. The King has also written to the same effect, so he and his favourite are united in their condemnation. Buckingham must have turned against him, and turned the King. In vain does Francis now protest, in vain does he now pour out conciliating words of self-defence, plead truth and fidelity to justify himself.

His only reward is a tight and nasty little message from the Earl: I have received your Lordship's letter by your man, but having so lately imparted my mind to you in my former letters, I refer your Lordship to those letters, without making a needless repetition.

Then Sir Henry Yelverton, now Attorney General, sends Francis word from the returning court, which is at Coventry. Yelverton says that Sir Edward Coke, as if he were already upon his wings, triumphs exceedingly, and he works by the weightiest instrument, the Earl of Buckingham, who as I see sets him as close to him as his shirt. As for the Earl, he professeth openly against you as forgetful of his kindness, and unfaithful to him in your love and in your actions, as if it were an inveterate custom with you, to be unfaithful to him as you were to the Earls of Essex and Somerset... it is too common in every man's mouth in court, that your greatness shall be abated, and as your tongue hath been as a razor to some, so shall theirs be to you.

And Yelverton adds a telling postscript: I beseech your Lordship burn this letter.

This is a disaster.

On 28 September Sir Edward Coke is restored to the Privy Council. The following day, Sir John Villiers and Frances Coke are married. It is a lavish affair, held at the royal palace of Hampton Court.

There are nine carriages to take the wedding party to the chapel. The bride's father walks her up the aisle before giving her hand to the King, who bestows her on her husband.

No one can miss the symbolism. Nor can they miss the length of time Coke spends in converse with His Majesty over dinner.

Elizabeth Hatton is not present at the wedding, but lies in the house of Alderman Bennet, where she has been confined by a warrant sought by her husband and granted by her friend and cousin Francis Bacon. She is crazy in body and sick in mind; she will never be reconciled to her husband. Nor are any other members of the Cecil family there.

Francis himself has escaped censure and humiliation. Given the insults he has inflicted, the Earl of Buckingham says, the King had a rigorous resolution to place some public exemplary mark of disgrace upon him, out of a deep-conceived indignation, but that Buckingham himself got upon his knees to beg His Majesty, and so turned aside and quenched his wrath.

Buckingham has been gracious to Francis; as he does not forebear to say, it was no small grief unto me to hear the mouths of so many upon this occasion open to load you with innumerable malicious and detracting speeches, as if no music were more pleasing to my ears than to rail of you; which made me rather regret the ill nature of mankind, that like dogs love to set upon him that they see once snatched at.

Yet these are not words to put a troubled heart at ease. Francis has seen how the wind is blowing, and now warmly supports the Villiers–Coke marriage. But the Earl's price has been a high one: Francis's offer of submission to him, he says, is met by a fair occasion so to make good hereafter your reputation by your sincere service to His Majesty, as also by your firm and constant kindness to your friends.

Yes, Buckingham is Francis Bacon's master now. Of that there can be no doubt.

91

THE PALACE OF WHITEHALL, AUTUMN 1617–18

Looking back on recent events, the Earl of Buckingham is well pleased. All has worked out to his advantage, indeed far better than he could ever have hoped. The Coke girl is married, and she has brought £30,000 with her to his family. Brother John is delighted. Their mother, Lady Compton, fusses happily over the couple; it cannot be long before her own rank is raised to suit her station.

The King, too, is more than happy. For him at least, his Scottish progress has been a great success. It troubles him not that the progress required many months of planning, and drained moneys from his own Exchequer and from the Scottish lairds alike. Prohibitions were made in Scotland on killing game, deer, hares and wildfowl, that His Majesty might hunt well and his court be fed. Vagabonds and beggars were sent home and otherwise suppressed on pain of the stocks, or worse. The palaces at Holyrood, Stirling and Falkland were much improved and adorned.

There were complaints and petitions, it is true: from the city of Edinburgh, asked to accommodate and feed a train of five thousand and their horses; from parishes charged with mending and making roads; from churchmen who see defilement of the great and equal Presbyterian Church of Scotland from the King's steady zeal to spread the liturgy, the hierarchy and symbols of the English Church above the border. In older days the King had often expressed his admiration for the Scottish Church. Yet of it he is but a member; whereas he is supreme head of the Church of England, which he likes much better.

In any case, the King hears little that is not pleasant wherever he goes, and that suits him very well. Every Scotsman of consequence has felt the touch of the royal hand upon his shoulder – or in his purse. And His Majesty is not displeased to find Sir Edward Coke resurgent on his return. He likes a measure of confusion and rivalry around him for it breeds dependency... provided always that his dearest Steenie is close.

As for the Earl of Buckingham, he cares not for religion. What he desires is power, wealth and glory, and the progress has been a triumph for him as much as for the King. But the power Buckingham seeks is not merely personal; he is not like Somerset or the King's other former favourites, who acted purely for themselves and their kin. No; more and more, Buckingham seeks to shape the policy and instruments of government for his country, and for himself.

Know a man's desires, know his lusts, and you know how to control him, he is apt to say; the surprise is not that men can be bought; the surprise is how cheaply. The gentle word, the touch on the arm, the glance direct to a man you are about to destroy, these things are breakfast, dinner and supper to Buckingham. He has an unsurpassed capacity to please, and to control. He sees men's dreams, their hopes and vanities as if they lie at the bottom of a rock pool fed only by spring water, and he knows at once what will move them.

A case in point: on the eve of the wedding of Frances Coke, with no bidding or other occasion for it, seemingly from sheer exuberant love, His Majesty convened the Privy Council and said to them I, James, am neither a god nor an angel, but a man like any other. Therefore I act like a man, and confess to loving those dear to me more than other men. You may be sure that I love the Earl of Buckingham, more than anyone else, and more than you who are here assembled. I wish to speak in my own behalf, and not to have it thought to be a defect, for Jesus Christ did the same, and therefore I cannot be blamed. Christ had his John and I have my George.

Christ had his John and I have my George. Men can hardly believe their ears.

❧

Or consider a second case, contrariwise: that of Sir Francis Bacon.

One courtier notes that Lord Keeper Bacon attended two days at the Earl of Buckingham's chamber, being not admitted to any better place than the room where trencher-scrapers and lackeys attended, there sitting upon an old wooden chest with his purse and seal lying by him on the chest. A servant told him they had been commanded it must be so.

After two days – two days! – Bacon had admittance, and at his first entrance fell down flat on his face at the Earl's foot, kissing it, vowing never to rise till he had his pardon. Then was he again reconciled, it was reported, and since that time he has been so very much a slave to the Earl, and all that family, that he durst not deny the command of the meanest of the kindred, nor oppose anything.

First the price, then the payment. Of late Buckingham has tended to write letters to Bacon on behalf of suitors in the Court of Chancery. Who are these men? Friends, would-be friends, projectors, those who would ease the cares of the King, those with money to give and an interest to protect.

There have always been these suitors buzzing about like bluebottle flies. What is new is where the flies settle: on cases now pending in the court, cases where land and gold and reputations are at stake. The Earl is careful to qualify his requests, saying such as I desire your Lordship's favour on the plaintiffs' behalf so far only as the justice of their cause shall require. But why should he write at all, if justice is what he seeks? And what has he received, or what does he expect, that makes him write?

Bluebottles do not ratiocinate; the syllogism is a stranger to them. But whether by odour, obedience or observation, they throng thicker than ever around these two men.

If Bacon is now the creature of Buckingham, then Buckingham must be a sure path to success in the Court of Chancery. And if Buckingham is Bacon's master, then there must lie a sure path through Bacon to the King. So the letters multiply.

These paths grow surer still in October, when Secretary Winwood sickens over the course of a week and dies. He is cut open, and the doctors find his spleen and kidneys rotted away. Much beloved at court, and a close friend to Coke, he has been an enemy to Bacon, and Francis does not mourn him. But the King appoints no successor. He says he was never so well served as when he was his own secretary, and delivers the Secretary's seals of office to the custody of the Earl of Buckingham.

It is a further confirmation of power on the Earl. All that remains is formal recognition. On New Year's Day the King gives Buckingham a marquessate; and the following Sunday, at a great feast of celebration, he raises Sir Francis Bacon from Lord Keeper to Lord Chancellor. And on 12 July 1618, Bacon is created Baron Verulam, after the ancient Roman settlement of Verulamium close to Gorhambury.

A year earlier Francis had left Dorset House for York House, his childhood home. Now at last he has surpassed his father; in rank, in office, in title. He is Sir Francis Bacon, Lord Verulam. He inherited an ageing house at Gorhambury, and plans to build a second house to his own design, with gorgeous walks and terraces and water gardens. He is attended everywhere he goes by his own liverymen.

He has helped Archbishop Abbot to establish a great new library at Lambeth Palace, from the bequest of Bancroft who had preceded him. Nor is this all, for over many years Francis has also improved the gardens at Gray's Inn. There too he lays out walks, there too he plants elms and birches, beeches and sycamore, cherry trees and oziers, pinks and violets and woodbine, eglantine and roses. He does good work, and enjoys all that life has to offer.

He is fifty-seven years of age; just fifteen years ago, he reflects, he had none of this. He was despised, ignored, confined, indebted, a man of no future and no consequence. In vain had he petitioned and petitioned again, almost begged, his uncle Burghley for prefer-ment. What had he written in that letter? *I have as vast contempla-tive ends, as I have moderate civil ends. For I have taken all knowledge to be my province.* See how these moderate civil ends alone have taken him to the Lord Chancellorship! Yet he has never given up his vast contemplative ambitions; indeed he has continued to write and reflect privately on natural philosophy and other subjects. Im-agine what might have been made of these works, what may still be!

Now Francis is closer than ever to Buckingham, and to the King. He continues to prepare a great scheme for reformation of the laws, and of the sciences. Salisbury is dead, Coke has been ruined in his profession. For the first time he feels fully in control of his own fortune. The seas are calm, the future is set fair.

92

GORHAMBURY, SUMMER 1618

And, for some time, the seas of politics remain calm for Francis Bacon. There are great ruptions in the state over the next two years, events that engage and involve him as Lord Chancellor, but as a man they hurt him not.

That summer of 1618, the Earl of Suffolk is suspended from his position of Lord Treasurer for extorting and taking bribes in office and other matters, and he and his wife are sent for trial. That is another score for Buckingham, another potential source of power removed, the Howard faction further reduced in influence. How the Howards must rue the fall of Somerset!

But the main talk is of Sir Walter Raleigh. Ever since his conviction in 1603 Raleigh had been held in the Tower of London, condemned but neither executed nor pardoned, the axe held over his head, and so kept captive at the King's pleasure. He had written poetry and many pages of a great history of the world, composed treatises, baited churchmen with ideas of atheism, conducted his chemical experiments... even fathered a son, Carew, while in the Tower.

Yet Raleigh's dreams and his persuasions have been of gold, a great but undiscovered mine of gold on the banks of the Orinoco in the New World, of which he says he alone has the information. Over the years he has regularly petitioned the King without success; until at last at the urging of Secretary Winwood the King consents, and in August 1616 Raleigh is commissioned to lead an expedition. But there is one strict condition. Gondomar, the ambassador of Spain, has insinuated that this whole enterprise is but cover for a raiding expedition against the ships or settlements of the Spanish King, and His Majesty has given him an undertaking that Raleigh shall do no such thing, indeed shall not intrude upon ground occupied by any civilised nation, on pain of death. To this Sir Walter has given his solemn pledge in turn.

A fleet of fourteen ships, equipped and victualled, with a land force as might be necessary to deal with any heathen and savage people, had set sail the following June, amid great rejoicing and excitement. But they had failed to find the mine, fought with the Spanish, burned and pillaged a town, and finally returned to England disgraced, depleted and without reward. Raleigh's own eldest son Wat is dead, and his old friend Captain Kemys has taken his own life at the shame of it.

Gondomar is in a fury, and the King no less so, fearing to lose the greater amity he seeks with Spain. Raleigh is arraigned, examined and swiftly beheaded, in the Old Palace Yard at Westminster. They say that before his end he ran his finger along the blade of the executioner's axe, saying this is a fair sharp medicine to cure me of all my diseases and miseries.

But Francis Bacon knows no misery in these days. As Lord Keeper he had inherited a vast accumulation of old cases in the Court of Chancery. Ellesmere is dead at last, but he left behind him a court so bogged down in repetitious taking of evidence and superfluous procedure as to lose all power of decision. In Francis's eyes, such unnecessary delay is an offence to law. So he had retrenched, and put the clerks and masters of Chancery to work through its ancient inventory.

It was with immense satisfaction that, just three months after becoming Lord Keeper, Francis could write to Buckingham, saying that this day I have made even with the business of the kingdom for common justice. Not one cause unheard. The lawyers drawn dry of all the motions they were to make. Not one petition unanswered. And this I think could not be said in our age before.

But this was the previous summer, and that work is all done. Now Francis can give himself to pleasure, and to contemplation and the life of the mind. He is a great man at last and can, nay must, live splendidly, as a great man does. How he has looked forward to this moment!

His household has grown to suit. How many servants do I have? he asks himself. Answer: as many as are needed. There seem to be many more than in my father's day... but then my father was not Lord Chancellor, and had not so many petitioners to feed and young gentlemen to educate and nurture. It is sweet and sour at once for Francis to recall his former life, when he lodged with his brother Anthony at Gray's Inn: surrounded by debts, hiding tallies from his steward Henry and that great leather book of accounts, constantly dealing with creditors, enduring the unsought advice of his mother and her ceaseless suspicion of the servants. And if at night a harrowing fear returns, and the sense that those were blessed years, years before the Fall, before he gave himself to ambition and worldly power, then he must swallow that fear, or somehow drown it in physic and fatigue.

I am become the mask. Where is the graceful bright-eyed boy of my youth?

Now he has his diligent secretaries Young and Meautys to deal with his papers. He has Phillips as his auditor, to test and check accounts. He has chaplains to attend his private prayer, remembrancers for benefices, ushers, a receiver of casual fines, six handsome young men of the chamber, pages, a barber, a messenger, cooks, yeomen of the wardrobe, Pilkington who keeps the wine, butlers, men of the ewery and pantry, wards, gentlemen of the horse, Richard his bottleman.

Sharpeigh says it is more than a hundred in all, and we must make economies. But what of it? So must expense be with the King, and Lord Buckingham; every man of consequence in history has had expense. I am minded to build an aviary at York House.

Besides, there is work enough for all the servants, for the household is like a little empire in its trade. Just this summer there have been gifts of bucks, stags, ducks, hares, hawks, horses, wethers, strawberries and cherries, the bearers of them all to be tipped and thanked. There have been payments for quail and salmon, turkeys and orange flowers and sweetmeats, books and physic, a present of seeds from Lady Hatton. The trumpeters of the King and the Prince have been thanked and paid for their service.

As for trades, there have been payments, direct and on account, to Mr Markham, Mr Askew and Mr Pemberton, all silkmen; to Mr Davies the mercer, Mr King the apparelmaker, Mr Corbett and Mr Glover, tailors, Mr Young for the hangings, Mr Harwood the perfumer, Mr Parkinson the linen draper, Mr Bate the haberdasher of small wares, Mr Neave the upholsterer and Mr Miller the woollen draper. And Francis remains ever willing to make payment to those who bring him brightly coloured stones for his ponds.

This is a style of living old Lusty Pakington in his pomp could never have dreamed of. There had been a moment the previous year when Lusty and his lady's fight had again grown so intense that she took it to the High Commission, which then referred the matter to... Francis himself as Lord Keeper.

A testing moment indeed! Especially since he had found for Lusty. But Francis's relations could be little worse with Lady Pakington in any case, and she is nothing if not a battler. She has gone in her marriages from gentleman to knight as husband. At some point Lusty will die, and his lady can continue her ascent in society.

And, as Lady Pakington can see, Francis has not forsworn his promise to Alice before their wedding. To the contrary, Alice seems quite content. She is now Alice, Lady Verulam, which pleases her excessively; and she has esteemed her husband all the more that, even when she was just Lady Bacon, he sought to petition the King directly to recognise her precedence ahead of every other lady below the rank of Baroness in the kingdom.

As for him, he is Baron Verulam of Verulam, and in celebration he has commissioned a new house, a place of pleasure in which to enjoy the summer months, to be built by Mr Dobson of St Albans to Francis's own long-meditated design. It is set less than a mile away from Gorhambury itself, within the estate but close to the turnpike.

In the days of Sir Nicholas every room in the old house was served with water, coming by a great leaded pipe from the ponds by the Prae Wood a mile off. There were cisterns and wells too, but many of these works have fallen into disrepair, and Verulam House will have its own supply, from the River Ver. The new house is much smaller than Gorhambury but it rises higher, in the compacted modern style, with a grand central staircase intricately carved in wood, giving at the top on to a flat roof, from which Francis can look out upon the parkland, the walks and alleys, the gardens, fishponds and water gardens.

Mr Phillips is perpetually fretful about the debt it must incur, for he puts the final cost at £9,000–£10,000. Hard to conceive the scale of such an expense, yet it is a work of art that is full of works of art, and such things do not come cheaply, Francis reflects.

And to sit out on that roof of a drowsy summer evening with his dear friend Tobie Matthew by his side... to see the swallows skim the water, glimpse a flash of silver in the ponds as a trout takes the fly, and smell the waft of honeysuckle and jasmine, that is a kind of heaven on Earth.

As he will sometime write, God Almighty planted a garden. And indeed it is the purest of human pleasures.

93

WESTMINSTER, 1619–20

Music and poetry is his delight;
Therefore I'll have Italian masques by night,
Sweet speeches, comedies, and pleasing shows;
And in the day, when he shall walk abroad,
Like sylvan nymphs my pages shall be clad;
My men, like satyrs grazing on the lawns,
Shall with their goat-feet dance an antic hay.
Sometime a lovely boy in Dian's shape,
With hair that gilds the water as it glides,
Crownets of pearl about his naked arms,
And in his sportful hands an olive tree
To hide those parts which men delight to see,
Shall bathe him in a spring; and there, hard by,
One like Actaeon, peeping through the grove,
Shall by the angry goddess be transformed,
And running in the likeness of a hart
By yelping hounds pulled down and seem to die.
Such things as these best please his majesty.

Yet the heavenly perfection of God's garden is not to be met with on the Earth below. On Earth there is corruption and decay.

Though his spirits are light, Francis cannot disguise that he feels the changes in his own body more and more. His constitution has always been nervous, prone to bouts of weakness, but of late these bouts are grown harsher and more frequent. He has days of torturous pain, in his side from the stone, and in his feet and hands from gout.

As the agony comes on, it is all he can do not to cry out. He cannot bear to be touched, but must lie shivering or sweating in his bed till the physic takes effect and sleep overcomes him. Yet sometimes too the physic itself will not settle, but causes an emetic convulsion of the stomach and bowel. The black bile of melancholy is uppermost, he thinks; I am in the ebbing tide of my days.

When a Lord Chancellor suddenly withdraws from business there can be no dealings in Star Chamber, so Francis's absences are quickly noted. As one man says, the general opinion is that he hath so tender a constitution both of body and mind that he will hardly be able to undergo the burden of so much business as his place requires. If he do not rouse and force himself beyond his natural inclination, both private subjects and the Commonwealth will suffer much.

The coming man is Sir Lionel Cranfield, the Master of the Court of Wards, a mercer by trade and well known for his acumen in matters of finance. Introduced by the old Earl of Northampton, he has lately been picked up by the Marquess of Buckingham, as Villiers now is. Cranfield has sat with Bacon on the commission to reform and reduce the King's expenditures. But if Bacon cannot do all the business, then why should the King not choose Cranfield as his new Lord Keeper?

In March 1619 Queen Anne dies, at Hampton Court, at just forty-four years of age. She had borne her husband seven children in all, and miscarried others. There was strength enough for her to embrace Prince Charles at her end, but she was never the same after the death of Prince Henry, her eldest, a boy first taken away from her protection and love at just two days old, for whom she had fought her husband so long and so hard.

The Queen had despised the King's succession of favourites, but she made her own court a place of art and beauty. In her later

years she hated Somerset and assisted the advancement of Buckingham, only to suffer the disregard of Buckingham in turn. She
ceased her masques, slowed her patronage and, as illness overtook
her, cut herself off from company. Now, near her mortal end, sick
and blind, her limbs swollen with dropsy, she is attended only by
her closest maids. Her body is transported after death to lie in state
at Denmark House; where it remains, slowly putrefying, for two
months before the money can be found for a state funeral, where
the final mourner in the train of followers is her friend and adviser,
Sir Edward Coke.

The playhouses are closed, and entertainments forbidden. The
King too has been grievously sick; it must be so, for he attends his
wife of thirty years neither at her death nor her funeral.

Decay and corruption, corruption and decay. It is as though the
canker is spreading through the body politic, seeping into its mys-
terious channels and infecting its organs.

Earlier that year of 1619 the Secretary of State, Sir Thomas
Lake, had fallen from office, brought down by a most sordid and
protracted family quarrel with the Earl of Exeter. Lake's daughter
Anne had been married to Lord Roos, grandson of Exeter; Lake
has long been close to the Howards, and the union was intended to
strengthen the tie, for Roos's sister is married to a son of the Earl
of Suffolk.

But the marriage was unhappy and brief, and when it ended
there was a dispute over the conveyance of lands from Exeter. Lord
Roos was then attacked by Lake's son Arthur, and threatened that
if consent was not given, he would be the subject of a scandalous exposure. Roos left the country, whereupon his Howard wife
forged letters purporting to implicate him in an incestuous intimacy with the young Countess of Exeter, the Earl's second wife,
whom for good measure the Lakes also accused of an attempted

poisoning. The Countess then in turn filed suit against Lady Lake, her daughter Anne and two sons for slanderous defamation, and much else.

The matter is so complex that the court papers run into the thousands, and the King insists on hearing the evidence himself over five days. At the end the judgment goes heavily against the Lakes, who are found guilty of forgery and subornation of witnesses. They are fined, imprisoned, and forced to apologise and pay great damages. Secretary Lake was not the prime mover, so much is clear; and this is in any case a man who they say lives in terror of his wife. But prime mover or no, he loses the seals of office and is ruined.

Then in November the trial of the Earl of Suffolk himself at last reaches Star Chamber. The charges against him include not only the extortion and receipt of bribes, but defrauding the King of many thousands of pounds of jewels, diverting money for the army and navy in Ireland for his own use, and much else. The Countess of Suffolk has clearly been leading her husband, with her confederate, Sir John Bingley, but that fact does not protect the Earl. Francis Bacon presides over the case as Lord Chancellor, and he is careful to keep Buckingham informed on the trial; there is a wealth of evidence and confession. The Earl and Countess are fined £30,000 and sent to the Tower.

And the new year brings no relief from the succession of scandals. In June 1620 it is the turn of the Attorney General, Sir Henry Yelverton, to be arraigned. Once a supporter of Somerset, Yelverton has long been an object of suspicion to Buckingham. The charge is that as Attorney he enlarged a patent given to the City of London further than the warrant allowed.

Yelverton and he were once friends, but Francis Bacon presses the seriousness of the matter. A patent is, he insists, nothing less than the grant of a monopoly, that grant being under the Great Seal, and at the instruction of the Attorney as adviser and officer at law to the King. If the King's own Attorney be suffered to expand the scope of the warrant, Bacon insists, the Crown will be undone in a short time. The Signet, Privy Seal, Great Seal, all these follow the Attorney's hand.

In Francis's words, *He that thinks more of the greatness of his place than of the duty of his place, will soon commit misprisions.* There can be no excuse that Yelverton did not know the law, or had not read the warrant, for he is the Attorney; the King's authority has been flouted, and many men might be enriched by such an excess of monopoly. Who knows what bribes Yelverton may have received for this delinquency?

This is humiliating talk. Yelverton takes such treatment hard, and all the more when it comes directly from a man he has defended in the face of Buckingham. In vain does he confess his error and seek to avoid a trial; his case is remitted to the Star Chamber. In vain does he protest that his was an error of judgement, negligence and credulity, with no trace of deceit or corruption; he is fined £4,000 and discharged from his office.

Corruption and decay. It is as though the state itself is now so rotten that it must ruin men from time to time, that it can take their revenues for its own sustenance.

Is there a common thread between these cases? Francis does not trouble himself to ask. But if he did, he might distinguish between a cause and a trigger. The cause of these trials is that each man has done wrong, in his own way.

And the trigger? For that, one might perhaps ask the Marquess of Buckingham. None of these ruined men is his friend; all are thought to have crossed him in different ways. That lesson is not lost on others.

94

YORK HOUSE, 1620–21

But Francis does not see the canker, nor note the spread of this infection. How can he? His omnicapacious mind is filled with matters of the cloth trade, the supply of corn, the treatment of informers, Ireland and a hundred other things. And he is himself lodged in the core of the infected body. He cannot step back from it, cannot observe the tumours or run his finger down the limbs for signs of swelling.

But in matters of the mind, of the imagination, of the quest-ing spirit that asks not what is but what might be? Well, that is a different story. There is distemper there too, one that dates back to Aristotle and the Greeks, and so deep-seated as to exercise an unseen empire over men's reason. So Francis understands it; and he understands it better than any man alive. He has tracked that distemper for more than thirty years, from his earliest days of hope, through the long ageing of his ambition, to the late moment of his worldly success.

Even now, amid all his present glory, his wealth and rank and retinue, his true heart lies where it has always lain: in his dreams, to build a new method and a new foundation of discovery in natural philosophy. In 1592, in writing to his uncle Burghley, he had not merely confessed his vast contemplative ends, taking all knowledge to be his province. No: he had also shown the danger, the need to purge knowledge itself both of frivolous disputations, confutations, and verbosities, and of what he called blind experiments, auricular traditions and impostures. And he had set out his object: to bring in industrious observations, grounded conclusions, and profitable inventions and discoveries; what he called the best state of that province.

In 1605, Francis's *Advancement of Learning* had laid out a vast plan of reformation across the whole field of human knowledge. But both before and since that date there have been other works from his pen, some published, some privately circulated, that have unfolded his ideas and arguments. In them and through them he has sought to explore and interpret nature, to examine the wisdom of the ancients and refute old philosophies that have outworn their use, to set out a new theory of the heavens, and much else. Together, they form a great arch of thought. He has come to call the whole span *Instauratio Magna*, the *Great Renewal*, using the Latin words to signify the greatness of his conception.

Of this work, the *Advancement* is but one chapter, one stone in the arch. Now in 1620 at last Francis publishes what is to be the keystone: the *Novum Organum*, or *New Instrument*. By design, the title echoes the great works of Aristotle that were gathered together into an *organon*, a logic or method of thinking; and here too Francis seeks to set out a new method of his own, what he calls the method of induction. This is no sterile formality in the style of the scholastics, he insists, no system of deductions or syllogisms that arises purely in the mind. It is not contemplative; nay, it is active. It requires the careful and extensive gathering from nature itself of instances of the subject to be investigated, the rigorous tabulation of these instances, and from them the formulation of the hidden formal causes or laws of nature that are at work beneath the surface.

For Francis, such a labour is not the product of a single mind, but of the minds and hands of many. It is not derived from inspiration, but from tools and work; tools that multiply effort, and work that can become a kind of mechanism, which does not require the intervention of man in order to proceed. His new method of induction may, he insists, be of entirely general application, fit not merely for natural philosophy but for ethics and politics and law, indeed all science, even logic itself.

And its purpose is not simply learning or scholarship, and the interpretation of nature, though for many that would be ambition enough. No, it is utility, the common wealth, the conquest and direction of nature to suit the good ends of humankind. As he says, look, see the force of discoveries unknown to antiquity: printing, gunpowder and the compass. These three have changed the whole face and state of things throughout the world; so much that no empire, no sect, no star seems to have exerted greater power and influence in human affairs than these mechanical discoveries. And as the world is changed, and men found a real model of the world in the understanding and not in the apish imitations of their fancies, so they will learn the difference between the idols of the human mind and the ideas of the divine mind. Truth and utility are here perfectly identical.

For there are, Francis avers, three kinds or degrees of human ambition. The first is the ambition of those who are greedy to increase their personal power in their own country; which is common and base. The second is the ambition of those who strive to extend the power and empire of their country among the human race; this surely has more dignity, but no less greed.

The third is to renew and extend the power and empire of the human race itself over the universe of things, and that ambition is, he says, without a doubt both more sensible and more majestic than the others. And the empire of man over things lies solely in the arts and sciences. For one does not have empire over nature except by obeying her laws.

As befits its status, Francis writes the *New Instrument* not in English but in Latin, in all its greater clarity and precision. Latin is the universal language of scholars across Europe, and he intends the book to be a work for them, and for the ages.

At the front of the book, he places an image that captures his ambition: two ships which have set forth far beyond the Pillars of Hercules and the known world, across a vast and fathomless ocean in search of new regions of knowledge, and which now it seems return to port, their holds laden with treasures of the mind. Even thus it must be for the exploration and conquest of human thought, to venture out into the unknown and then to return; to master nature by obeying her, and turn her capacities to productive purpose.

Yet just as ships are driven back by squalls, or overturned by monsters, so are there hazards that block the method of induction. Among them are humans' often deceptive senses, their foolish beliefs, too confident habits of mind, poorly designed experiments and sophistical and superstitious philosophies.

But at the head of these hazards, Francis has long identified four illusions, or vices of the human intellect.

He calls them *idols*: of the tribe, the cave, the marketplace, and the theatre. The *idols of the tribe* are the distortions and corruptions that are innate to the human understanding. The *idols of the cave* are the variable and irregular illusions of a man, derived from his upbringing, his education or his reading.

The *idols of the marketplace* are the words, the common standards and conventions that come from men's association with each other; these are the most troublesome and hardest to extirpate of all. And finally, *the idols of the theatre* are the false and fictitious worlds of the philosophers that make their homes in men's minds.

All these idols are empty apparitions, Francis says, which must be rejected and renounced and the mind totally liberated and cleansed of them, so that there will be only one entrance into the kingdom of man, which is based upon the sciences; as there is into the kingdom of heaven, into which, except as an infant, there is no way to enter.

In its language, in its depth, in its direction, this is a philosophy like none other.

Francis Bacon celebrates his sixtieth birthday on its eve, 21 January 1621, and holds a great dinner at York House to mark the occasion. He has now been made Viscount St Alban by His Majesty, and the King, the Prince of Wales, the Marquess of Buckingham and a host of other peers of the realm are in attendance.

There is much carousing and levity, and the evening is made perfect when Francis's friend Ben Jonson stands and declaims an ode he has composed in honour of the host, addressing not the Lord Chancellor but York House itself:

> *Hail, happy GENIUS of this ancient pile!*
> *How comes it all things so about thee smile?*
> *The fire, the wine, the men! And in the midst*
> *Thou stand'st as if some mystery thou didst!*
> *Pardon, I read it in thy face, the day*
> *For whose returns, and many, all these pray;*
> *And so do I. This is the sixtieth year,*
> *Since BACON, and thy lord was born, and here;*
> *Son to the grave wise Keeper of the Seal,*
> *Fame and foundation of the English weal.*
> *What then his father was, that since is he,*
> *Now with a title more to the degree;*
> *England's high Chancellor: the destin'd heir,*
> *In his soft cradle, to his father's chair:*
> *Whose even thread the fates spin round and full,*
> *Out of their choicest and their whitest wool.*

'Tis a brave cause of joy, let it be known,
For 'twere a narrow gladness, kept thine own.
Give me a deep-crown'd bowl, that I may sing
In raising him, the wisdom of my king.

Francis is now Sir Francis Bacon, Baron Verulam, Viscount St Alban, Lord Chancellor and Keeper of the Great Seal. In all, he has been elevated eight times by His Majesty. He stands at the pinnacle of government, and power.

It is his greatest moment of joy and pride. And his last.

95

ENGLAND, 1621

But this still lies in the future. For the present, the canker of decay continues to work its way through the body politic, and will not be abated. It is spreading into the foreign affairs of the realm. Now that too begins to rot and rankle.

The King has long prided himself on the peace he made with Spain in 1604. He rejoices in his place as the leading Prince of the reformed Church across the continent of Europe, a status confirmed by the marriage of his daughter Elizabeth to Count Frederick, the Elector Palatine of the Rhine, in 1613.

Yet James has also been careful to conciliate the Catholics both at home and abroad. He has acted with moderation against the milder sort of recusant, and sought to build an alliance with the Spanish, despite fierce opposition from the brief and obstreperous parliament of 1614.

A French marriage for Prince Charles would come, he had thought, with a vast dowry, and at a time of such exigency in his finances that was hardly to be ignored. But over time the King had begun to favour the idea of a Spanish match with the young Infanta; there is talk of a dowry of £600,000, a stupendous sum, which would pay off all his debts. The heat of his interest has been fanned by the Howards, with their Catholic sympathies, and by Count Gondomar, who has played upon the King's feelings and needs with the delicate precision of a Byrd upon the virginals.

It was the Spanish ambassador's insistence, and the King's desire to please the court of Madrid, that did for Raleigh. Now Buckingham too seems to have been captured by Spain, for he has married Lady Katherine Manners, sole heir of the Earl of Rutland, a noted Catholic peer and among the very richest women in the kingdom. She has abjured her faith to make the marriage, but no one doubts she may return to it in time.

The King has sought to be a peacemaker between the religions, and to hold the balance of power where he can across a continent dominated by Spain and the Habsburgs. But as he is well aware, this is but a feeble construct, held up by hope and expediency.

In 1618 the whole edifice begins to fail. The election of the Catholic Ferdinand as King of Bohemia has spread alarm among the much more numerous Protestants in his country. There is a Protestant revolt, which spreads to Silesia and the lands toward Vienna. Two of Ferdinand's Lords Regent are ejected from office in the traditional Bohemian fashion, by bodily defenestration from the upper windows of Prague Castle.

Then to James's dismay, Ferdinand is elected Emperor of the Holy Roman Empire, and Count Frederick is offered the Kingship of Bohemia, which he foolishly accepts. At once James finds himself in an impossible position. Catholic Spain will surely support her Habsburg neighbours, while the clamour at home becomes ever more insistent for him to stand behind the Protestant cause, and the rule and safety of his own daughter and son-in-law. It is known that an invasion of Bohemia is being prepared, in appearance under an Imperial banner, but in reality under the command of the brilliant Spanish general Ambrosio Spinola.

James's fervent hope is that Spain can be prevented from entering the war, but his hope is smashed at the end of August 1620, when her true intentions become clear and Spinola, after marching along the course of the Rhine, suddenly thrusts his army not at Bohemia to the east, but south, directly into the lower Palatinate.

It is a devastating blow, aimed directly at the heart of Frederick's power, and a grave embarrassment to James's policy. Where is the great *rex pacificus* now? Where are his arts of peace and mediation? The King has been gulled, his weakness has been revealed to all, and he is enraged by the Spaniards' treachery.

Such is James's hatred of arms that even now he hesitates. But the clamour at home grows ever greater, only to be replaced by open rejoicing in the streets and in the shires when he issues a public declaration pledging to go to war for the Palatinate in the spring if it is not restored. So too is there celebration around the King; as one remarks, there was never so joyful a court here as this declaration hath made.

An army will surely be needed, though of what size and kind, and to what purpose, is not yet clear. For that there must be new revenue, and in October the King asks Lord Chancellor Bacon to make preparations for a parliament, through a special commission to include Hobart and Montagu, the Chief Justices, Crew who was the Speaker of the previous parliament, and Sir Edward Coke.

In the meantime, to take advantage of the high spirits among his people, the King calls for a new benevolence from his leading subjects. This is led by young Prince Charles, who gives £10,000; the Privy Councillors follow, each contributing £1,000. In all, £30,000 is quickly raised; a fine beginning. Let the others pay in as well, the barons and the bishops and esquires, and perhaps this sum may be doubled, or more. Royal pursuivants are sent out across the counties, to prick the Sheriffs and rouse the gentry.

But then, as is so often the way, a gap is discovered between fine words and full purses. The times have been difficult, prices are high, trade not what it was. The apologies multiply. And there is the ever-lurking fear that if the benevolence succeeds, it may become the practice, and men may be rated, assessed and exacted as they stand. But then what are rights of property? What need of a parliament, or of any place to air men's grievances and seek justice?

Barely £6,000 is raised outside London from the benevolence. But in November news comes that Count Frederick has been decisively defeated outside Prague, and the fever for war at home is redoubled.

There can be no escaping it: both to assuage men's feelings and to raise a revenue, the King must call a parliament. Bacon's special commission goes about its work; it drafts a proclamation, and reviews lists of sound gentlemen to be returned at the election; Councillors, courtiers, men to be relied upon. But Francis is also careful to ensure that there will be provided for the new parliament some Commonwealth Bills; not wooing Bills to make the King and his graces cheap, he says, but good matter to set the parliament to work, that an empty stomach do not feed upon humour.

The Members of Parliament will surely seek to air their grievances, and at their head will be the matter of patents and monopolies, the special concessions and licences that enrich their holders and bleed the common man dry of his pennies.

Desiring to see off such discontent in advance, Bacon's commission conducts a careful review of the patents. Francis's advice to the King is moderate and wise. To take away all the noxious patents, he says, will give more scandal that such things were granted, than cause thanks that they be now revoked. And to do so by Act of Parliament would cause a flood of suitors to court wishing for compensation. Yet there must be action from the King, or action from the parliament will surely follow.

Francis therefore offers a measured, twofold remedy: to withdraw the most offensive patents before the parliament and then, once the parliament is convened, to have some grave and discreet country gentlemen make a modest motion to withdraw certain other patents, that the King may give his assent and show his justice.

The trial of Yelverton has surely shown the danger, for patents are becoming ever more obnoxious to men, an affront not merely to their purses but to their dignity and freedoms. Let Parliament seek a remedy by this gentle means, let the King grant them out of his royal discretion, as a matter of grace and not of right. Then may Parliament grant the necessary subsidy, and all will be well.

Yet before the passage of these sober well-considered plans, there stands a rock: the Marquess of Buckingham.

The Marquess and his family have long been sunk in patents, and they are covetous for more. The most talked-of patents are those of the licences for alehouses and inns, which belong one each to his brother Edward Villiers, and to Sir Giles Mompesson, his creature and relative by marriage. Mompesson has sent his agents to spy on inns and close the ones that do not pay the fees. He also owns the patent for gold and silver thread; for that too he has gained an evil reputation. And even now Buckingham is seeking to procure a patent for another brother, Kit Villiers, for the drawing-up of wills in the prerogative Court of Canterbury.

Francis raises these matters with Buckingham, then raises them again. He presents the report of his commission to the King, but His Majesty is in such thrall to his favourite that he gives no sign of assent to its recommendations. This is a rock that will not be removed. Finally, gently and wistfully, Francis puts the matter one last time by letter to his patron; to this there is no reply.

It is evident that nothing can be allowed to impede the enrichment of the Marquess and his family. Eventually, Francis himself certifies the Canterbury patent for Kit Villiers in December, alongside Sir Henry Montagu, who is now Lord Mandeville and the new Lord Treasurer.

Thus it is, to Francis's alarm, that the matter of patents, the central point of likely grievance to the new parliament, goes unaddressed. For the King, for his country and above all for his Lord Chancellor, that is a momentous omission.

96

THE PALACE OF WESTMINSTER, JANUARY 1621

Parliament is opened on Tuesday, 30 January. The day is bitterly cold, the air sharp enough to cut through broadcloth. There are no boats to ferry men to the opening, for the river is frozen solid, with great pieces of ice that jut above the surface. And the crowds as well are large and thickly packed between the two palaces of Whitehall and Westminster.

At 11 a.m. the King rides out, resplendent, crowned, accompanied by the Lords Temporal and Spiritual and the justices of the realm. There are fifes and drums to beat a slow march as he proceeds in state to Westminster, and as he goes he stops and speaks often and lovingly to the people that press in around him, saying to them all God bless ye! God bless ye! Not since '88 have hearts been so stirred and fears so raised: against the Spanish menace, against the loss of the reformed faith in Europe, against the danger to Count Frederick and the lovely Princess Elizabeth.

Yet for all this warmth, there are early signs that disconcert the onlooker. In the draft of his proclamation to call the new parliament, despite the urgings of Lord Chancellor Bacon, the King had insisted on inserting words certain to anger and provoke, calling on the electors not to choose curious and wrangling lawyers who may seek reputation by stirring needless questions.

And indeed the King's words seem to have had an effect opposite to that intended, for the lists of new Members are short on stalwarts for His Majesty, and long on just the captious common lawyers whom he so evidently despises. Each electoral return is carefully weighed and scrutinised. After just a few weeks, Bacon is forced to confess that the prognostics are not so good as I expected. Even Privy Councillors are struggling to be elected in their county seats.

As expectation builds over Christmastime, the sermons against the Spanish multiply both in number and in violence. To calm tempers, the Bishop of London instructs his clergy to omit any mention of Spain at the pulpit, but all to no avail. At last the King issues a further proclamation, against lavish talk of matters of state, instructing his loving subjects from the highest to the lowest to take heed how they intermeddle by pen and speech with causes of state and secrets of empire either at home or abroad. It is a salutary precaution against public disorder.

And there are further signs to disconcert. The day of the opening of Parliament had to be delayed. Such was then the crush of onlookers that two scaffolds specially erected for the ceremony collapsed, and several people were injured. When the King at last dismounted from his horse that day, his legs were seen to be so bad from gout that he could not walk even the few yards into the Chamber of the Lords, but had to be carried in a chair. Are these things portents? What do they mean?

For Francis, the first days of the new parliament pass broadly as expected. The King's speech is a long tour around his usual haunts: the royal prerogative, the purposes and duties of a parliament, the duties he lays on its Members never to touch on matters of state or meddle with religion.

Kings make laws, he says, parliaments are the advisers, councillors and confirmers of them. I have laboured as a woman in travail, not ten months but ten years, and therefore am full time to come to be delivered of my wants.

No king, he plaintively insists, had yet required less of his subjects: just six subsidies and four fifteenths in the full course of eighteen years. Yes, his bounty had in years past been somewhat abused, but there had been economy in spending by the royal household, and it had learned that every day was not to be a Christmas. As for grants and patents, some have complained of monopolies, and if rightly informed, he will give redress. But let men not hunt after grievances.

The speech is well received, and then the House quickly loses itself for several days in debates over men's freedom to speak as they would. All recall how after the last parliament several Members were sent to the Tower, and all know that what should be their secret proceedings are reported on the streets and quickly retailed to the King.

James then sends a soft and wooing message that he does not intend in any way to lessen the lawful and free liberty of speech which appertains unto the House of Commons, and the tumult recedes. When the House turns itself to recusants, however, when it approves a stern petition calling for them to be expelled from London and confined to within five miles of their homes except by royal licence, when it prays in aid the support of the Lords, it is a different matter. The King sternly reproves and chastises the Commons. His message is heard in complete silence.

All this is to be expected, on these and other subjects, as the new parliament relieves itself of many years of complaint. The foreign legates and ambassadors around the court are gloomy and dismissive. This parliament will be like the last, they say, a mess of rancour and disagreement, certain of an early dissolution.

But what do they really know of a parliament, of its deep currents of trust and personal disdain, of animosity and respect? What do they know, who have only sat in their perfumed salons and caught the wafty airs of hearsay, while others stand in that chilly chapel of St Stephen and debate the greatest matters of a nation?

Lodged now as Viscount St Alban in the House of Lords, Francis Bacon can no longer take part in, nor even observe, the debates of the Commons. But like the King whom he advises, he gathers intelligence from others as to its words and actions.

He hears that Sir Edward Coke has been elected and is now Chairman of the Grand Committee on Recusants and Supply, and that Coke has carefully delayed the matter of financial supply and subsidy till tempers have receded. It is good fortune indeed to have a Privy Councillor in such a place to guide the hotheads and the troublemakers!

And both the King and his Lord Chancellor are delighted when the committee reports on 15 February that there was granted a gift of two subsidies; which were offered freely and with none gainsaying, not on any consideration or condition for or concerning the Palatinate. Two subsidies! That is £160,000, more than was ever levied in a single year before, and early in the session as well, not extracted with pain like a rotten tooth at the very end, as would be normal.

The King quickly accepts the offer. It is confirmed by a unanimous vote of the House. The foreign legates and ambassadors are confounded.

97

THE PALACE OF WESTMINSTER, FEBRUARY 1621

And then, suddenly, the curtain is drawn back, and everything is altered. The great dream Francis has so long entertained, that glimpse of palaces amid the clouds and a new Zion to unite wisdom and science, the arts of peace and war, with him as the wisest of legislators at its head, guiding the nation to wealth and prosperity, all this dissolves to nothing before his eyes.

The mighty platform of rank and wealth and connection on which he has been standing drops away in just a few short days, and he is left alone like a man on the scaffold, with none to serve or save him.

At first, to be sure, all goes as Francis has foreseen. Now that the subsidies have been so readily disposed of, it is to be expected that the House will occupy itself with patents and monopolies. A Committee for Grievances has also been established, and Coke elected as its Chairman. Now it takes up the matter of patents and quickly directs itself to Sir Giles Mompesson and the much-reviled patent of inns. The Members hear how, in addition to a stipend, Mompesson as promoter and patent-holder has been entitled to receive one-fifth of the money collected for the licences he issues, creating every inducement to a scandalous enforcing and oppressive collection of fees. Some say it is more than a scandal; it is a subversion of the law.

Mompesson is himself a Member of Parliament. He is called before the committee and testifies that the patent was referred twice: once for law, to Justices Crooke, Winch and Nichols, and to Bacon, who was then the Attorney General; and once for convenience to Lord Treasurer Suffolk, Secretaries Lake and Winwood and Serjeants Montagu and Finch, whereafter it was finally drawn up by Bacon, Finch and Solicitor Coventry.

The name of Bacon is thus spoken twice. But these are all august personages, and that name does not particularly obtrude, while the abuse of the patent is roundly condemned.

The patent for alehouses is next, and there the Committee for Grievances takes two further steps. It condemns not merely the abuse but the patent itself, which required the judges to act as assistants to the promoters and serve papers on their behalf; and it demands that all the patent-holders and beneficiaries be summoned to the bar of the House. These men include Kit Villiers, younger brother of the Marquess. The King's men in the Commons vigorously protest against the demand, but in vain.

The power of the committee is confirmed, and the waters of a rising tide of parliamentary anger start to lap gently at the outer edges of the royal court itself.

Yet now the Committee for Grievances finds itself in a quandary. By agreement it sits two days a week, Monday and Friday, though in reality it has started to dominate the proceedings of the Commons. It has the promoters of these evil patents at its mercy, and the tempers of its own Members and those of the wider House are inflamed for punishment against the malefactors. Yet the actual powers of the House are very limited. Void the patent so it is of no effect and benefit? Send a man to the Tower for a few days, whence the King will swiftly free him? These are hardly remedy enough. So, what to do?

In response, on 27 February the committee sends William Noye

and another of its Members into the archives to review the precedents. Noye is the great Gamaliel of the law, famed for his knowledge of cases, and the following day he returns armed with a sheaf
of them, ranging from the time of the first King Edward to that of
Henry VI.

These precedents suggest that if the House joins with the Lords
in condemnation, then Mompesson may be punished not merely
for any offence he has given the Commons, but for matters deemed
to be of general grievance. After all, the House of Lords is in its
origins a high court; nay, it is the highest court of all. It has long,
perhaps always, had judicial functions. The precedents show how it
may serve as a court once more, to impeach men in high office and
bring them to justice.

Yet still the Lord Chancellor senses no danger. He is like a town
mayor on a hot summer's day, who busily directs the drays with
water hither and yon to put out small fires, yet does not see a vast
and creeping conflagration till it is upon him.

He has Chancery business to attend to, the King to counsel, the
Marquess to conciliate, the Lords to guide. Yet even their Lordships, normally so placid, are becoming more and more infected
by a querulous indisposition that will brook no hindrance. They
quickly adopt the habit of the Commons of transforming themselves into a committee, a stratagem which allows men to speak
more than once to the question and so gathers power around a few
leading figures.

When a Commons petition for better execution of the laws
against recusants comes before the peers, Francis speaks against
it, as does Prince Charles, the Marquess and the Archbishop of
Canterbury. These are all mighty voices, yet the Lords will not be
gainsaid and vote the petition their support. Just a few days later,
Francis cannot control their Lordships in a further debate on the

matter. He tries to adjourn the House, and then to read a Bill. It is all to no avail. The debate will proceed, whether the Lord Chancellor wishes it or no.

Barely a month of the new parliament has passed, and rumours now run every day as rampant as the vermin that infest the Palace of Westminster. The Court of Chancery has long been a source of grievance for the stricter sort of common lawyer in the House. Now these legal men have meat to feed on, for it is revealed that the registrars of Chancery have been falsifying orders in order to increase their fees, which causes outrage.

How has this been allowed to happen? Had the Lord Chancellor not spoken of reforms, of clearing the inventory of past cases, of smoothing and accelerating the process of decision? What has he to say to all of this?

The mills of rumour have also been grinding vigorously against the Marquess of Buckingham, for all the world knows how he has used patents to fill the coffers of his family.

Is not Bacon his creature, and did Bacon not sign the patents as referee? And now the Chancellor has presided over these frauds in Chancery! Did he know of them? Was he too distant to pay them any heed? Or was he there, but only slumbering while his own clerks picked men's unsuspecting pockets?

98

THE PALACE OF WESTMINSTER, MARCH 1621

Be not deceived; God is not mocked: for whatsoever a man soweth,
that shall he also reap. For he that soweth to his flesh shall
of the flesh reap corruption; but he that soweth to the
Spirit shall of the Spirit reap life everlasting.

Then, suddenly, on 3 March the congested heat of Parliament breaks into a violent and unexpected storm. It is found that Sir Giles Mompesson has escaped from the Tower of London, getting away through his wife's private chamber where the Serjeant dared not follow him. Mompesson may already be out of the country.

Bewildered and enraged, the Commons petitions the Lords to have warrants sent forthwith for his arrest. But this carries an immediate further implication, that Buckingham must answer yea or nay in the Lords for Mompesson, who is his man.

What had Francis written to the younger Buckingham, when he still stood as adviser, nay almost father-confessor to him?

The King himself is above the reach of his people, but cannot be above their censures, and you are his shadow if either he commit an error, and is loath to avow it, or you commit the fault, or have willingly permitted it. So perhaps you may be offered as a sacrifice to appease the multitude…

This you cannot now avoid unless you will adventure a precipice, to fall down faster than you rose. Opinion is a master wheel in these cases.

Men in high places cannot bear to be judged. And empty men bear it least.

Buckingham is at risk, and there can be little doubt as to what he will do. He directly joins his name to the warrant, and gives an open and ingenuous account to their Lordships of his association with the fugitive. Yes, he had introduced Mompesson to the King, yet if there were deception and wrong here he would be the first to set his hand against the man. He too might have been deceived, as might any other, but he knows little of law, and the patents had been sealed and certified on the authority of the best and most learned legal men in the kingdom.

By this means he turns attention away from himself and to the referees of the patents, those who allowed and approved them in law. No man could take the Marquess for a lawyer; he acted on good authority, yet who were his advisers?

While the Lords ponder this question, there is another convulsion in the lower house on the matter of monopolies. The Committee for Grievances uncovers details of the patent for gold and silver thread. Their informer is none other than Sir Henry Yelverton; once Attorney General, but now in the Tower following his trial.

Yelverton is a man with a grievance, but even so the testimony of a former law officer is not to be ignored. He states on oath that he had advised the King against a patent and in favour of a lesser instrument that might be readily discarded if it proved inconvenient. But the King referred it back to him, with Bacon and Suffolk, and they all approved it. That name of Bacon again!

And there is worse from Yelverton to follow. He reports that Sir Edward Villiers, half-brother to the Marquess, had pressed Yelverton to imprison the men who resisted the patent. He had done so, but only on condition that they would be released if their arrests were not confirmed by Lord Chancellor Bacon. Bacon had so confirmed them.

The men then spent three weeks languishing in the Fleet prison before being questioned by the Lord Chancellor, but, remaining obstinate, they were sent back again. Yet when their wives and children made a petition to the Lord Mayor of London, and he in turn informed the King, His Majesty quickly ordered their release.

These further revelations move the Commons to outrage. To the exactions and oppressions of patents are added the charge of wrongful imprisonment. The names of Bacon and Villiers are joined yet again in men's mouths, and this time there is a clear imputation of personal dishonour in the Lord Chancellor. Disfavour too: for did the King not immediately contradict the Chancellor's decision, in order to do justice?

Come to that, did not the King's favourite say that he would give up any man who deceived his master? Surely deception is exactly what the patent referees have practised; and Bacon is one of those referees.

The hunt moves ever onwards. It is in quest of new prey, yet still Francis cannot see where the hounds are headed. How strange to think that, if another were at risk, he would be the first to spot the danger! But in his own case he is blind.

Some men have talked loosely over the past weeks of pursuing those who refereed the patents, but they have gained no respectable following in the House. The referees are great figures who serve the King, and no man can look into the sun unharmed. They have never yet been formally named in Parliament. Besides, the committee has had little enough to go on: simply the unsupported words of Mompesson, a charlatan, and Yelverton, who has been disgraced and speaks with a grudge. The Lords will throw the matter out. Or if not, the King or the Marquess will guide them away from any adverse conclusion.

But even so, Francis feels a sudden chill of anxiety. He writes to

Buckingham on 7 March, noting a prominent Member's motion not to have the referees meddled with, and the intent not to look back, but to the future. I do hear, he adds, almost all men of judgement in the House wish now that way. I woo nobody: I do but listen, and I have doubt only of Sir Edward Coke, who I wish had some round *caveat* given him from the King, that he should beware. For your Lordship hath no great power with him; but I think a word from the King mates him.

Now, however, it is too late. Such is their anger that the Members have started to move as a pack. Let all the patents be suppressed, they mutter; all the patents, with a *praemunire* laid on the backs of the projectors, and throw in the referees as well!

So when the Commons sends its carefully drafted document up to the Lords for review, it is not merely a petition to the King for redress of grievances. Nor is it a mere case for action against Mompesson. It is an indictment, by which their Lordships may impeach and prosecute both the promoters of these odious patents and the referees that authorised them, in the House of Lords, which is the highest court in the land.

Every day the pressure grows. By 10 March matters have become so adverse that the King himself decides to intervene.

The Commons had sought to rehearse its conference with the Lords two days earlier. Five of its leading Members had been due to make the argument, but at just ten o'clock in the morning the Speaker had suddenly risen from his chair, loudly declared the House adjourned and quit the Chamber. It is a foolish, disruptive stratagem, evidently designed to please the King, but it works. The Members are disturbed and ineffective when they address the Lords later in the day. The best they can do is to lodge the case in outline, but they cannot bring themselves to name the referees, which is the essence of the matter.

Proceedings in the Commons are supposed to be secret, yet no one doubts that between them the Speaker, the Privy Councillors, the place-seekers, the flatterers and gossips all make sure to keep the King informed. He seems to know exactly what has taken place, and now, when he suddenly appears in the House of Lords, he is master of his brief.

As he sees, the task is a delicate one: to dispel this mischief without injury to himself or the prerogative, yet with respect enough that Parliament will proceed to final passage of the subsidy which is his chief concern. Without that money, he has no foreign policy; and he will need much more still if he is to send an army to support Frederick.

The King's thoughts are not hard to read. *God alone knoweth where all these proceedings will end. Might these wretches even seek to indict the Marquess of Buckingham, darling Steenie who is my John the Evangelist? At all costs, no! Who can care what may be lost, if only Steenie be saved? If Bacon must be given up, then so be it.*

Striding into the House of Lords, the King bids Lord Chancellor Bacon read aloud the charges made in conference.

It is perhaps only at this moment that Francis at last grasps, grasps fully, grasps not merely in his mind but in his viscera, the danger that threatens him. Ah, the irony of it, that he had so pressed the King to avoid this trouble, only now to be caught up in it himself! He speaks from a paper in a faltering voice, knowing that every word threatens to entangle him more closely.

Then the King is away and running in his own speech. As is his wont, he mixes concession with dispute and defence. Yes, let there be laws against the patents; he had already declared his opposition to monopolies such as that on alehouses. But let not their Lordships rely on precedents from the times of bad Kings like Henry VI, Kings that are not to be compared to the present. Their Lordships' house is one of record, but how far it may punish, what its privileges be, is a question. He, James, is their King, and he scorns to be compared in his actions to usurpers and tyrants' times; let the man who would say so be punished.

As for the patent for gold and silver thread, the King says blithely, if it were a trade before, then he too has been wronged, by his referees. And as for the things objected against the Chancellor and the Treasurer, he says, I leave them to answer for themselves, and stand or fall as they equip themselves; for if they cannot justify themselves, they are not worthy to hold and enjoy those places they have under me.

I leave them to answer for themselves, and stand or fall as they equip themselves. Every word lands on Francis like the stroke of an axe. He can feel himself being cut off from his connection with the King. He is like a great ship's mast blown over in a tempest – a mast that was much needed in calmer seas but is now a useless encumbrance, to be hacked away lest it drag in the water with all its rigging and pull the vessel and its captain down with it.

Once the King has spoken, Francis is given leave to speak to his own case. It is all he can do to say a few plain and simple words. He will submit his conduct to the judgment of his peers, and asks only time to consult his papers.

That was two days before. Now, on the 10th, the Lords have a second conference with the Commons. This time the Members do not forget their lines, but lay the names of the referees formally before the House, the name of Lord Chancellor Bacon foremost among them.

Francis's position has become exquisitely difficult, in its procedure as in its substance. As Lord Chancellor, he must conduct the business of the House of Lords with a scrupulous care for good order and impartiality, from his central seat; but as a peer now named to be the subject of a proceeding, he yearns to defend himself. To do that, he must quit his central seat and speak from the benches.

It is a desperate, unhappy dance, to which he nevertheless tries to lend a sense of gravity. Moving now to take his place among the peers, he disclaims responsibility for any abuses in the execution of the patents, which is nothing to the referees. He had imprisoned those men for their contempt, and so as not to disable the authority of the Attorney. As for Yelverton's claims, the testimony of a discontented person is but poor in value.

A simple, inoffensive speech, yet Coke instantly seizes upon it. Do these words, he asks, reflect the settled will and vote of the House of Lords? The answer is, unanimously, No, for what else can their Lordships say? But the effect is lethal. To all appearance Francis now stands before them quite alone, open to investigation and prosecution, bereft of supporters or defence. The King has put him at a distance, while the Marquess of Buckingham has actively pledged himself to join the hunters.

In vain may Privy Councillors urge the view that Ministers of the Crown are responsible not to Parliament but only to His Majesty. The two Houses are ambitious, for their own powers and for themselves. They have their prey where they want him, and they mean to kill, and feast.

99

THE PALACE OF WESTMINSTER, MARCH 1621

Within this sty here now doth lie
A hog well bred with bribery
A pig, a hog, a boar, a bacon
Whom God hath left, and the Devil taken

Yet, at the end, the final stroke of the axe comes from quite another direction. The Committee for Courts of Justice has been
very active in its investigations into abuses of the Court of Chancery. But all this business is suddenly pushed aside by scandalous
new charges of bribery against the Lord Chancellor.

Francis has had wind for some days of a petition from one
Christopher Aubrey, saying that when he was Lord Keeper Francis
had taken money from him to bring forward his case in Chancery.
He has tried to keep the man silent, without success. On 14 March
this matter is brought before the House, together with another of
which he has had no inkling: from a former client of his, Edward
Egerton, that he took a great sum of money from him, £400 in
gold, in connection with a disputed will, a case in which a favourable result was expected but not given by the court.

To the committee, the question is not whether his actions were
sound or the judgments just. It is whether he took money from
suitors whose cases were still pending in the court. Some men
particularly recall that Sir Francis Bacon as Lord Chancellor had

himself given a speech not four years before, when Serjeant Hutton was called to become a judge of the Common Pleas, in which he had laid out the lines and portraitures of a good judge.

There Bacon had charged Hutton that your hands, and the hands of your hands (I mean those about you), be clean, and uncorrupt from gifts, from meddling in titles, and from serving of turns, be they of great ones or small ones. Yet see what the Lord Chancellor is charged with now!

In desperation, Francis writes to the Marquess of Buckingham, to say My very good Lord, your Lordship spake of Purgatory. I am now in it, but my mind is in a calm; for my fortune is not my felicity. I know I have clean hands and a clean heart; and I hope a clean house for friends or servants. But the King and your Lordship will, I hope, put an end to these miseries one way or other. And in truth that which I fear most is lest continual attendance and business, together with these cares, and want of time to do my weak body right this spring by diet and physic, will cast me down; and then it will be thought feigning or fainting. But I hope in God I shall hold out. God prosper you.

The committee reports to the House that it has found matter for a charge of corruption against the Lord Chancellor. On 15 and 17 March the House hears the particulars of the Aubrey and Egerton petitions, and it debates what should be done. The 18th is a Sunday, and the House does not sit. On Monday the 19th, it sends word to the House of Lords for another conference, having found abuses in certain eminent persons.

Such is the appetite to proceed, that the conference meets that very afternoon.

All this is witnessed by the King, with still greater alarm than before. His intervention has not checked the Lords, while the Commons grows ever more turbulent.

The Lord Chancellor will not survive in his place, indeed he must not survive if Steenie is to be saved; there are other men who will serve. But for the Lords henceforth to have a revived power of impeachment of ministers? For the King's officials to be forced to render account to Parliament, and not to their master?

To James this is all a manifest absurdity, for Parliament is but the moon, which derives its light from the sun of his own majesty. But even so, these matters require delicate handling, for they directly touch his prerogative and royal power. To concede on them now will surely be thought to grant a precedent. Yet to hold fast may spend all the goodwill he has enjoyed, and lose the subsidy.

Time is pressing, and over that weekend the King consults with the Privy Council on a new method of treating with Parliament. On Monday, he makes a handsome offer through his agents in the Commons. Lest matters be dragged out, he will establish and authorise a special commission, consisting of twelve Members of the Commons and six from among the Lords, to be chosen by the Houses and not by him, to expedite and examine proceedings against the Lord Chancellor on oath. If it is desirable, this commission can sit through the Easter recess, and report quickly back in the new session.

It is a most tempting proposal, and some in the Commons favour it. But after debate the House decides to refer it to the Lords and make a joint response, and no more is heard of the suggestion. Meanwhile, the case against the Lord Chancellor is quickly offered up, and quickly accepted by the House of Lords, which appoints three further committees to examine witnesses and take evidence.

Now there is no hope. Francis sees how it all must end. He has enemies as well as friends in the Lords.

There is the Earl of Suffolk. He will never forgive Francis the role he played in presiding at his trial.

And then there is Henry Wriothesley, the Earl of Southampton: the beautiful young man to whom Shakespeare had dedicated his poem *The Rape of Lucrece* with the words, The love I dedicate to

your Lordship is without end... What I have done is yours; what I
have to do is yours; being part in all I have, devoted yours.

Southampton is older now, and no longer the lovely youth he
was. He is a man of many interests and honours, restored to great
wealth and position by King James soon after His Majesty's accession. But Southampton loved the Earl of Essex above all men;
his boon companion, almost a brother, the friend beside whom he
stood in Westminster Hall to face a capital charge of treason.

As for Francis Bacon, Southampton mocked and despised him
before Essex while Essex lived. He blamed him for betraying Essex
after his death, and he has spent twenty years sustaining what remains of the Essex faction in Parliament. He is no friend of Buckingham, for they have quarrelled, and that is one more reason to
damn Francis, who is Buckingham's man.

*Can it really be doubted that Southampton hates me, hates me still,
and will not be assuaged?*

These men are leaders in the House of Lords, thinks Francis,
and they will make my indictment prolonged and full of pain. Now
that I am so publicly wounded, now that the blood of my reputation is spilled on the ground and the hounds can smell it, others
are coming forward.

The latest is this man Churchill who alleges bribery and corruption. But there will be more. This is no true legal process. There
will be no testing of the evidence, no cross-examination, no chance
for me to see or weigh the charges beforehand, no separate jury
to reach a verdict. The House has made up its mind already, it
considers every gratuity a bribe, it is drunk on its new power of
impeachment yet lacks all experience of law, it has scores to settle
and precedents to lay, and it will be judge and jury on me all in one.

Now Francis writes again to the King, through Buckingham, to
show his suffering, to renew his credit, and to send a signal that he
will not make trouble but wishes to be kindly dealt with.

He is not yet ready to make confession, but comes close to it,
saying And for the briberies and gifts wherewith I am charged,

when the books of hearts shall be opened, I hope I shall not have the troubled fountain of a corrupt heart in a depraved habit of taking rewards to pervert justice; howsoever I may be frail, and partake of the abuse of the times. And therefore I am resolved when I come to my answer, not to trick up my innocency by cavillations or voidances, but to speak to them the language that my heart speaketh to me, in excusing, extenuating, or ingenuous confessing.

He closes piteously, telling the King I have been ever your man, and counted myself but a usufructuary of myself, the property being yours... resting as clay in your Majesty's gracious hands, Francis St Alban.

Parliament adjourns for Easter. Greatly afflicted in mind and body, exhausted both from his toils and the use of physic, Francis makes his will. He bequeaths his soul to God above, his body to be buried obscurely, his name to the next ages, and to foreign nations. Entirely missing is any lingering hope of fame and reputation here and now, in England.

And, knowing he is lost, he prays, 'Most gracious Lord God, my merciful Father, from my youth up, my Creator, my Redeemer, my Comforter. Thou O Lord soundest and searchest the depths and secrets of all hearts, Thou acknowledgest the upright of heart, Thou judgest the hypocrite, Thou ponderest men's thoughts and doings as in a balance, Thou measurest their intentions as with a line, vanity and crooked ways cannot be hid from thee.

'Thousand have been my sins, and ten thousand my transgressions; but thy sanctifications have remained with me, and my heart, through thy grace, hath been an unquenched coal upon thy altar. O Lord, my strength, I have since my youth met with thee in all my ways... As thy favours have increased upon me, so have thy corrections; so as thou hast been always near me, O Lord.

'And now when I thought most of peace and honour, thy hand is heavy upon me, and hath humbled me, according to thy former loving-kindness, keeping me still in thy fatherly school, not as a bastard, but as a child. Just are thy judgments upon me for my sins, which are more in number than the sands of the sea, but have no proportion to thy mercies.'

Francis asks, and asks again, for an audience with the King, who hesitates. At last his request is granted on 16 April, the day before Parliament resumes. It is a desultory affair. Francis begs to be given particulars of the charges against him, and the King refers him back to their Lordships, making no sign of his own desires or favour.

On 19 April, the Lords' committees make their reports, which list between thirty and forty examinations taken of witnesses. On the 21st, Francis begs the King in a letter to save him from a sentence, with the good liking of the House, and that cup may pass from me; it is the utmost of my desires.

On the 22nd, he writes a formal message of pleading and apology to the Lords of the Parliament, in the upper house assembled. In it, he says I hope I may say and justify with Job in these words: *I have not hid my sin as did Adam, nor concealed my faults in my bosom.* It resteth therefore that, without fig-leaves, I do ingenuously confess and acknowledge, that having understood the particulars of the charge, not formally from the House, but enough to inform my conscience and memory, I find matter sufficient and full, both to move me to desert the defence, and to move your Lordships to condemn and censure me.

My humble desire is, he goes on, that His Majesty would take the seal into his hands, which is a great downfall, and may serve I hope in itself for an expiation of my faults. Therefore, if mercy and mitigation be in your power, and do no ways cross your ends, why should I not hope of your Lordships' favour and commiseration?

The letter is read out to the Lords, first by the clerk and then by the Lord Chief Justice, and is heard in silence. They note its passion and eloquence. But they also note that it is artful. It admits fault, but does not acknowledge and formally confess to each of the charges made, which now number over twenty.

As the Earl of Southampton says, he is charged with corruption; and there is no word of confession of any corruption in his submission. The Earl of Suffolk insists that the punishment is far short of what we expect, and he must be summoned to the bar of the House to make public account.

But Francis has not yet even seen the charges, so how can he plead to them? They are at last sent to him in written form, and he replies in writing on 30 April. He makes a full declaration and confession to each of twenty-eight counts, saying Upon advised consideration of the charge, descending in to my own conscience, and calling my memory to account so far as I am able, I do plainly and ingenuously confess that I am guilty of corruption; and do renounce all defence, and put myself upon the grace and mercy of your Lordships.

Yet even this, they say, is artfully done. It is a confession of circumstances, rather than of his personal guilt in each case. The Lords then send to him to confirm whether he stands by his own guilt or not.

Francis replies, My Lords, it is my act, my hand, my heart. I beseech your Lordships, be merciful to a broken reed.

The King then commissions the Lord Treasurer, the Lord Steward, the Lord Chamberlain and the Earl of Arundel to receive, take charge and sequester the Great Seal. Seeing Francis so sick in body, they move to comfort him, but he says The worse the better. By the King's great favour I received the Great Seal; by my own great fault I have lost it.

This is the moment of *tesis*, of punishment. *Quisque faber fortunae suae*?

On 3 May, Sir Francis Bacon, Viscount St Alban, having been removed from his place as Lord Chancellor, is fined £40,000, sent for imprisonment in the Tower of London during the King's pleasure, rendered incapable of any future office, place, or employment in the State and Commonwealth, and banned from ever sitting in Parliament or sitting within the verge of the court.

He sought office for twenty-five years, and held it for fifteen. To fall from power, be tried and sentenced and leave the highest place in the land in disgrace, has taken barely twelve weeks.

VI

SYNTHESIS:
1621–1626

100

INNER TEMPLE, MAY 1621

'**C**ome. Albert, it may be spring but we must have a fire lit if I
am to do any work this evening.'

A few minutes later Edward Coke has settled himself in his favourite chair by the hearth, candlestick to one side, a large pile of
books and papers to the other. He is now in his seventieth year.
Threescore years and ten, he reflects, the days of our lives, as it
sayeth in the Psalms, and if by reason of strength they be fourscore
years, yet is their strength labour and sorrow, for it is soon cut off,
and we fly away. So it is in the King's new Bible.

But enough of musing: he has work to do, a mass of work. He
has been framing a new series of books in his mind, *Institutes* of
the common law that he hopes will exceed even his own *Reports*
in their authority and renown. Littleton on feudal tenures and the
law of property, Magna Carta itself… these are among the greatest
of all men's works. But they will be greater still for his commentary
upon them.

In his mind, Edward Coke feels undiminished by the passage of
years. His beard and moustaches are now full grey, and thin as new
hay; long gone are the days of their trimmed and barbered elegance. The hair on his head, likewise, has fallen back from his tem-
ples. Yet his body is hale and he still rides his horses for pleasure,
though he misses all those old days in the saddle. Seventy years!
He must seem like a Methuselah to the young pups of the House
of Commons as they plunge and rush about their business. When

he looks across the Chamber at the other Members, or at his fellows round the Privy Council table, there are few to rival him for age.

Yet it is not age that wears a man away, but resignation and loss of hopes. Coke notes his fellows' progression and decay: how listless, even vacant so many of them become, long before their time, as they settle down to lives of beef, port wine and self-regard. And still the pups come on! Little wonder that flatterers and sycophants dog the court in greater proportion than ever. Little wonder the King has never struggled to find men of the modest capacity he prefers to do his bidding.

But I, I have kept lean while they grow fat. I am still hungry.

The old Queen was never like this, he thinks. She had her chosen councillors, her favourites, of course, but they were men of real energy and capability. Leicester, Walsingham, even Raleigh, above all Burghley. And she kept them in good order.

By God but she could be fierce! Coke vividly recalls how she summoned him nearly thirty years before, flayed him to the bone in front of others for taking cases for money that if won would thwart and infringe her revenue... and then spoke kindly and said he would be her new Solicitor General. He was so wholly appalled and had such incomparable grief that she suspected his loyalty that his heart shook and his body trembled so as he could make no speech, but gushed out with tears, of shame and mortification and gratitude.

Now that was a woman, and a prince. She could weigh a man's worth to the ounce. Perhaps it was no accident that the Queen never gave any preferment to Francis Bacon. She knew his father Sir Nicholas, and trusted him, as did we all. Not so the son; and she had watched the boy grow up, so there were few secrets there. She could see the boy was like a ship without a keel, blown in all directions by his wants and schemes. It was all to come so easily to him. The arrogance, the presumption!

And yet beneath it, a fawning creature desperate to please. What did the man say in his essay *Of Judicature?* 'Let judges be lions, but yet lions under the throne; being circumspect that they do not check or oppose any points of sovereignty.' Not quite Coke's own view, to be sure! Bacon would have the judges be not lions but kittens mewling at the feet of His Majesty. Yet at times the man seemed to think himself another Justinian, fit to write a whole new code of law.

Coke has the *Essays* there before him, interleaved with his notes, scribbled with comments. The man wrote all these books, and for what? Full of fine words, yes, but many misplaced, and all as nothing to a man of action. God gave man ambition, that he should dream and achieve great things, whereof high office is but a recognition and grant of power. But an ambition just for one's own self is a paltry unworthy thing. It makes a man biddable, and known to be biddable. He will be turned by gold, or office, or rank, and others will know it. Men smell the absence of true friendship. When the moment of judgment comes, they will not defend him.

There are other works of Bacon's on his table. One is the *Novum Organum*, which Bacon had pressed into his hand after a Council meeting a few months earlier, with an earnest request to tell him his opinion of it. Coke knows what he thinks of it, knew before he opened it. He wrote inside it, *Edw. C. ex dono auctoris*, Edward Coke, by gift of the author, and then a Latin couplet:

> *Auctori consilium*
> *Instaurare paras veterum documenta sophorum*
> *Instaura leges, iustitiamque prius*

Which he could render

> *Advice to the author*
> *You plan to set up wisdom of the ancient sages;*
> *First set up laws, and justice for the ages.*

And then, on that title page, with its ships returning from beyond the Pillars of Hercules, Coke has written:

It deserves not to be read in schools
But to be freighted in the Ship of Fools.

Let Bacon's sailors, his navigators of new knowledge, let them read it and rejoice on their voyages! The book is good for little more than ballast.

Why has Coke had these works to hand? Why have they been his ready companions these past six months? The answer is simple: to succeed, it is well to be prepared.

It was the Lord Treasurership that had finally tipped the balance. But that is to run ahead.

Even now Coke still smarts at the pain of his removal from the Court of King's Bench four long years before. Not just the injustice of it, which was pain enough, for when had a Chief Justice last been so displaced, let alone one of such an eminence? Nor just the loss of income, or even the end of his *Reports*. No, it was the manner of his dismissal: a slow, inexorable fall, a fall by degrees, each step worse than the last, a torture of public humiliation.

Coke was crushed, true enough, but only briefly; like a cat, as one wag remarked, throw him down never so often, he'll still light upon his legs. If anything, his fall had given him new life, for he became filled like a volcano with a furious molten anger longing to burst forth, an indignant need to recover his place as a Privy Councillor and regain the King's favour.

But that was not all. Coke had always considered Francis Bacon a fool, at bottom, a squanderer, a mewler, a petitioner for the favour of others. He had derided Bacon's claims to knowledge of the law, and mocked his pretensions to an equality with himself.

Let me see him day upon night and night upon day among the law-books; he hath not done the hours. This was a man to be despised, not hated.

It has not been pleasant for Coke to revise this judgment, but the past events have made it inevitable. Bacon was not what Coke thought he was; that is the truth of it. These last years have given Coke ample time, and he has reconstructed in detail every step by which Bacon had, quietly and with subtle care, contrived Coke's own gradual destruction.

The advice to His Majesty as to points of law adverse to Coke, the fuelling of distrust between the King and his Chief Justice, the questioning of judges in the Privy Council by their juniors, the deliberate confusion between a judge's general duty to advise the King and discussion of specific cases pending before the courts, the setting of each man to give advice one by one, *seriatim*... all were steps designed to coerce and oppress the judges into compliance. None of this would have happened in the reign of Elizabeth, for she knew the proper limits of princely power.

Every part of it designed to sow division, damage Coke and advance Bacon himself! And Coke notes, unpleasant though it is to note, the artful way in which his adversary exploited Coke's pride for his own malapert purposes.

The Lord Chancellor thus acquired new dignity in Coke's estimation, a dignity Coke disliked to grant, but could not disavow. There could be no room now for condescension, for his old chaffing dismissals.

No: Coke had come to burn with an inexhaustible rage for revenge over Francis Bacon. Bacon, whose twisted counsel brought about Coke's removal from Common Pleas; Bacon, whose sly hatred for him had only been magnified and sharpened by high office; Bacon, whose muttering campaign to humiliate Coke and detach and separate him from the King had finally yielded its ugly harvest.

At first the very idea of revenge was unthinkable. Coke had not the means, for he lacked any standing with the King, and little with Buckingham.

So he had spent nigh on a year working to arrange the marriage of his daughter Frances to Sir John Villiers, despite her mother's vain attempts to interfere. It had cost Coke dearly in the purse, but the expense was worth it to secure the support of Buckingham, which was vital for him to regain favour with His Majesty.

It was a great comfort that Bacon had made a fool of himself in the matter; but Coke's own victory had been short-lived and bittersweet. He had been raised again to the Privy Council, but had failed in his attempt to be made Lord Keeper; and had been forced to watch close by as Bacon himself was advanced to Baron, to Lord Keeper over Coke, to Lord Chancellor, and to Viscount, while Coke himself remained firmly bound to earth.

Yet even this might have been tolerable to Coke if he himself had come by any other preferment. God knows how much he deserved it! As Lord Chief Justice he had moved mountains to conduct the interrogatories in the trials of the Earl and Countess of Somerset, only for these labours to come to naught when he was dismissed from office.

Once he had returned as Privy Councillor, he sat on the King's commission to make economies, and spent countless hours reviewing accounts and expenditures. He led the Councillors in contributing to the King's benevolence, though he hated to part with the money, and still more that it was taxation in disguise and levied without the approval of Parliament. Just recently he had served on the commission, under Bacon, to plan the new parliament and manage the elections.

Coke had, in short, done everything the King had asked of him and more. And then, in December 1620, on the eve of the new parliament, he watched as the King made Sir Henry Montagu, Coke's successor as Chief Justice of King's Bench, a man his junior in the law, his inferior in every kind of human capability, into the new Lord Treasurer; and saw the King raise Montagu way above him in rank, into the body of the peerage as Viscount Mandeville and Baron Montagu of Kimbolton.

Raised up, that is, for a second time on the recommendation of Sir Francis Bacon, who is now Lord Chancellor. The Treasurer's stave, given to a man before whom as a mere Serjeant Edward Coke had been forced to justify himself! What can be the reason? A deal of flattery, a compliant soul, and a payment of £20,000 to His Majesty. Promoted by Buckingham, this disease of ruining men and selling their offices to the highest bidder has become epidemic. As with all dishonesty, once begun it has turned men inside out in their ambition, so that truth and merit are discarded. So it was here. Bacon had advanced a friend, and damned Coke's prospects once again.

So: it was the Lord Treasurership that tipped the balance. Hitherto Coke had believed, half from hope, half from desire, that his restoration to the Privy Council would prefigure his return to high office, and he had devoted all his more than human efforts to that end. But the news of Montagu's elevation struck him like a lightning bolt, and by its flash he saw in an instant that there was nothing left for him.

The cause of it mattered little. All his efforts and expense had been in vain. In fact if not in appearance, his life as an Officer of the Crown was over; there was no Salisbury any more, no Queen Anne to vouch for him. And with his dreams had disappeared any chances to avenge himself on Francis Bacon.

Or so it had seemed.

But, as Coke thinks on it now, seated in his chair before the fire, he gradually comes to understand, to his amazement, that in reality the elevation of Montagu was a colossal stroke of good fortune.

Far from being denied to Coke, all had now been offered to him. With care and industry he could achieve everything he wanted: if not through the King, then through Parliament.

101

INNER TEMPLE, MAY 1621

Looking back, it seems almost too easy. From the start, Coke had had a guiding hand in every part of Bacon's downfall.

As a member of Bacon's commission that met the previous autumn to plan the parliament, he was privy to information about the most offensive patents and monopolies, and knew where were the tenderest places to press. So he was well prepared for the parliamentary turbulence that followed.

Yet it is always hard labour to make a complex matter easy. The first thing was to be elected himself. It was twenty-eight years since Coke had been an MP, in the parliament of 1593 in which he held the Speakership. There was a convention that former Speakers should not stand again, but he ignored it and was nominated by the Council for the old stannary town of Liskeard in Cornwall. Not a place he knew, had lived in or ever set his foot, but when voices were raised ten days into the parliament to exclude Sir George Hastings for not living in his constituency, Coke quoted the mediaeval law of elections so persuasively that the motion was thrown out and he was generally applauded.

Coke had feared that he would be too old, too detached, too rough in his manner and now too little known to make an impression in the new parliament. In fact, his effect was marked from his very first day, in which he made a speech of great power demanding proper enforcement of the laws against recusants, who would deny the true Church in England.

The old Parliament men have long known Coke to be sound and true on recusants. Did he not prosecute their treasons to the hilt in the 1590s, till the worst were hung and drawn or their heads put on pikes above the city? Had he not been hot against recusancy when he was at King's Bench? Coke had sensed all this of course, and the subject was carefully chosen to gain favour among the vast majority of Members of Parliament.

As for the speech, the Members admired the evident sincerity of his words, and the gravity of his demeanour, but still more that he did not shrink from criticism of his own government. A Privy Councillor with the courage to speak thus! Can it be that the policy is changing, and the King is less willing than before to cosset the recusants in hopes of a Spanish match? And all this from the man they called the Oracle of the Law, his notebook to hand as his trusted *vademecum*, always ready to cite case and statute when the moment demanded.

It did not hurt that, far from being thought too rough with others, Coke was soon discovered to have a quick wit and an easy humour to lighten his grey hairs and Abrahamic tones. He had pressed to lead the delegation to the Lords on recusancy, and it seemed only natural and inevitable for him then to be elected Chairman of the Committee of Recusants and Supply. His high reputation was made certain when he signed and presented the petition against recusants in person. That the King hated the petition only raised Coke's reputation still further in his colleagues' minds.

Yet even the King soon had cause to thank Coke. By delaying any debate, garnering support and using his new eminence to good purpose, Coke ensured the passage of the subsidy. Somehow, all sides were left well satisfied.

All in all, it took Edward Coke barely two weeks to establish himself as the dominant man in the House of Commons.

He could feel the sap rising within him, feel how the flow of debate ran along the benches and through his body, filling his lungs with spirit and his mind with ideas. Many of the old great figures had gone, men like Fuller, Neville and Owen, leaving a huge void which he could fill. He worked closely and effectively with the leading Members that remained, notably Sandys and Phelips, and even with the rising man Cranfield, making friends and building alliances.

Coke had long noted that many Members of Parliament had spent time at the Inns of Court; perhaps half of the total, a huge number. Amid all their revelry, fencing, masqueing and time in town, they must have picked up a smattering of the common law, he thinks: a sense at least of its structure and values. Those are things on which to build.

But Coke also saw how the House of Commons had changed since he was Speaker. In her later years Queen Elizabeth had kept her parliaments short and well tasked. Yet now they plainly were more confident and regular. Now the two Houses kept records of their proceedings, and used antiquaries to search for old documents. Procedures for reading Bills and reviewing petitions were more settled.

There were more points of continuity between parliaments, as well; the end of a parliament was no longer an abrupt caesura, but men looked forward and held over unfinished business for the next. There is now, too, a steady current of resentment against the Crown, which carries through from earlier sessions: the King's extravagance has led to huge debts, the Great Contract was aborted, economies in the household have been modest at best, now His Majesty seeks new subsidies. It is this larger passion that sustains the continuity.

And Coke had noted how the influence of the government, and the scope and power of the Privy Councillors within the Commons, had waned since the time of Elizabeth, even while the power of committees was augmented. Just as it had been with the Earl of

Salisbury in 1610, Lord Chancellor Bacon had been elevated, and now found it impossible to lead and guide the Commons, or even to detect its shifting moods, from his high seat in the House of Lords.

For Coke, all this was to the good. The greater use of committees in the Commons gave him greater licence to speak in debates, magnifying his presence, and to the chair of the Committee of Recusancy and Petitions was added that of Grievances, so that he presided over two of the leading committees in the House.

He used his new positions ably, and persuaded the House that Mondays and Fridays should be used to hear grievances. These were days when fewer Members were present, and in any case the business of grievances was steadily expanding, so the total effect was to consolidate Coke's control over the order paper of business in the Commons.

Position, and procedure. These would be the essential instruments of his revenge.

Coke had other long-standing business to transact: measures as to recusants, measures to rectify and curb the Court of Chancery, and most notably measures on patents and monopolies. But in the weeks that followed, a much deeper project revealed itself to, and through, the old Chief Justice: to resurrect the powers of Parliament itself as a court, indeed as the highest court in the land. He calls them the powers of judicature, of which impeachment is but a part.

Did Coke see all the possibilities before, or did they emerge through force of events? Who can know? But more than any man alive, Coke had a sense of them. What had Bracton said all those years before? *Rex non debet esse sub homine, sed sub Deo et Lege.* The King should not be under any man, but under God and the law. Coke himself had written those words in his fourth *Reports*, quoted them at the King to his face – and been threatened with violence for his trouble.

But Parliament? To make Parliament the equal of the King, or even in some matters his superior? To make the privileges of free speech and immunity from arrest, not grants graciously awarded by His Majesty at the opening of every session, but rights inherent in and inseparable from Parliament itself?

To bring back into use the ancient process of impeachment for high crimes in public office? Above all, to make Parliament and not the King into the instrument and agent of the nation, possessed of a general care for the nation's welfare? And Coke himself into the leading voice in Parliament? Surely, these are matters too great for any man's imagination.

As a judge and legislator, even as a young lawyer when he first learned of the history and grew to love the power of Magna Carta and the writ of *habeas corpus*, Edward Coke has always had one single and consistent project, to protect the ordinary common subject of the realm in the exercise of his traditional rights and freedoms from the oppressions of an over-mighty government. To replace personal discretion and arbitrary power with a common, settled and universal rule of law.

If Coke can no longer achieve this through the courts of common law, then he will do so through the High Court of Parliament.

102

INNER TEMPLE, MAY 1621

It was the matter of patents and monopolies, and specifically the case of Sir Giles Mompesson, that gave Coke the opportunity to isolate, to name and to pursue Francis Bacon.

Coke was scrupulously careful throughout to spare the King and the Marquess of Buckingham from any accusation, or even implication, of misconduct. It was not to his purpose to do so, for the offence given would be vast and immediate, and if men could blame His Majesty or the Marquess then it would blur the responsibility of the legal referees, who were his true target.

So, as the King had done, Coke carefully distinguished between the King's prerogative absolute, which none might question, and his disputable prerogative, which might be the subject of court proceedings, and which governed the grant of patents. For these, he said, the sole fault lies in the referees. As for Mompesson himself, Coke declared forthrightly that His Majesty was free from all blame in bestowing the patent for inns, and no king in Christendom but would have granted it, given the advice he had received. The effect of these remarks was to allow Members a free rein to attack Mompesson and the referees, without impugning the King.

But Coke was also careful never to accuse or attack Lord Chancellor Bacon in person. As he said of Bacon in connection with the Chancery, I speak not because he is in a cloud but according to the liberty of a true subject.

Again, what need? Coke's committee did his bidding, and its course was clear to him: moving from the revelation of malpractices with patents to a direct criticism of Mompesson, avoiding a mere petition for redress but advancing a much more serious formal indictment on a matter of general grievance.

Coke it was who had the patent-holders summoned to account for themselves at the bar of the Commons, so all could feel the power of his committee. When Sir Henry Yelverton testified that Lord Chancellor Bacon had refused to release the recalcitrants who would not pay the licence fees for gold and silver, it was Coke who immediately invoked Chapter 29 of Magna Carta to press for their release.

Mompesson had fled, confirming his guilt, but by then Coke had assembled the procedure for an indictment. Investigations, interrogatories, a case to answer, a petition from the Commons to the Lords as high court, a joint conference, and then a trial; it was all a vast body of work, from the compilation of examinations of fact to the search for precedents in law, to the preparation of the legal proceedings.

And at every stage, Coke was the driving force; the unnamed, unmoved mover. Condemn not merely Mompesson and the other patent-holders, but the patents themselves and their referees as well? Coke arranged it. Send the brilliant Noye into the archives to find precedents for impeachment? Coke made it so. Steady his colleagues with a long and careful speech, when the tenderer souls were dithering whether to name the referees before the House of Lords? Coke did that too, and more. Much more.

Position and procedure; and now precedent.

Coke had sent Noye into the archives, true enough. And rightly so, for judicature – the powers of Parliament to act as a court – was a wide field, he could see, in which it would be easy to stray from the right path. Pursue Bacon in the Commons only, and he would get away too lightly. Pursue him directly in the Lords, and the Commons might lose control. Refer him to the King, and the man might as well already be acquitted.

No: what was required was to use both Houses in a joint procedure: the Commons to impeach and accuse, to hear the initial grievances and lay general charges, the Lords to investigate, hear evidence, refine the charges, and give judgment.

And as it proved, the vital precedent was one Coke had long had in his own hands. He had come across it in his researches for the trial of Lord Treasurer Suffolk, four years before: William, 4th Baron Latimer, had been impeached by the parliament of 1376 for arranging Crown loans at exorbitant cost, extorting moneys in Brittany and selling merchants exemptions from the duty on exports of wool. The charges were begun in the Commons and judged in the Lords. Latimer was condemned, fined, put out of office and imprisoned. This was all Coke needed.

It helped that men were hot against the Court of Chancery and the prerogative courts, with their single judges and potential for corruption. But Coke had already had all the necessary legal armaments massed and prepared when the moment came to turn them upon Francis Bacon. And, what was no less satisfying, not just on Bacon but on Lord Mandeville as well, for he too as Henry Montagu had been a referee and had signed obnoxious patents. As for Yelverton, who had dealt pertly with Coke in Council and reviewed his *Reports* so ill before the King... well, who can care? The man has already been ruined.

First, Bacon was named as referee in the patent for inns, and he lived. Then he was named as presiding over the corruptions of the Court of Chancery, and he lived. Then he was named as Buckingham's creature, as the man who would not discharge the innocents from the Tower, and he lived.

What he could not survive were the charges of bribery from Aubrey and Egerton which at that very moment suddenly appeared, as if from nowhere. These were supported by reputable

437

witnesses, one for each charge. Many men knew that Bacon had taken money in relation to proceedings; that could not be denied. And Bacon himself had condemned the act of bribery on numerous occasions, as recently in the trials of Suffolk and Yelverton. So there could be no demur, and no defence.

What had Bacon said of Yelverton? *He that thinks more of the greatness of his place than of the duty of his place, will soon commit misprisions.* So too had Bacon thought, so too had he most evidently done.

103

INNER TEMPLE, MAY 1621

It is still light outside. Coke throws a few more logs upon the fire, then settles down once more in his chair to reflect.

Nulli vendemus rectum aut iustitiam. To none will we sell right or justice. The law is plain, was ever plain. It is Magna Carta, Chapter 29.

The timing of the bribery charges against Bacon had proven to be exquisite; no doubt of that. Coke smiles at the thought. Yet they too had required careful preparation. Men do not come forward to lay public accusation against powerful men, men of quality, just of their own accord. They must be encouraged, shielded, instructed, reassured that they will succeed and be rewarded. In each case the documents had to be reviewed and marshalled, the witnesses tested and proven.

Bacon had seen the plaintiff Aubrey coming, tried to get to him and silence him, and it had been all Coke and his colleague Sir Robert Phelips could do to keep the fellow on his track. But the plaintiff Egerton had stepped forward entirely new and undetected by the Lord Chancellor. The claims of both men had been ruinous: for their substance, for their implications and, in particular, for the public stir they created. It was like a piece of theatre... how fitting for this masqueing man!

Phelips had made a report to the Commons soon thereafter, saying I am commanded from the Committee for Abuses in Courts of Justice to render account of some abuses... the person is no less than the Lord Chancellor, a man so endued with all parts both of nature and art as that I will say no more of him because I am not able to say enough. The matter alleged is corruption...

Even then there had been obstacles. Bacon had many connections in the House of Commons. Now that they saw the danger, these men had thrown up every kind of objection. In particular Secretary Calvert, now the King's leading minister in the Commons, questioned whether so great a man might be examined by the two Houses. Other Members had put the point of principle, whether the evidence of a single witness on each charge could really be enough for any proper accusation?

Time for Coke to reach for his books! He had had to move quickly to give colleagues the necessary reassurance, that *Newarke's Case* in the late Queen's reign showed that even where there was but a single witness in each instance, the similarity of several instances together could be held sufficient for a conviction. As for greatness, no man however mighty could stand above the common law, all must know that.

In retrospect, the King's offer of a special commission had been a last cast of the dice. It had been an artful, flattering proposal, come direct from the mouth of His Majesty, to set aside delay and expedite justice, bring the Houses together, and examine Lord Chancellor Bacon on his oath. Coke had been dismayed to hear of it, fearful of its plausibility, and aghast when several of his leading colleagues, including Perrot and Alford, had given it their approval. To accept the offer would be ruin to Coke's wider project, for Parliament would not be asserting its own right to try Bacon, but yielding it up. It would be taking a purely temporary power from the King, and even that a power merely of investigation. The final power, the power of judgment, the power to condemn or to reprieve, would remain with His Majesty.

It had to be stopped, but how? The King could not be controverted, nor have his sweet words met with sour, and there were no legal precedents to use against such an innovation. In the end, Coke had merely counselled the House not to set aside its earlier resolutions, that this gracious message taketh not away our parliamentary proceeding. Sir Robert Phelips should proceed to file the charges against Bacon, and the House return a joint answer with the Lords, once they had considered the matter. To his immense relief, his colleagues had taken the hint, and the proposal had died away.

After such convulsions, the upper house proved to be a place of calm. Yet even here Coke had had a hand. For the leading men of the Lords included the Earls of Suffolk and Southampton. Both now led committees of investigation into the Lord Chancellor, and both had separate cause to hate him. With Suffolk the cause was proximate and livid, for he still burned with anger at his own trial and fall, over which Bacon had presided. Suffolk had little kindness of feeling for Coke, but he would do what was necessary.

Southampton was a different case, however; for this was the same Earl of Southampton who was bosom friend to the great Earl of Essex, that rose against the Queen. He had disliked Bacon in his youth, but after the trial of Essex he loathed him, that was clear. It gave Southampton great satisfaction now to work closely with his friend and kinsman Edwin Sandys, an ally of Coke, for the destruction of the Lord Chancellor.

They had proved to be a very effective pair: Suffolk the ageing ranter, hot for Bacon to be summoned to the bar of the Lords; Southampton, the cooler spirit, who simply insisted that Bacon acknowledge and plead to every single one of the charges.

It was the final humiliation for the Chancellor. And even then Coke had been on hand to remind their Lordships that three judges had been hanged for bribery, so that legal precedents might inform their righteous indignation.

Coke snorts, and stands. All this reflection is but wasted time, and he has work to do that evening. The ruin of his enemy has been sweet, both the matter and the manner of it. Hard to imagine that Bacon would have been convicted, without Coke's guiding hand on the proceedings. And not unmeet that the man was forced to say in terms I am guilty of corruption, a broken man, and abase himself before their Lordships! From such a place there can be no returning.

But, he thinks, what, all for all, has been achieved these past three months? The ending of some malpractices in patents, some curbing of abuses in the Court of Chancery, the restitution of an ancient process of impeachment, a growing power for Parliament to hold the King's ministers to account. It is not nothing, it could be something great in time, but it is not enough. It is not an end.

Coke cannot say what that end will be. But he has much more to do, of that he is certain. The power of the law is to bring peace and order to men's lives, and prosperity to their dealings. Magna Carta and the writ of *habeas corpus* serve as their shield and sword.

For no man is above the law, not even a king, and no man may rightfully check its spread. It is a silver current that spends itself in innumerable and unnamed channels throughout the land. It serves not just the great and mighty but the mass of men and women who act without renown or recompense for themselves and for each other, through its diffusive good.

That is true advancement. But the law must have its champions in every age, or it is no living, active force.

As Coke leaves the room he pauses, and picks up Bacon's book of *Essays*. What does it say? *All rising to great place is by a winding stair*. Not so in Coke's own case, he reflects. It was ever upwards for him, directly and with no winding about, under two sovereigns, Elizabeth and James, by his own merit and not with any pleaded patronage, at least till the end. How like Bacon to make a general law of his own case!

As for Bacon, he ascended slowly, late and by degrees. But when he fell from greatness there was no winding stair to slow his fall.

No: his was a sudden desperate plunge into a yawning void. He sowed the wind, and reaped the whirlwind.

A man is apt to discover virtue after vice has ceased to pay him. Let him do so now, and good luck to him.

As for himself, Coke thinks, there is rising still to come. Of that he is certain. Perhaps Parliament will prove a surer means of ascent.

VII

CATHARSIS: 1671

104

LONDON, NOVEMBER 1671

PROSPERO
I have bedimmed
The noontide sun, called forth the mutinous winds,
And 'twixt the green sea and the azured vault
Set roaring war; to the dread rattling thunder
Have I given fire, and rifted Jove's stout oak
With his own bolt; the strong-based promontory
Have I made shake, and by the spurs plucked up
The pine and cedar; graves at my command
Have waked their sleepers, oped, and let 'em forth
By my so potent art.
But this rough magic
I here abjure, and when I have required
Some heavenly music, which even now I do,
To work mine end upon their senses that
This airy charm is for, I'll break my staff,
Bury it certain fathoms in the earth,
And deeper than did ever plummet sound
I'll drown my book.

A BRIEF NOTICE OF THE LATER LIFE OF FRANCIS BACON, KNIGHT, PRIVY COUNCILLOR, BARON VERULAM AND VISCOUNT ST ALBAN, WRIT FOR THE PRIVATE ENJOYMENT AND USE OF THE EARL OF DEVONSHIRE

Your Lordship hath bid me set down some details of my acquaintance with the late Lord Chancellor Bacon, Viscount St Alban, a man known for his most rare and excellent parts in his own time, and celebrated for them in our own. I had but little knowledge of him, some few occasions of meeting apart, till I was resident at Gorhambury House as one of his secretaries under Mr Meautys, who was latterly Sir Thomas Meautys. That was in the year 1623, if memory serves.

As the world knoweth, his Lordship had been expelled from office two years previous, disgraced, set a fine of £40,000 to be paid, imprisoned in the Tower, barred from any public honour and station, and forbidden to approach the verge, that is within twelve miles of the court, except by permission of the King. Which in truth meant permission of the Marquess, later the Duke, of Buckingham, who had been his Lordship's patron.

As it transpired, the former Lord Chancellor had spent but a few days in the Tower, and had treated with His Majesty to allay his creditors; yet despite this success he took the loss of Parliament after forty years a Member very ill, and found the prohibition on his movements a grievous burden, which more and more confined him to his estate and disabled any return to greater fortune.

He was especially vexed to be obliged to defend his house in London against the predatory desire of Buckingham, his former patron, who tried without cease to use his Lordship's weakened condition to prise it from him. Eventually his Lordship was obliged to give the house up to Sir Lionel Cranfield, who promptly remitted it to the Duke his patron, avoiding any regrettable necessity whereby the Duke might incur a personal obligation to his Lordship.

In outward appearance, his Lordship took care not to be disheartened, couching his change of circumstance as but a temporary one, as befell Seneca the Stoic, who was banished from the city of Rome and then restored. As his Lordship once said, *my genius calleth me to retire from the stage and betake myself to letters.* At other times, he was more sombre, and wont to remark that Lethe is but the river of time, which bringeth oblivion to all things.

But, as I judge now, he never gave up hopes of a return to favour. He sought to be Provost of Eton, but was denied. He sued for a pension from the King, and for a pardon; and though he got the one after a fashion, he never had the other, or at least not signed. Yet still his Lordship chose to dedicate his *Essays* in their final expansion to the Duke a few years later.

When I arrived at Gorhambury, some two years after his fall, I found my new master engaged in the composition of numerous discourses and writings by which he sought to win the esteem of posterity and advance the progression of natural philosophy. It was as though the drought of increasing age had forced his great tree of knowledge to flower and fruit of a sudden, producing some good seed, some poor, and all of it scattered around to grow new shoots of thought and learning. Indeed one wit remarked, not without truth, that his disgrace made his later glory.

At that time the main house was in much disrepair. By all account it had been kept like a palace in his Lordship's latter years, his servants shod in boots of Spanish leather, and clad in his livery with a running boar as his crest. I heard tell how three of his servants kept coaches of their own, and some had race horses, and men used to take as they pleased from great chests of plate and gold and jewels to pay their own debts, with no record or accompt kept of it.

Some said his Lordship had favourites to attend him and ganymedes for his delight. But by the time of my arrival most of the servants had gone, which he said was like the flying of the vermin when a house was failing.

My station in the household was to assist his Lordship with

translations of some of his *Essays*, attending his person on his daily walks around the estate, and taking notes of his conversation. His strength at this time was most variable, and he addressed himself to it through the taking of physic, by three grains of nitre in a thin warm broth every morning. Once in six or seven days he would imbibe a maceration of rhubarb, infused into a draught of white wine and beer, immediately before his meal, as he said so as to carry away the grosser humours of the body, but not diminish or carry away any of the spirits, as sweating doth.

He liked well, too, to experiment with opiates, whether by infusion or inhalation or ingestion, which he deemed essential aids for the prolongation of life. As he remarked in his *Sylva Sylvarum*, There be two things, which (inwardly used) do cool and condense the spirits; and I wish the same to be tried outwardly in vapours. The one is nitre... The other is, the distilled water of wild poppy; which I wish to be mingled, at half, with rose-water, and so taken with some mixture of a few cloves, in a perfuming-pan.

In these medications he evidently met with much success. For, on our walks, so rich and varied were his remarks, darting from one subject to another, full of hints and images and allusion, that it was all I could do to capture even a part of them. Yet reading through my notes afterwards, he was kind to say that of his secretaries he preferred to have me by him, for some had no Latin, and as to others he could make little sense of what they had writ.

It was about this time that he had composed his *History of the Reign of King Henry VII*, which hath done much to amend and improve the writing of history, for the pleasure of the King and the Prince. There was also, if I recall, a discourse of a war with Spain, a dialogue concerning an holy war, a history of the winds and some other histories of elements of natural philosophy, and a digest of the laws of England.

Many of these works, and others, may be found in your library of Chatsworth Hall. So too may the translations into Latin which his Lordship prepared, including that of his work *De Augmentis*

Scientiarum, the elaboration of his earlier work *The Advancement of Learning*, designed for the better information and edification of scholars across the continent of Europe. All of these writings earned for their author a just and lasting renown. Though he never completed his *Great Instauration*, the master-work of which these others are but opuscules, yet there are treasures in what remains.

Few men would choose among their children, could they avoid it. Yet I have ever felt that his Lordship had a special affection for the history he called *The New Atlantis*, though he never finished it. It is a very pretty tale, of an island of peace and contentment where lieth Salomon's House, a place wherein are to be found every device and gin or project for the increase of men's knowledge. For his Lordship held that such increase could only come by collective inquiries into particular matters, and that men should be as bees in the hive, all working together to gather the pollen of their experiments and transform it into the honey of science. His Lordship sometimes used to describe himself as *buccinator*, the trumpeter of knowledge to come, and *The New Atlantis* is a work not of the past, but of the future.

He had writ once that knowledge itself is power, as it might be here the power to preserve and prolong life, or to make ships for going under water, or perhaps an hundred other tasks as yet undreamt of. There was for him in metaphysics a kind of magic. For nature is God's word on Earth, he said, and true science would read it, vex it to reveal its secrets, shape it and force it to obey man's will, just as poesy may conceive and give life to monsters and other such things as are not found among us.

His Lordship used to remark to me that art and science spring alike from the human fancy, and that despair is the enemy of the pursuit of knowledge. From which arise these questions: What should a man admire? Should there be limitation to man's passion to control nature itself? Or may he like Midas come to curse his own audacity?

His Lordship looked into these questions, but perhaps not

enough. Perhaps, like Shakespeare's Prospero, man must abjure unearthly power to be content, and find other cures for his despair.

From our converse, it appeared that his Lordship had been of a mind to stablish such a House of Salomon himself, even from his youth. He had long developed a contempt for the scholastic teachings of Aristotle, or rather for their mortifying effects on men's minds. But that contempt was matched by his desire to write out a constructive philosophy of nature, and to realise such a plan through the creation of a new college.

Mankind is living in the autumn of the world, he said, and a great house of learning must have through lights or windows, that permit no shadows or corners unlit by the sun, and allow men to see both backwards and forwards in time. Would that such an enterprise had succeeded, to challenge the authority by which some at the universities do champion false and foolish notions!

Yet his Lordship could not win the support of the late Queen or her councillors for his college scheme, though Lord Burghley was his close relation. He recalled to me with some pain once hearing that King James had remarked of his *Novum Organum* that like the peace of God it passeth all understanding. And his fortunes did not improve when Prince Charles acceded to the throne. It seemeth that a want of good patrons was ever his Lordship's defect, throughout his life. He was apt to say that hope is a good breakfast but an ill supper, and though he always breakfasted well on the words of his patrons, yet he never seemed to sup well on their deeds.

But despite his Lordship's labours the *Novum Organum* is by no means a perfected work. It is a curiosity that of the great discoveries of compass, printing and gunpowder that he noted with praise, all came from chance and trial, from the workshop or manufactory, and none came from any system of practical tabulation as he offered; it is yet to be proven that they may be. His Lordship was wont to wax on the importance of collective inquiries, yet I do not recall that he was ever in direct communication with the leading men of natural philosophy across Europe, men such as Brahe, Kepler and Galileo.

When I myself encountered Sig. Galileo in Florence in the year 1636, the Italian, who is to me the greatest philosopher not only of our own but of all time, remarked that his Lordship's new method of induction in no wise described his own passages of thought, or mathematical conjectures, nor could they be fitted to it. Something similar might be said for the precise mathematical measurements and instrumental inventions of Sig. Sanctorius of Padua.

It has ever seemed to me that his Lordship's speculations applied more fitly to his botanical and geological investigations than to the rarer matter of physics and mathematics. But I confess I struggled to answer questions that arose in my mind, in particular as to how a man may tabulate instances securely, without already knowing or imagining what it is of which they may be instances? To me this has ever seemed a formidable objection to the new method as his Lordship conceived it.

But the *Novum Organum* was not I think intended for men of genius, but to give an instrument by which all might uncover Nature's laws and render human knowledge more certain, as if by a mechanical aid. He used to say that he held it enough to have constructed the machine, though he might not succeed in setting it on work. For that his Lordship is rightly celebrated among the men of our modern Royal Society, who profess to aim at the improvement of all useful sciences and arts, not by mere speculations but by exact and faithful observations and experiments – however absurd and feeble-minded some of them may otherwise be. And the time may come when such an instrument of thought, and indeed other such mechanical aids, may prove their worth to men's inquiries.

His Lordship's ambition also stretched from the laws of nature to the laws of men, of which he had long meditated a reformation, with the purpose to remove redundancy and error, and to ease men's understanding by placing the laws in a more composed and reasonable order. More than once I heard him comment in dismay at events in Parliament, whereby men challenged the prerogative right and earthly power of His Majesty, which his Lordship ever sought to defend.

He seemed to reserve a special disrelish for Sir Edw. Coke, though he lived not to see his rival's most flagrant act in 1628, some months before the murder of the Duke of Buckingham. Then it was that Sir Edw. Coke acted as prime author and procurer of what men have called the Petition of Right, which sought to bind the new King Charles and his successors by statute not to levy any tax without the consent of Parliament, and sundry other things, all contradictory to right principles of regal power and law.

Coke and his like all averred that the government of England was not an absolute but a mixed monarchy, and they infected the nation as a whole with this disease.

Can it be doubted that such thwarting and confronting actions – actions taken in the name of Magna Carta and the common law, but which in their effects emptied the King's coffers and weakened the realm – can it be doubted that these actions set the frame for the rebellion that followed, barely twelve years afterwards, in which men of nobility and quality, gentlemen and merchants alike were lured to join with the worse sort of Parliament men and with Adamites and Quakers and Presbyterians and other preachers of sedition in a foul and deceitful assault on the King, to their own disgrace and the general ruin?

To return: Sir Edw. Coke was buried in 1634, in Norfolk, next to the tomb of his first wife, Mistress Paston. They say that at his funeral there was much pomp, and a long procession which included his wife, Lady Hatton, with whom he regularly fought, and at the end she said We shall not see his like again, thanks be to God.

With this sentiment Viscount St Alban would have agreed. His own end came in a way both unexpected and yet of a piece with his beliefs. Some impudent souls have said that it resulted from too much of an inhalation of the life-preserving opiates with which he regularly experimented in the cause of natural philosophy. But

I have heard what seemeth far more fitting, that he was taking the air by coach on a snowy day near Highgate with Doctor Witherborne, who attended the King, when they fell to debating whether snow might not be used to preserve flesh. Come, let us put the matter to the test, sayeth his Lordship, and stopping by a house at the foot of the hill, they purchased a hen and had it exenterated. Then they stuffed the cavity within with snow.

But the cold and perhaps the effort of it were so great that his Lordship immediately fell ill, and they took him to the house of his friend the Earl of Arundel nearby. There he lay for some few days, where he steadily worsened, and all their efforts could not save him from a peripneumonia by which he was suffocated. This took place on 9 April 1626, which was Easter Sunday. They say that near his death his mind wandered and he spoke with longing of the birds in his father's house, and of pebbles of bright colours. He was in his sixty-sixth year, and was buried near his mother in St Michael's Church by Verulam, with a memorial of white marble; though I have not visited it.

His Lordship often remarked that *quisque faber fortunae suae*, every man maketh his own fortune. So it proved: in his fame and his disgrace, on the public stage and in his home, in life and in death. Truly, as his friend Mr Jonson remarked, no man ever spake more neatly, more pressly, more weightily, or suffered less emptiness, less idleness, in what he uttered. The fear of every man that heard him was lest he should make an end.

His Lordship was celebrated after his death in a memorable lyric of the Revd Mr Herbert:

> *While thou dost groan 'neath weight of sickness slow,*
> *And wasting life with doubtful step doth go,*
> *What wise fates sought I see at last fulfill'd;*
> *There needs must die in April – so they will'd;*
> *That here the flowers their tears might weep forlorn*
> *And there the Nightingale melodious mourn,*

Such dirges only fitting for thy tongue,
Wherein all eloquence most surely hung.

His widow the Viscountess had been the daughter of a London merchant and a querulous lady, who herself rose steadily by her four marriages, from Gent. to Knight to Viscount and at last to Earl.

Viscountess Verulam had lived much in London in his Lordship's retirement, and latterly in Chiswick where she kept a separate household. Shortly before his end his Lordship made a great amendment of his will, which utterly revoked and avoided any bequests to her, leaving her to her right only. For her part, within but a few days of his death she married Underhill, a gentleman usher, whom my friend Aubrey informeth me she made deaf and blind with too much of Venus.

Faithfully subscribed by the hand of James Wheldon, amanuensis, in London this eighteenth day of November, 1671.

THOMAS HOBBES

105

THE WORLD'S A BUBBLE

THE WORLD'S a bubble, and the life of man
                  less than a span;
In his conception wretched, from the womb
                  so to the tomb:
Curst from the cradle, and brought up to years
                  with cares and fears.
Who then to frail mortality shall trust,
But limns the water, or but writes in dust.

Yet since with sorrow here we live opprest,
                  what life is best?
Courts are but only superficial schools
                  to dandle fools.
The rural parts are turned into a den
                  of savage men.
And where's the city from all vice so free,
But may be termed the worst of all the three?

Domestic cares afflict the husband's bed,
                  or pains his head.
Those that live single take it for a curse,
                  or do things worse.
Some would have children; those that have them moan,
                  or wish them gone.

What is it then to have or have no wife,
But single thraldom, or a double strife?

Our own affections still at home to please
                    is a disease:
To cross the seas to any foreign soil
                        perils and toil.
Wars with their noise affright us: when they cease,
                    we are worse in peace.
What then remains, but that we still should cry
Not to be born, or being born to die.

F. B.

VIII

TELOS

EPILOGUE

If parts allure thee, think how Bacon shined
The wisest, brightest, meanest of mankind!
ALEXANDER POPE, ESSAY ON MAN, *1733*

Bacon, Locke and Newton. I consider them as the three greatest men
that have ever lived, without any exception, and as having
laid the foundation of those superstructures which have
been raised in the physical and moral sciences.
THOMAS JEFFERSON, LETTER TO JOHN TRUMBULL, PARIS,
15 FEBRUARY 1789

For my part I had rather be damned with Plato and Lord Bacon,
than go to Heaven with Paley and Malthus.
PERCY BYSSHE SHELLEY, PREFACE TO PROMETHEUS UNBOUND, *1820*

The founding of the Royal Society represents both Bacon's deification
as a philosopher and the final victory of the Baconian project of
collaboration, utility, and progress in natural inquiries.
PROF. ANTONIO PEREZ-RAMOS, UNIVERSITY OF MURCIA

It is difficult to resist the comparison of Coke with his eminent
contemporaries Bacon and Shakespeare; what they were to
philosophy and literature, Coke was to the common law.
SIR JOHN BAKER, DOWNING PROFESSOR OF LAW EMERITUS,
CAMBRIDGE UNIVERSITY, *1972*

The seventeenth century was a period of turmoil over the relationship between the Stuart kings and Parliament, which culminated in civil war. That political controversy did not deter the courts from holding, in the Case of Proclamations (1611) 12 Co Rep 74, that an attempt to alter the law of the land by the use of the Crown's prerogative powers was unlawful. The court concluded that 'the King hath no prerogative, but that which the law of the land allows him', indicating that the limits of prerogative powers were set by law and were determined by the courts.

UK SUPREME COURT, JUDGMENT IN THE CASE OF
MILLER V. THE PRIME MINISTER, 24 SEPTEMBER 2019

I understand that the Law requires that I should, at My Accession to the Crown, take and subscribe...

OATH OF HM KING CHARLES III RELATING TO THE SECURITY OF THE
CHURCH OF SCOTLAND, ACCESSION COUNCIL, 10 SEPTEMBER 2022

ACKNOWLEDGEMENTS

I have amassed a wide array of debts in writing this book. I should especially like to thank the warden and fellows of All Souls College, Oxford, for electing me to a visiting fellowship and then a two-year fellowship, both of which have greatly assisted this work; and the School of History at St Andrews University; the History of Parliament Trust; the House of Commons Library; University College London Library; the Liberty Fund; and the Selden Society.

I thank the Earl and Countess of Leicester for their warm welcome to Holkham Hall, and Mac Graham, Katherine Hardwick, Lucy Purvis and especially Laura Nuvoloni for their expert assistance while I was visiting Coke's library there. I thank the Marquess of Salisbury for allowing me to consult the Cecil archives at Hatfield House, and Sarah Whale and Robin Harcourt-Williams for their very helpful guidance. Sara Foster, the church warden at St Mary, Tittleshall, kindly arranged for me to see the Coke memorials there in an out-of-hours visit. Giles Mandelbrote and the staff of the Lambeth Palace Library were extremely helpful with correspondence by and relating to Anthony and Francis Bacon.

I am hugely grateful to John Baker, Harry Bingham, Kate Bingham, Richard Bourke, Nell Butler, Alan Cromartie, Claudia Daventry, George Garnett, Simon Green, James Harris, John Hudson, Colin Kidd, Michael Lobban, Diarmaid MacCulloch, Ian Maclean, Noel Malcolm, Bobby Monks, Sam Norman, Richard Ovenden, Peter Phillips, Stuart Proffitt, Paul Seaward, Alan Stewart, Brian Vickers, John Vickers, Richard Whatmore, Mike Webb and David Womersley for their ideas, comments, help and conversation. I am much indebted to the work of previous biographers of Bacon and Coke, most notably to that indefatigable nineteenth-century Baconian James Spedding, and to the more recent work of Paul Brand, Wolfgang Ernst, Alexandra Gajda, John Guy, Paul Hammer, the late Lisa Jardine, the late Graham Rees and other specialists in related historical, legal, scientific and literary fields.

This book particularly benefitted from the careful early comments of two superlative scholars, John Baker and Brian Vickers. Needless to say, neither bears responsibility for any errors of fact or divergences in interpretation that remain.

I thank my peerless agent, Caroline Michel, and her colleagues at PFD; and James Stephens, Olivia Beattie, Ryan Norman and Suzanne Sangster at Biteback. So too my brilliant constituency team in Hereford and London over the years: Gill, Susie, Wendy, Aliya and Grant.

Finally, I thank Kate, Sam, Nell and Noah, without whom nothing would be possible.

Jesse Norman
Hereford, March 2023